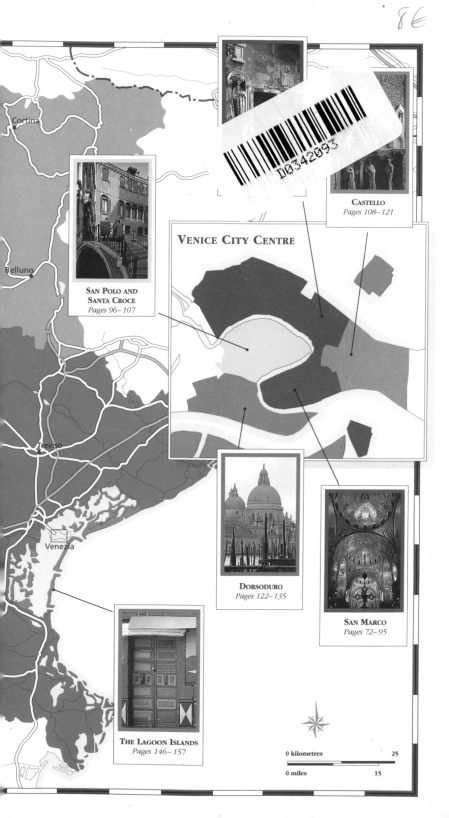

8€

Cortina

Belluno

SAN POLO AND
SANTA CROCE
Pages 96–107

CASTELLO
Pages 108–121

VENICE CITY CENTRE

Treviso

Venezia

DORSODURO
Pages 122–135

SAN MARCO
Pages 72–95

THE LAGOON ISLANDS
Pages 146–157

0 kilometres   25

0 miles   15

EYEWITNESS *TRAVEL GUIDES*

VENICE
& THE VENETO

EYEWITNESS *TRAVEL GUIDES*

VENICE
& THE VENETO

Main contributors:
SUSIE BOULTON
CHRISTOPHER CATLING

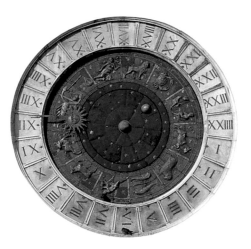

DORLING KINDERSLEY

LONDON • NEW YORK • STUTTGART • MOSCOW

www.dk.com

A DORLING KINDERSLEY BOOK

www.dk.com

Produced by Pardoe Blacker Publishing Limited,
Lingfield, Surrey
PROJECT EDITOR Caroline Ball
ART EDITOR Simon Blacker
EDITORS Jo Bourne, Molly Perham, Linda Williams
DESIGNERS Kelvin Barratt, Dawn Brend, Jon Eland,
Nick Raven, Steve Rowling
PICTURE RESEARCH Jill De Cet
MANAGING EDITOR Alan Ross
PROJECT SECRETARY Cindy Edler

Dorling Kindersley Limited
DEPUTY EDITORIAL DIRECTOR Douglas Amrine
DEPUTY ART DIRECTOR Gaye Allen
MAP CO-ORDINATORS Simon Farbrother, David Pugh
PRODUCTION Hilary Stephens

CONTRIBUTOR (TRAVELLERS' NEEDS) Sally Roy

MAPS
Phil Rose, Jennifer Skelley, Jane Hanson
(Lovell Johns Ltd, Oxford UK)
Street Finder maps based upon digital data, adapted
with permission from L.A.C. (Italy)

PHOTOGRAPHERS
John Heseltine (Venice), Roger Moss (Veneto)

ILLUSTRATORS
Arcana Studios, Donati Giudici Associati srl,
Robbie Polley, Simon Roulstone
•
Film outputting by The Best Bureau Centre Limited
(East Grinstead)
Reproduced by Colourscan (Singapore)
Printed and bound by G. Canale & C. (Italy)

First published in Great Britain in 1995
by Dorling Kindersley Limited
9 Henrietta Street, London WC2E 8PS
Reprinted with revisions 1995, 1997 (twice), 1999

A CIP CATALOGUE RECORD IS AVAILABLE FROM THE BRITISH LIBRARY.

ISBN 0-7513-0103-5
•

Every effort has been made to ensure that the information in this
book is as up-to-date as possible at the time of going to press.
However, details such as telephone numbers, opening hours,
prices, gallery hanging arrangements and travel information are
liable to change. The publishers cannot accept responsibility for
any consequences arising from the use of this book.

We would be delighted to receive any corrections and
suggestions for incorporation in the next edition.
Please write to the Deputy Editorial Director,
Eyewitness Travel Guides, Dorling Kindersley,
9 Henrietta Street, London WC2E 8PS.

CONTENTS

HOW TO USE
THIS GUIDE 6

The Venetian explorer Marco Polo

INTRODUCING VENICE AND THE VENETO

PUTTING VENICE AND
THE VENETO ON
THE MAP 10

A PORTRAIT OF THE
VENETO 16

VENICE AND THE
VENETO THROUGH
THE YEAR 32

THE HISTORY OF
VENICE AND
THE VENETO 36

**Palazzo Pisani Moretta on the
Grand Canal**

VENICE
AREA BY AREA

VENICE AT A GLANCE *54*

A VIEW OF THE
GRAND CANAL *56*

SAN MARCO *72*

The Rialto Bridge, on the
Grand Canal

SAN POLO AND
SANTA CROCE *96*

CASTELLO *108*

DORSODURO *122*

CANNAREGIO *136*

THE LAGOON
ISLANDS *146*

Veronese's *Passion and Virtue* in
the Villa Barbaro at Masèr

THE VENETO
AREA BY AREA

THE VENETO AT A
GLANCE *160*

THE VENETO PLAIN *162*

VERONA AND
LAKE GARDA *186*

THE DOLOMITES *210*

The medieval Palio dei Dieci Comuni at Montagnana

TRAVELLERS'
NEEDS

WHERE TO STAY *222*

RESTAURANTS, CAFÉS
AND BARS *234*

SHOPS AND
MARKETS *248*

ENTERTAINMENT IN
THE VENETO *254*

SURVIVAL GUIDE

PRACTICAL
INFORMATION *260*

TRAVEL
INFORMATION *270*

VENICE STREET
FINDER *280*

GENERAL INDEX *294*

Anguilla in umido

ACKNOWLEDGMENTS
309

PHRASE BOOK *311*

VAPORETTO ROUTES
AROUND VENICE
Inside back cover

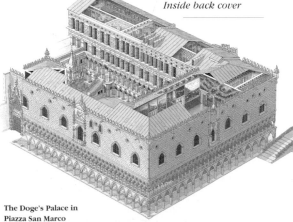

The Doge's Palace in
Piazza San Marco

HOW TO USE THIS GUIDE

THIS GUIDE helps you get the most from your stay in Venice and the Veneto. It provides both expert recommendations and detailed practical information. *Introducing Venice and the Veneto* maps the region and sets it in its historical and cultural context. *Venice Area by Area* and *The Veneto* describe the important sights, with maps, pictures and detailed illustrations. Suggestions for food, drink, accommodation, shopping and entertainment are in *Travellers' Needs*, and the *Survival Guide* has tips on everything from the Italian telephone system to travelling around Venice by *vaporetto*.

VENICE AREA BY AREA

The city has been divided into five sightseeing areas. The lagoon islands make up a sixth area. Each area has its own chapter, which opens with a list of the sights described. All the sights are numbered and plotted on an *Area Map*. The detailed information for each sight is presented in numerical order, making it easy to locate within the chapter.

Sights at a Glance lists the chapter's sights by category: Churches; Museums and Galleries; Historic Buildings; Palaces; Streets, Bridges and Squares.

Each area of Venice can be quickly identified by its colour coding.

A locator map shows where you are in relation to other areas of the city.

1 **Area Map**
For easy reference, the sights are numbered and located on a map. The sights are also shown on the Venice Street Finder *on pages 280–89.*

2 Street-by-Street Map
This gives a bird's eye view of the heart of each sightseeing area.

Stars indicate the sights that no visitor should miss.

A suggested route for a walk covers the more interesting streets in the area.

3 Detailed information on each sight
All the sights in Venice are described individually. Addresses, telephone numbers, nearest vaporetto *stop, opening hours and information on admission charges are also provided.*

The Veneto Area by Area

In this book, the Veneto has been divided into three regions, each of which has a separate chapter. The most interesting sights to visit have been numbered on a *Pictorial Map*.

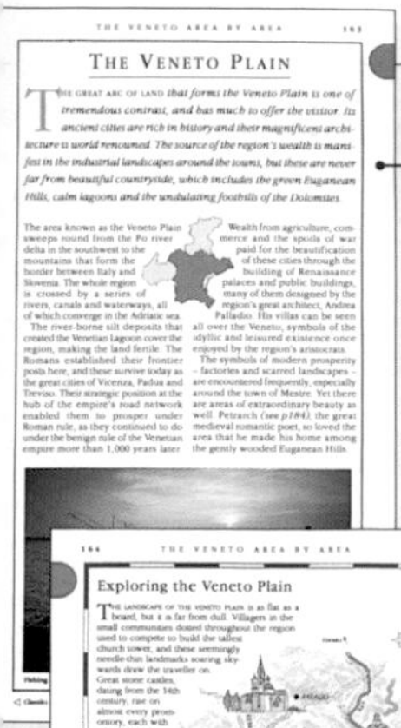

1 Introduction

The landscape, history and character of each region is described here, showing how the area has developed over the centuries and what it offers to the visitor today.

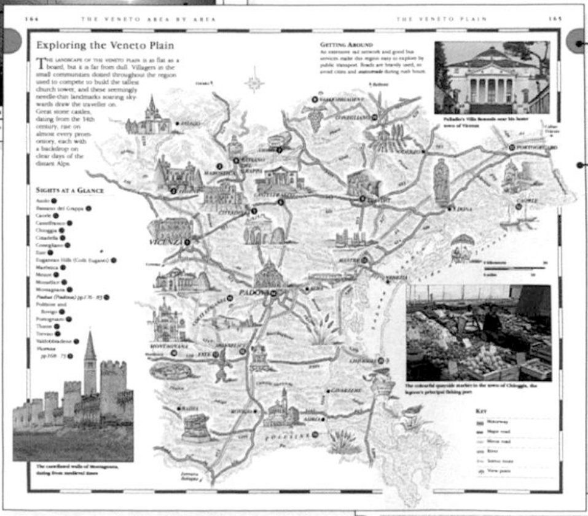

Each area of the Veneto can be quickly identified by its colour coding.

2 Pictorial Map

This shows the road network and gives an illustrated overview of the whole region. All the sights are numbered and there are also useful tips on getting around the region by car, bus and train.

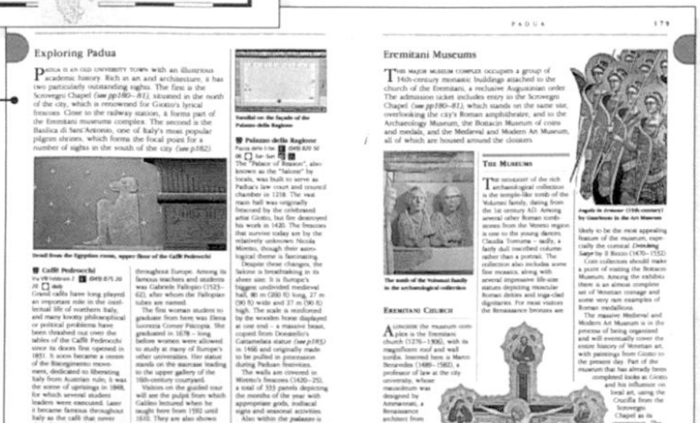

3 Detailed information on each sight

All the important towns and other places to visit are described individually. They are listed in order, following the numbering on the Pictorial Map. *Within each town or city, there is detailed information on important buildings and other sights.*

Stars indicate the best features and works of art.

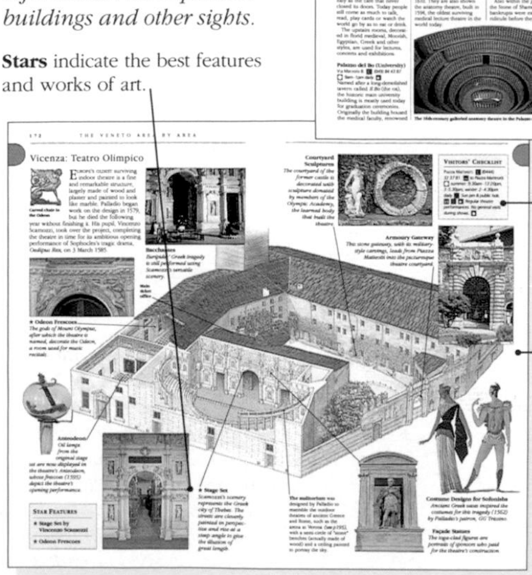

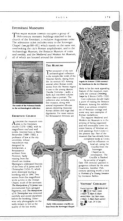

For all the top sights, a Visitors' Checklist provides the practical information you will need to plan your visit.

4 The top sights

These are given two or more full pages. Historic buildings are dissected to reveal their interiors; museums and galleries have colour-coded floorplans to help you locate the most interesting exhibits.

INTRODUCING
VENICE AND
THE VENETO

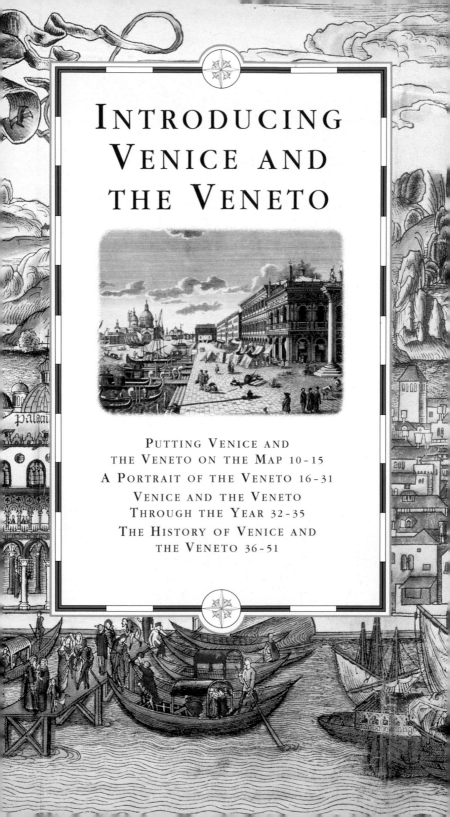

PUTTING VENICE AND
THE VENETO ON THE MAP 10-15
A PORTRAIT OF THE VENETO 16-31
VENICE AND THE VENETO
THROUGH THE YEAR 32-35
THE HISTORY OF VENICE AND
THE VENETO 36-51

Putting Venice and the Veneto on the Map

THE VENETO LIES in the northernmost sector of Italy, and stretches from the Dolomite mountains in the north to the flatlands of the Venetian lagoon in the south. One of the most prosperous regions of Italy, the Veneto covers an area of 47,562 sq km (18,364 sq miles), and has a population of 4.5 million. Rail and road links with the rest of Europe are excellent, and three international airports serve the region: Valerio Catullo in Verona, Marco Polo on the edge of the lagoon, and Treviso.

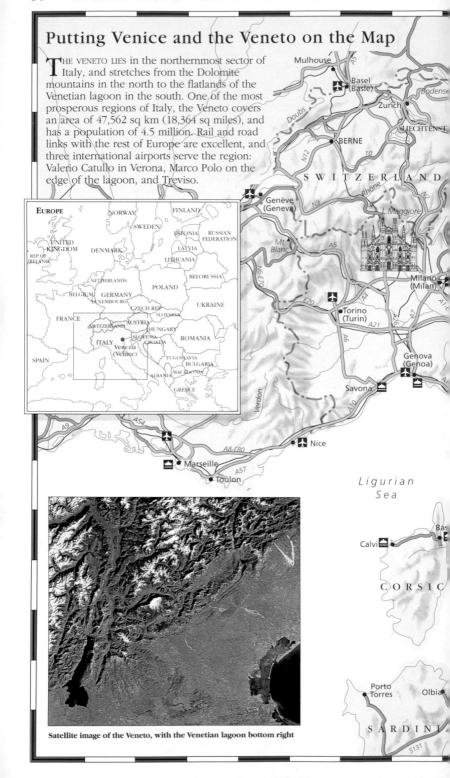

EUROPE

NORWAY, SWEDEN, FINLAND, UNITED KINGDOM, REP OF IRELAND, DENMARK, NETHERLANDS, BELGIUM, LUXEMBOURG, GERMANY, POLAND, ESTONIA, LATVIA, LITHUANIA, RUSSIAN FEDERATION, BELORUSSIA, UKRAINE, CZECH REP, SLOVAKIA, FRANCE, SWITZERLAND, AUSTRIA, HUNGARY, SLOVENIA, CROATIA, ROMANIA, ITALY, Venezia (Venice), YUGOSLAVIA, BULGARIA, ALBANIA, MACEDONIA, GREECE, SPAIN

Mulhouse, Basel (Basle), Bodense, Zurich, LIECHTENST, BERNE, SWITZERLAND, Genève (Geneva), L. Maggiore, Mt Blanc, Milano (Milan), Torino (Turin), Genova (Genoa), Savona, Nice, Marseille, Toulon

Ligurian Sea

Calvi, Bas, CORSIC, Porto Torres, Olbia, SARDINI

Satellite image of the Veneto, with the Venetian lagoon bottom right

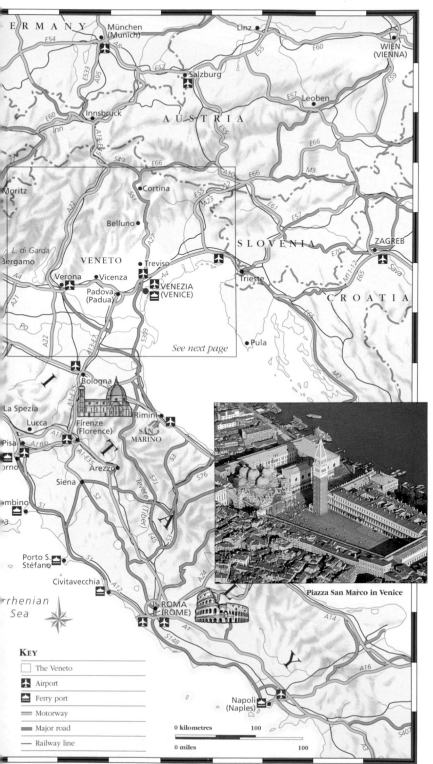

Piazza San Marco in Venice

See next page

KEY

☐ The Veneto

✈ Airport

⛴ Ferry port

══ Motorway

━━ Major road

── Railway line

0 kilometres   100

0 miles   100

Road Map of the Veneto

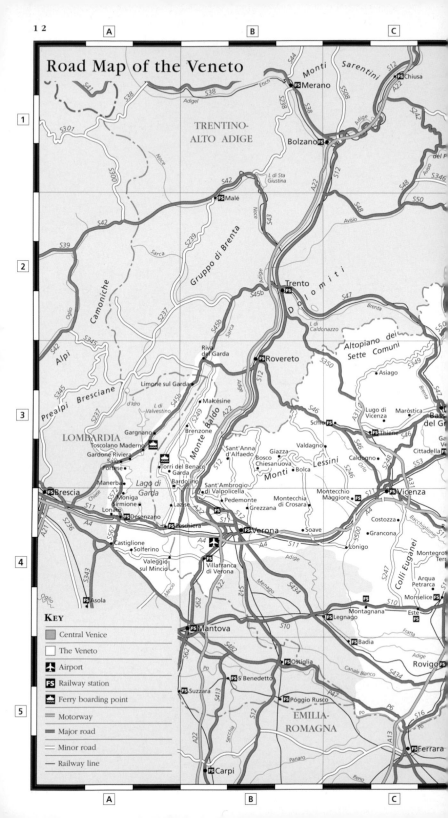

Monti Sarentini

FS Chiusa

Merano

S44

S508

TRENTINO-ALTO ADIGE

S238 S38

Adige

Bolzano FS

del P

S346

Aviso

S12

S42

L di Sta Giustina

Malé

S43

S48

S50

S239

Noce

S42

Sarca

Gruppo di Brenta

Avisio

S45b

Trento FS

S47

Brenta

Dolomiti

L di Caldonazzo

S350

Altopiano dei Sette Comuni

S349

Riva del Garda

Rovereto FS

Asiago

S12

Limone sul Garda

Prealpi Bresciane

S345

Alpi

Oglio

Camoniche

S345

S237

S12

Makésine

Lugo di Vicenza

Maròstica

Bassa del Gr

S344

Schio FS

S46

S246

Ga Ve

Thiene FS

S248

Cittadella FS

LOMBARDIA

Gargnano

Toscolano Maderno

Gardone Riviera

Salò

Portese

Manerba

Brenzone

Sant'Anna d'Alfaedo

Valdagno

Caldogno

Torri del Benaco

Garda

Bardolino

Sant'Ambrogio di Valpolicella

Lago di Garda

Lazise

Pedemonte

Grezzana

Giazza

Bosco Chiesanuova

Monti Lessini

Bolca

Montecchio Maggiore FS

Montecchia di Crosara

S53

Vicenza FS

S11

A4

Costozza

Grancona

Brescia FS

Moniga

Sirmione

Lonato

Desenzano

Peschiera

Verona FS

Soave

Lonigo

S500

Colli Euganei

Montegrotto Terme

Castiglione

Solferino

Valeggio sul Mincio

Villafranca di Verona

S247

Arquà Petrarca

Monselice FS

Este FS

Asola

Montagnana

Legnago FS

Mantova FS

Badia

Rovigo FS

Ostiglia FS

S'Benedetto FS

Pòggio Rusco FS

Suzzara FS

EMILIA-ROMAGNA

Ferrara FS

Carpi FS

KEY

	Central Venice
	The Veneto
✈	Airport
FS	Railway station
⛴	Ferry boarding point
═	Motorway
━	Major road
━	Minor road
—	Railway line

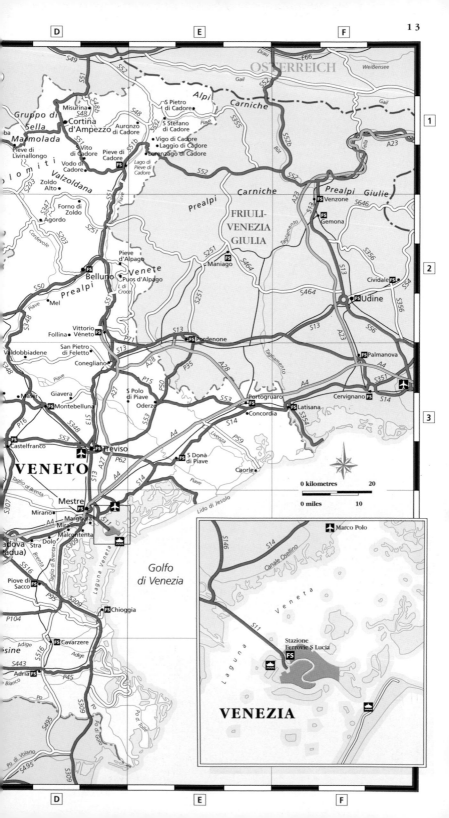

Central Venice

VENICE IS DIVIDED into six ancient administrative districts or *sestieri*. The areas described in this book for the most part follow the *sestieri* boundaries, with San Polo and Santa Croce combined. Visitors usually start with the Piazza San Marco, heading for the Doge's Palace and the breath-taking basilica, but each district has its own distinct character, and time spent exploring each will be fully rewarded.

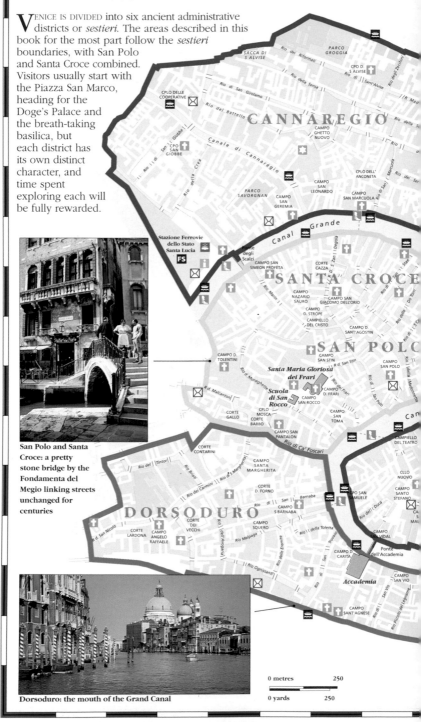

San Polo and Santa Croce: a pretty stone bridge by the Fondamenta del Megio linking streets unchanged for centuries

Dorsoduro: the mouth of the Grand Canal

| 0 metres | 250 |
| 0 yards | 250 |

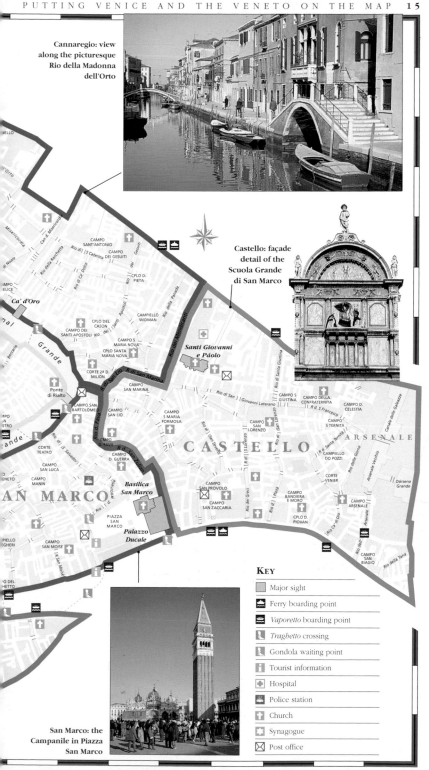

Cannaregio: view along the picturesque Rio della Madonna dell'Orto

Castello: façade detail of the Scuola Grande di San Marco

Ca' d'Oro

Grande

Ponte di Rialto

Santi Giovanni e Paolo

Basilica San Marco

Palazzo Ducale

SAN MARCO

CASTELLO

ARSENALE

San Marco: the Campanile in Piazza San Marco

KEY

	Major sight
	Ferry boarding point
	Vaporetto boarding point
	Traghetto crossing
	Gondola waiting point
	Tourist information
	Hospital
	Police station
	Church
	Synagogue
	Post office

A PORTRAIT OF THE VENETO

Venice and the Veneto form, *on the face of it, an unlikely part nership. Venice is a romantic tourist city frozen in time, the Veneto a forward-thinking and cosmopolitan part of the new Europe. Yet the commercial dynamism of the mainland cities is a direct legacy of the Old Lady of the Lagoon who, in her prime, ruled much of the Mediterranean.*

Venice is one of the few cities in the world that can truly be described as unique. It survives against all the odds, built on a series of low mud banks amid the tidal waters of the Adriatic and regularly subject to floods. Once a powerful commercial and naval force in the Mediterranean, Venice has found a new role. Her *palazzi* have become shops, hotels and apartments, her warehouses have been transformed into museums and her convents have been turned into centres for art restoration. Yet little of the essential fabric of Venice has altered in 200 years. A prewar guide to the city is just as useful today as when it was pub-

The lion of St Mark, symbol of imperial Venice

lished, a rare occurrence on a continent scarred by the aerial bombing of World War II and the demands of postwar development. More than 12 million visitors a year succumb to the magic of this improbable city whose streets are full of water and where the past has more meaning than the present.

For all this Venice has had a price to pay. So desirable is a Venetian apartment that rents are beyond the means of the Venetians themselves. Many of the city's apartments are owned by wealthy foreigners who use them perhaps for two or three weeks a year – unlit windows at night are indicative of absent owners.

Children attending their first communion at Monte Berico, outside Vicenza

◁ Venice's Carnival, an historic celebration revived in 1979

An elderly Venetian in an ageing Venice

In 1994 the population of the city was 70,000 (compared with 150,000 in 1950) and death carries off another 2,000 a year. The average age of the Venetian population is nearly 50 and the city's schools and maternity hospitals are closing for lack of use – pampered children, ubiquitous everywhere else in Italy, are markedly absent from the streets of Venice. One reason why the city shuts down so early at night is that the waiters, cooks and shop assistants all have to catch the last train home across the causeway to Mestre.

Mestre, by contrast, is a bustling city of 340,000 inhabitants, with a busy oil terminal and an expanding industrial base, as well as some of the liveliest discos in Italy. Governed by the same mayor and city council, Mestre and Venice have been described as the ugliest city in the world married to the most beautiful. Yet Mestre, founded by Venetians who foresaw a day when development land would run out in the lagoon, is simply an

Fruit seller in Sirmione, on Lake Garda

extension of that same entrepreneurial spirit that characterized mercantile Venice in her heyday, a spirit that is now typical of the region as a whole.

THE INDUSTRIOUS NORTH

The creativity and industry demonstrated by the people of the Veneto contradict all the clichés about the irrationality and indolence of the Italian character. For a tiny area, with a population of 4.5 million, the Veneto is remarkably productive. Many worldrenowned companies have manufacturing bases in the area, from Jacuzzi Europe, manufacturers of whirlpool baths, to Benetton, Zanussi, Olivetti

Benetton shop in Treviso

and Iveco Ford. As a result, poverty is rare, and the region has successfully progressed from its prewar agricultural base to a modern manufacturing and distribution economy.

Unencumbered by the rest of Italy, the three northern provinces of Piedmont, Lombardy and Venetia alone would qualify for membership of the G10 group of the world's richest nations, a fact exploited by the region's politicians in separatist calls for independence from Rome. Coldshouldering the rest of the Italian peninsula, the Veneto looks east to Slovenia for an example of a small state which has recently achieved independence, and north to Germany as a model of political federalism and sound economic management.

Valle di Cadore in the Dolomites, close to the Austrian border

Despite the ferocity of battles fought against them down the ages, the people in the north of the Veneto have a close relationship with their Germanic neighbours. Today, German signs, language and food dominate the towns around Lake Garda and the Dolomites. Here, the pretty Tyrolean farmsteads and onion-domed churches are a marked contrast to the isolated fishing communities of the lagoon, where Venice's maritime heritage is still evident. Between these two extremes, however, the urbane and likeable cities of the Veneto plain, with their wealth of culture, provide a more typical view of Italian life.

Traditional Venetian rowing

ITALIAN TRADITION

Padua is a perfect example of the *città salotto*, a city built like a salon on a human scale, where the streets are an extension of the home and where the doorless Caffè Pedrocchi is treated like the city's main square. Here Paduans come to drink coffee or write a letter, read a newspaper or talk to friends. Just like the salons of old, the café provides a meeting place for intellectual discourse and entertainment.

It is not just the Paduans who treat their streets and squares like so many corridors and rooms in one vast communal palace. After 5pm crowds throng Verona's Via Mazzini, taking part in the evening stroll, the *passeggiata*. Against the backdrop of the Roman arena or medieval *palazzi* they argue, swap gossip, forge alliances and strike deals. Younger strollers dress to impress, while young mothers bring their babies out to be admired. For all their modernity, the people of the Veneto still understand the powerful part played by ancient rituals such as this in cementing a strong sense of community.

Wedding Ferrari decorated with typical Italian style

The Building of Venice

VENICE IS BUILT on a patchwork of more than 100 low-lying islands in the middle of a swampy lagoon. To overcome these extremely challenging conditions, early Venetian builders evolved construction techniques unique to the city, building with impermeable stone supported by larchwood rafts and timber piles. This method proved effective and most Venetian buildings are remarkably robust, many having stood for at least 400 years. By 1500 the city had taken on much of its present shape and only in the 20th century has further building begun to alter the outline.

Campo Santa Maria Mater Domini *is a typical medieval square, with its central wellhead and its business-like landward façades – decoration on buildings was usually reserved for the canal façades.*

Campaniles often lean because of compaction of the underlying subsoil.

Pinewood piles *were driven 7.5 m (25 ft) into the ground before building work could begin. They rest on the solid* caranto *(compressed clay) layer at the bottom of the lagoon.*

Istrian stone, a type of marble, was used to create damp-proof foundations.

Bricks

Closely packed piles do not rot in the waterlogged subsoil because there is no free oxygen, vital for microbes that cause decay.

Water grilles

Sand acting as a filter

The well was the source of the fresh water supply. Rainwater was channelled through pavement grilles into a clay-lined cistern filled with sand to act as a filter.

Ornate wellheads, *such as this one in the Doge's Palace courtyard photographed in the late 19th century, indicate the importance of a reliable water supply for the survival of the community. Strict laws protected the purity of the source, prohibiting "beasts, unwashed pots and unclean hands".*

THE CAMPANILE FOUNDATIONS

When the Campanile in the Piazza San Marco *(see p76)* collapsed in 1902, the ancient pilings, underpinning the 98.5-m high (323-ft) landmark, were found to be in excellent condition, after 1,000 years in the ground. Like the Campanile, all buildings in Venice are supported on slender oak and pine piles, harvested in the forests of the northern Veneto and floated downriver to the Venetian lagoon. Once driven through the lagoon subsoil, they create an immensely strong and flexible foundation. Even so, there is a limit to how much weight the piles can carry – the Campanile, its height having been increased several times, simply grew too tall and collapsed. When the tower was rebuilt, timber foundations were again used, but this time more than double the size.

Strengthening the Campanile foundations

Palazzo roofs, built of light, glazed tiles, had gutters to channel rainwater to the well.

Façades were built of light-weight rose-coloured bricks, sometimes left bare, sometimes weatherproofed with plaster.

Bridges were often privately owned and tolls were charged for their use. Originally, none had railings, creating a night-time hazard for the unwary in the dark streets.

High water level

Low water level

Accumulated rubbish is regularly removed by dredging to prevent the canal silting up.

Sand and clay

Caranto is compacted clay and sand in alternate layers, which provides a stable base for building.

THE CAMPO (SANTA MARIA MATER DOMINI)

The fabric of Venice is made up of scores of self-contained island communities, linked by bridges to neighbouring islands. Each has its own water supply, church and bell-tower, centred on a *campo* (square), once the focus of commercial life. *Palazzi*, with shops and warehouses at ground floor level, border the *campo* which is connected to workshops and humbler houses by a maze of side alleys.

The Venetian Palazzo

Baroque statue

VENETIAN HOUSES EVOLVED to meet the needs of a city without roads. Visitors usually arrived by boat, so the façade facing the canal was given lavish architectural treatment, while the landward side, which was accessible from a square or alley, was rarely so ornate. Most Venetian houses were built with three storeys, with kitchens located on the ground floor for ready access to water, or in the attic to enable cooking smells to escape. Typically, a *palazzo* served as a warehouse and business premises, as well as a family home, reflecting the city's mercantile character.

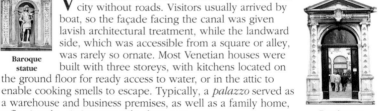

Renaissance doorcase with lion

BYZANTINE (12TH AND 13TH CENTURIES)

The earliest surviving private *palazzi* in Venice date from the 13th century and reflect the architectural influence of the Byzantine world. Façades are recognizable by their ground-floor arcades and arched open galleries which run the entire length of the first floor. Simple motifs feature leaves or palm trees.

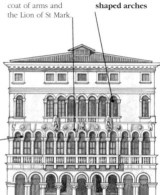

Byzantine roundel, Fondaco dei Turchi

The Byzantine arcades of the Fondaco dei Turchi (built 1225)

Façade carvings feature the owner's coat of arms and the Lion of St Mark.

Byzantine horseshoe-shaped arches

Cushion capitals have only simple motifs.

Palazzo Loredan (see p64) *has an elegant ground floor arcade and first floor gallery typical of a 13th-century Byzantine palace.*

GOTHIC (13TH TO MID 15TH CENTURIES)

Elaborate Gothic *palazzi* are more numerous than any other style in Venice. Most famous of all is the Doge's Palace *(see pp82–3)*, with elegant arches in Istrian stone and fine tracery which give the façade a delicate, lace-like appearance. This style, emulated throughout the city, can be identified through its use of pointed arches and carved window heads.

Palazzo Foscari (see p66) *is a fine example of the 15th-century Venetian Gothic style, with its finely carved white Istrian stone façade and pointed arches.*

The interlacing ribs of pointed ogee arches create a delicate tracery.

Trefoil "three leaved" window heads are typically Gothic.

Quatrefoil patterns on elegant gallery windows

Gothic capitals are adorned with foliage, animals and faces.

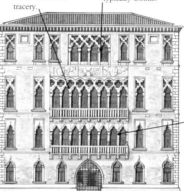

Gothic capitals (Doge's Palace)

RENAISSANCE (15TH AND 16TH CENTURIES)

Houses of the Renaissance period were often built in sandstone rather than traditional Venetian brick. The new style was based on Classical architecture, with emphasis on harmonious proportions and symmetry. The new decorative language, borrowing motifs from ancient Rome and Greece, typically incorporated fluted columns, Corinthian capitals and semi-circular arches.

Palazzo Grimani (see p64) *has lavish stone carving which none but the wealthy could afford; massive foundations were constructed to bear the incredible weight.*

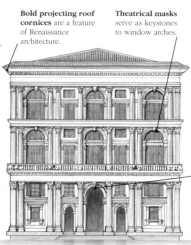

Bold projecting roof cornices are a feature of Renaissance architecture.

Theatrical masks serve as keystones to window arches.

Corinthian pilasters on the portal to San Giovanni Evangelista

The Venetian door, a very popular Renaissance motif, has a rounded central arch flanked by narrower side openings. This combination was also used for windows.

BAROQUE (17TH CENTURY)

Venetian Baroque has its roots in the Renaissance Classical style but is far more exuberant. Revelling in bold ornamentation that leaves no surface uncarved, garlands, swags, cherubs, grotesque masks and rosettes animate the main façades of buildings such as the 17th-century Ca' Pesaro.

Baroque cartouche

Semi-circular window head of Palazzo Balbi with two lights and spandrel decorated with a circle.

Massive blocks with deep ridges give solidity to the lower walls.

Ca' Pesaro (see p62) *is an example of Baroque experimentation, with its flat façade broken into a three-dimensional stone pattern of deep recesses and strong projections.*

Cherubs and plumed heads are carved into Baroque stone window heads.

Recessed windows and column clusters create an interesting play of light and shadow.

THE VENETIAN HOUSE

The layout of a typical *palazzo* (often called Ca', short for *casa*, or house) has changed little over the centuries, despite the very different styles of external decoration.

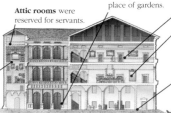

Attic rooms were reserved for servants.

Offices, used for storing business records, evolved into libraries.

Courtyards took the place of gardens.

The upper floor housed the family.

The *piano nobile* (grand floor), often lavishly decorated, was used to entertain visitors.

The ground floor storerooms and offices were used for the transaction of business.

The Villas of Palladio

Andrea Palladio

WHEN IT BECAME fashionable in the 16th century for wealthy Venetians to acquire rural estates on the mainland, many turned to the prolific architect, Andrea Palladio (1508–80) for the design of their villas. Inspired by ancient Roman prototypes, described by authors such as Vitruvius and Virgil, Palladio provided his clients with elegant buildings in which the pursuit of pleasure could be combined with the functions of a working farm. Palladio's designs were widely imitated and continue to inspire architects to this day.

The façade is symmetrical; dovecotes and stables in the wings balance the central block.

The Room of the Little Dog is ornate and lavishly decorated with frescoes by Veronese. Look closely to see the detail of a spaniel in one of the panels.

The Nymphaeum combines utility with art; the same spring that feeds the statue-lined pool also supplies water to the villa.

KEY

☐ Crociera	☐ Room of the Little Dog
☐ Bacchus Room	☐ Room of the Oil Lamp
☐ Room of the Tribunal of Love	☐ Nymphaeum
☐ Hall of Olympus	☐ Non-exhibition space

THE VILLA BARBARO

Palladio and Veronese worked closely to create this splendid villa (commissioned in 1555, *see p167*). Lively frescoes of false balconies, doors, windows and rural views create the illusion of greater space, perfectly complementing Palladio's light, airy rooms.

DEVELOPMENT OF THE VILLA

Palladio experimented with many different designs which he published in his influential *Quattro Libri (Four Books)* in 1570, illustrating the astonishing fertility of his mind and his ability to create endless variations on the Classical Roman style.

The portico statues reflect Palladio's study of ancient Roman buildings.

The pedimented pavilion is all that survives of Palladio's ambitious design; the main residence was never built.

Stables and storerooms

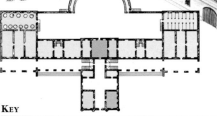

Villa Thiene (1546), now the town hall, Quinto Vicentino

The Hall of Olympus *shows Giustiniana, mistress of the house and wife of Venetian ambassador Marcantonio Barbaro, with her youngest son, wetnurse and family pets.*

In the Crociera, *the cross-shaped central hall, servants peer round false doors, while imaginary landscapes blur the boundary between the house interior and the garden.*

The Room of the Oil Lamp *symbolizes virtuous behaviour; here Strength, with the club, leans on Truth, with the mirror.*

The Bacchus Room, *with its winemaking scenes and chimneypiece carved with the figure of Abundance, reflects the bucolic ideal of the villa as a place of good living and plenty.*

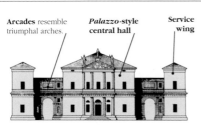

Arcades resemble triumphal arches.

***Palazzo*-style central hall**

Service wing

Villa Pisani (1555), Montagnana *(see p184)*

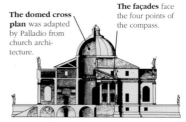

The domed cross plan was adapted by Palladio from church architecture.

The façades face the four points of the compass.

Villa Capra "La Rotonda" (1569), Vicenza *(see p171)*

Styles in Venetian Art

VENETIAN ART grew out of the Byzantine tradition of iconographic art, designed to inspire religious awe. Because of the trade links between Venice and Constantinople, capital of Byzantium, the Eastern influence lasted longer here than elsewhere in Italy. Andrea Mantegna introduced the Renaissance style to the Veneto in the 1460s, and his brother-in-law Giovanni Bellini became Venice's leading painter. In the early 16th century Venetian artists began to develop their own style, in which soft shading and dramatic use of light distinguishes the works of Venetian masters Titian, Giorgione, Tintoretto and Veronese. The development of this characteristic Venetian style, which the prolific but lesser known artists of the Baroque and Rococo periods continued, can be seen in the chronological arrangement of the Accademia *(see p130–33)*.

Detail from Veneziano's *Coronation of the Virgin*

The Last Judgment *(12th century) from Torcello: in the damp climate, mosaics, not frescoes, were used to decorate Venetian churches.*

BYZANTINE GOTHIC

Paolo Veneziano is credited with the move from grand-scale mosaics to more intimate altarpieces. His painting mixes idealized figures with the hairstyles, costumes and textiles familiar to 14th-century Venetians. The typically lavish use of jewel colours and gold, symbol of purity, can also be seen in the work of Veneziano's pupil (and namesake) Lorenzo, and in the gilded warrior angels of Guariento *(see p179)*.

Veneziano's entire dazzling polyptych (1325) of which this is the centrepiece, is in the Accademia (see p132).

The Madonna's gentle face reinforces the courtly refinement of Veneziano's work.

The composition and colours reflect the style of the early Byzantine icons which influenced the artist.

Arabesque patterns on the tunics reflect Moorish influence.

Musicians like these played at grand ceremonies in San Marco.

Paolo Veneziano's *Coronation of the Virgin*

TIMELINE OF VENETIAN ARTISTS

1300	1350	1400	1450
1338–c.1368 Guariento	**1356–72 (active)** Lorenzo Veneziano	**1430–1516** Giovanni Bellini / **1431–1506** Andrea Mantegna	**1483–1539** Giovanni Pordenone
		1415–84 Antonio Vivarini	**1450–1526** Vittore Carpaccio / **1480–1528** Palma il Vecchio / **1480–1556** Lorenzo Lotto
	1321–62 (active) Paolo Veneziano	**1395–1455** Antonio Pisanello / **1400–71** Jacopo Bellini	**1429–1507** Gentile Bellini / **1467–1510** "Il Morto da Feltre"
		1432–99 Bartolomeo Vivarini	**1477–1510** Giorgione
		1441–1507 Alvise Vivarini	**1487–1576** Titian

☐ **Byzantine Gothic**   ☐ **Early Renaissance**

Early Renaissance

Renaissance artists were fascinated by Classical sculpture and developed new techniques of perspective and shading to give their figures a three-dimensional look. Using egg-based tempera gave crisp lines and bold blocks of colour, but with little tonal gradation. The Bellini family dominated art in Renaissance Venice, and Giovanni, who studied anatomy for greater accuracy in his work, portrays the feelings of his subjects through their facial expressions.

In Bellini's 1488 Frari altarpiece, the Madonna is flanked by Saints Peter, Nicholas, Benedict and Mark (see p102).

Illusionistic details fool the eye: the real moulding copies the painted one.

St Benedict carries the Benedictine book of monastic rule.

Musical cherubs playing at the feet of the Virgin are a Bellini trademark; music was a symbol of order and harmony.

Giovanni Bellini's *Madonna and Child with Saints*

High Renaissance

Oil-based paints, developed in the late 15th century, liberated artists. This new medium enabled them to create more fluid effects, an advantage Titian exploited fully. The increasingly expressive use of light by Titian and contemporaries resulted in a distinctive Venetian style, leading to Tintoretto's masterly combination of light and shade *(see p106–7).*

Titian began this **Madonna** *in 1519 for the Pesaro family altar in the great Frari church (see p102), after his* Assumption *was hung above the high altar.*

The Virgin is placed off centre, contrary to a centuries-old rule, but Titian's theatrical use of light ensures that she remains the focus of attention.

Saint Peter looks down at Venetian nobleman Jacopo Pesaro, who kneels to give thanks to the Virgin.

Titian's *Madonna di Ca' Pesaro*

Members of the Pesaro family, Titian's patrons, attend the Virgin; Lunardo Pesaro, gazing outwards, was heir to the family fortune.

		1600–38 Francesco Maffei		**1712–93** Francesco Guardi
1500–71 Paris Bordone				**1707–88** Francesco Zuccarelli
				1708–85 Pietro Longhi
1518–94 Tintoretto				
				1696–1770 Giambattista Tiepolo
1500	**1550**	**1600**	**1650**	**1700**
	1548–1628 Palma il Giovane		**1675–1758** Rosalba Carriera	
			1676–1729 Marco Ricci	
	1528–88 Paolo Veronese	**1581–1644** Bernardo Strozzi		
			1697–1768 Canaletto	
1517–92 Jacopo Bassano				
			1727–1804 Giandomenico Tiepolo	

High Renaissance   ☐   **Baroque, Rococo & Later Artists**

Gondolas and Gondoliers

Gondoliers are part of the symbolism and mythology of Venice. Local legend has it that they are born with webbed feet to help them walk on water. Their intimate knowledge of the city's waterways is passed down from father to son (this is still very much a male preserve). The gondola, with its slim hull and flat underside, is perfectly adapted to negotiating narrow, shallow canals. Once essential for the transport of goods from the markets to the *palazzi*, gondolas today are largely pleasure craft and a trip on one is an essential part of the Venetian experience *(see p276)*. It gives an entirely different perspective on the city, gliding past grand palatial homes, using a form of transport that dates back over 1,000 years.

Hippocampus (sea horse) ornament

Squero San Trovaso (see p129) is the oldest of Venice's three surviving squeri *(boatyards). Here, new wood is seasoned, while skilled craftsmen build new gondolas and repair some of the 400 craft in use.*

Traditional dress for a gondolier is a beribboned straw hat, striped vest and black trousers.

The gondolier, unusually for an oarsman, stands upright and pushes on the oar to row the boat in the direction he is facing.

Passengers sit on upholstered cushions and low stools.

The rowlock *(forcola)* can hold the oar in eight different positions for steering the craft.

The oar has a ribbed blade.

The asymmetrical shape of the gondola counteracts the force of the oar. Without the leftward curve to the prow, 24 cm (9.5 inches) wider on the left than the right, the boat would go round in circles.

Continuing a Tradition

Gondolas are hand-crafted from nine woods – beech, cherry, elm, fir, larch, lime, mahogany, oak and walnut – using techniques established in the 1880s. A new gondola takes three months to build and costs £10,000.

Gondola Decoration

Black pitch, or tar, was originally used to make gondolas watertight. In time this sombre colour gave way to bright paint-work and rich carpets, but such displays of wealth were banned in 1562. Today all except ceremonial gondolas are black, ornamented only with their *ferro*, and a golden hippocampus on either side. For special occasions such as weddings, the *felze* (the traditional black canopy) and garlands of flowers appear, while funeral craft, now seldom seen, have gilded angels.

Ceremonial gondolas

Upper Reaches of the Grand Canal *(c.1738) is one of many paintings by Canaletto to capture the everyday life of gondoliers and their craft. Since they were first recorded in 1094, gondolas have been a Venetian institution, inspiring writers, artists and musicians.*

Races and parades *are part of the fun during Venice regattas. Professional gondoliers race in pairs or in teams of six, using boats specially designed for competition. Many amateur gondoliers also participate in the events.*

The *ferro* with its metal teeth symbolizes the six *sestieri* of Venice, beneath a doge's cap.

Seven layers of black lacquer give the gondola its gloss.

The main frame is built of oak.

More than 280 separate pieces of wood are used in constructing a gondola.

Mooring posts *and channel markers feature prominently in the crowded waterways of Venice. The posts may be topped with a family crest, to indicate a private mooring.*

Funeral gondola approaching S Michele *(see p149)*

Wedding gondola

Venetian Masks and the Carnival

THE VENETIAN GIFT for intrigue comes into its own during the Carnival, a vibrant, playful festival preceding the abstinence of Lent *(see p32)*. Masks and costume play a key role in this anonymous world; social divisions are dissolved, participants delight in playing practical jokes, and anything goes.

Flamboyant Carnival costume

The tradition of Carnival in Venice began in the 11th century and reached its peak of popularity and outrageousness in the 18th century. Industrialization left little leisure time and Carnival fell into decline, but was successfully revived in 1979.

Modern Carnival Revellers
Since 1979, each year sees more lavish costumes and impromptu celebrations.

Laws forbidding the wearing of costly lace were suspended at Carnival.

The high spirits of Venetian women scandalized many foreign observers.

The Plague Doctor
This sinister Carnival garb is based on the medieval doctor's beaked face-protector and black gown, worn as a precaution against plague.

TRADITIONAL MASK CELEBRATION

Carnival in the 18th century began with a series of balls in the Piazza San Marco, as in this fresco on the walls of Quadri's famous café in the square *(see p74)*.

Gambling at the Ridotto
Fortunes were squandered every night of Carnival at the state-run casino depicted in Guardi's painting (c.1768).

Street Entertainers
Musicians and comedians attract the crowds in the piazza San Marco.

The satyr-like profile of this dancer hints that he is the devil in disguise.

Columbine
A classic Carnival figure, Columbine wears lace and an apron, but no mask.

MAKING A MASK

Many masks, and the characters they represent, are deeply rooted in Venetian history. Though instantly recognizable by such features as the beaked nose of the Plague Doctor, each character can be interpreted in a style that is unique to its maker, making each piece a true work of art.

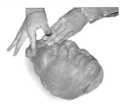

① *The form of the mask is first modelled out of clay. Then a plaster of Paris mould is made using the fired clay sculpture as a pattern.*

② *Papier mâché paste, made from a pulpy fibrous mixture of rags and paper dipped in glue, is used to make the mask itself.*

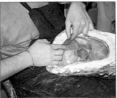

③ *To shape the mask, papier mâché paste is pushed into the plaster mould, then put aside to set. It becomes hard yet flexible as it dries.*

④ *The size, or glue, used to make the papier mâché gives the mask a smooth, shiny surface, similar to porcelain, when it is extracted.*

⑤ *An abrasive polish is used to buff the surface of the mask, which is then ready to receive the white base coat.*

⑥ *Cutting the eye holes and other features requires the mask maker to have a steady hand.*

⑦ *The features are painted on the mask and the final touches are added with a few clever brushstrokes.*

⑧ *The finished mask is ready to wear at the Carnival or to hang on a wall – the perfect Venetian souvenir.*

VENICE AND THE VENETO THROUGH THE YEAR

VENICE IS A CITY that can be enjoyed at all times of the year. Even winter's mists add to the city's romantic appeal, though clear blue skies and balmy weather make spring and autumn the best times to go. This is especially true if you combine a visit to Venice with a tour of the Veneto, where villa gardens and alpine meadows put on a colourful

Festive flag throwers in Feltre

display from the beginning of April. Autumn sees the beech, birch and chestnut trees of the region turn every shade of red and gold. In summer the waters of Lake Garda, fed by melted snow from the Alps, serve to moderate the heat. Winters are mild, allowing some of the crops typical of the southern Mediterranean, like lemons and oranges, to grow.

Winter in the delta of the River Po

WINTER

ONCE A QUIET time of year, winter now brings an increasing number of visitors to the city of Venice, especially over Christmas, New Year and Carnival. Many a day that begins wet and overcast ends in a blaze of colour – the kind of sunset reflected off rain-washed buildings that Canaletto liked to paint. In the resorts of the Venetian Dolomites, popular for winter sports, the conditions are perfect for skiing from early December throughout the winter months.

DECEMBER

Nativity. Churches all over Venice and the Veneto mount elaborate Nativity scenes in the days leading up to Christmas. Attending mass is a moving experience at this time, even for non-Christians.

Canto della Stella. In Desenzano, on Lake Garda (see p204), Christmas is marked by open-air processions called *Canto della Stella*, literally "singing to the stars".

JANUARY

Epiphany (6 Jan). Children of the Veneto get another stocking full of presents at Epiphany, supposedly brought by the old witch Befania (also known as Befana, Refana or Berolon). She forgot about Christmas, according to the story, because she was too busy cleaning her house. Good children traditionally get sweets, but naughty children get cinders from her hearth. Images of the witch appear in cake-shop windows, along with evil-looking biscuits made to resemble charcoal.

FEBRUARY

Carnival (ten days up to Shrove Tuesday). The pre-Lent festival of Carnevale (see p30), which means "farewell to meat", is celebrated throughout the Veneto. First held in Venice in the 11th century, it consisted of two months of revelry every year. Carnival fell into decline during the 18th century, but was revived in 1979 with such success that the causeway has to be closed at times to prevent overcrowding in the city.

Today the ten-day festival is mainly an excuse for donning a mask and costume and parading around the city. Various events are organized for which the Tourist Board will have details, but anyone can buy a mask and participate while watching the gorgeous costumes on show in the Piazza San Marco (see pp74–5).

Bacanal del Gnoco (11 Feb). Traditional masked procession in Verona, with groups from foreign countries and allegorical floats from the Verona area. Masked balls are held in the town's squares.

Masked revellers at the Carnival

AVERAGE DAILY HOURS OF SUNSHINE

Sunshine Chart
Few days are entirely without sunshine in Venice and the Veneto. The amount of sunshine progressively builds up to mid-summer, when it is dangerous to venture out without adequate skin protection.

Spring wisteria in Verona's Giardini Giusti *(see p203)*

SPRING

THIS IS THE SEASON when many fine gardens all over the Veneto and round Lake Garda come into their own. As the snow melts, there is time to catch the brief glory of the alpine meadows and the region's nature reserves, renowned for rare orchids and gentians. Verona holds its annual cherry market and many other towns celebrate the arrival of early crops.

MARCH

La Vecia *(mid Lent)*. Gardone and Gargnano, villages on Lake Garda *(see p204)*, play host to festivals of great antiquity, when the effigy of an old woman is burnt on a bonfire. The so-called Hag's Trials are an echo of the darker side of medieval life.
Su e zo per i ponti *(second Sun in Mar)*. A gruelling marathon-style race in Venice. Participants run through the city's streets *su e zo per i ponti* (up and down the bridges).

APRIL

Festa di San Marco *(25 Apr)*. The feast of St Mark, patron saint of Venice, is marked by a gondola race across St Mark's Basin between Sant' Elena *(see p121)* and Punta della Dogana *(see p135)*, and by the consumption of the traditional dish of *risi e bisi* *(see p236)*. Men give their wives or lovers a red rose.

MAY

Festa della Sparasea *(1 May)*. Festival and regatta for the new season's asparagus held on Cavallino, in the lagoon, where the crop is grown.

Spring produce in the Rialto's vegetable market

La Sensa *(Sun after Ascension Day)*. The ceremony of Venice's Marriage with the Sea draws huge crowds, as it has every year since Doge Pietro Orseolo established the custom in AD 1000. Once the ceremony was marked with all the pomp that the doge and his courtiers could muster. Today the words: "We wed thee, O Sea, in token of true and lasting dominion" are spoken by a local dignitary who then casts a laurel crown and ring into the sea.

Celebrating La Sensa, Venice's annual Marriage with the Sea

Vogalonga *(Sun following La Sensa)*. Hundreds of boats take part in the Vogalonga (the "Long Row") from the Piazza San Marco to Burano *(see p150)* and back – a distance of 32 km (20 miles).
Festa Medioevale del vino Soave Bianco Soave *(5 May)*. Sumptuous medieval-style celebration of the investiture of the Castillian of Suavia. There is a procession with a historical theme, music in the town square, theatrical performances and displays of various sports.
Valpollicellore *(8 May)*. Festival of local wine in Cellore with exhibitions and displays.

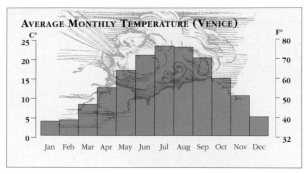

Temperature Chart
Venice, being by the sea, rarely suffers from frost in winter, but summers in the city can be unbearably humid. Temperatures in the Dolomites are considerably lower, with snow and freezing conditions from November to March.

SUMMER

SUMMER BRINGS the crowds to Venice. Queues for museums and popular sites are long, and hotels are frequently fully booked. Avoid visiting the city during the school holidays (mid Jul–end Aug). Verona, too, will be full of opera lovers attending the famous festival, but elsewhere in the Veneto it is possible to escape the crowds and enjoy the spectacular countryside.

JUNE

Sagra di Sant'Antonio *(13 Jun)*. The Feast of St Anthony has been celebrated in Padua for centuries. The day is marked by a lively fair in Prato della Valle *(see p183)*.
Biennale *(Jun–Sep)*. The world's biggest contemporary art exhibition takes place in Venice in odd-numbered years *(see p256)*.
Festa di Santi Pietro e Paolo *(end Jun)*. The feast day of Saints Peter and Paul is celebrated in many towns with fairs and musical festivals.
Regata di Santi Giovanni e Paolo *(third Sun in Jun)*. Adriatic Classic sailing regatta in Caorle *(see p175)*.

Exhibit by Japanese artist Yayoi Kusama at the Biennale

Boats for hire at Sirmione on Lake Garda

JULY

Opera Festival *(Jul–Sep)*. Verona's renowned opera festival overlaps with the equally famous **Shakespeare Festival**, providing culture lovers with a feast of music, drama, opera and dance in the stimulating setting of the Roman Arena and the city's churches *(see pp256–7)*.
Festa del Redentore *(third Sun in Jul)*. The city of Venice commemorates its deliverance from the plague of 1576. An impressive bridge of boats stretches across the Giudecca Canal so that people can walk to the Redentore church to attend mass. On the Saturday night, crowds line the Zattere or row their boats into the lagoon to watch a spectacular firework display *(see p154)*.
Sardellata al Pal del Vo *(22 Jul)*. Moonlit sardine fishing displays on Lake Garda at Pal

del Vo. Boats are illuminated and decorated, and the catch is cooked and distributed to guests and participants.

AUGUST

Village Festivals. The official holiday month is marked by local festivals throughout the Veneto, giving visitors the chance to sample food and wines and see local costume and dance. Around Lake Garda these are often accompanied by firework displays and races in boats like large gondolas.
Palio di Feltre *(first week in Aug)*. Medieval games, horse-racing and feasts commemorate Feltre's inclusion in the Venetian empire *(see p219)*.
Festa dell'Assunta *(6–14 Aug)*. Spectacular nine-day celebration in Treviso *(see p174)*. The colourful festivities feature dance, poetry, cabaret and music competitions.

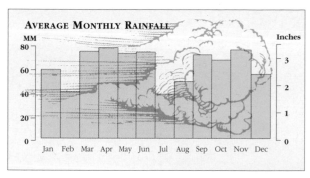

AVERAGE MONTHLY RAINFALL

Rainfall Chart
The mountains and sea combine to give Venice and the Veneto higher rainfall than is normal in the rest of Italy, with the possibility of rain on just about any day of the year. The driest months are February and July.

AUTUMN

Expect to see a profusion of market stalls selling a huge range of wild fungi as soon as the climatic conditions are right for them to grow. Local people go on expeditions to harvest them, and mushroom dishes will also feature high on the restaurant menus along with game. Another feature of autumn is the grape harvest, a busy time of year in the wine-producing regions of Soave, Bardolino and Valpolicella *(see pp208–9)*.

Grapes ripening in the Bardolino area

Medieval costume at Montagnana's Palio dei Dieci Comuni

SEPTEMBER

Venice Film Festival *(early Sep)*. The International Film Festival attracts an array of filmstars and paparazzi to the Lido *(see p157)*.
Regata Storica *(first Sun in Sep)*. Gondoliers and other boatsmen compete in a regatta which starts with an historic pageant down the Grand Canal.

Partita a Scacchi *(second weekend in Sep, alternate years)*. In Maròstica's chequerboard main square, a human chess game is re-enacted in medieval costume *(see p166)*.
Palio dei Dieci Comuni *(first Sun in Sep)*. The liberation of the town of Montagnana is celebrated with a pageant and horse race *(see p184)*.

OCTOBER

Bardolino Grape Festival *(first Sun in Oct)*. A festival for wine lovers, held to celebrate the completion of the harvest.
Festa del Mosto *(first weekend in Oct)*. The Feast of the Must on Sant'Erasmo, the market-garden island in the lagoon *(see p149)*. Here, grapes are still pressed underfoot by bare-legged dancers.

NOVEMBER

Festa della Salute *(21 Nov)*. Deliverance from the plague is celebrated with the erection of a pontoon bridge across the Grand Canal to La Salute *(see p135)*. Venetians light candles in the church to give thanks for a year's good health.

PUBLIC HOLIDAYS
New Year (1 Jan)
Epiphany (6 Jan)
Easter Monday (variable)
Liberation Day (25 Apr)
Labour Day (1 May)
Assumption (15 Aug)
All Saints (1 Nov)
Immaculate Conception (8 Dec)
Christmas Day (25 Dec)
St Stephen (26 Dec)

Rowers practising for the Regata Storica

THE HISTORY OF VENICE AND THE VENETO

THE WINGED LION of St Mark is a familiar sight to anyone travelling in the Veneto. Mounted on top of tall columns in the central square of Vicenza, Verona, Chioggia and elsewhere, it is a sign that these cities were once part of the proud Venetian empire. The fact that the lion was never torn down as a hated symbol of oppression is a credit to the benign nature of Venetian authority.

Doge Giovanni Mocenigo (1478–85)

In the 6th century AD, Venice had been no more than a collection of small villages in a swampy lagoon. By the 13th century she ruled Byzantium and, in 1508, the pope, the kings of France and Spain and the Holy Roman Emperor felt compelled to join forces to stop the advances of this powerful empire. As the League of Cambrai, their combined armies sacked the cities of the Veneto, including those such as Vicenza which had initially sided with the League. Venetian territorial expansion was halted, but she continued to dominate the Eastern Mediterranean for another 200 years.

The Venetian system of government came as close to democracy as anyone was to devise until the 19th century, and it stood the city and its empire in good stead until the bumptious figure of Napoleon Bonaparte dared to intrude in 1797. But by then Venice had become a byword for decadence and decline, the essential mercantile instinct that had created and sustained the Serene Republic for so long having been extinguished. As though exhausted by 1,376 years of independent existence, the ruling doge and his Grand Council simply resigned, but their legacy lives on, to fascinate visitors with its extraordinary beauty and remarkable history.

A map dated 1550, showing how little Venice has changed in nearly 500 years

◁ Tintoretto's *Triumph of Doge Nicolò da Ponte* (1580–84), Sala del Maggior Consiglio, Doge's Palace

Roman Veneto

THE VENETO TAKES ITS NAME from the Veneti, the pre-Roman inhabitants of the region, whose territory fell to the superior military might of the Romans in the 3rd century BC. Verona was then built as a base for the thrusting and ambitious Roman army which swept northwards over the Alps to conquer much of modern France and Germany. While the Roman empire remained intact the Veneto prospered, but the region bore the brunt of fierce and destructive barbarian attacks that began in the 4th century AD. Riddled by in-fighting and the split between Rome and Constantinople, the imperial administration began to crumble.

A Roman bust in Vicenza

Horsemen in Roman Army
Goths, Huns and Vandals served as mercenaries in the Roman cavalry but later turned to plunder.

Horse-Drawn Carriage
Finds from the region show the technological skills and luxurious lifestyles of the inhabitants.

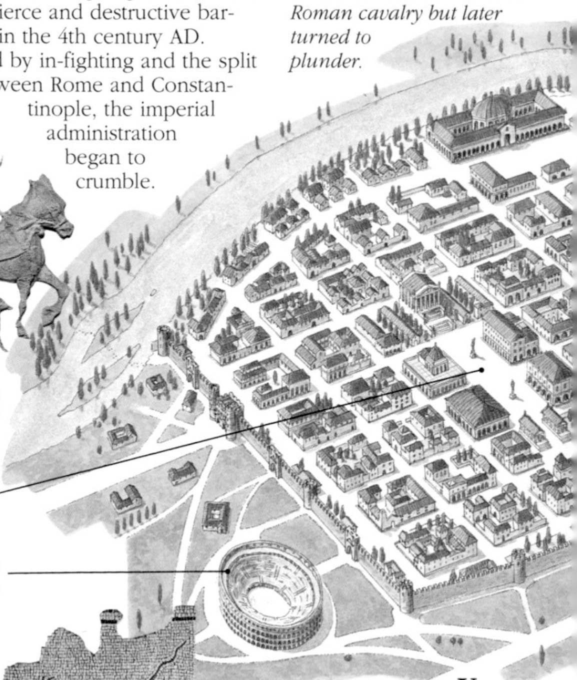

The Forum (market square)

The Arena was completed in AD 30 to entertain the troops stationed in Verona. It could hold 30,000 spectators.

Chariot Racing
A pre-Roman chariot in Adria's museum (see p185) suggests the Romans adopted the sport from their predecessors.

VERONA
Securely fortified and moated by the River Adige, Roman Verona was divided into square blocks (*insulae* or "islands"). The Forum has since been filled in by medieval palaces, but several landmarks are still discernible today *(see p192)*.

TIMELINE

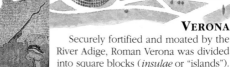

6th century BC Veneto region occupied by the Euganei and the Veneti

87 BC Catullus, Roman love poet, born in Veron

89 BC The citizens of Verona, Padua, Vicenza, Este and Treviso granted full rights of Roman citizenship

600 BC	500	400	300	200	10

3rd century BC Veneto conquered by the Romans. The Veneti and Euganei adopt Roman culture and lose their separate identities

Catullus (87–c.54 BC)

Hunting in the Lagoon

The wild lagoon, future site of Venice, attracted fishermen and huntsmen in pursuit of game and wildfowl. It also became a place of refuge during raids by Huns and Goths.

WHERE TO SEE ROMAN VENETO

Verona *(p192)* has the highest concentration of Roman sites in the region; the archaeological museum *(p202)* is full of fine mosaics and sculptures, and Castelvecchio *(p193)* has some very rare early Christian glass and silver. Good museums can also be found at Este *(p184)*, Adria, Treviso *(p174)* and Portogruaro, situated near Concordia *(p175)*.

This fine mosaic of a nightingale in Treviso Museum is from Trevisium, the town's Roman predecessor.

The theatre, built in the 1st century BC, is still used for open-air performances *(see p256)*.

Two arches of the Ponte Romano *(see p202)* survive intact.

Gladiators

Bloodthirsty citizens flocked to the gladiatorial contests in which prisoners of war, criminals and Christian martyrs were put to the sword.

Verona's Arena is an awe-inspiring home for the city's opera festival, despite the loss of its outer wall to earthquakes.

Fierce Visigoth

AD 100 The Arena, Verona's amphitheatre, is built. Far Eastern merchants bring Christianity to the region

401 Led by Alaric, the Goths invade northern Italy; the Veneto bears the brunt of the attack

360 The Roman Empire's northern borders under attack from Slavic and Teutonic tribes

AD 1	100	200	300	400

9 BC Livy, Roman historian, born in Padua

313 Constantine the Great grants official status to Christianity

331 Constantinople takes over from Rome as capital of the Roman Empire

395 Roman Empire splits into eastern and western halves

410 Alaric succeeds in sacking Rome itself, but dies the same year

The Birth of Venice

9th-century Venetian coin

FLEEING THE GOTHS, who were systematically looting and burning their way southwards to Rome, the people of the Veneto sought refuge among the wild and uninhabited islands of their marshy coast. There they formed villages, and from the ashes of the Roman past rose the city of Venice (founded, as tradition has it, in AD 421). Exploiting its easily defended maritime position, important trade links with Byzantium were created. Venice proclaimed its brash self-confidence by brazenly stealing the relics of St Mark the Evangelist from Alexandria, in Egypt.

Early Venetian Settlements
The Rialto Bridge (from Rivo Alto, or "high bank") marks the spot of one of many early settlements.

San Marco as it was before 14th-century rebuilding.

The First Crusade *(1095–9)*
Venice cunningly used the Crusades to her advantage, gaining valuable trading rights in captured cities such as Antioch and Tripoli.

The Bishop of Altino
The cathedral at Torcello was founded in AD 639, when Altino's bishop led a mass exodus to the lagoon island, fleeing Lombardic invaders.

THE ARRIVAL OF THE RELICS
This 13th-century mosaic from the façade of San Marco depicts the body of St Mark being carried into the newly built basilica for reburial in AD 832. By securing the relics of such an important saint, Venice signalled its ambition to be considered one of the foremost cities in Christendom, on a par with Rome.

TIMELINE

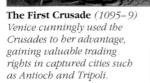

421 Venice founded, traditionally – and conveniently – on St Mark's Day, 25 April

452 Attila the Hun invades Italy and plunders the Veneto

570 The Lombards' first invasion of northern Italy; beginning of mass migration from the cities of the Veneto to lagoon islands

Charlemagne (742–814)

726 First documented doge, Orso Ipato

400	500	600	700

So-called "Attila's throne" in Torcello

552 Totila the Goth invades Italy and destroys many towns in the Veneto

639 Torcello cathedral founded

697 According to legend, Paoluccio Anafesta is elected first doge

774 Charlemagne invited to drive Lombards from Italy

800 Charlemagne is crowned first Holy Roman Emperor by Pope Leo III

Diplomacy
Strategically placed between the powers of Rome and Byzantium, Venice was continually exerting her powers of diplomacy. Here, Doge Ziani receives Holy Roman Emperor Frederick I, whom he reconciled with Pope Alexander III in 1177.

WHERE TO SEE EARLY VENICE

The cathedral at Torcello *(pp152–3)* is the oldest surviving building in Venice, and the Basilica San Marco *(pp78–83)* has many period treasures. Early Venetian coins are in the Correr Museum *(p77)*. The original statue of St Theodore is in the Doge's Palace courtyard.

Looting the remains of St Mark from Alexandria was seen as an act of anti-Moslem piety.

Torcello cathedral's jewel-like mosaics (11th century) are masterpieces of Byzantine art, probably the work of craftsmen from Constantinople.

The doge and his entourage are wearing Byzantine-style caps and robes.

St Theodore
The Byzantine emperor nominated Theodore as the patron saint of Venice. Venice chose St Mark instead, an act of defiance against Byzantine rule.

The Pala d'Oro, St Mark's 10th-century altarpiece, shows merchants bringing St Mark's plundered relics to Venice.

900	1000	1100	1200

?4 First Venetian coins minted; ?rk begins on first Doge's Palace

?32 First Basilica San ?Marco completed

888 King Berengar I of Italy chooses Verona as his seat

?28 Venetian merchants steal ?ody of St Mark from Alexandria

1000 Doge Pietro Orseolo rids the Adriatic of pirates, commemorated by the first Marriage of Venice to the Sea ceremony

1095 First Crusade; Venice provides ships and supplies

1104 Arsenale founded

1128 First street lighting in Venice

1171 Six districts *(sestieri)* of Venice established

1120 Verona's San Zeno church begun

1173 First Rialto Bridge built

1177 Emperor Frederick I Barbarossa agrees to peace terms with Pope Alexander III

1202 Venice diverts the Fourth Crusade to its own ends, the conquest of Byzantium

The Growth of the Empire

D URING THE MIDDLE AGES, Venice expanded in power and influence throughout the eastern Mediterranean, culminating in the conquest of Byzantium in 1204. At home, in contrast to the fractional strife of most of the area, Venice enjoyed a uniquely ordered administration headed by the doge, an elected leader whose powers were carefully defined by the Venetian constitution. Real power lay with the Council of Ten and the 2,000 or so members of the Grand Council, from whose number the doge and his advisers were elected.

The doge's hat, the *zogia*

Bocca di Leone
Such letterboxes were used to report crimes anonymously and were often abused (p89).

Doge Enrico Dandolo boldly led the attack on Constantinople, despite being over 90 and completely blind.

Cangrande I
Founder of the Veronese Scaligeri dynasty (see p207), Cangrande I ("Big Dog") typified the totalitarian rule of most Italian cities.

Marco Polo in China
Renowned Venetian merchant, Marco Polo (see p143) spent over 20 years at the court of Kublai Khan.

SIEGE OF CONSTANTINOPLE
Facing financial difficulties, the leaders of the Fourth Crusade agreed to attack the capital of Byzantium, as payment for warships supplied by Venice. The city fell in 1204, leaving Venice ruler of Byzantium.

TIMELINE

1204 Conquest of Constantinople; Venice's plunder includes four bronze horses	**1260** Scaligeri family rules Verona	**1309** Present Doge's Palace begun
1222 University of Padua founded	**1271–95** Marco Polo's journey to China	**1325** The names of Venice's ruling families are fixed and inscribed in the Golden Book

1200	1250	1300	1350

The Four Horses of San Marco

1284 Gold ducats first minted in Venice

1301 Dante, exiled from his native Florence, is welcomed to Verona by the Scaligeri rulers

1310 The Venetian Constitution is passed; Council of Ten formed

1304–13 Giotto paints the Scrovegni Chapel frescoes (pp180–81) in Padua

1348–9 Black Death plague kills half Venice's population

WHERE TO SEE IMPERIAL VENICE

The Doge's Palace combines ceremonial splendour and the grimmer business of imprisonment and torture (*pp84–9*). Aspects of the constitution are on display in the Correr Museum (*p77*). A *bocca di leone* survives on the Zattere (*p129*).

Decapitation
Doge Marin Falier was beheaded in 1355 for plotting to become absolute ruler of Venice. His execution was a warning to future doges.

Imperial treasures and ancient buildings were lost when the 900-year-old city was looted and burned.

Electing the Doge
This pointer was used for counting votes during dogal elections, using a convoluted system designed to prevent candidates bribing their way to power.

Troops scaled the fortifications from galleys moored against the city walls.

Many doges are commemorated by Renaissance-style monuments in the church of Santi Giovanni e Paolo (*pp116–17*).

Queen of Cyprus
Venice shamelessly gained Cyprus in 1489 by arranging for Caterina Cornaro, from one of Venice's noblest families, to marry the island's king, then poisoning him.

Meetings of the Grand Council, dominated by the merchant class, were held in the Sala del Maggior Consiglio (*p87*) in the Doge's Palace.

Battle of Chioggia

1489 Cyprus ceded to Venice by Queen Caterina Cornaro

1518 Titian's *Assumption* hung in Frari (*p102*)

1400	1450	1500	

1380 Battle of Chioggia: Venice defeats Genoa to win undisputed maritime supremacy in the Adriatic and Mediterranean

1453 Constantinople falls to the Turks; Venice's empire reaches its zenith

1508 Andrea Palladio, architect, born in Vicenza

1430 Giovanni Bellini born, greatest of the artistic family

Titian (1487–1576)

The Queen of the Adriatic

B Y THE 16TH CENTURY, Venice held a monopoly on Mediterranean trade and had colonized the whole of northeastern Italy, from the Adriatic to the Alps. Keeping hold of such a vast empire meant being in a constant state of war. The League of Cambrai, dedicated to destroying Venice, was formed in 1508 by the most powerful men in Europe, Pope Julius II and the Holy Roman Emperor Maximilian. Their troops sacked the cities of the Veneto, but the region remained loyal to Venice's relatively benign rule. Far more of a threat were the Turks. They carved out the Ottoman Empire from 1522, driving Venice from the eastern Mediterranean and eventually taking Cyprus in 1570.

16th-century armour from the Doge's Palace

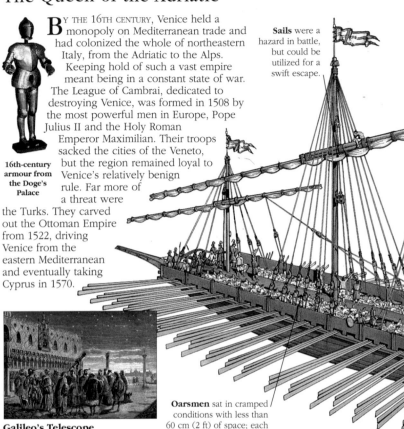

Sails were a hazard in battle, but could be utilized for a swift escape.

Oarsmen sat in cramped conditions with less than 60 cm (2 ft) of space; each team was led by a foreman.

Galileo's Telescope
Galileo, professor at Padua University from 1592 to 1610, demonstrated his telescope to Doge Leonardo Donà in 1609.

Battle of Lepanto
Venice led the combined forces of the Christian world in this bloody victory over the Turks, fought in 1571.

TIMELINE

1500			1550		16(?)
1514 Fire destroys the original timber Rialto Bridge	**1516** Jews confined to the Venetian Ghetto. End of League of Cambrai wars			**1585** First performance at Vicenza's Teatro Olimpico *(p172)*	**1592** Galileo appointed professor of mathematics at Padua University
	1518 Tintoretto born	**1528** Paolo Veronese born	**1570** Cyprus lost to the Turks		
	1501 Doge Leonardo Loredan, great diplomat, begins 20-year rule	**1529** Death of Luigi da Porto of Vicenza, author of the story of Romeo and Juliet	**1571** Battle of Lepanto: decisive victory for the western fleet, led by Venice, over the Turks	**1595** Shakespeare's *Romeo and Juliet*	
				1577 Palladio designs the Redentore church *(p154)* to mark the end of the plague that took 51,000 lives	

Celebrating the End of the Plague
More deadly than any opposing army, plague hit Venice in 1575 and again in 1630, carrying off Titian among its 100,000 victims.

WHERE TO SEE MARITIME VENICE

The triumph of Venice over the sea is celebrated in the Museo Storico Navale *(p118)*. For a glimpse of the extensive and disused Arsenale shipyard in Castello, take a trip on *vaporetto* route No. 52 or 23 *(p275)*.

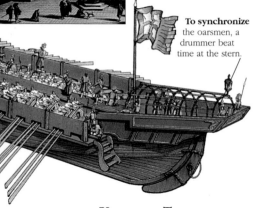

The Venice Arsenale
Venice was at the forefront of maritime construction. Her heavily defended shipyards were capable of turning out warships at the rate of one a day.

To synchronize the oarsmen, a drummer beat time at the stern.

***Arsenale lions**, plundered from Piraeus in 1687, guard the forbidding gates of the Arsenale shipyard (p119).*

The trireme was so named because the oars were grouped in threes. Each trireme had up to 150 oars.

VENETIAN TRIREME

Venetian naval supremacy was based on the swift and highly manoeuvrable trireme, used to sink enemy ships by means of its pointed battering ram and its bow-mounted cannon.

***Santa Maria della Salute** was built in thanksgiving for deliverance from the 1630 plague (p135).*

teverdi 1567– -43)

1613 Monteverdi appointed choirmaster at Basilica San Marco

1630 Plague strikes Venice again, reducing the city's population to 102,243, its smallest for 250 years

1669 Venice loses Crete to the Turks

1678 Elena Piscopia receives doctorate from Padua University, the first woman in the world ever to be awarded a degree *(p178)*

Elena Piscopia (1646–84)

1708 In a bitter winter, the lagoon freezes over and Venetians can walk to the mainland

1703 Vivaldi joins La Pietà as musical director

1718 Venetian maritime empire ends with the surrender of Morea to the Turks

| 1650 | 1700 |

Glorious Decadence

NO LONGER A MAJOR POWER, 18th-century Venice became a byword for decadence, as aristocratic Venetians frittered away their inherited wealth in lavish parties and gambling. All this crumbled in 1797 when the city was besieged by Napoleon, who demanded the abdication of the doge. Napoleon granted the city to his allies, the Austrians, whose often authoritarian rule drove many people of the Veneto to join the vanguard of the revolutionary Risorgimento. This movement, led in Venice by Daniele Manin, was dedicated to creating a free and united Italy, a dream not fully realized until 1870, four years after Venice was freed from Austrian rule.

Casanova, the Venetian libertine

The State-Run Casino
The notorious Ridotto, open to anyone wearing a mask, closed in 1774 as many Venetians had bankrupted themselves.

Gambling fever so gripped the city that gaming tables were set up between the columns in the Piazza.

Caffè Pedrocchi
Several intellectuals who had used this lavishly decorated café (see p178) in Padua as their base, were executed for leading a revolt against Austrian rule in 1831.

The Horses of St Mark
Among the art treasures looted by Napoleon were the Four Horses of St Mark, symbols of Venetian liberty. The horses were returned in 1815.

IMPERIAL RITUAL
Canaletto's *St Mark's Basin on Ascension Day* (c.1733) captures the empty splendour of Venice on the eve of her demise. The doge's gold and scarlet barge has been launched for the annual ceremony of Venice's Marriage to the Sea.

TIMELINE

1720 Caffè Florian opens in Venice (p246)	**1752** Completion of sea walls protecting the lagoon entrances	**1755** Casanova imprisoned in Doge's Palace	**1789** The Dolomites named after Déodat Dolomieu (1750–1801)
1725 Casanova born in Venice		**1775** Caffè Quadri (p246) opens in Venice	

1720 | **1770**

Florian's café

1757 Canova, Neo-Classical sculptor, born in Venice

1790 Venetian opera house, La Fenice, opens

1797 Napoleon invades the Veneto; Doge Lodovico Manin abdicates; Venetian Republic ends

1798 Napoleon grants Venice and its territories to his Austrian allies in return for Lombard

Antonio Vivaldi
(1678–1741)
Fashionable Venetians flocked to hear the red-haired priest's latest compositions, performed by the orphan girls of La Pietà. Vivaldi's most famous work, The Four Seasons *(1725), was a great success throughout Europe.*

The Bucintoro, the doge's ceremonial barge

Sumptuary laws, passed in 1562, decreed that all Venetian gondolas must be black to prevent lavish displays of wealth.

No Longer an Island
Venice lost its isolation in 1846 when a causeway joined the city to the mainland and the Italian rail network.

WHERE TO SEE 18TH-CENTURY VENICE

The Museo Storico Navale *(p118)* displays a beautifully crafted model of the Bucintoro and its original banner. Vivaldi concerts are a regular feature at La Pietà church *(p112)*. Paintings by Guardi, Canaletto and Longhi capture the spirit of the age and are found in the Accademia *(pp130–3)*, Correr Museum and Ca' Rezzonico *(p126)*.

Fortunes were spent *on opulent wigs, jewels and clothing for costume balls and the theatre. This high-heeled shoe is in the Correr Museum (p77).*

The comic antics *of Harlequin and Pantaloon at La Fenice (p93) ensured the popularity of the theatre with opera-loving Venetians.*

---

804 Napoleon crowned King of Italy and takes back Venice

1814–15 Austrians drive French from Venice; Congress of Vienna returns the Veneto to Austria

Daniele Manin (1804–57)

1859 Second War of Italian Independence; after Battle of Solferino, Red Cross founded

1861 Vittorio Emanuele crowned King of Italy

1820				1870

1818 Byron swims up the Grand Canal

1846 Venetian rail causeway links the city to the mainland for the first time

1848 First Italian War of Independence. Venice revolts against Austrian rule

1853 Ruskin publishes *The Stones of Venice*

1849 Hunger and disease force Venetian rebels, led by Daniele Manin, to surrender

1866 Venice and Veneto freed from Austrian rule

Venice in Vogue

FROM BEING AN INTROVERTED and unchanging city, Venice developed with remarkable speed. The opening of the Suez Canal in 1869 brought new prosperity; a new harbour was built for ocean-going ships and Venice became a favourite embarkation point for colonial administrators and rich Europeans travelling east. The fashion for sea-bathing and patronage by wealthy socialites reawakened interest in the city, and the founding of the Biennale attracted Europe's leading artists, who expressed their enthusiasm for the city in novels, paintings and music.

Peggy Guggenheim *(1898–1979) Patron of the avant garde, Peggy Guggenheim brought her outstanding art collection (see p134) to Venice in 1949.*

The Hotel Excelsior's Moorish exterior is distinctive.

Bathing huts, designed for modesty in the 1920s, are still a feature of the Lido.

Igor Stravinsky *(1882–1971) Along with Turgenev, Diaghilev and Ezra Pound, Stravinsky was one of many émigrés enchanted by the magic of Venice.*

Hotel Excelsior *When it was built in 1907, the Hotel Excelsior (see p231) was the world's largest hotel.*

THE LIDO

From the turn of the century, grand hotel developments along the sandy Adriatic shore turned the Lido into Europe's most stylish seaside resort. The island has since given its name to bathing establishments the world over.

TIMELINE

1883 Wagner dies in Palazzo Vendramin-Calergi

Richard Wagner (1813–83)

1902 Collapse of campanile in Piazza San Marco

1912 Opening of rebuilt campanile; Thomas Mann writes *Death in Venice*

1870	1880	1890	1900	1910

1881 Venice becomes second largest port in Italy after Genoa

1889 Poet Robert Browning dies in Ca' Rezzonico

1895 First Biennale art exhibition

1903 Patriarch Sarto of Venice becomes Pope Pius X

The International Exhibition of Modern Art
Venice became a showcase for all that was new in world art and architecture when the Biennale was launched. The first exhibition, in 1895, showed work by Renoir and Monet.

The manicured beaches of the Lido became a catwalk for style-conscious holidaymakers.

The Campanile
After the appearance of ominous warning cracks, the 1,000-year-old bell tower crashed to the ground in 1902. It was rebuilt within a decade (see p76).

WHERE TO SEE TURN-OF-THE-CENTURY VENICE

Regular *vaporetto* services link Venice to the Lido *(p156)*, with its deluxe hotels, sports facilities and beaches. The pavilions of the Biennale *(p121)* are usually only open during the exhibition. A lift carries visitors to the top of the rebuilt Campanile *(p76)* for panoramic views of Venice.

***San Michele**, the cemetery isle (p151), is the last resting place of eminent foreigners, such as Serge Diaghilev, Igor Stravinsky and Ezra Pound.*

***The exclusive** Grand Hôtel des Bains (p231) on the Lido has retained its Art Deco style and private section of beach.*

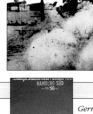

German travel poster from 1936

1917 Work starts on constructing the port of Marghera	**1926** Mestre is formally granted town status		**1954** Britten's *Turn of the Screw* premièred in Venice		**1959** Patriarch Roncalli elected Pope John XXIII
			1943–5 Mussolini rules a puppet state, the Salò Republic		
1920	**1930**	**1940**		**1950**	**1960**
1918 Fierce fighting in mountain passes of the Veneto in the last weeks of World War I	**1932** First Venice Film Festival	**1951** Stravinsky's *The Rake's Progress* premièred in Venice			**1960** Venice airport opens
	1931 Venice is linked to the mainland by a road causeway		**1956** Cortina d'Ampezzo hosts Winter Olympics		

Venice Preserved

IN NOVEMBER 1966 Venice was hit by the worst floods in its history, sparking worldwide concern for the future of the city's delicate and decaying fabric. Major steps have since been taken to protect Venice and its unique heritage, though some difficult issues remain, including the erosion caused by large numbers of visitors to the city and pollution from the economically buoyant mainland. However, the allure of Venice, set in its watery lagoon, is as compelling as ever.

Pink Floyd in Venice
Pink Floyd's 1989 rock concert threatened the city's equilibrium.

Venice as Film Set
Venice has served as the backdrop to countless films, including Fellini's Casanova *(1976) and* Indiana Jones and the Last Crusade *(1989).*

The Regata Storica, held in September, is an annual trial of strength and skill for gondoliers.

After the Flood
During the 1966 floods, the waters rose nearly 2 m (6 ft). Great damage was done by fuel oil, washed out of broken tanks. It is now banned from the city in favour of gas.

TOURISM

Venetian regattas are part of a rich tradition that enhances the city's attraction to tourists, providing employment for many on the mainland as well as in Venice itself. Even so, some complain that tourism has turned Venice from a living city into one vast museum.

TIMELINE

1966 Floods cause devastation in Venice. UNESCO launches its Save Venice appeal

Visconti and Dirk Bogarde on the set of Death in Venice

1978 Patriarch Luciani of Venice elected Pope John Paul I, but dies 33 days later

1960

1970

1968 Protestors prevent part of the lagoon being drained to extend Marghera's industrial zone

1970 Luchino Visconti's film, *Death in Venice*

1973 Laws passed to reduce pollution, subsidence and flooding.

Benetton
*The famous clothing firm,
originating in Treviso,
represents the modern
face of Veneto industry.*

Venice plays host to
over 12 million visitors
every year.

Glass Blowing
*This age-old tradition still
contributes to the economy.*

Water is now piped into
Venice to combat subsidence
caused by water extraction
from the subsoil.

The Acqua Alta
*High tides cause frequent
flooding in San Marco.
Plans to complete a flood
barrier across the lagoon
are subject to controversy.*

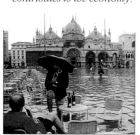

RESTORATION IN VENICE

One positive result of the
1966 floods was a major
international appeal for
funds to pay for the cleaning
of historic buildings, statues
and paintings. Funds raised
are coordinated under the
auspices of UNESCO, with
offices in

***Restorers** learn how to repair
and conserve fragile works of
art at the School of Craftsmanship on San Servolo (p154).*

***Madonna dell'Orto** (p140)
was restored by the Italian Art
and Archives Rescue Fund
(later renamed Venice in Peril).*

1979 Venetian
Carnival is
revived

1988 First experimental stage of MOSE,
the lagoon flood barrier, is completed

1983 Venice officially stops
sinking after extraction of
underground water prohibited

*1932–1992 Venice
Film Festival poster*

1992 Venice Film
Festival celebrates
60 years

1995
Centenary
of Biennale
Exhibition

1980

1990

*Carnival
reveller*

1990 Plans to hold Expo 2000 in
Venice defeated by Italian parliament
after massive international pressure

1992 Venice rocked by corruption
scandals. Metro network beneath
lagoon proposed

1994 Voters
decide against a
divorce between
Venice and
Mestre, which
share a mayor
and city council

VENICE AREA BY AREA

VENICE AT A GLANCE 54–55
A VIEW OF THE GRAND CANAL 56–71
SAN MARCO 72–95
SAN POLO AND SANTA CROCE 96–107
CASTELLO 108–121
DORSODURO 122–135
CANNAREGIO 136–145
THE LAGOON ISLANDS 146–157

Venice at a Glance

Venice is small and most of the sights can be comfortably visited on foot. The heart of the city is the Piazza San Marco, which is overlooked by the great Basilica and the Doge's Palace. For many, these are attractions enough, but there are delights worth exploring beyond the Piazza, such as the galleries of the Accademia, Ca' Rezzonico and the imposing Frari church. Unique to Venice are the naval Arsenale to the east and the Ghetto in the north.

Ghetto
Established in the early 16th century, this fascinating quarter was the world's first ghetto (see p145).

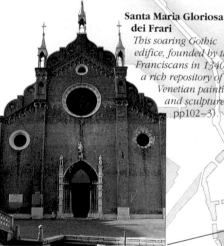

Santa Maria Gloriosa dei Frari
This soaring Gothic edifice, founded by the Franciscans in 1340, is a rich repository of Venetian painting and sculpture (see pp102–3).

CANNAREGIO
Pages 136–45

SAN POLO AND SANTA CROCE
Pages 96–107

DORSODURO
Pages 122–35

SAN MAR
Pages 72–

| 0 metres | 500 |
| 0 yards | 500 |

Ca' Rezzonico
The splendid rooms of this palace, overlooking the Grand Canal, are decorated with 18th-century furniture and paintings (see p126).

Accademia
Carpaccio's St Ursula cycle (1490–5) is one of the treasures of the Accademia, which has a comprehensive collection of Venetian art (see pp130–3).

Rialto Bridge
*The bustling Rialto Bridge
(see p100) was named after
the ancient commercial seat
of Venice, where the first
inhabitants settled.*

Ca' d'Oro
*This ornate palace is the
finest example of Venetian
Gothic style* (see p142).

Basilica San Marco
*Magnificent mosaics
sheathe the domes, walls
and floor of the Byzantine
Basilica (see pp78–83).*

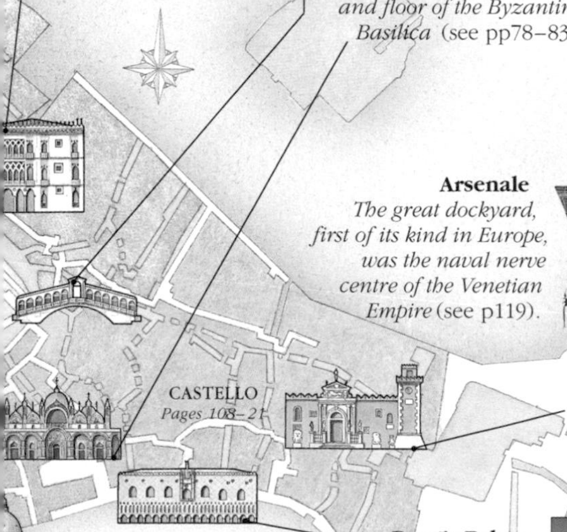

Arsenale
*The great dockyard,
first of its kind in Europe,
was the naval nerve
centre of the Venetian
Empire* (see p119).

CASTELLO
Pages 108–21

Doge's Palace
*The colonnaded Gothic
palace was the seat of
government as well as
home to the doge and his
family* (see pp84–89).

Santa Maria della Salute
*Marking the southern end of the Grand
Canal, this great Baroque church is one
of the city's landmarks* (see p135).

A VIEW OF
THE GRAND CANAL

KNOWN to the Venetians as the *Canalazzo*, the Grand Canal sweeps through the heart of Venice, following the course of an ancient river bed. Since the founding days of the empire it has served as the city's main thoroughfare. Once used by great galleys or trading vessels making their stately way to the Rialto, it is nowadays teeming with *vaporetti*, launches, barges and gondolas. Glimpses of its glorious past, however, are never far away. The annual re-enactment of historic pageants, preserving the traditions of the Venetian Republic, brings a blaze of colour to the canal. The most spectacular is the Regata Storica held in September *(see p35)*,

Venetian gondolier

a huge procession of historic craft packed with crews in traditional costumes, followed by boat and gondola races down the Grand Canal.

The parade of palaces bordering the winding waterway, built over a span of around 500 years, presents some of the finest architecture of the Republic. Historically it is like a roll-call of the old Venetian aristocracy, with almost every *palazzo* bearing the name of a once-grand family. Bright frescoes may have faded, precious marbles worn, and foundations frayed with the tides, but the Grand Canal is still, to quote Charles VIII of France's ambassador in 1495, "the most beautiful street in the world".

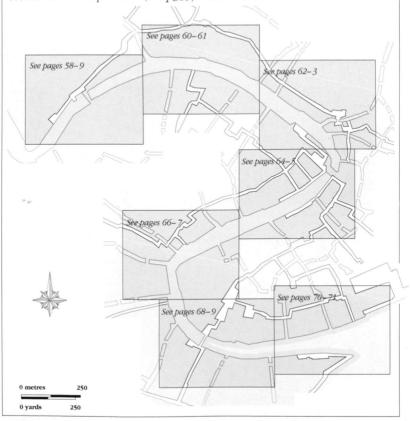

See pages 60–61

See pages 58–9

See pages 62–3

See pages 64–5

See pages 66–7

See pages 70–71

See pages 68–9

| 0 metres | 250 |
| 0 yards | 250 |

◁ **The Grand Canal at its most colourful, during the Regata Storica**

Santa Lucia to Palazzo Flangini

Vaporetto ticket office, Grand Canal

THE GRAND CANAL is best admired from a gondola or, more cheaply, from a *vaporetto*. Several lines travel the length of the canal *(see p275)* but only the No. 1 goes sufficiently slowly for you to take in any of the individual palaces. The journey from the station to San Zaccaria takes about 40 minutes. Ideally you should take a return trip, absorbing one bank at a time. Nearly 4 km (2½ miles) long, the canal varies in width from 30 to 70 m (98 to 230 ft) and is spanned by three bridges, the Scalzi, the Rialto and the Accademia.

LOCATOR MAP

Santa Maria di Nazareth is known today as the Scalzi, after the supposedly "shoeless" Carmelites who founded it (see p145). Within is the tomb of Ludovico Manin, last of the doges.

Santa Lucia railway station (see p272), *built in the mid 19th century and remodelled in the 1950s, links the city with the mainland.*

La Direzione Compartimentale, *the administration offices for the railway, was built at the same time as the station, on the site of the church of Santa Lucia and other ancient buildings.*

Ferrovia

Palazzo Diedo, *also known as Palazzo Emo, is a Neo-Classical palace of the late 18th century. It is believed to be the birthplace of Angelo Emo (1731– 92), the last admiral of the Venetian fleet. The palace was built by Andrea Tirali, an engineer who worked on the restoration of San Marco.*

Palazzo Calbo Crotta is now the 4-star Hotel Principe. Fine antiques and fabrics which once decorated the palace are now in Ca' Rezzonico (see p126).

Palazzo Flangini was designed by Giuseppe Sardi, a leading 17th-century architect.

Palazzo Gritti was built in the 16th century. The Grittis were a wealthy family who produced one of the most intelligent doges, Andrea Gritti (reigned 1523–38).

The Scalzi Bridge was built in 1934, replacing the original wrought iron bridge.

Campo San Simeone Grande, named after the nearby church (otherwise called San Simeone Profeta), is one of the few campi overlooking the canal.

Casa Adoldo and Palazzo Foscari-Contarini were both rebuilt in the 16th century. According to local tradition, the great Doge Francesco Foscari (ruled 1423–57) was born in the original Foscari-Contarini palace.

San Simeone Piccolo is a large church, despite its name (piccolo means small). Built in 1738, its design was based partly on the Pantheon in Rome. It is only open for concerts.

San Geremia to San Stae

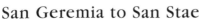

THIS STRETCH sees the start of the great palaces. The most remarkable is the Vendramin Calergi, which became a model for other Venetian palaces.

LOCATOR MAP

San Geremia houses the relics of St Lucy, formerly preserved in Santa Lucia where the station now stands.

Palazzo Labia, frescoed with Tiepolo's Venetian-style Story of Cleopatra, is open to the public (see p143).

Palazzo Querini has the family coat of arms on the façade.

Palazzo Corner-Contarini is also called Ca' dei Cuori after the hearts in the family coat of arms.

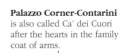

Palazzo Giovanelli, a restored Gothic palace, was acquired by the Giovanellis in 1755. This titled non-Venetian family had been admitted into the Great Council in 1668 for a fee of 100,000 ducats.

Fondaco dei Turchi was a splendid Veneto-Byzantine building before last century's brutal restoration. Today it houses the Natural History Museum (see p105).

Palazzo Donà Balbi, built in the 17th century, is named after two great Venetian families who intermarried. The Donà family produced four doges.

Deposito del Megio, a crenellated building with a reconstructed Lion of St Mark, was a granary in the 15th century.

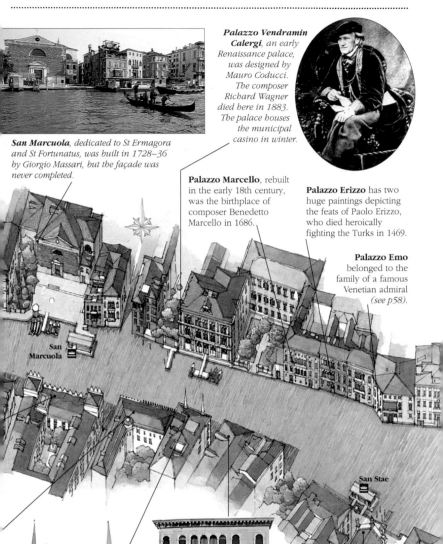

Palazzo Vendramin Calergi, *an early Renaissance palace, was designed by Mauro Coducci. The composer Richard Wagner died here in 1883. The palace houses the municipal casino in winter.*

San Marcuola, *dedicated to St Ermagora and St Fortunatus, was built in 1728–36 by Giorgio Massari, but the façade was never completed.*

Palazzo Marcello, rebuilt in the early 18th century, was the birthplace of composer Benedetto Marcello in 1686.

Palazzo Erizzo has two huge paintings depicting the feats of Paolo Erizzo, who died heroically fighting the Turks in 1469.

Palazzo Emo belonged to the family of a famous Venetian admiral *(see p58).*

San Marcuola

San Stae

Palazzo Tron, *built in the late 16th century, hosted a famous ball in 1775 in honour of Emperor Joseph II of Austria.*

Palazzo Belloni Battagia, *with its distinctive pinnacles, was built by Longhena in the mid 17th century for the Belloni family, who had bought their way into Venetian aristocracy.*

San Stae *is striking for its Baroque façade, graced by marble statues. It was funded by a legacy left by Doge Alvise Mocenigo in 1709 (see p105).*

Palazzo Barbarigo to the Markets

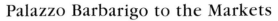

Here the canal is flanked by stately palaces, built over a period of five centuries. The most spectacular is the Gothic Ca' d'Oro, whose façade once glittered with gold.

Palazzo Barbarigo retains the vestiges of its 16th-century frescoed façade paintings.

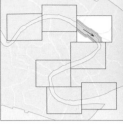

LOCATOR MAP

Palazzo Gussoni-Grimani's façade once had frescoes by Tintoretto. It was home to the English ambassador in 1614–18.

Palazzo Fontana Rezzonico was the birthplace of Count Rezzonico (1693), the fifth Venetian pope

■ San Stae

Ca' Foscarini, a Gothic building of the 15th century, belonged to the Foscari family before it became the residence of the Duke of Mantua in 1520.

Ca' Pesaro, *a huge and stately Baroque palace designed by Longhena (see p23), today houses the Gallery of Modern Art and the Oriental Museum (see p105). It was built for Leonardo Pesaro, a Procurator of San Marco.*

Casa Favretto (Hotel San Cassiano) was the home of the painter Giacomo Favretto (1849–87).

Palazzo Morosini Brandolin *belonged to the Morosini family, one of the Case Vecchie families, deemed to be noble before the 9th century.*

Ca' Corner della Regina *is named after Caterina Cornaro, Queen of Cyprus, who was born here in 1454. The present building (1724–7) was designed by Domenico Rossi.*

The Pescheria *has been the site of a busy fish market for six centuries. Today it takes place in the striking mock-Gothic market hall, built in 1907.*

Ca' d'Oro, *the most famous of Venetian Gothic palaces (see p144), houses paintings, frescoes and sculpture from the collection of Baron Giorgio Franchetti, who bequeathed the palace and all its contents to the State.*

CANALETTO

Antonio Canale (Canaletto) (1697–1768) is best known for his *vedute* or views of Venice. He studied in Rome, but lived here for most of his life. One of his patrons was Joseph Smith *(see below)*. Sadly there are very few of his paintings left on view in the city.

Palazzo Sagredo *passed from the Morosini to the Sagredo family in the early 18th century. The façade shows characteristics of both Veneto-Byzantine and Gothic styles.*

Palazzo Foscarini *was the home of Marco Foscarini, a diplomat, orator and scholar who rose to the position of doge in 1762.*

Palazzo Michiel dalle Colonne was named after its distinctive colonnade.

Palazzo Michiel del Brusà was rebuilt and named after the great fire *(brusà)* that swept the city in 1774.

Palazzo Mangili Valmarana *was designed by Antonio Visentini (above) in Classical style for Joseph Smith, who became the English consul in Venice. Smith (1682–1770) was a patron of both Visentini and Canaletto.*

Ca' da Mosto *is a good example of 13th-century Veneto-Byzantine style. Alvise da Mosto, the 15th-century navigator, was born here in 1432.*

...Oro

Tribunale Fabbriche Nuove, Sansovino's market building (1555), is now the seat of the Assize Court.

The Rialto Quarter

THE AREA AROUND THE RIALTO BRIDGE is the oldest and busiest quarter of the city. Traditionally a centre of trade, crowded quaysides and colourful food markets still border the canal south of the bridge.

LOCATOR MAP

Palazzo Papadopoli, *formerly known as Coccina-Tiepolo, was built in 1560. Its splendid hall of mirrors has been preserved.*

Riva del Vin *is one of the few spots where you can sit and relax on the banks of the Grand Canal (see p98).*

Ca' Corner-Martinengo-Ravà *became the Leon Bianco Hotel in the 19th century. The American writer, James Fenimore Cooper, stayed here in 1838.*

Palazzo Barzizza, rebuilt in the 17th century, still preserves its early 13th-century façade.

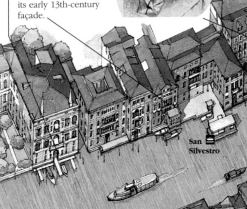

San Silvestro

Palazzo Grimani, *a fine, if somewhat austere looking, Renaissance palace (see p23), was built in 1556 by Michele Sanmicheli for the Procurator, Girolamo Grimani. The State purchased the palace in 1807 and it is now occupied by the city's Court of Appeal.*

Palazzo Farsetti and Palazzo Loredan, *both occupied by the City Council, were built around 1200 and finally merged in 1868. Palazzo Farsetti became an academy for young artists, one of whom was Canova.*

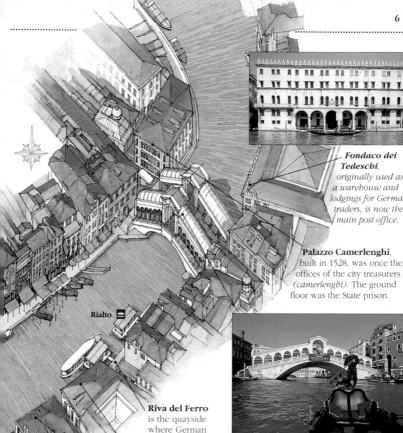

***Fondaco dei Tedeschi**, originally used as a warehouse and lodgings for German traders, is now the main post office.*

Palazzo Camerlenghi, built in 1528, was once the offices of the city treasurers *(camerlenghi)*. The ground floor was the State prison.

Rialto

Riva del Ferro is the quayside where German trading barges offloaded iron *(ferro)*.

The Rialto Bridge (see p100) *was built to span the Grand Canal in what was, and still is, the most commercial quarter of the city.*

Casetta Dandolo's predecessor is said to have been the birthplace of Doge Enrico Dandolo (ruled 1192–1205).

Palazzo Manin-Dolfin *was built by Sansovino in 1538–40 but only his Classical stone façade survives. The interior was completely transformed for Ludovico Manin, last doge of Venice (died 1797). He intended to turn the house into a magnificent palace extending as far as Campo San Salvatore.*

***Palazzo Bembo**, a 15th-century Gothic palace, was the birthplace of the Renaissance cardinal and scholar, Pietro Bembo, who wrote one of the earliest Italian grammars.*

THE DANDOLO FAMILY

The illustrious Dandolo family produced four doges, 12 procurators of San Marco, a patriarch of Grado and a queen of Serbia. The first of the doges was Enrico who, despite being old and blind, was the principal driving force in the Crusaders' plan to take Constantinople in 1204 *(see p42)*. The other remarkable doge in the family was the humanist and historian, Andrea Dandolo (died 1354).

Doge Enrico Dandolo

La Volta del Canal

THE POINT WHERE THE CANAL doubles back sharply on itself is known as La Volta – the bend. This splendid curve was long ago established as the finishing stretch for the annual Regata Storica *(see p35)*.

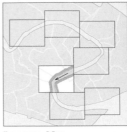

Palazzo Marcello, *which belonged to an old Venetian family, is also called "dei Leoni" because of the lions either side of the doorway.*

Palazzo Persico, on the corner of Rio San Polo, is a 16th-century house in Lombardesque style.

Palazzo Civran-Grimani is a Classical building of the early 17th century.

Palazzo Balbi, *seat of the regional government, was built for Nicolô Balbi, who is said to have died of a chill surveying its construction. From here, Napoleon viewed the 1807 regatta, held in his honour.*

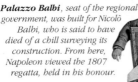

Ca' Foscari *was built for Doge Francesco Foscari in 1437(see p22). It is now part of the University of Venice.*

Palazzo Giustinian was the residence of Wagner in 1858–9, when he was composing the second act of *Tristan and Isolde.*

Ca' Rezzonico, *now the museum of 18th-century Venice (see p126), became the home of the poet Robert Browning and his son, Pen, in 1888.*

San Tomà

San Samuele

Ca' Rezzonico

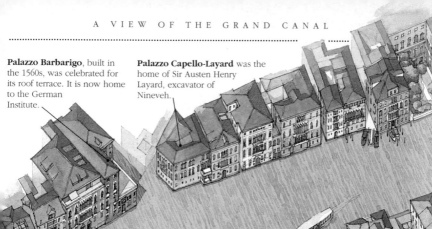

Palazzo Barbarigo, built in the 1560s, was celebrated for its roof terrace. It is now home to the German Institute.

Palazzo Capello-Layard was the home of Sir Austen Henry Layard, excavator of Nineveh.

Sant' Angelo

Palazzo Corner Spinelli, Mauro Coducci's outstanding Renaissance palace, built in 1490–1510, became a prototype for other mansions in Venice.

Palazzo Garzoni, a renovated Gothic palace, is now part of the university. The traghetto service, which links the neighbouring Calle Garzoni to San Tomà on the other side of the canal, is one of the oldest in Venice.

Palazzo Mocenigo, formed by four palaces linked together, has a plaque to the poet Byron who stayed here in 1818.

Palazzo Moro Lin, also known as the "palace of the 13 windows", was created in the 17th century for the painter Pietro Liberi by merging two Gothic houses.

Palazzo Grassi, built in the 1730s, was bought by Fiat in 1984 and turned into a venue for art exhibitions.

Palazzo Capello Malipiero, a Gothic palace, was reconstructed in 1622. Beside it, in Campo di San Samuele, stands the church of San Samuele which has a 12th-century Veneto-Byzantine campanile.

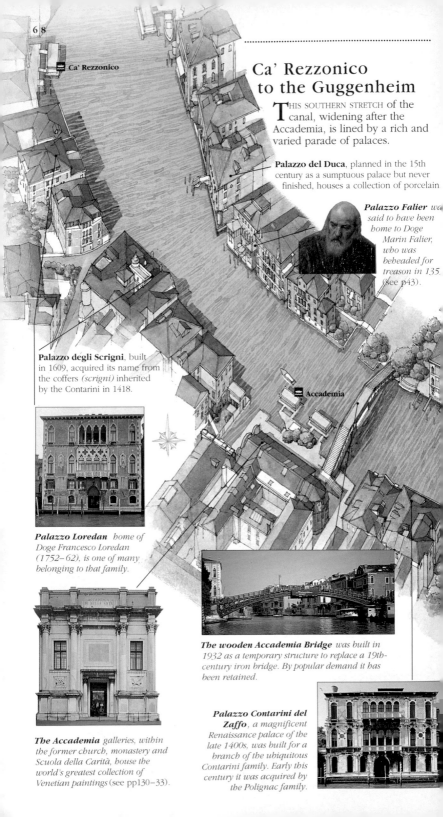

Ca' Rezzonico

Ca' Rezzonico to the Guggenheim

THIS SOUTHERN STRETCH of the canal, widening after the Accademia, is lined by a rich and varied parade of palaces.

Palazzo del Duca, planned in the 15th century as a sumptuous palace but never finished, houses a collection of porcelain

Palazzo Falier was said to have been home to Doge Marin Falier, who was beheaded for treason in 1355 (see p43).

Palazzo degli Scrigni, built in 1609, acquired its name from the coffers *(scrigni)* inherited by the Contarini in 1418.

Accademia

Palazzo Loredan home of Doge Francesco Loredan (1752–62), is one of many belonging to that family.

The wooden Accademia Bridge was built in 1932 as a temporary structure to replace a 19th-century iron bridge. By popular demand it has been retained.

Palazzo Contarini del Zaffo, a magnificent Renaissance palace of the late 1400s, was built for a branch of the ubiquitous Contarini family. Early this century it was acquired by the Polignac family.

The Accademia galleries, within the former church, monastery and Scuola della Carità, house the world's greatest collection of Venetian paintings (see pp130–33).

LOCATOR MAP

Palazzo Franchetti Cavalli
belonged to Archduke Frederick
of Austria, who died here in 1836.

Palazzo Barbaro comprises two
palaces, one of which was
bought by the Curtis
family in 1885. Monet
and Whistler painted
here and Henry James
(right) wrote The
Aspern Papers.

Ca' Grande, a huge Classical
palace, was designed in 1545
by Sansovino for Giacomo
Cornaro, nephew of the Queen
of Cyprus. The family was one of
the richest in Venice and spared
no expense in the palace's decoration. This family tree illustrates
the extent of the Cornaro's wealth
and influence in Venice.

Casetta delle Rose, one of the
smallest houses on the canal,
was the home of Italian poet
Gabriele d'Annunzio during
World War I. Canova (above)
had his studio here in 1770.

Palazzo
Barbarigo, beside the
Campo San Vio, stands out for
the harsh mosaics, added in 1887.

Peggy Guggenheim
established her collection
of modern art in Venice
in 1951 (see p134). She
chose as her venue the
Palazzo Venier dei Leoni,
which had been built in
1749 and never finished.

Palazzo Dario,
built in 1487, is a
charming but
strangely ill-fated
palace (see p135).

To La Salute and San Marco

THE VIEW ALONG THE FINAL STRETCH of the canal is one of the finest – and most familiar – in Venice. Near the mouth rises the magnificent church of La Salute with busy St Mark's Basin beyond.

LOCATOR MAP

Palazzo Contarini Fasan, a tiny 15th-century palace with an elegant façade, is popularly known as the House of Desdemona from Shakespeare's play.

The Palazzo Gritti-Pisani, where Ruskin stayed in 1851, is better known today as the luxurious 5-star Hotel Gritti Palace (see p229).

Santa Maria Del Giglio

Salute

The mock-Gothic mansion, Ca' Genovese, was built in 1892 in the place of the second Gothic cloister of the San Gregorio monastery.

The deconsecrated Gothic brick church of Abbazia San Gregorio and a little cloister are all that survive of what was for centuries a powerful monastic centre. The church is now used as a laboratory for the renovation of large-scale paintings.

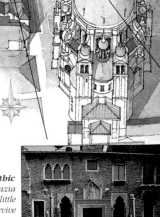

Palazzo Salviati is the head-quarters of the Salviati glass-producing company, hence the glass mosaics on the façade.

Palazzo Tiepolo, *the Hotel Europa and Regina, was formerly owned by the Tiepolo family, associated with an unsuccessful uprising in 1310.*

Harry's Bar (see p92) *was popular with Hemingway and other writers. This was the very first Harry's Bar in the world.*

Palazzo Giustinian, head-quarters of the Biennale, used to be a hotel, where Turner, Verdi and Proust stayed.

San Marco Vallaressa

Giardinetti Reali, the Royal Gardens, were created by Napoleon to improve his view from the Procuratie Nuove.

Palazzo Treves Bonfili, a Classical building of the 17th century, is decorated with Neo-Classical frescoes, paintings and statuary.

***The view from the Dogana**, taking in the Doge's Palace, the Campanile of San Marco and the Zecca, is one of the most memorable in Venice.*

Santa Maria della Salute, *a Baroque church of monumental proportions, is supported by over a million timber piles. Built to commemorate the end of the 1630 plague, it was the work of Baldassare Longhena (see p135).*

Dogana di Mare, *the customs house, is topped by a weathervane figure of Fortune (see p135).*

SAN MARCO

HOME OF THE POLITICAL and judicial nerve centres of Venice, the *sestiere* of San Marco has been the heart of Venetian life since the early days of the Republic. The great showpiece of the Serenissima was the Piazza San Marco, conceived as a vista for the Doge's Palace and the Basilica. The square, described by Napoleon as "the most elegant drawing room in Europe",

Adam and
Eve on the
corner of the
Doge's Palace

was the only one deemed fit to be called a piazza – the others were merely *campi*, or fields.

The San Marco area has the bulk of luxury hotels, restaurants and shops. It is also home to several imposing churches, three theatres, including the famous Fenice, and a wealth of handsome *palazzi*. Many of these line the sweeping southern curve of the Grand Canal which borders the *sestiere*.

SIGHTS AT A GLANCE

Churches
Basilica San Marco
  pp78– 83 **3**
Santa Maria Zobenigo **13**
San Moisè **11**
San Salvatore **18**
Santo Stefano **16**
San Zulian **21**

Museums and Galleries
Libreria Sansoviniana **5**
Museo Archeologico **6**
Museo Correr **8**
Museo Fortuny **17**

Palaces
Doge's Palace pp84–9 **4**
Palazzo Contarini
  del Bovolo **12**

Historic Buildings and Monuments
Campanile **1**
Columns of San Marco
  and San Teodoro **7**
San Giorgio Maggiore **22**
Torre dell'Orologio **2**

Streets and Squares
Campo San Bartolomeo **19**
Campo Santo Stefano **15**
Mercerie **20**

Bars
Harry's Bar **9**

Theatres
La Fenice **14**
Ridotto **10**

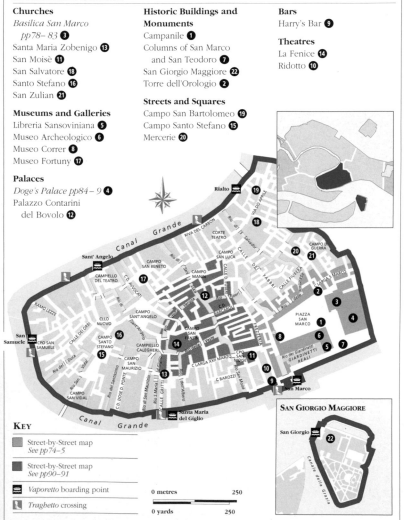

KEY

■ Street-by-Street map
  See pp74–5

■ Street-by-Street map
  See pp90–91

■ *Vaporetto* boarding point

■ *Traghetto* crossing

0 metres   250
0 yards   250

SAN GIORGIO MAGGIORE

◁ **Central dome of the Basilica San Marco**

Street-by-Street: Piazza San Marco

Lion of St Mark

THROUGHOUT ITS long history the Piazza San Marco has witnessed pageants, processions, political activities and countless Carnival festivities. Tourists flock here in their thousands, for the Piazza's eastern end is dominated by two of the city's most important historical sights – the Basilica and the Doge's Palace. In addition to these magnificent buildings there is plenty to entertain, with elegant cafés, open-air orchestras and smart boutiques beneath the arcades of the Procuratie. So close to the waters of the lagoon, the Piazza is one of the first points in the city to suffer at *acqua alta* (high tide). Tourists and Venetians alike can then be seen picking their way across the duckboards which are set up to crisscross the flooded square.

Gondolas customarily moor in the Bacino Orseolo, named after Doge Pietro Orseolo who established a hospice for pilgrims here in 977.

Quadri's café was the favourite haunt of Austrian troops during the Occupation *(see p48).*

Museo Correr
Giovanni Bellini's Pietà *(1455–60) is one of many Renaissance masterpieces hanging in the picture galleries of the Correr* **8**

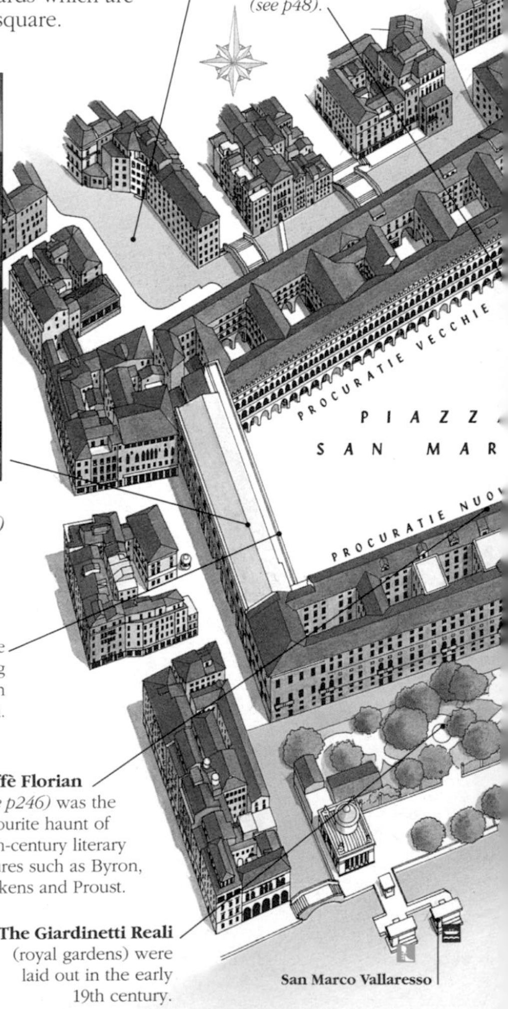

The Ala Napoleonica is the most recent wing enclosing the square, built by Napoleon to create a new ballroom.

PROCURATIE VECCHIE

PIAZZA SAN MARCO

PROCURATIE NUOVE

0 metres   75
0 yards   75

STAR SIGHTS

★ Basilica San Marco

★ Doge's Palace

★ Campanile

Caffè Florian
(see p246) was the favourite haunt of 19th-century literary figures such as Byron, Dickens and Proust.

The Giardinetti Reali (royal gardens) were laid out in the early 19th century.

San Marco Vallaresso

Torre dell'Orologio
The Madonna on the clock tower is greeted each Epiphany and Ascension by clockwork figures of the Magi ②

Piazzetta dei Leoncini
was named after the pair of porphyry lions which stand in the square.

LOCATOR MAP
See Street Finder, map 7

★ **Basilica San Marco**
The remarkable Basilica of St Mark is a glorious reflection of the city's Byzantine connection ③

★ **Doge's Palace**
Once the Republic's seat of power and home to its rulers, the Doge's Palace, beside the Basilica, is a triumph of Gothic architecture ④

★ **Campanile**
Today's tower replaced the one that collapsed in 1902. The top provides spectacular views of the city ①

Museo Archeologico
The museum sculptures had a marked influence on Venetian Renaissance artists ⑥

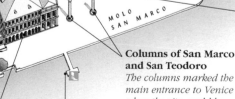

Columns of San Marco and San Teodoro
The columns marked the main entrance to Venice when the city could be reached only by sea ⑦

San Marco Giardinetti

The Zecca, designed by Sansovino and started in 1537, was the city mint until 1870, and gave its name to the *zecchino* or Venetian ducat.

Libreria Sansoviniana
The ornate vaulting of the magnificent library stairway is decorated with frescoes and gilded stucco ⑤

Campanile ❶

Piazza San Marco. **Map** 7 B2.
📞 (041) 522 40 64. 🚏 San Marco.
🕐 9:30am–3:45pm daily. ● Jan. ♿

F ROM THE TOP of St Mark's
campanile, high above the
Piazza, visitors can enjoy
sublime views of the city, the
lagoon and, visibility permitting, the peaks of the
Alps. It was from this
viewpoint that Galileo

The spire, 98.5 m (323
ft) high, is topped with
a golden weathervane
which was designed
by Bartolomeo Bon.

The five bells in
the tower each
had their role
during the
Republic. The
marangona
tolled the start
and end of the
working day; the
malefico warned
of an execution;
the *nona* rang at
noon; the
mezza terza
summoned
senators to the
Doge's Palace;
and the *trottiera*
announced a
session of the
Great Council.

An internal lift,
installed in 1962,
provides visitors
with access to
one of the most
spectacular views
across Venice.

The Loggetta
was built in the
16th century
by Jacopo
Sansovino. Its
Classical
sculptures
celebrate the
glory of the
Republic.

**The allegorical
reliefs** in red marble
from Verona depict
Justice representing
Venice, Jupiter as
Crete and Venus as
Cyprus. All were
carefully rebuilt after
the campanile's
collapse in 1902.

demonstrated his telescope to
Doge Leonardo Donà in
1609. To do so he would
have climbed the internal
ramp. Access these days is
achieved far less strenuously
via a lift which can carry 14
people. Nevertheless there is
almost always a queue. If you
are at the top of the tower on
the hour, beware the resonant
ringing of the five bells.

The first tower, completed
in 1173, was built as a light-
house to assist navigators in
the lagoon. It took on a less
benevolent role in the Middle
Ages as the support for a
torture cage where offen-
ders were imprisoned and
in some cases left to die.
The tower's present
appearance dates from
the early 16th century,
when it was restored
by Bartolomeo Bon
after an earthquake.

The tower survived
the vicissitudes of
time until 14 July
1902 when, with little
warning, its founda-
tions gave way and it
suddenly collapsed.
The only casualties
were the Loggetta at
the foot of the tower
and the custodian's
cat. Donations for
reconstruction came
flooding in and the
following year the
foundation stone was
laid for a campanile
"dov'era e com'era"
("where it was and
how it was"). The new
tower was finally
opened on 25 April (St
Mark's Day) 1912.

**The highly ornamented clock face
of the Torre dell'Orologio**

Torre dell'Orologio ❷

Piazza San Marco. **Map** 7 B2. 🚏 San
Marco. ● for restoration.

T HE RICHLY decorated
Renaissance clock tower
stands on the north side of
the Piazza, over the archway
leading to the Mercerie *(see
p95)*. It was built in the late
15th century, and the central
section is thought to have
been designed by Mauro
Coducci. Displaying the
phases of the moon and the
zodiac, the gilt and blue
enamel clock was originally
designed with seafarers in
mind. A story was spread by
scandalmongers that once the
clock was complete, the two
inventors of the complex
clock mechanism had their
eyes gouged out to prevent
them creating a replica.

During Ascension Week,
crowds gather on the hour to
watch the figures of the Magi
emerge from side doors to
pay their respects to the Virgin
and Child, whose figures are
set in the niche above the
clock. On the upper level, the
winged lion of St Mark stands
against a star-spangled blue
backdrop. At the very top the
two huge bronze figures,
known as the *Mori*, or Moors,
because of their dark patina,
strike the bell on the hour.

Basilica San Marco ❸

See pp78–83.

Doge's Palace ❹

See pp84–9.

Libreria Sansoviniana 5

Piazzetta. **Map** 7 B3. 📞 *(041) 520 87 88.* 🚌 *San Marco.* 🕐 *for guided tours only; tours start at 10am, 11am & noon.* ● *public hols.* ⓧ

PRAISED BY Andrea Palladio as the finest building since antiquity, the library was designed in the Classical style by the Tuscan architect, Jacopo Sansovino. A graceful building, it is surmounted by a procession of statues of mythological gods. During construction (1537–88) the vaulting collapsed: Sansovino was blamed and imprisoned. He was freed only after appeals from eminent acquaintances.

Today the national library of St Mark, the Biblioteca Marciana, is housed here. Its greatest treasure is the Grimani Breviary, a manuscript illuminated by 15th- and 16th-century Flemish artists. The salon is sumptuously decorated, and two fine ceiling paintings by Paolo Veronese, *Arithmetic and Geometry* and *Music*, won for the artist the prize of a golden necklace.

Museo Archeologico 6

Piazzetta. **Map** 7 B3. 📞 *(041) 522 59 78.* 🚌 *San Marco.* 🕐 *9am–2pm daily.* ● *1 Jan, 1 May, 25 Dec.* 🖼 📷

HOUSED IN ROOMS in both the Libreria Sansoviniana and the Procuratie Nuove, the museum provides a quiet retreat from the bustle of San Marco. The collection owes its existence to the generosity of Domenico Grimani, son of Doge Antonio Grimani, who bequeathed all of his Greek, Roman and earlier sculpture, together with his library, to the State in 1523.

Columns of San Marco and San Teodoro 7

Piazzetta. **Map** 7 C3. 🚌 *San Marco.*

ALONG WITH ALL the bounty from Constantinople came the two huge granite columns which now tower above the Piazzetta. These were said to have been erected in 1172 by the engineer Nicolò Barattieri, architect of the very first Rialto Bridge. For his efforts he was granted the right to set up gambling tables between the columns. A more gruesome spectacle on the same spot was the execution of criminals, which took place here until the mid 18th century. Even today, superstitious Venetians will not be seen walking between the columns.

The western column is crowned by a marble statue of St Theodore, who was the patron saint of Venice before St Mark's relics were smuggled from

Columns of San Marco and San Teodoro

Alexandria in AD 828. The statue is a modern copy – the original is kept for safety in the Doge's Palace *(see p88)*.

The second column is surmounted by a huge bronze of the Lion of St Mark. Its origin remains a mystery, though it is thought to be a Chinese chimera with wings added to make it look like a Venetian lion. In September 1990 the 3,000-kg (3-ton) beast went to the British Museum in London for extensive restoration, and was returned with great ceremony and skill to the top of the column.

Fragment from a monumental statue, in the Museo Archeologico

***A Portrait of a Young Man in a Red Hat* by Carpaccio (c.1490)**

Museo Correr 8

Procuratie Nuove. Entrance in Ala Napoleonica. **Map** 7 B2. 📞 *(041) 522 56 25.* 🚌 *San Marco.* 🕐 *Apr–Oct: 9am–7pm daily; Nov–Mar: 9am–5pm daily.* ● *1 Jan, 25 Dec.* 🖼 ⓧ

THE WEALTHY Abbot Teodoro Correr bequeathed his extensive collection of works of art and documents to the city in 1830. This forms the nucleus of the civic museum.

The first rooms form a suitably Neo-Classical backdrop for early statues by Antonio Canova (1757–1822). The rest of the floor covers the history of the Venetian Republic, with maps, coins, armour and a host of doge-related exhibits.

On the second floor, the Museo del Risorgimento is devoted to the history of the city, until Venice became part of unified Italy in 1866. Also here is the Quadreria, or picture gallery. The paintings are hung chronologically and the rooms have the bonus of explanations in English. The collection enables you to trace the evolution of Venetian painting, and to see the influence that Ferrarese, Paduan and Flemish artists had on the Venetian school. The most famous works in the gallery are the Carpaccios: *A Portrait of a Young Man in a Red Hat* (c.1490), and *Two Venetian Ladies* (c.1507). The latter is traditionally, but probably incorrectly, known as *The Courtesans* because of the ladies' décolleté dresses.

Basilica San Marco ❸

THIS AWESOME BASILICA, built on a Greek cross plan and crowned with five huge domes, is the third church to stand on this site. The first, built to enshrine the body of St Mark in the 9th century, was destroyed by fire. The second was pulled down in the 11th century in order to make way for a more spectacular edifice designed by an unknown architect (1063–94), reflecting the escalating power of the Republic. The basilica continued to be remodelled over the following centuries, and in 1807 it succeeded San Pietro in the *sestiere* of Castello *(see p120)* as the cathedral of Venice; it had until then served as the doge's private chapel for State ceremonies.

The Pentecost Dome, showing the Descent of the Holy Ghost as a dove, was probably the first dome to be decorated with mosaics.

St Mark and Angels
The statues crowning the central arch are additions from the early 15th century.

★ **Horses of St Mark**
The four horses are replicas of the gilded bronze originals (see p80), now protected inside the Basilica.

★ **Central Doorway Carvings**
The central arch features 13th-century carvings of the Labours of the Month. The grape harvester represents September.

★ **Façade Mosaics**
A 17th-century mosaic shows the body of St Mark being taken from Alexandria, reputedly smuggled out under slices of pork.

Ciborium
The fine alabaster columns of the altar canopy, or ciborium, are adorned with scenes from the New Testament.

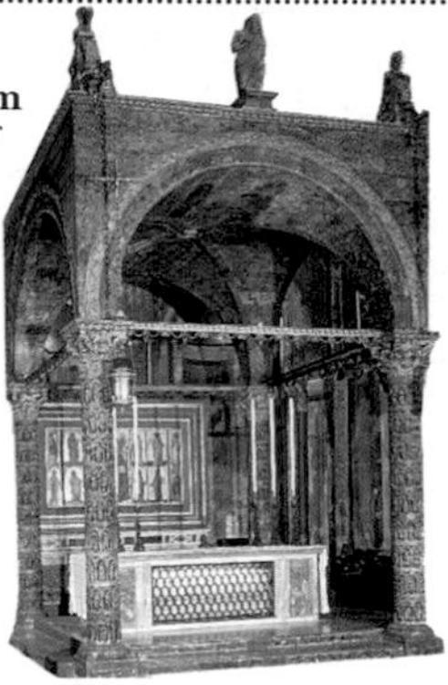

VISITORS' CHECKLIST

Piazza San Marco. **Map** 7 B2. *(041) 522 52 05.* *San Marco.* **Basilica, Treasury and Pala d'Oro** *Oct–May: 9:45am–4pm Mon–Sat, 2–4pm Sun; Jun–Sep: 9:45am–5:30pm Mon–Sat, 2–5:30pm Sun.* **Museum** *as above, but also 9:45am–2pm Sun.* *Museum, Treasury and Pala d'Oro only.* *9 times a day. Sightseeing is limited during services.* *in English twice a week in season.*

The Ascension Dome features a magnificent 13th-century mosaic of Christ surrounded by angels, the 12 Apostles and the Virgin Mary.

St Mark's body, believed lost in the fire of AD 976, supposedly reappeared in this spot in 1094, when the new church was consecrated.

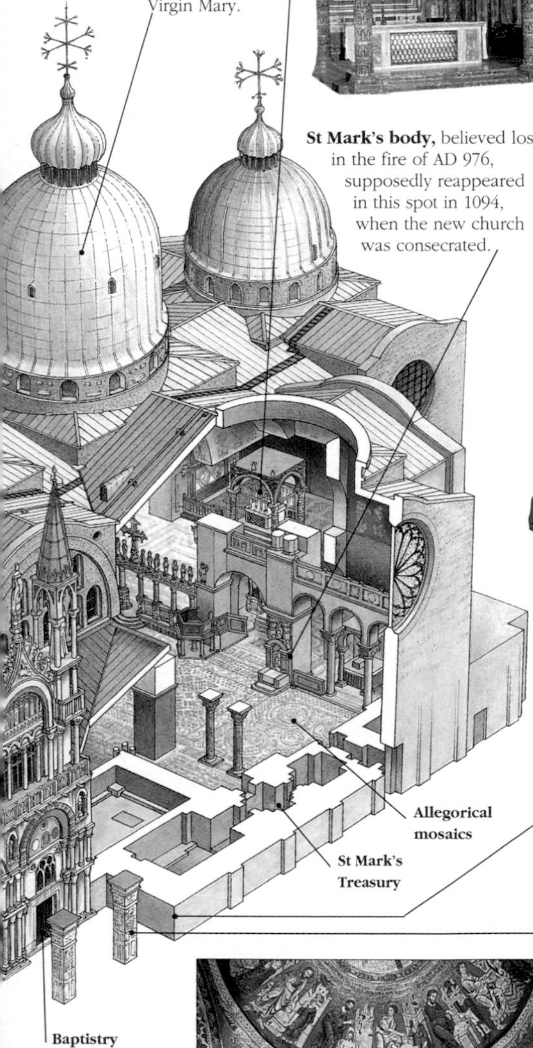

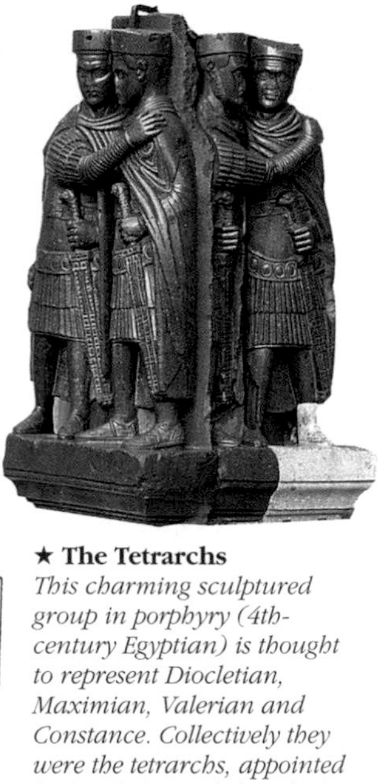

★ The Tetrarchs
This charming sculptured group in porphyry (4th-century Egyptian) is thought to represent Diocletian, Maximian, Valerian and Constance. Collectively they were the tetrarchs, appointed by Diocletian to help rule the Roman Empire.

The so-called Pilasters of Acre in fact came from a 6th-century church in Constantinople.

Baptistry Mosaics
Herod's Banquet *(1343–54) is one of the mosaics in a cycle of scenes from the life of St John the Baptist.*

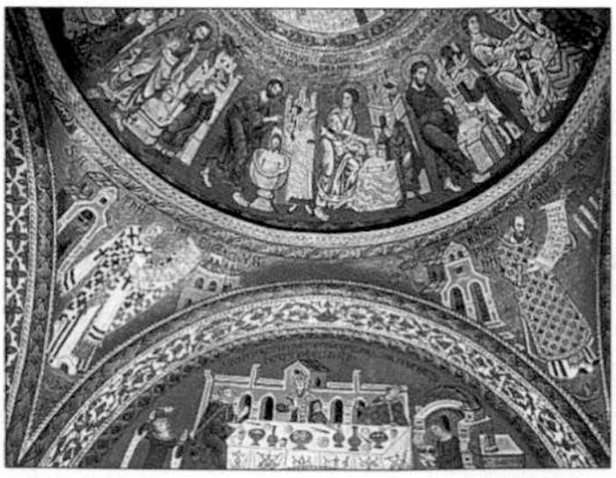

STAR FEATURES

- ★ **Façade Mosaics**
- ★ **Horses of St Mark**
- ★ **The Tetrarchs**
- ★ **Central Doorway Carvings**

Inside the Basilica

D ARK, MYSTERIOUS and enriched with the spoils of conquest, the Basilica is a unique blend of Eastern and Western influences. This oriental extravaganza, embellished over a period of six centuries with fabulous mosaics, marble and carvings, made a fitting location for the ceremonies of the Serene Republic. It was here that the doge was presented to the city following his election, that heads of State, popes, princes and ambassadors were received, and where sea captains came to pray for protection before embarking on epic voyages.

Mascoli Chapel
Formerly called the "New Chapel", this is named after an all-male confraternity, or mascoli.

North Aisle
The gallery leading off the museum affords visitors a splendid overall view of the mosaics.

The Porta dei Fiori or Gate of Flowers is decorated with 13th-century reliefs.

★ **Pentecost Dome**
Showing the Apostles touched by tongues of flame, the Pentecost Dome was decorated in the 12th century.

The columns of the inner façade are thought to be fragments of the first basilica.

Main entrance

★ **Atrium Mosaics**
In the glittering Genesis Cupola the Creation of the World is described in concentric circles. Here, God creates the fish and birds.

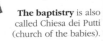

The baptistry is also called Chiesa dei Putti (church of the babies).

The Altar of the Virgin has a 10th-century icon of the Madonna of Nicopeia, which came with the spoils of war in 1204 (see p42).

The Chapel of St Peter has a 14th-century altar screen relief of St Peter worshipped by two Procurators.

★ **Pala d'Oro**
The magnificent altarpiece, created in the 10th century by medieval goldsmiths, is made up of 250 panels such as this one, each adorned with enamels and precious stones.

The sacristy door (often locked) has fine bronze panels by Sansovino, which include portraits of himself with Titian and Aretino.

★ **Ascension Dome**
A mosaic of Christ in Glory decorates the enormous central dome. This masterpiece was created by 13th-century Venetian craftsmen, who were strongly influenced by the art and architecture of Byzantium.

The Altar of the Sacrament is surrounded by mosaics of the parables and miracles of Christ dating from the late 12th or early 13th century.

 South aisle

★ **Treasury**
A repository for precious booty from Constantinople, the Treasury also houses ancient Italian works of art, such as this 12th- or 13th-century incense burner.

STAR FEATURES
★ Pala d'Oro
★ Atrium Mosaics
★ Treasury
★ Ascension and Pentecost Domes

Exploring the Basilica

THE BASILICA cannot comfortably be covered in one visit. The glittering mosaics, the rich store of bounty from the east, the dim, mysterious lighting and the sheer size of the place create a feeling of confusion for first-time visitors. To get the most out of it, make several visits, ideally at different times of the day. The mosaics look especially splendid during the hour 11:30am–12:30pm when the church is fully illuminated. Visitors are often led towards the (fee-paying) Pala d'Oro and Treasury and miss out on other sections of the church. To avoid the crowds, visit early in the morning or in the evening. If a mass is in progress visitors are expected to be silent and will only be able to visit certain areas.

The Genesis Cupola of the atrium

Stories of Joseph and of Moses in the domes at the north end. The figures of saints on either side of the main doorway date from the 11th century and are among the earliest mosaics in the church. Just in front of the central doorway there is a lozenge of porphyry to mark the spot where the Emperor Frederick Barbarossa was obliged to make peace with Pope Alexander III in 1177 (see p41).

MUSEO MARCIANO

A PRECARIOUS STAIRWAY from the atrium, marked *Loggia dei Cavalli*, takes you up to the church museum. The gallery gives a splendid view into the basilica, while from the exterior loggia you can survey the Piazza San Marco and take a close look at the replica horses on the church façade. It was from this panoramic balcony that doges and dignitaries once looked down on ceremonies taking place in the square. The original gilded bronze horses, housed in a room at the far end of the museum, were stolen from the top of the Hippodrome (ancient racecourse) in Constantinople in 1204 but their origin, either Roman or Hellenistic, remains a mystery. In the same room is Paolo Veneziano's 14th-century *pala feriale*, painted with stories of St Mark, which once covered the Pala d'Oro. Also on show are medieval

MOSAICS

CLOTHING THE DOMES, walls and floor of the basilica are over 4,000 sq m (40,000 sq ft) of gleaming golden mosaics. The earliest, dating from the 12th century, were the work of mosaicists from the east. Their techniques were adopted by Venetian craftsmen who gradually took over the decoration, combining Byzantine inspiration with western influences. During the 16th century, sketches and cartoons by Tintoretto, Titian, Veronese, and other leading artists were reproduced in mosaic. The original iconographical scheme, depicting stories from the Testaments, has more or less been preserved by careful restoration.

Among the finest mosaics in the basilica are those decorating the 13th-century central Dome of the Ascension and the 12th-century Dome of the Pentecost over the nave.

The *pavimento*, or basilica floor, spreads out like an undulating Turkish carpet. Mosaics, made of marble, porphyry and glass are used to create complex and colourful geometric

patterns and beautiful scenes of beasts and birds. Some of these scenes are allegorical. The one in the left transept of two cocks carrying a fox on a stick was designed to symbolize cunning vanquished by vigilance.

ATRIUM (VESTIBULE)

THE 13TH-CENTURY mosaics decorating the cupolas, vaults and lunettes of the atrium are among the finest in the basilica. The scenes depict Old Testament stories, starting at the southern end with the Genesis Cupola (showing 26 detailed episodes of the Creation), to the

The Quadriga, the original gilded bronze horses in the museum

Noah and the Flood – atrium mosaics from the 13th century

illuminated manuscripts, fragments of ancient mosaics and antique tapestries.

SANCTUARY AND PALA D'ORO

BEYOND THE CHAPEL of St Clement, tickets are sold to view the most valuable treasure of San Marco: the Pala d'Oro. This jewel-spangled altarpiece situated behind the high altar consists of 250 enamel paintings on gold foil, enclosed within a gilded silver Gothic frame. Originally commissioned in Byzantium in AD 976, the altarpiece was embellished over the centuries. Following the fall of the Republic, Napoleon helped himself to some of the precious stones, but the screen still gleams with pearls, rubies, sapphires and amethysts.

Statue of St Mark on the iconostasis

The iconostasis, the screen dividing nave from chancel, is adorned with marble Gothic statues of the Virgin and Apostles, and was carved in 1394 by the Dalle Masegne brothers. Above the high altar the imposing green marble baldacchino is supported by finely carved alabaster columns featuring scenes from the New Testament.

BAPTISTRY AND CHAPELS

THE BAPTISTRY (closed to the public) was added in the 14th century by Doge Andrea Dandolo (1343–54) who is buried here. Under his direction the baptistry was decorated with outstanding mosaics depicting scenes from the lives of Christ and John the Baptist. Sansovino, who designed the font, is buried by the altar.

The adjoining Zen Chapel (currently closed for restoration) originally formed part of the atrium. It became a funeral chapel for Cardinal Zen in 1504 in return for his bequest to the State.

In the left transept of the basilica the Chapel of St Isidore, normally accessible only for worship, was also built by Dandolo. Mosaics in the barrel vault ceiling tell the tale of the saint, whose body

The archangel Michael, a Byzantine icon from the 11th century in the Treasury

was stolen from the island of Chios and transported to Venice in 1125. To its left the Mascoli Chapel, used in the early 17th century by the confraternity of Mascoli (men), is decorated with scenes from the life of the Virgin Mary. The altarpiece has statues depicting the Virgin and Child between St Mark and St John.

The third chapel in the left transept is home to the icon of the Madonna of Nicopeia. Looted in 1204, she was formerly carried into battle at the head of the Byzantine army.

The revered icon of the Nicopeia Madonna, once a war insignia

TREASURY

ALTHOUGH PLUNDERED after the fall of the Republic and much depleted by the fund-raising sale of jewels in the early 19th century, the treasury nevertheless has a precious collection of Byzantine silver, gold and glasswork. Today, most of the treasures are housed in a room whose remarkably thick walls are believed to have been a 9th-century tower of the Doge's Palace. Exhibits include chalices, goblets, reliquaries, two intricate icons of the archangel Michael and an 11th-century silver-gilt reliquary made in the form of a five-domed basilica (see p81). The sanctuary, with over 100 reliquaries, is normally closed to the public.

Doge's Palace ❹

THE PALAZZO DUCALE started
life in the 9th century as a
fortified castle, but this and
several subsequent buildings
were destroyed by a series of
fires. The existing palace owes
its external appearance to the
building work of the 14th and
early 15th centuries. The
designers broke with tradition
by perching the bulk of the
pink Verona marble palace on lace-like Istrian
stone arcades, with a portico supported by
columns below. The result is a light and airy
masterpiece of Gothic architecture.

Arco Foscari
*The Adam and
Eve figures on this
triumphal arch in
the courtyard are
copies of the 15th-
century originals
by Antonio Rizzo.*

★ Porta della Carta
*This 15th-century Gothic gate
was the principal entrance to
the palace. From it, a vaulted
passageway leads to the
Arco Foscari and the
internal courtyard.*

Exit

STAR FEATURES

★ Giants' Staircase

★ Porta della Carta

The balcony on
the west façade was
added in 1536 to mirror
the early 15th-century balcony
looking on to the quay.

★ Giants' Staircase
*This late 15th-century staircase by Antonio
Rizzo was used for ceremonial purposes. It
was on the landing at the top that the doges
were crowned with the glittering zogia.*

Torture Chamber
"The court of the room of the Cord" recalls the practice of interrogating suspects as they hung by their wrists.

Sala dei Tre Capi
(Chamber of the Three Heads of the Council of Ten)

Sala della Bussola
("Compass" Room)

Bridge of Sighs
The famous bridge once crossed by offenders on their way to the State interrogators.

Drunkenness of Noah
This early 15th-century sculpture, symbolic of the frailty of man, is set on the corner of the palace.

Ponte della Paglia
(see p113)

Main entrance

Adam and Eve
with the serpent are depicted in stone on the corner of the Piazzetta.

Sala del Maggior Consiglio
An entire wall of the Great Council Hall is taken up by Domenico and Jacopo Tintoretto's Paradise (1588–92).

Inside the Doge's Palace

Intricate carved Gothic capital

From the early days of the Republic, the Doge's Palace was the seat of the government, the Palace of Justice and the home of the doge. For centuries this was the only building in Venice entitled to the name palazzo (the others were merely called Ca', short for Casa). The power of the Serenissima is ever present in the large and allegorical historical paintings which embellish the walls and ceilings of the splendid halls and chambers. These ornate rooms are testament to the glory of the Venetian Republic, and were designed to impress and overawe visiting ambassadors and dignitaries.

STAR FEATURES

★ **Sala del Maggior Consiglio**

★ **Collegiate Rooms**

★ **Prisons**

Colonnade
Sunlight streams through the arches of the Loggia on the first floor of the palace.

Mars
The Giants' Staircase is named after Sansovino's monumental figures, statues of Mars and Neptune, sculpted in 1567.

Ground floor

Scala d'Oro
Visitors enter the palace via Sansovino's lavish staircase, built between 1554 and 1558. The arched ceiling is embellished with gilded stucco by Alessandro Vittoria.

Exit through Porta della Carta

KEY TO FLOORPLAN

- ☐ State Apartments
- ☐ Collegium and Senate Rooms
- ☐ Council of Ten and Armoury
- ☐ Great Council Rooms
- ☐ Prisons
- ☐ Non-exhibition space

Wellhead
The two 16th-century bronze wellheads in the courtyard are considered to be the finest in Venice.

★ **Collegiate Rooms**
Bacchus and Ariadne Crowned by Venus is the finest of four mythological scenes by Tintoretto in the Anticollegio.

Third floor

The Sala del Consiglio dei Dieci has a ceiling decorated with paintings by Veronese (1553–54).

Sala dello Scudo
The walls of this room are covered with maps of the world. In the centre are two huge 18th-century globes.

First floor

Second floor

★ **Sala del Maggior Consiglio**
The first 76 doges, with the exception of the traitor Marin Falier, are portrayed on a frieze round the upper walls of the room.

★ **Prisons**
These 16th-century cells were mainly used for petty offenders. Serious criminals were lodged in the dank pozzi (wells).

THE SECRET ITINERARY

The fascinating, though poorly publicized, Secret Itinerary (Itinerari Segreti) tour (see Visitors' Checklist p85) takes you behind the scenes in the palace to the offices and Hall of the Chancellery, the State Inquisitors' room, the Torture Chamber and the prisons. It was from these cells that Casanova made his spectacular escape in 1755. Tours are available in Italian, English and French. Each is limited to 20 people and lasts for 90 minutes.

Casanova's cell door

Exploring the Doge's Palace

A TOUR OF THE PALACE takes you through a succession of richly decorated chambers and halls. The rooms are on three floors and, unless you are visiting the state apartments (only accessible during exhibitions), you start at the top and work your way down.

The rooms within the palace are neither named nor numbered, and without a guide, the place can be very confusing. The latest equipment available is the Light and Man infra-red Walkman which you can hire for a commentary on the whole palace or just the areas which interest you.

St Theodore in the palace courtyard

COURTYARD

THE COURTYARD is reached via a vaulted passage from the Porta della Carta. At the top of the Giants' Staircase, which rises to the first floor, new doges were crowned with the *zogia* or dogal cap.

SCALA D'ORO AND STATE APARTMENTS

THE SUMPTUOUS Scala d'Oro (golden staircase) takes its name from the elaborate gilt stucco vault by Alessandro Vittoria (1554–58). The doge's private apartments on the first floor can be seen only when they are being used for temporary exhibitions (a separate ticket is usually required). The apartments, built after the fire of 1483 and later looted on the orders of Napoleon, are bare of furnishings, but the lavish ceilings and colossal carved chimney-pieces in some of the rooms give you an idea of the doges' lifestyle. The most ornate is the Sala degli Scarlatti, with a richly carved gilt ceiling, a fireplace (c.1501) designed by Antonio and Tullio Lombardo and a relief (1501–21) by Pietro Lombardo of Doge Leonardo Loredan at the feet of the Virgin.

The Sala dello Scudo, or map room, contains maps and charts. The picture gallery further on features works by Vittore Carpaccio and Giovanni Bellini, and some incongruous wooden demoniac panels by Hieronymous Bosch.

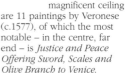

A *bocca di leone* used for denouncing tax evaders

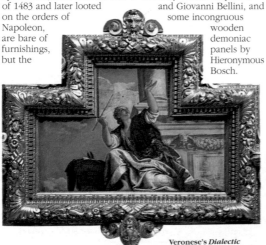

Veronese's *Dialectic* (c.1577), Sala del Collegio

SALA DELLE QUATTRO PORTE TO SALA DEL SENATO

THE SECOND FLIGHT of the Scala d'Oro leads to the third floor and its council chambers. The first room, the Sala delle Quattro Porte, was completely rebuilt after the 1574 fire, its ceiling designed by Andrea Palladio and frescoed by Tintoretto.

The next room, the Anticollegio, was the waiting room. The end walls are decorated with mythological scenes by Tintoretto: *Vulcan's Forge*; *Mercury and the Graces*; *Bacchus and Ariadne* and *Minerva Dismissing Mars*, all painted in 1578. Veronese's masterly *Rape of Europa* (1580), opposite the window, is one of the most eyecatching works in the palace.

Off the Anticollegio, the Sala del Collegio was the hall where the doge and his counsellors met to receive ambassadors and discuss matters of State. Embellishing the magnificent ceiling are 11 paintings by Veronese (c.1577), of which the most notable – in the centre, far end – is *Justice and Peace Offering Sword, Scales and Olive Branch to Venice*.

It was in the next room, the Sala del Senato, that the doge would sit with some 200 senators to discuss matters such as foreign affairs or nominations of ambassadors. The wall and ceiling paintings, by pupils of Tintoretto or the master himself, are further propaganda for the Republic.

SALA DEL CONSIGLIO DEI DIECI TO THE ARMERIA

THE ROUTE RETURNS through the Sala delle Quattro Porte to the Sala del Consiglio dei Dieci. This was the meeting room of the awesomely powerful Council of Ten, founded in 1310 to investigate and prosecute crimes concerning the security of the State. Napoleon pilfered some of the Veroneses from the ceiling but two of the finest found their way back here in 1920: *Age and Youth* and *Juno Offering the Ducal Crown to Venice* (both 1553–54).

In the next room, the Sala della Bussola, offenders awaited their fate in front of the Council of Ten. The room's *bocca di leone* (lion's mouth), used to post secret denunciations, was just one of several within the palace. The wooden door here leads to the rooms of the Heads of the Ten, the State Inquisitors' Room and thence to the torture chamber and prisons. This is the route taken by those on the Secret Itinerary.

Age and Youth (1553–54) by Veronese

Others follow the flow to the Armoury – one of the finest collections in Europe, thanks in part to bequests by European monarchs.

SALA DEL MAGGIOR CONSIGLIO

ANOTHER STAIRCASE, the Scala dei Censori, takes you down again to the second floor, along the hallway and past the Sala del Guariento with fresco fragments of *The Coronation of the Virgin* by Guariento (1365–67). From the *liagò*, or veranda, where Antonio Rizzo's marble statues of Adam and Eve (1480s) are displayed, you pass into the magnificent Sala del Maggior Consiglio or Hall of the Great Council. A chamber of monumental proportions, it was here that the Great Council convened to vote on constitutional questions, to pass laws and elect the top officials of the Serene Republic. The hall was also used for State banquets. When Henry III of France paid a royal visit, 3,000 guests were entertained in this spectacular room.

By the mid 16th century the Great Council had around 2,000 members. Any Venetian of high birth over 25 was entitled to a seat – with the exception of those married to a commoner. From 1646, by which time the Turkish wars had depleted state coffers, nobility from the *terra firma* or those from merchant or professional classes with 100,000 ducats to spare could purchase their way in.

Tintoretto's huge, highly restored work called *Paradise* (1587–90) occupies the eastern wall. Measuring 7.45 by 24.65 m (25 by 81 ft) it is one of the largest paintings in the world. For a man in his late seventies, albeit assisted by his son, it is a remarkably vigorous composition.

The ceiling of the hall is decorated with panels glorifying the Republic. One of the finest is Veronese's *Apotheosis of Venice* (1583). A frieze along the walls illustrates 76 doges by Tintoretto's pupils. The portrait covered by a curtain is Marin Falier, beheaded for treason in 1355. The other 42 doges are portrayed in the Sala dello Scrutinio, where new doges were nominated.

PRISONS

View of the lagoon through a grille on the Bridge of Sighs

FROM THE Sala del Maggior Consiglio a series of passageways and stairways leads to the Bridge of Sighs *(see p113)* which links the palace to what were known as the New Prisons, built between 1556 and 1595.

Situated at the top of the palace, just below the leaded roof, are the *piombi* cells (*piombo* means lead). These cells are hardly inviting but prisoners here were far more comfortable than the criminals who were left to fester in the *pozzi* – the dark dank dungeons at ground level. The windowless cells of these ancient prisons are still covered with the graffiti of the convicts. Visitors on the Secret Itinerary tour are shown Casanova's cell in the *piombi* and told of how he made his daring escape from the palace through a hole in the roof.

Visits end with the offices of the Avogaria, where the state prosecutors *(avogadori)* prepared the trials.

The splendid Sala del Maggior Consiglio, the hall of the Great Council

Street-by-Street: Around La Fenice

WEST OF THE HUGE EXPANSE of the ever-crowded Piazza San Marco there is a labyrinth of alleys to explore. At the centre of this part of the *sestiere* is Campo San Fantin, flanked by the Renaissance church of San Fantin. Nearby is the Ateneo Veneto, formerly a *scuola* whose members had the unenviable role of escorting prisoners to the scaffold. The narrow streets around these sights have some wonderfully exotic little shops, while the more recent Calle Larga XXII Marzo further south boasts big names in Italian fashion. The quarter in general has some excellent restaurants but, being San Marco, you will find that prices in the majority of establishments are steep.

Campo San Fantin has a late Renaissance church, San Fantin, with a particularly beautiful apse designed by Jacopo Sansovino.

★ **La Fenice**
The opera house gained its name (the phoenix) after a fire in 1836. Sadly, it was again destroyed by fire in 1996 ⓮

The Rio delle Veste leads past the rear of the theatre. This is the route taken by those fortunate enough to arrive for their night out by gondola.

KEY

– – –   Suggested route

| 0 metres | 75 |
| 0 yards | 75 |

STAR SIGHTS

★ La Fenice

★ San Moisè

Santa Maria Zobenigo
The carvings feature the Barbaro family who paid for the church façade. Ground-level reliefs show towns where the family held high ranking posts ⓭

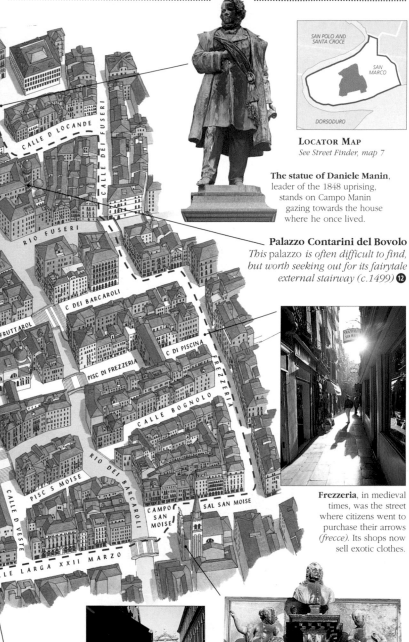

LOCATOR MAP
See Street Finder, map 7

The statue of Daniele Manin, leader of the 1848 uprising, stands on Campo Manin gazing towards the house where he once lived.

Palazzo Contarini del Bovolo
This palazzo is often difficult to find, but worth seeking out for its fairytale external stairway (c.1499) 12

Frezzeria, in medieval times, was the street where citizens went to purchase their arrows *(frecce)*. Its shops now sell exotic clothes.

Calle Larga XXII Marzo was named after 22 March 1848, the day of Manin's rebellion. Today the street is best known for its trendy designer boutiques.

★ **San Moisè**
The exuberant Baroque façade of San Moisè (c.1668) was funded by a legacy from the patrician Vincenzo Fini, whose bust features above a side door 11

Harry's Bar ❾

Calle Vallaresso 1323. **Map** 7 B3.
San Marco. See also **Restaurants, Cafés and Bars** pp246–7.

CELEBRATED FOR cocktails, *carpaccio* and American clientèle, Harry's Bar is famous throughout Venice. Founded in 1931 by the late Giuseppe Cipriani, it was financed by a Bostonian called Harry who thought Venice had a dearth of decent bars. They chose a storeroom at the Grand Canal end of the Calle Vallaresso as their location, conveniently close to the Piazza San Marco. Since then, the bar has seen a steady stream of American visitors, among them Ernest Hemingway who used to come here after shooting in the lagoon. The bar became the most popular venue in Venice, patronized by royalty, film stars and heads of state.

Ernest Hemingway, a regular at Harry's Bar

These days there are far more American tourists than famous figures, often there to sample the Bellini cocktail that Cipriani invented *(see p239)*. Aesthetically, the place is unremarkable and there is no terrace for meals *al fresco*.

Ridotto ❿

Calle del Ridotto, 1332 San Marco.
Map 7 B3. (041) 522 29 39.
San Marco. to the public.

IN AN EFFORT to control the gambling mania that swept the city of Venice in the 17th century, the State gave Marco Dandolo permission to use his palace as the first public gaming house in Europe. In 1638 the Ridotto was opened, with the proviso that players came disguised in a mask. In 1774 the Great Council closed the casino's doors on account of the number of Venetians ruined at its tables.

In 1947 the old Palazzo Dandolo was converted into a theatre which staged Italian plays, but today the building is closed to the public.

San Moisè ⓫

Campo San Moisè. **Map** 7 A3.
(041) 528 58 40. San Marco.
3:30–7pm daily.

ONE OF the churches in Venice that people love to hate, San Moisè displays a ponderous Baroque façade. Completed in 1668, it is covered in grimy statues, swags and busts. John Ruskin, in a characteristic anti-Baroque outrage, described it as the clumsiest church in Venice. The interior has a mixed collection of paintings and sculpture from the 17th and 18th centuries. In the nave is the tombstone of John Law, a financier from Scotland who founded the Compagnie d'Occident to develop the Mississippi Valley. His shares collapsed in 1770 in the notorious South Sea Bubble, and he fled to Venice, surviving on his winnings at the Ridotto.

Façade of San Moisè, encrusted with Baroque ornamentation

Palazzo Contarini del Bovolo ⓬

Corte Contarini del Bovolo. **Map** 7 A2.
(041) 521 75 21. Rialto or Sant'Angelo. Apr–Oct: 10:30am–5:30pm daily.

TUCKED AWAY in a maze of alleys (follow signs from Calle della Vida), the Palazzo Contarini del Bovolo is best known for its graceful external

The external stairway of the Palazzo Contarini del Bovolo

stairway. The word *bovolo* in Venetian dialect means snail shell, appropriate to the spiral shape of the Lombardesque stairway. The Contarini, who had the 15th-century palace built, were a learned Venetian family, known as "the philosophers". The collection of wellheads within the enclosure belongs to the present owners.

Santa Maria Zobenigo ⓭

Campo Santa Maria del Giglio.
Map 6 F3. (041) 522 57 39.
Santa Maria del Giglio.
10am–5:30pm Mon–Sat, 3–5:30pm Sun & public hols.

NAMED AFTER the Jubanico family who are said to have founded it in the 9th century, this church is also referred to as "del Giglio" ("of the lily"). The exuberant Baroque façade was financed by the affluent Barbaro family and was used to glorify their naval and diplomatic achievements.

Inside is a tiny museum of church ornaments and paintings including *The Sacred Family* attributed to Rubens and two works by Tintoretto.

La Fenice 🔴

Campo San Fantin. **Map** 7 A3.
🚇 *San Marco.* 📞 *(041) 520 40 10
(Palafenice booking office).* **Theatre**
⬤ *until further notice.*

THEATRE HOUSES were enormously popular in the 18th century and La Fenice, the city's oldest theatre, was no exception. Built in 1792 in Classical style, it was one of several privately owned theatres showing plays and operas to audiences from all strata of society. In December 1836 a fire destroyed the interior but a year later it was resurrected, just like the mythical bird, the phoenix *(fenice)* which is said to have arisen from its ashes.

Another fire in early 1996 again destroyed the theatre, except for the façade. La Fenice's season is currently being held at Palafenice, a temporary structure near the parking area just outside the city, while the theatre is rebuilt.

Throughout the 19th century the name of La Fenice was linked with great Italian composers. The many operatic premières that took place here include Verdi's *La Traviata* (1853) and Rossini's *Tancredi* (1813) and *Semiramide* (1823). During the Austrian Occupation *(see p48)* red, white and green flowers, symbolizing the Italian flag, were thrown on stage, to shouts of "Viva Verdi" – the letters of the composer's name standing for Vittorio Emanuele Re d'Italia. More recently, the theatre saw premières of Stravinsky's *The Rake's Progress* (1951) and Britten's *Turn of the Screw* (1954).

Shop in Campo Santo Stefano selling antiques and masks

Campo Santo Stefano 🔴

Map 6 F3. 🚇 *Accademia or Sant'Angelo.*

ALSO KNOWN as Campo Francesco Morosini after the 17th-century doge who once lived here, this *campo* is one of the most spacious in the city. Bullfights were staged until 1802, when a stand fell and killed some of the spectators. It was also a venue for balls and Carnival festivities. Today it is a pleasantly informal square where children play and visitors drink coffee in open-air cafés.

The central statue is Nicolò Tommaseo (1802–74), a Dalmatian scholar who was a central figure in the 1848 rebellion against the Austrians.

At the southern end of the square the austere-looking Palazzo Pisani, overlooking the Campiello Pisani, has been the Conservatory of Music since the end of the 19th century. In summer months, music wafts from its open windows. On the opposite side of the square No. 2945, Palazzo Loredan, is the home of the Venetian Institute of Sciences, Letters and Arts.

The ceiling of Santo Stefano, in the form of a ship's keel

Santo Stefano 🔴

Campo Santo Stefano. **Map** 6 F2.
📞 *(041) 522 50 61.* 🚇 *Accademia or Sant'Angelo.* ⏱ *10am–5:30pm Mon–Sat, 7:30am–12:30pm, 3–5:30pm Sun & public hols.* 📷

DECONSECRATED six times on account of the murder and violence that took place within its walls, Santo Stefano today is remarkably serene. Built in the 14th century and radically altered in the 15th, the church has a notable carved portal by Bartolomeo Bon and a campanile which has a typical Venetian tilt. The interior has a splendid ship's keel ceiling, carved tie-beams and tall pillars of Veronese marble. The most notable works of art, including some paintings by Tintoretto, are housed in the damp sacristy.

La Fenice, destroyed by fire in 1996

Courtyard of the Palazzo Pesaro, where Fortuny lived

Museo Fortuny **⓱**

Palazzo Pesaro degli Orfei, Campo San Benedetto, San Marco 3958. **Map** 6 F2. *(041) 520 09 95.* 🚤 *Sant'Angelo.* 🔵 *Temporarily for restoration, but occasionally open for exhibitions.* 🖼 🚫

KNOWN PRINCIPALLY for his fantastic pleated silk dresses, Fortuny was also a painter, sculptor, set designer, photographer, and scientist. One of his inventions was the Fortuny Dome which is used in theatre performances to create the illusion of sky.

Mariano Fortuny y Madrazo, or Don Mariano as he liked to be called, was born in 1871 in Granada and moved to Venice in 1889. In the early 20th century he purchased the Palazzo Pesaro, a late Gothic *palazzo* which had originally been owned by the fabulously rich and influential Pesaro family. Fortuny spent the remainder of his life here and the house and its contents

were bequeathed to the city by his wife in 1956.

The large rooms and *portego* make a splendid and appropriate setting for the precious Fortuny fabrics. Woven with gold and silver threads, these were created by Fortuny's reintroduction of Renaissance techniques and use of ancient dyes. The collection also includes paintings by Fortuny (less impressive than the fabrics), decorative panels and a few of the finely pleated, clinging silk dresses regarded as a milestone in early 20th-century women's fashion.

San Salvatore **⓲**

Campo San Salvatore. **Map** 7 B1. *(041) 523 67 17.* 🚤 *Rialto.* 🔵 *10am–noon, 4–6:30pm daily.*

THE INTERIOR of the church of San Salvatore is a fine example of Venetian Renaissance architecture. If the main door is closed you can enter

by the side entrance, which is squeezed between shops along the Mercerie. The present church was designed by Giorgio Spavento in the early 16th century, and continued by Tullio Lombardo and Jacopo Sansovino. The pictorial highlight is Titian's *Annunciation* (1566) over the third altar on the right. Nearby, Sansovino's monument to Doge Francesco Venier (1556–61), is one of several Mannerist tombs in the church.

On the high altar is Titian's *Transfiguration of Christ* (1560). The end of the right transept is dominated by a vast monument to Caterina Cornaro, Queen of Cyprus *(see p43)*. Executed by the sculptor Bernardino Contino in 1580–84, the tomb shows the queen handing over her kingdom to the doge.

Campo San Bartolomeo **⓳**

Map 7 B1. 🚤 *Rialto.*

CLOSE TO the Rialto, the square of San Bartolomeo bustles with life, particularly in the early evening when young Venetians rendezvous here. They meet at cafés, bars or by the statue of Carlo Goldoni (1707–93), Venice's prolific and most celebrated playwright. His statue, in a fitting spot for a writer who drew his inspiration from daily social intercourse, is by Antonio del Zotto (1883).

The beautiful Renaissance interior of the church of San Salvatore

St George and Dragon bas-relief on a corner of the Mercerie

Mercerie ⑳

Map 7 B2. 🚤 San Marco or Rialto.

DIVIDED INTO the Merceria dell'Orologio, Merceria di San Zulian and Merceria di San Salvatore, this is, and always has been, a principal shopping thoroughfare. Linking Piazza San Marco with the Rialto, it is made from a string of narrow, bustling alleys, lined by small shops and boutiques. The 17th-century English author, John Evelyn, described it as "the most delicious streete in the World for the sweetnesse of it . . . tapisstry'd as it were, with Cloth of Gold, rich Damasks & other silk." He wrote of perfumers, apothecary shops and nightingales in cages. Today all this has been replaced with fashions, footwear and glass.

At the southern end, the relief over the first archway on the left portrays the woman who in 1310 accidentally stopped a revolt. She dropped her pestle out of the window, killing the standard-bearer of a rebel army. They retreated, and the woman was given a guarantee that her rent would never be raised.

San Zulian ㉑

Campo San Zulian. **Map** 7 B2. 🚤 San Marco. 📞 (041) 523 53 83. ◯ 8:30–11:45am. ✝ Mass in English 11am Sun (summer only).

ON THE BUSY Mercerie, the church of San Zulian (or Giuliano) provides a refuge from the crowded shopping alleys. Its interior is rich with gilded woodwork, 16th- and 17th-century paintings, and sculpture. The central panel of the frescoed ceiling portrays *The Apotheosis of St Julian*, painted by Palma il Giovane in 1585. The 16th-century church façade was designed by Sansovino and financed by the rich and immodest physician, Tommaso Rangone. His bronze statue, surrounded by books, stands out against the white Istrian stone walls.

Bronze statue of Tommaso Rangone

San Giorgio Maggiore ㉒

Map 8 D4. 📞 (041) 528 99 00. 🚤 San Giorgio. ◯ 9:30am–12:30pm, 2:45–5pm. Phone in advance for visits to the Foundation (closed Sat & Sun). 📷 **Campanile** ◯ 9:30am–12:30pm, 2:45–5pm (phone to check).

APPEARING LIKE a stage set across the water from the Piazzetta, the little island of San Giorgio Maggiore has been captured on canvas countless times.

The church and monastery, built between 1559–80, are among Andrea Palladio's greatest architectural achievements. The church's temple front and the spacious, serene interior with its perfect proportions and cool beauty are typically Palladian in that they are modelled on the Classical style of ancient Rome. Within the church, the major works of art are the two late Tintorettos on the chancel walls: *The Last Supper* and *Gathering of the Manna* (both 1594). In the Chapel of the Dead is his last work, *The Deposition* (1592–94), finished by his son Domenico.

The top of the tall campanile, reached by a lift, affords a superb panorama of the city and lagoon.

Centuries ago, when Benedictines occupied the original monastery, it was known as the Isle of Cypresses. The monastery was rebuilt in the 13th century following an earthquake and later became a centre of learning and a residence for eminent

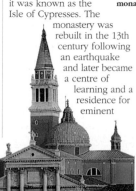

Palladio's church of San Giorgio Maggiore on the island of the same name

Cloisters designed by Palladio in the monastery of San Giorgio Maggiore

foreign visitors. Following the Fall of the Republic in 1797 (see p48) the monastery was suppressed and its treasures plundered.

In 1829 the island became a free port, and in 1851 the headquarters of the artillery. By this time it had changed out of recognition. The complex regained its role as an active cultural centre when the monastery, embracing Palladio's cloisters, refectory and library, was purchased in 1951 by Count Vittorio Cini (see p134). Today it is a thriving centre of Venetian culture, with international events and exhibitions. There is also a small open-air theatre. Visits are arranged by appointment.

SAN POLO AND SANTA CROCE

THE SESTIERI of San Polo and Santa Croce, bordered by the upper sweep of the Grand Canal, were both named after churches which stood within their boundaries. The first inhabitants are said to have settled on the cluster of small islands called *Rivus Altus* (high bank) or Rialto. When markets were established in the 11th century, the quarter became the commercial hub of Venice. San Polo is still one of the liveliest *sestieri* of the city, with its market stalls, small shops and

Shuttered window in Campo Sant'Aponal

local bars. The bustle of the market gives way to a maze of narrow alleys opening on to squares. Focal points are the spacious Campo San Polo, the Frari church and the neighbouring Scuola di San Rocco. Santa Croce for the most part is a *sestiere* of very narrow, tightly packed streets and squares where you will see the humbler side of Venetian life. Its grandest *palazzi* line the Grand Canal. Less alluring is the Piazzale Roma, the city's giant car park, lying to the west.

SIGHTS AT A GLANCE

Churches
San Cassiano ❹
San Giacomo dell'Orio ⓮
San Giacomo di Rialto ❷
San Giovanni Evangelista ⓭
Santa Maria Gloriosa dei Frari pp102–3 ❽
San Nicolò da Tolentino ⓬
San Pantalon ⓫
San Polo ❻
San Rocco ❿
San Stae ⓰

Museums and Galleries
Ca' Mocenigo ⓱
Ca' Pesaro ⓲
Fondaco dei Turchi (Natural History Museum) ⓯
Museo Goldoni ❼
Scuola Grande di San Rocco pp106–7 ❾

Streets and Squares
Campo San Polo ❺

Bridges
Rialto Bridge ❶

Markets
Rialto Markets ❸

KEY

Street-by-Street map
See pp98–9

Vaporetto boarding point

Traghetto crossing

0 metres   250
0 yards   250

◁ **Ponte del Megio, in a quiet corner of Santa Croce**

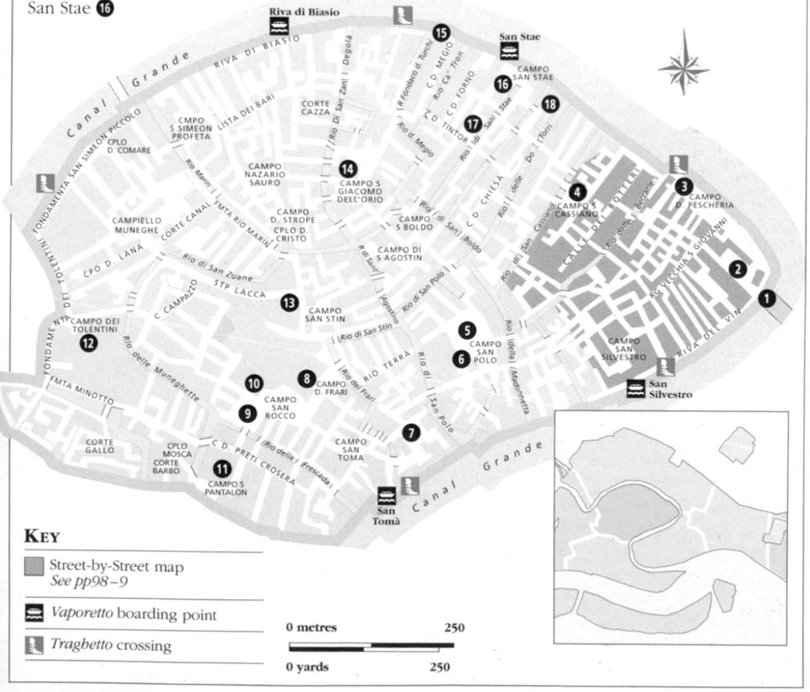

Street-by-Street: San Polo

THE RIALTO BRIDGE and markets make
this a magnet for tourists. Traditionally the city's commercial quarter, it
was here that bankers, brokers and
merchants conducted their affairs.
Streets are no longer lined with stalls
selling spices and fine fabrics, but the
food markets and pasta shops are a
colourful sight. The old-fashioned
standing-only bars called *bacari* are
packed with locals. In contrast, Riva
del Vin to the south, by the Grand
Canal, is strictly tourist territory.

San Cassiano
*Inside this church is a
carved altar (1696) and
a* Crucifixion
*by Tintoretto
(1568)* ❹

Ponte Storto is
crooked, like many
bridges in the city. It
leads under a portico to
Calle Stretta, a narrow
alley that is only 1 m (3 ft)
wide in places.

Sant'Aponal, founded
in the 11th century,
rebuilt in the 15th, is
now deconsecrated.
Gothic reliefs decorate
the façade.

Riva del Vin, where wine was
offloaded from boats, is one of
the few accessible quaysides
along the Grand Canal.

San Silvestro

STAR SIGHTS

★ **Rialto Bridge**

★ **Rialto Markets**

★ **Rialto Markets**
The Rialto markets have been in operation for centuries. The Pescheria (above) sells fresh fish and seafood, and the Erberia sells fruit and vegetables ❸

LOCATOR MAP
See Street Finder, maps 2, 3, 7

The statue of Gobbo of the Rialto, the hunchback, was sculpted in 1541 *(see p100).*

San Giacomo di Rialto
Since its installation in 1410, the clock on this church has been a notoriously poor time-keeper ❷

KEY

- – – Suggested route

0 metres   75
0 yards   75

Trattoria alla Madonna is a popular seafood restaurant *(see p240).*

★ **Rialto Bridge**
A beloved landmark of the Grand Canal, the bridge marks the geographical centre of the city. The balustrades afford fine views of the canal ❶

Rialto Bridge ❶

Ponte di Rialto. **Map** 7 A1. 🚤 *Rialto.*

THE RIALTO BRIDGE has been a busy part of the city for centuries. At any time of day you will find swarms of crowds jostling on the bridge, browsing among the souvenirs or taking a break to watch the constant swirl of activity on the Grand Canal from the bridge's balustrades.

Stone bridges were built in Venice as early as the 12th century, but it was not until 1588, after the collapse, decay or sabotage of earlier wooden structures, that a solid stone bridge was designed for the Rialto. One of the early wood crossings collapsed in 1444 under the weight of spectators at the wedding ceremony of the Marchese di Ferrara.

Vittore Carpaccio's painting *The Healing of the Madman* (1496, *see p133*) in the Accademia shows the fourth bridge – a rickety looking structure with a drawbridge for the tall-masted galleys. By the 16th

Busy canalside restaurant near the Rialto Bridge

century this was in a sad state of decay and a competition was held for the design of a new bridge to be built in stone. Michelangelo, Andrea Palladio and Jacopo Sansovino were among the eminent contenders, but after months of deliberation it was the aptly named Antonio da Ponte who won the commission. The bridge was built between 1588 and 1591 and, until 1854, when the Accademia Bridge was constructed, this remained the only means of crossing the Grand Canal on foot.

San Giacomo di Rialto ❷

Campo San Giacomo, San Polo. **Map** 3 A5. ☎ *(041) 522 47 45.* 🚤 *Rialto.* ○ *10:30am–noon, 4–5:30pm daily.* ● *Sun afternoon.*

THE FIRST CHURCH to stand on this site was allegedly founded in the 5th century, making it the oldest church in Venice. The present building dates from the 11th–12th centuries, with major restoration in 1601. The original Gothic portico and huge 24-hour clock are the most striking features.

The crouching stone figure on the far side of the square is the so-called Gobbo (hunchback) of the Rialto. In the 16th century this was a welcome sight for minor offenders who were forced to run the gauntlet from Piazza San Marco to this square at the Rialto.

***Traghetto* ferrying passengers across to the Erberia**

Rialto Markets ❸

San Polo. **Map** 3 A5. 🚤 *Rialto.* **Erberia** *(fruit and vegetable market) until noon Mon–Sat,* **Pescheria** *(fish market) until noon Tue–Sat.*

VENETIANS HAVE come to the Erberia to buy fresh produce for hundreds of years. Heavily laden barges arrive at dawn and offload their crates on to the quayside by the Grand Canal. Local produce includes red radicchio from Treviso, and succulent asparagus and baby artichokes from the islands of Sant'Erasmo and Vignole *(see p149)*. In the adjoining fish market are sole, sardines, skate, squid, crabs, clams and other species of seafood and fish. To see it all in full swing you must arrive early in the morning – by noon the vendors are packing up.

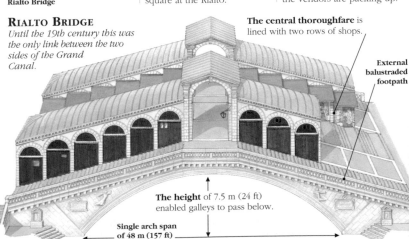

RIALTO BRIDGE
Until the 19th century this was the only link between the two sides of the Grand Canal.

The central thoroughfare is lined with two rows of shops.

External balustraded footpath

The height of 7.5 m (24 ft) enabled galleys to pass below.

Single arch span of 48 m (157 ft)

San Cassiano ❹

Campo San Cassiano, San Polo.
Map 2 F5. ☎ *(041) 72 14 08.*
🚤 *San Stae.* ⏰ *8am–noon,
4:30–6pm daily (phone to check).*

THE MEDIEVAL CHURCH of San Cassiano suffered heavily at the hands of 19th-century restorers and the building is a bizarre mix of architectural styles. Of the original church, only the campanile survives. The highlight of the interior is Jacopo Tintoretto's immensely powerful *Crucifixion* (1568), which is in the sacristy.

The campo in which the church stands was notorious for prostitutes in the 1500s – as was the Rialto in general.

Campo San Polo ❺

Map 6 F1. 🚤 *San Silvestro.*

THE SPACIOUS SQUARE of San Polo has traditionally been host to spectacular events. As far back as the 15th century it was the venue for festivities, masquerades, ceremonies, balls and bullbaiting.

The most dramatic event was the assassination of Lorenzo de' Medici in 1548. He took refuge in Venice after brutally killing his cousin Alessandro, Duke of Florence. Lorenzo was stabbed in the square by two assassins who were in the service of Cosimo de' Medici, and both were handsomely rewarded by the Florentine duke.

On the eastern side of the square is the beautiful Gothic Palazzo Soranzo. This was originally two palaces – the one on the left is the older. The building is still owned by the Soranzo family.

Palazzo Corner Mocenigo, which is situated in the north-west corner (No. 2128), was once the residence of the eccentric English writer Frederick Rolfe (1860–1913), alias Baron Corvo. He was thrown out of his lodgings when his English hostess read his manuscript of *The Desire and Pursuit of the Whole* – a

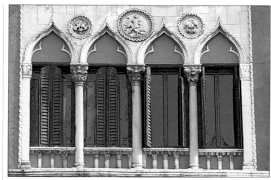
A detail of the Gothic façade of Palazzo Soranzo, Campo San Polo

cruel satirization of English society in Venice.

Since 1979 the square has enjoyed a revival of Carnival festivities. This wide open space is also a haven for local youngsters, who ride bikes, rollerskate or play football. Such activities would not have gone down well in the 17th century – a plaque on the apse of the church, dated 1611, forbids all games (or selling merchandise) on pain of prison, galley service or exile.

San Polo ❻

Campo San Polo. **Map** 6 F1.
☎ *(041) 523 76 31.* 🚤 *San Silvestro.* ⏰ *10am–5:30pm Mon–Sat, 3–5:30pm Sun & public hols.* 🏛

FOUNDED IN THE 9th century, rebuilt in the 15th and revamped in the early 19th in Neo-Classical style, the church of San Polo lacks any sense of homogeneity. Yet it is worth visiting for individual features such as the lovely Gothic portal and the Romanesque lions at the foot of the 14th-century campanile – one holds a serpent between its paws, the other a human head.

Inside, follow the signs for the *Via Crucis del Tiepolo* – fourteen canvases of the Stations of the

Cross by Giandomenico Tiepolo. The church also has paintings by Veronese, Palma il Giovane (the Younger) and a dark and dramatic *Last Supper* by Tintoretto.

Carlo Goldoni 1707–93

Museo Goldoni ❼

Palazzo Centani, Calle dei Nomboli, San Polo 2794. **Map** 6 E1.
☎ *(041) 523 63 53.* 🚤 *San Tomà.*
⏰ *for restoration.*

CARLO GOLDONI, one of the city's favourite sons, wrote over 250 comedies, many based on Commedia dell'Arte figures. Goldoni was born in the beautiful Gothic Palazzo Centrani (or Zantani) in 1707. The house was left to the city in 1931 and is now a centre for theatrical studies and has a collection of theatrical memorabilia. The house is currently closed for restoration, but peep into the enchanting courtyard with its 15th-century open stairway and see a magnificent wellhead, which features carved lions and a coat of arms bearing a hedgehog.

A lion at the foot of the campanile, Church of San Polo

Santa Maria Gloriosa dei Frari ❽

K NOWN BY ALL simply as the Frari (a corruption of *Frati*, meaning brothers), this huge, plain Gothic church dwarfs the eastern section of San Polo. The first church was built by Franciscan friars in 1250–1338, but was replaced by a larger building which was completed by the mid 15th century. The interior is striking for its sheer size and for the quality of its works of art. These include masterpieces by Titian and Giovanni Bellini *(see pp26–7)*, a statue by Donatello and a number of imposing monuments to famous Venetians.

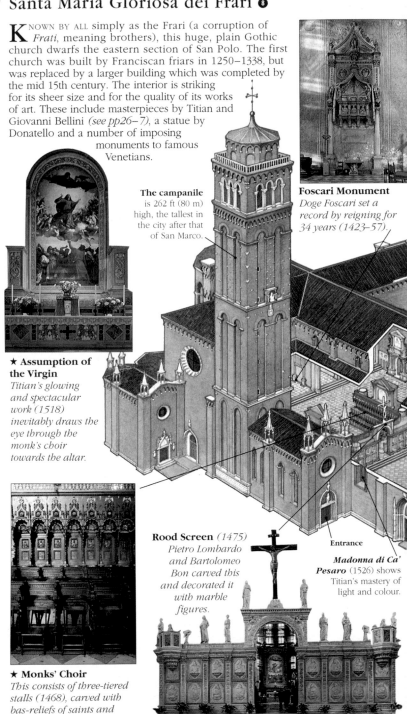

The campanile is 262 ft (80 m) high, the tallest in the city after that of San Marco.

Foscari Monument
Doge Foscari set a record by reigning for 34 years (1423–57).

★ **Assumption of the Virgin**
Titian's glowing and spectacular work (1518) inevitably draws the eye through the monk's choir towards the altar.

Rood Screen *(1475)*
Pietro Lombardo and Bartolomeo Bon carved this and decorated it with marble figures.

Entrance

Madonna di Ca' Pesaro *(1526)* shows Titian's mastery of light and colour.

★ **Monks' Choir**
This consists of three-tiered stalls (1468), carved with bas-reliefs of saints and Venetian city scenes.

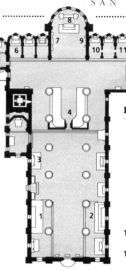

FLOORPLAN

Exploration of the huge
interior can be daunting.
The floorplan pinpoints
12 highlights that should
not be missed.

KEY TO FLOORPLAN

1 Canova's tomb
2 Monument to Titian
3 Titian's *Madonna di Ca' Pesaro*
4 Choir stalls
5 Corner Chapel
6 Tomb of Monteverdi
7 Tomb of Doge Nicolò Tron
8 High altar with Titian's *Assumption
   of the Virgin*
9 Tomb of Doge Francesco Foscari
10 Donatello's *John the Baptist*
   (c.1450)
11 B Vivarini's altar painting (1474),
   Bernardo Chapel
12 Giovanni Bellini's *Madonna
   Enthroned with Saints* (1488)

VISITORS' CHECKLIST

Campo dei Frari. **Map** 6 D1.
(041) 522 26 37. San
Tomà. 9am–6pm Mon–Sat,
3–6pm Sun & religious hols.
except for those attending
mass and on public hols.
frequent.

Monument to Titian *(1853)*
*Canova's pupils, Luigi and Pietro
Zandomeneghi, built this monument to Titian in place of the one
conceived by Canova himself.*

The former monastery,
which houses the State
Archives, has two cloisters, one
in the style of Sansovino,
another designed by Palladio.

Canova's Tomb
*Canova designed, but
never actually made,
a Neo-Classical
marble pyramid like
this as a monument
for Titian. After
Canova's death in
1822, his pupils used
a similar design for
their master's tomb.*

STAR FEATURES

★ **Assumption of the
Virgin by Titian**

★ **Monks' Choir**

Scuola Grande di San Rocco **9**

See pp106–7.

San Rocco **10**

Campo San Rocco, San Polo.
Map 6 D1. **C** *(041) 523 48 64.*
San Tomà. **O** *Apr–Oct:
7:30am–12:30pm, 2–4pm daily;
Nov–Mar: 7:30am–12:30pm daily.*

S HARING THE LITTLE square
with the celebrated Scuola
Grande di San Rocco is the
church of the same name.
Designed by Bartolomeo Bon
in 1489 and largely rebuilt in
1725, the exterior is a mix of
architectural styles. The façade,
similar in concept to the
Scuola, was added in 1765–71.

Inside, the main interest lies
in Tintoretto's paintings in the
chancel, which depict scenes
from the life of St Roch,
patron saint of contagious
diseases. Of these the most
notable is *St Roch Curing the
Plague Victims* (1549).

San Pantalon **11**

Campo San Pantalon, Dorsoduro.
Map 6 D2. San Tomà.
O *4–6pm Sun–Fri.*

**Fumiani's ceiling painting (1680–
1704), San Pantalon**

T HE OVERWHELMING feature of
this late 17th-century
church is the painted ceiling,
dark, awe-inspiring and
remarkable for its illusionistic

effects. The ceiling comprises
a total of 40 scenes (admirers
claim this makes it the world's
largest work of art on canvas),
depicting the martyrdom and
apotheosis of the physician St
Pantalon. The artist, Gian
Antonio Fumiani, took 24
years (1680–1704) to achieve
this masterpiece, but then
allegedly fell to his death
from the scaffolding.

Paolo Veronese's emotive
painting *St Pantalon Healing
a Boy* (second chapel on the
right) was his final work of art
(1587). If you would like to
see Antonio Vivarini and
Giovanni d'Alemagna's
Coronation of the Virgin (1444)
and *The Annunciation* (1350)
attributed to Paolo Veneziano,
ask the custodian for access
to the Chapel of the Holy Nail
(Cappella del Sacro Chiodo).

San Nicolò da Tolentino **12**

Campo dei Tolentini, Santa Croce.
Map 5 C1. **C** *(041) 522 21 60.*
Piazzale Roma. **O** *9:30–
11:30am, 4:30–6pm Mon–Sat.*

C LOSE TO Piazzale Roma
(see p271), San Nicolò da
Tolentino is an imposing
17th-century church with a
Classical portico. The interior,
decorated with 17th-century
paintings, is the resting place
of Francesco Morosini (d.1694),
the great Venetian admiral. A
cannonball embedded in the
façade is a memento of an
Austrian bombardment during
the siege of 1849.

San Giovanni Evangelista **13**

Campiello de la Scuola, San Polo.
Map 6 D1. **C** *(041) 71 82 34.*
San Tomà. *No official entry for the
public. Phone for an appointment or
ring the bell.*

A CONFRATERNITY of flagellants
founded the Scuola of St
John the Evangelist in 1261.
The complex, just north of
the Frari *(see pp102–3)*, has a
church, *scuola* and courtyard.
Separating the square from
the street is Pietro Lombardo's
elegant white and grey screen

**Lombardo's marble screen and
portal, San Giovanni Evangelista**

and portal (1480) and in the
arch crowning the portal, the
carved eagle is the symbol of
St John the Evangelist.

The main hall of the Scuola
is reached via a splendid 15th-
century double stairway by
Mauro Coducci (1498). Large,
dark canvases decorate the
ceiling and walls of the 18th-
century hall. The Scuola's
greatest art treasure, the cycle
of paintings depicting *The
Stories of the Cross*, is now on
display in the Accademia
gallery *(see p133)*. It formerly
embellished the oratory (off
the main hall) where the
Reliquary of the True Cross is
still carefully preserved.

San Giacomo dell'Orio **14**

Campo San Giacomo dell'Orio, Santa
Croce. **Map** 2 E5. **C** *(041) 524 06 72.*
Riva di Biasio or San Stae. **O**
*10am–5:30pm Mon–Sat, 3–5:30pm
Sun & public hols.*

T HIS CHURCH is a focal point
of a quiet quarter of Santa
Croce. The name "dell'Orio"
(locally dall'Orio) may derive
from a laurel tree *(alloro)* that
once stood near the church.

Founded in the 9th century,
rebuilt in 1225 and repeatedly
modified, the church is a mix
of architectural styles. The
campanile, basilica ground
plan and Byzantine columns
survive from the 13th century.
The ship's keel roof and the
columns are from the Gothic
period, and the apses are
Renaissance. For access to the
Veronese ceiling and altar
paintings in the new sacristy,
apply to the custodian.

Fondaco dei Turchi 🕦

Canal Grande, Santa Croce 1730.
Map 2 E4. ((041) 524 08 85.
San Stae. ● for renovation.

THE BUILDING that now contains Venice's natural history museum has a chequered history. In the 13th century it was one of the largest *palazzi* on the Grand Canal. In 1381 it was bought by the state for the Dukes of Ferrara and its lavishly decorated rooms were used for banquets and state functions. In 1621 the Turks set up a warehouse *(fondaco)*, and the spacious portico was used for loading merchandise. As commerce with the Orient declined further, the structure fell into disrepair until, roused by Ruskin's passionate interest, the Austrians began restoration work in the 1850s.

Since 1924 the Fondaco has housed the natural history museum (Museo di Storia Naturale). There is a collection of stuffed animals, crustacea and dinosaur fossils and a section on lagoon life. Prize exhibits include a skeleton of an *Ouranosaurus nigeriensis*, 7 m (23 ft) long and 3.6 m (12 ft) tall, and a fossil of an *Sarcosuchus imperator* – an ancestor of the crocodile.

Ouranosaurus skeleton in the Fondaco dei Turchi

San Stae 🕦

Campo San Stae, Santa Croce. **Map** 2 F4. San Stae. ○ 10am–5:30pm Mon–Sat, 3–5:30pm Sun. 🖼

RESTORED IN 1977–8 by the Pro Venezia Foundation, San Stae (or Sant'Eustachio) has a spick-and-span sculpted façade. It was built in 1709 by Domenico Rossi. Works by Piazzetta, Tiepolo and other 18th-century artists decorate the chancel. Near the second altar on the left is the bust of Antonio Foscarini, executed for treason in 1622 but pardoned the following year.

One of the finely furnished rooms of Ca' Mocenigo

Ca' Mocenigo 🕦

Salizzada San Stae, Santa Croce 1992.
Map 2 F5. ((041) 72 17 98.
San Stae. ○ 8:30am–1:30pm Mon–Sat. ● public hols. 🖼 🚫

ONE OF the oldest and greatest of all Venetian families, the Mocenigos produced no fewer than seven doges. There were various branches of the family, one of which resided in this handsome 17th-century mansion. Count Alvise Nicolò Mocenigo, the last of this particular branch, died in 1954, bequeathing the palace to the Comune di Venezia (city authorities). The entrance façade is unremarkable, but the interior is elegantly furnished and gives you a rare opportunity of seeing inside a *palazzo* preserved more or less as it was in the 18th century. The frescoed ceilings and other works of art are celebrations of the family's achievements. The illustrious Mocenigos are portrayed in a frieze around the portego on the first floor. The Museo del Tessuto e del Costume inside the house contains antique fabrics and exquisitely made costumes.

Ca' Pesaro 🕦

Canal Grande, Santa Croce 2076.
Map 2 F5. San Stae. **Galleria d'Arte Moderna** ((041) 72 11 27. ● for restoration. **Museo Orientale** ((041) 524 11 73. ○ 9am–2pm Tue–Sun. ● 1 Jan, 1 May, 25 Dec. 🖼 🚫

IT TOOK 58 YEARS to complete this magnificent Baroque palace. Built for the Pesaro family, it was the masterpiece of Baldassare Longhena, who worked on it until his death in 1682. Antonio Gaspari then took over Longhena's design, eventually completing the structure in 1710.

In the 19th century the Duchess of Bevilacqua La Masa bequeathed the palace to the city for exhibiting the works of unestablished Venetian artists. The Galleria d'Arte Moderna was founded in 1897. Today this features a permanent exhibition of work by artists such as Bonnard, Matisse, Miró, Klee, Klimt and Kandinsky, in addition to works by Italian artists of the 19th and 20th centuries.

The Museo Orientale has an idiosyncratic collection of Chinese and Japanese artifacts collected by the Count of Bardi during his 19th-century travels in the Far East.

Gustav Klimt's *Salome*, Gallery of Modern Art, Ca' Pesaro

Scuola Grande di San Rocco ➒

Pianta's caricature of Tintoretto

FOUNDED IN HONOUR of St Roch (San Rocco), the Scuola was set up as a charitable institution for the sick. Construction began in 1515 under Bartolomeo Bon and was completed in 1549 by Scarpagnino, financed largely by donations from Venetians who believed that St Roch, the patron saint of contagious diseases, would save them from the plague. In 1564 Tintoretto *(see p140)* was commissioned to decorate the walls and ceilings of the Scuola. His remarkable cycle of paintings starts in the Sala dell'Albergo *(see* Gallery Guide*).*

Restored main entrance to the Scuola di San Rocco

SALA DELL'ALBERGO

THE CRUCIFIXION
In this panorama of Calvary, Tintoretto reached a pitch of religious feeling never hitherto achieved in Venetian art.

A self-portrait was often a feature of Tintoretto's paintings.

The subsidiary figures are full of life but do not lessen the central drama.

Figure of Christ
The crucified figure of the Redeemer is raised and leaning, accentuating His divinity and saving grace.

A COMPETITION was held in 1564 to select an artist for the central ceiling panel of the Sala dell'Albergo. To the fury of his rivals, Tintoretto pre-empted his fellow competitors by installing his painting *in situ* prior to judging. He won the commission and was later made a member of the Scuola. Over the next 23 years, Tintoretto decorated the entire building.

The series of paintings, completed in 1587, reveals Tintoretto's revolutionary use of light, mastery of foreshortening and visionary use of colour. The winning painting, *St Roch in Glory* ①, can be seen on the ceiling of the Sala dell'Albergo. The most moving work in the cycle is the *Crucifixion* (1565) ②. Henry James wrote: "Surely no single picture contains more of human life; there is everything in it, including the most exquisite beauty." Of the paintings on the entrance wall, portraying the Passion of Christ, the most notable is *Christ Before Pilate* (1566–7) ③. The easel painting, *Christ Carrying the Cross,* once attributed to Giorgione, is now believed to be a Titian.

Sala dell'Albergo

UPPER HALL

S CARPAGNINO'S great staircase (1544–6), decorated with two vast paintings commemorating the plague of 1630, leads to the Upper Hall. The biblical subjects, decorating the ceiling and walls, were painted in 1575–81. The ceiling paintings (which can be viewed most comfortably with a hired mirror) portray scenes from the Old Testament. The three large and dynamic central square paintings represent: *Moses Striking Water from the Rock* ④, *The Miracle of the Bronze Serpent* ⑤ and *The Gathering of the Manna* ⑥, all alluding to the charitable aims of the Scuola in alleviating thirst, sickness and hunger respectively. All three paintings are crowded compositions with much violent movement.

The vast wall paintings in the hall feature episodes from the New Testament, linking with the ceiling paintings. Two of the most striking paintings are *The Temptation of Christ* ⑦, which shows a handsome young Satan offering Christ two loaves of bread, and *Adoration of the Shepherds* ⑧. Like *The Temptation of Christ*, the *Adoration* is composed in two halves, with a female figure, shepherds and ox below, and the Holy Family and onlookers above.

The beautiful carvings below the paintings were added in the 17th century by sculptor Francesco Pianta. The figures are allegorical and include (near the altar) a caricature of Tintoretto with his palette and brushes, which is meant to represent Painting. Near the entrance to the Sala dell'Albergo you can see a portrait of Tintoretto.

VISITORS' CHECKLIST

Campo San Rocco. **Map** 6 D1.
📞 *(041) 523 48 64.* 🚌 *San Tomà.* ⏰ *Apr–Oct: 9am–5:30pm daily; Nov & Mar: 10am–4pm daily, Dec–Feb: 10am–1pm Mon–Fri, 10am–4pm Sat & Sun.* ● *1 Jan, Easter, 25 Dec.* 🎫 🚫 📷 📹

GROUND FLOOR HALL

The Flight into Egypt (1582–7) (detail)

T HIS FINAL CYCLE, executed in 1583–7, consists of eight paintings illustrating the life of Mary. The series starts with an *Annunciation*, and ends with an *Assumption*, which has been poorly restored. The tranquil scenes of *St Mary of Egypt* ⑨, *St Mary Magdalene* ⑩ and *The Flight into Egypt* ⑪, painted when Tintoretto was in his late sixties, are remarkable for their serenity. This is portrayed most lucidly by the Virgin's isolated spiritual contemplation in the *St Mary of Egypt*. In all three paintings, the landscapes, rendered with rapid strokes, play a major role.

GALLERY GUIDE

The paintings, which unfortunately are not well lit, have no labels, but a useful plan of the Scuola is available (in several languages) free of charge at the entrance.

To see the paintings in chronological order, start in the Sala dell'Albergo (off the Upper Hall), followed by the Upper Hall and finally the Ground Floor Hall.

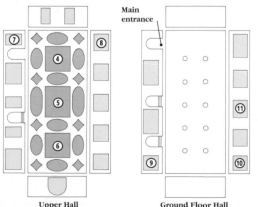

The Temptation of Christ, 1578–81 (detail)

Main entrance

Upper Hall

Ground Floor Hall

KEY

▢ Wall paintings

▢ Ceiling paintings

CASTELLO

THE LARGEST *sestiere* of the city, Castello stretches from San Marco and Cannaregio in the west to the modern blocks of Sant'Elena in the east. The area takes its name from the 8th-century fortress that once stood on what is now San Pietro, the island which for centuries was the religious focus of the city. The church here was the episcopal see from the 9th century and the city's cathedral from 1451 to

Water stoup, Santa Maria Formosa

1807. The industrial hub of Castello was the Arsenale, where the great shipyards produced Venice's indomitable fleet of warships. Castello's most popular and solidly commercial area is the Riva degli Schiavoni promenade. Behind the waterfront it is comparatively quiet, characterized by narrow alleys, elegantly faded *palazzi* and fine churches, including the great Santi Giovanni e Paolo *(see pp116–17)*.

SIGHTS AT A GLANCE

Churches
La Pietà ❸
San Francesco della Vigna ❹
San Giorgio dei Greci ❷
San Giovanni in Bragora ❿
Santi Giovanni e Paolo
  pp116– 17 ❶❷
San Lorenzo ❶❺
San Zaccaria ❶

Historic Buildings and Monuments
Arsenale ❶❾
Hotel Danieli ❹
Ospedaletto ❶❸
Statue of
  Colleoni ❶⓪

Streets, Bridges and Squares
Campo Santa Maria Formosa ❾
Ponte della Paglia and Bridge of
  Sighs ❻
Riva degli Schiavoni ❺

Walk
Exploring Eastern Castello ⓴

Museums, Galleries and Scuole
Fondazione Querini
  Stampalia ❽
Museo Diocesano d'Arte
  Sacra ❼
Museo Storico Navale ⓲
Scuola di San Giorgio degli
  Schiavoni ⓰
Scuola Grande di San
  Marco ⓫

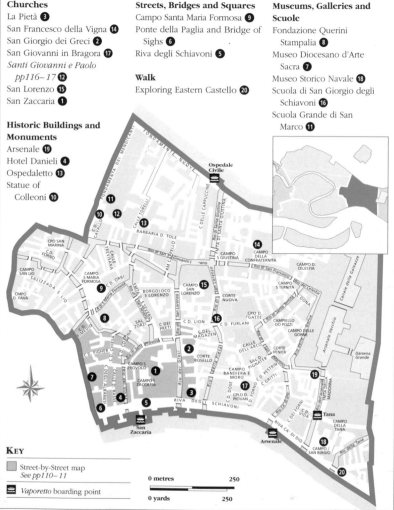

KEY

Street-by-Street map
  See pp110– 11

Vaporetto boarding point

0 metres   250
0 yards   250

◁ **Bas relief on Rio Terrà Garibaldi, eastern Castello**

Street-by-Street: Castello

A STROLL ALONG the Riva degli Schiavoni is an integral part of a visit to Venice. Glorious views of San Giorgio Maggiore compensate for the commercialized aspects of the quayside: souvenir stalls, excursion touts and an overabundance of tourists. Associations with literary figures are legion. Petrarch lived at No. 4145, Henry James was offered "dirty" lodgings at No. 4161, and Ruskin stayed at the Hotel Danieli. Inland, the quiet, unassuming streets and squares of Castello provide a contrast to the bustling waterfront.

13th-century Madonna in the Museo Diocesano

★ **Museo Diocesano**
The cloisters of the ancient Benedictine monastery of Sant'Apollonia herald the museum ❼

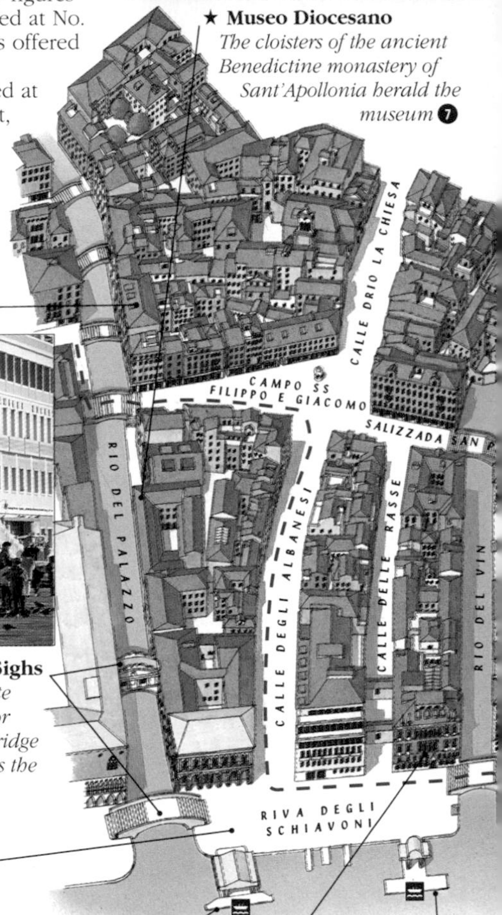

Palazzo Trevisan-Cappello, used as a showroom for Murano glass, was the home of Bianca Cappello, wife of Francesco de' Medici.

Ponte della Paglia and Bridge of Sighs
Crowds throng the Istrian stone Ponte della Paglia – the "straw bridge" – for the best views of the neighbouring Bridge of Sighs, the covered bridge that links the Doge's Palace to the old prisons ❻

Riva degli Schiavoni
This paved quayside was established over 600 years ago, and widened in 1782 ❺

San Zaccaria Jolanda

San Zaccaria Danieli

STAR SIGHTS

★ **La Pietà**

★ **San Zaccaria**

★ **Museo Diocesano**

Hotel Danieli
Joseph da Niel, after whom this hotel was named, turned the Palazzo Dandolo into a haunt for 19th-century writers and artists ❹

Palazzo Priuli, overlooking the quiet Fondamenta Osmarin, is a fine Venetian Gothic palace. The corner window is particularly beautiful, but the early 16th-century façade frescoes have long since disappeared.

San Giorgio dei Greci

Subsidence is the cause of the city's tilting bell-towers: San Giorgio dei Greci's looks particularly perilous ②

LOCATOR MAP
See Street Finder, maps 7, 8

★ **San Zaccaria**
Coducci added Renaissance details such as this panel to the Gothic façade ①

KEY

– – – Suggested route

| 0 metres | 75 |
| 0 yards | 75 |

Henry James stayed here and completed *Portrait of a Lady* (1881).

The Statue of Vittorio Emanuele II, the first king of a united Italy, was sculpted by Ettore Ferrari in 1887.

★ **La Pietà**
In Vivaldi's day, the church became famous for the superb quality of its musical performances ③

San Zaccaria ●

Campo San Zaccaria. **Map** 8 D2.
(*(041) 522 12 57.* 🚤 *San
Zaccaria.* ○ *10am–noon, 4–6pm
daily.* 🚫 *to chapels only.*

SET IN A QUIET square just a
stone's throw from the Riva
degli Schiavoni, the church of
San Zaccaria is a successful
blend of Flamboyant Gothic
and Classical Renaissance
styles. Founded in the 9th century, it was completely rebuilt
between 1444 and 1515.
Antonio Gambello began the
façade in Gothic style and,
when Gambello died in 1481,
Mauro Coducci completed the
upper section, adding all the
Classical detail.

The adjoining Benedictine
convent, which had close
links with the church, became
quite notorious for the riotous
behaviour of its nuns. The
majority were from families of
Venetian nobility, many of
them sent to the convent to
avoid the expense of a dowry.

Every Easter the doge came
with his entourage to San
Zaccaria – a custom which
originated as an expression of
gratitude to the nuns, who
had relinquished part of their
garden so that Piazza San
Marco could be enlarged.

The artistic highlight of the
interior (illuminate with coins
in the meter) is Giovanni
Bellini's sumptuously coloured
and superbly serene *Madonna
and Child with Saints* (1505)
in the north aisle.

On the right of the church
is a door to the Chapel of St
Athanasius which leads to the
Chapel of San Tarasio. The
chapel is decorated with vault
frescoes (1442) by Andrea del
Castagno of Florence, and

Gothic polyptychs painted in
1443–4 by Antonio Vivarini
and Giovanni d'Alemagna. The
relics of eight doges lie buried
in the waterlogged crypt.

**Distant view of San Giorgio dei
Greci's tilting campanile**

San Giorgio
dei Greci ●

Map 8 D2. 🚤 *San Zaccaria.* **Church**
(*(041) 523 95 69.* ○ *10am–1pm,
2:30–4:30pm Tue–Sun.* ● *Sun pm.*
Museo dei Icone **(** *(041) 522 65 81.*
○ *9am–12:30pm, 2–4:30pm.* 🚫 🚫

THE MOST remarkable feature
of this 16th-century Greek
church is the listing campanile
which looks as if it is about to
topple into the Rio dei Greci.
A characteristic feature of the
interior is the *matroneo* – the
gallery where, in keeping with
Greek Orthodox custom, the
women sat apart from men.
Note also the iconostasis, separating the sanctuary from the
nave. The nearby Scuola di San
Nicolò dei Greci, redesigned
by Baldassare Longhena in
1678, is now the museum of
icons of the Hellenic Institute.

La Pietà ●

Riva degli Schiavoni. **Map** 8 D2.
(*(041) 522 21 71.* 🚤 *San Zaccaria.*
○ *Jul–Aug: 9:30am–12:30pm,
3:30–6:30pm daily.*

THE CHURCH of La Pietà (or
Santa Maria della Visita-
zione) dates from the 15th
century. It was rebuilt in
1745–1760 by Giorgio Massari,
and the Classical façade was
added in 1906. The church has
a cool, elegant interior, with
an oval plan. The resplendent
ceiling fresco, *Triumph of
Faith* (1755), was painted by
Giambattista Tiepolo.

The Pietà started its life as a
foundling home for orphans.
It proved so popular that a
warning plaque was set up
(still to be seen on the side
wall), threatening damnation
to parents who tried to pass
off their children as orphans.

From 1703 until 1740
Antonio Vivaldi directed the
musical groups and wrote
numerous oratorios, cantatas
and vocal pieces for the Pietà
choir, and the church became
famous for its performances.

Today the church is a
popular venue for concerts –
with a strong emphasis on
Vivaldi. These are held
throughout the year, usually
on Mondays and Thursdays.

**Bas relief on La Pietà's early 20th-
century façade**

Hotel Danieli ●

Riva degli Schiavoni 4196. **Map** 7 C2.
🚤 *San Zaccaria. See also **Where to
Stay** p230.*

ONE OF THE MOST celebrated
hotels in Europe, the
Danieli's deep pink façade is
a landmark on the Riva degli
Schiavoni. Built in the 14th
century, it became famous as
the venue for the first opera
performed in Venice, Monteverdi's *Proserpina Rapita*

Detail from *The Nun's Parlour at San Zaccaria* by Francesco Guardi

(1630). The palace became a hotel in 1822 and soon gained popularity with the literary and artistic set. Its famous guests included Balzac, Proust, Dickens, Cocteau, Ruskin, Debussy and Wagner. In the 1830s Room 10 witnessed an episode in the love affair between the French poet and dramatist Alfred de Musset, and novelist George Sand: when de Musset fell ill after a surfeit of orgies, Sand ran off with his Venetian doctor.

Riva degli Schiavoni – the city's most famous promenade

Riva degli Schiavoni ❺

Map 8 D2. 🚉 *San Zaccaria.*

THE SWEEPING promenade that forms the southern quayside of Castello was named after the traders from Dalmatia (Schiavonia) who used to moor their boats and barges here. For those who arrive in Venice by water, this long curving quayside is a spectacular introduction to the charms of the city.

At its western end, close to Piazza San Marco, the broad promenade teems during the day with tourists thronging around the souvenir stalls and people hurrying to and from the *vaporetto* stops. Nothing can detract, however, from the glorious views across the lagoon to the island of San Giorgio Maggiore *(see p95)*.

The Riva degli Schiavoni has always been busy with boats. Canaletto's drawings in the 1740s and 1750s show the Riva bustling with gondolas, sailing boats and barges. The gondolas are still here, but it is also chock-a-block with water taxis, *vaporetti*, excursion boats, tugs, and – beyond the Arsenale – naval ships and ocean-going liners.

The modern annexe of the Hotel Danieli caused a great furore when it was built in 1948. Intruding on a waterfront graced by fine Venetian palaces and mansions, its stark outline is still something of an eyesore. The annexe marks the spot where Doge Vitale Michiel II was

stabbed to death in 1172. Three centuries earlier, in 864, Doge Pietro Tradonico had suffered the same fate in nearby Campo San Zaccaria.

Ponte della Paglia and Bridge of Sighs ❻

Map 7 C2. 🚉 *San Zaccaria.*

THE NAME OF the Ponte della Paglia may derive from the boats *(paglia)* that once moored here to offload their cargoes of straw. Originally built in 1360, the existing structure dates from 1847.

According to legend the Bridge of Sighs, built in 1600 to link the Doge's Palace with the new prisons, takes its name from the lamentations of the prisoners as they made their way to the offices of the

Ponte della Paglia behind the Bridge of Sighs

State Inquisitors. Access is available to the public via the Secret Itinerary tour in the Doge's Palace *(see p87)*.

Museo Diocesano d'Arte Sacra ❼

Sant'Apollonia, Ponte della Canonica. **Map** 7 C2. 📞 *(041) 522 91 66.* 🚉 *San Zaccaria.* ◯ *10:30am–12:30pm Mon–Sat.* ● *public hols.* ***Donations*** *appreciated.*

ONE OF the architectural gems of Venice, the cloister of Sant'Apollonia is the only Romanesque building in the city. Only a few steps from St Mark's, the cloister provides a quiet retreat from the hubbub of the Piazza.

The monastery was once the home of Benedictine monks, but its non-ecclesiastical uses have been manifold. In 1976 its cloisters became the home of the diocesan museum of sacred art, founded in order to provide a haven for works of art from closed or deconsecrated churches. The collection includes paintings, statues, crucifixes and many pieces of valuable silver. The museum has two workshops, staffed by volunteers who restore the paintings and statues. The collection is ever-changing, but among the major permanent exhibits are works by Luca Giordano (1634–1705), which came from the Church of Sant'Aponal, and a 16th-century wood and crystal tabernacle.

Fondazione Querini Stampalia **8**

Campiello Querini, Castello 4778.
Map 7 C1. **[** (041) 522 52 35.
San Zaccaria. **Museum** 10am–
1pm, 3–6pm Tue–Thu & Sun, 10am–
1pm, 3–10pm Fri & Sat. Mon.
Library 4–11:15pm Mon–Fri,
2:30–11:15pm Sat, 3–7pm Sun.

THE LARGE PALAZZO Querini
Stampalia was commis-
sioned in the 16th century by
the descendants of the old
Venetian Querini family. Great
art lovers, they filled the
palace with fine paintings.

In 1868 the last member of
the dynasty bequeathed the
palace and the family collection
of art to the foundation that
bears his name. The paintings
include works by Giovanni
Bellini, Giambattista Tiepolo,
and some vignettes by Pietro
and Alessandro Longhi. The
library on the first floor, which
is open to the public, contains
over 200,000 books.

Campo Santa Maria Formosa **9**

Campo Santa Maria Formosa.
Map 7 C1. Rialto.

LARGE, RAMBLING and
flanked by handsome
palaces, the market square
of Santa Maria Formosa is
one of the most characteristic *campi* of Venice. On
the southern side, distinctive for its swelling apses,
stands the church of Santa
Maria Formosa. Built on
ancient foundations, it was
designed by Mauro Coducci
in 1492 but took over a
century to assume its
current form. Unusually, it
has two main façades – one
overlooking the *campo*, the
other the canal. The cam-
panile was added in 1688.
Its most notable feature is
the truly grotesque stone
face that decorates its foot.

Inside, Palma il Vecchio's
polyptych, *St Barbara and
Saints* (c.1510), ranks
among the great Venetian
masterpieces and looks
particularly splendid since its
restoration by the American
Save Venice organization.

Palma il Vecchio's portrayal
of the handsome and dignified figure of St Barbara
glorifies Venice's ideal female
beauty. She is surrounded by
saints, with a central lunette
of the *pietà* above. St Barbara
was the patron saint of
soldiers: in wartime they
prayed to her for protection,
in victory they came for
thanksgiving.

Statue of Colleoni **10**

Campo Santi Giovanni e Paolo.
Map 3 C5. Ospedale Civile.

BARTOLOMEO COLLEONI, the
famous *condottiere* or
commander of mercenaries,
left his fortune to the Republic
on condition that his statue
was placed in front of San
Marco. A prominent statue in
the Piazza would have broken
with precedent, so the Senate
cunningly had Colleoni raised
before the Scuola di San Marco
instead of the basilica. A
touchstone of early Renaissance sculpture, the equestrian
statue of the proud warrior
(1481–8) is by the Florentine

**Palma il Vecchio's *St Barbara* in
Santa Maria Formosa**

Statue of Bartolomeo Colleoni

Andrea Verrocchio and, after
his death, was cast in bronze
by Alessandro Leopardi. The
statue has a strong sense of
power and movement which
arguably ranks it alongside
works of Donatello.

Scuola Grande di San Marco **11**

Campo Santi Giovanni e Paolo. **Map**
3 C5. Ospedale Civile. **Library [**
(041) 529 43 23. 8:30am–noon
Mon–Sat (ring bell). public hols.
Church [(041) 522 56 62.
7am–noon Mon–Sat, 8–10am Sun.

FEW HOSPITALS can boast as
rich and unusual a façade
as that of Venice's Ospedale
Civile. It was built originally
as one of the six great confraternities of the city *(see p127).*
Their first headquarters were
destroyed by fire in 1485, but
the Scuola was rebuilt at the
end of the 15th century.

The delightful asymmetrical
façade, with its arcades,
marble panels and *trompe
l'oeil* designs, was the work
of Pietro Lombardo working
in conjunction with his sons
and Giovanni Buora. The
upper order was finished by
Mauro Coducci in 1495. The
interior was revamped in the
last century and, since then,
most of the artistic masterpieces have been dispersed.

The library has a fine carved
16th-century ceiling, and the
hospital chapel, the Church of
San Lazzaro dei Mendicanti,
contains an early Tintoretto
and a work by Veronese.

Santi Giovanni e Paolo ⑫

See pp116–17.

Ospedaletto ⑬

Calle Barbaria delle Tole. **Map** 4 D5.
🄲 *(041) 520 06 33.* 🚤 *Ospedale Civile.* ⏰ *3–6pm Thu–Sat.*

BEYOND THE SOUTH flank of Santi Giovanni e Paolo *(see pp116– 17)* is the façade of the Ospedaletto or, more correctly, Santa Maria dei Derelitti. The Ospedaletto was set up by the Republic in 1527 as a charitable institution to care for the sick and aged, and to educate orphans and abandoned girls. Such an education consisted largely of the study of music. The girls became leading figures in choirs and orchestras, with concerts bringing in funds for the construction in 1630 of a *sala della musica,* which became the main performance venue. This elegant room, frescoed by Jacopo Guarana, can be visited on request.

The church, which formed part of the Ospedaletto, was built by Baldassare Longhena in 1662–74. John Ruskin regarded the huge, hideous heads on the façade as anti-Classical abominations, likening them to "masses of diseased figures and swollen fruit". The interior of the church is decorated with less

Fresco by Guarana in the *sala della musica* of the Ospedaletto

The decorative façade of the Scuola Grande di San Marco

provocative works of art and notable paintings from the 18th century, including *The Sacrifice of Isaac* (1715–16) by Giambattista Tiepolo.

San Francesco della Vigna ⑭

Ramo San Francesco. **Map** 8 E1. 🄲 *(041) 520 61 02.* 🚤 *Celestia.* ⏰ *8am–12:30pm, 3–7pm daily.*

THE NAME "della Vigna" derives from a vineyard which was bequeathed to the Franciscans in 1253. The church which the order built here in the 13th century was rebuilt under Jacopo Sansovino in 1534, with a façade added in 1562–72 by Palladio.

The interior has a rich collection of works of art, including sculpture by Alessandro Vittoria, Paolo Veronese's *The Holy Family with Saints* (1562) and Antonio da Negroponte's *Virgin and Child* (c.1450). The *Madonna and Child with Saints* (1507) by Giovanni Bellini hangs near the cloister.

San Lorenzo ⑮

Campo San Lorenzo. **Map** 8 D1. 🚤 *San Zaccaria.* ⏺ *for restoration.*

DECONSECRATED and closed for restoration, the church of San Lorenzo's only claim to fame is as the alleged burial place of Marco Polo *(see p143).* Unfortunately there is nothing to show for it because his sarcophagus disappeared during rebuilding in 1592. A collection of paintings was dispersed, and for many years the church was abandoned.

In 1987 restorers discovered the foundations of two earlier churches, dating from 850 AD and the late 12th century. The foundations of the present medieval structure, as well as substantial remains of the marble floor, have been damage by water seeping in from the adjacent canal. Restoration work funded by the British Venice in Peril Fund continues indefinitely.

Marco Polo

Santi Giovanni e Paolo ⑫

Figure in left transept

Mⁱᵒ ORE FAMILIARLY known as San Zanipolo, Santi Giovanni e Paolo vies with the Frari *(see pp102–3)* as the city's greatest Gothic church. It was built in the late 13th to early 14th centuries by the Dominican friars, and is striking for its huge dimensions and architectural austerity. Known as the Pantheon of Venice, it houses monuments to no less than 25 doges. Many of these are outstanding works of art, executed by the Lombardi family and other leading sculptors of the day.

★ Cappella del Rosario
The Adoration of the Shepherds *is one of many works by Paolo Veronese which decorate the Rosary Chapel.*

The sacristy has paintings that celebrate the Dominican Order.

★ Tomb of Nicolò Marcello
This magnificent Renaissance monument to Doge Nicolò Marcello (d.1474) was sculpted by Pietro Lombardo.

The doorway, which is decorated with Byzantine reliefs, is one of the earliest Renaissance architectural features in Venice. The portico carvings are attributed to Bartolomeo Bon.

The marble columns were taken from a former church on the island of Torcello.

★ Tomb of Pietro Mocenigo
Pietro Lombardo's great masterpiece (1481) commemorates the doge's military pursuits when he was Grand Captain of the Venetian forces. This west side wall is largely devoted to Mocenigo monuments.

STAR FEATURES

★ Doges' Tombs

★ Cappella del Rosario

★ Cappella di San Domenico

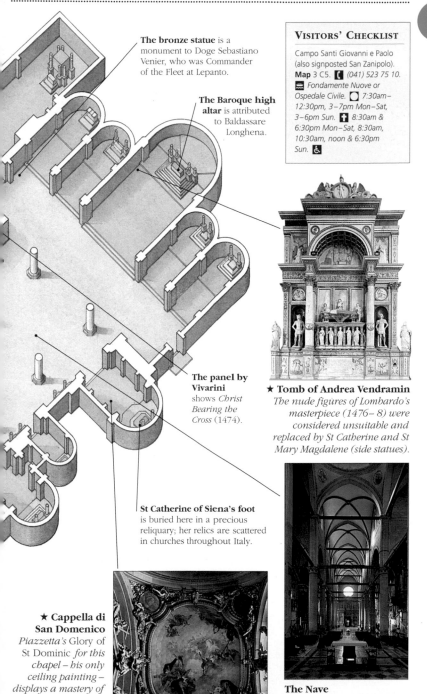

The bronze statue is a monument to Doge Sebastiano Venier, who was Commander of the Fleet at Lepanto.

The Baroque high altar is attributed to Baldassare Longhena.

★ Tomb of Andrea Vendramin
The nude figures of Lombardo's masterpiece (1476–8) were considered unsuitable and replaced by St Catherine and St Mary Magdalene (side statues).

The panel by Vivarini shows *Christ Bearing the Cross* (1474).

St Catherine of Siena's foot is buried here in a precious reliquary; her relics are scattered in churches throughout Italy.

★ Cappella di San Domenico
Piazzetta's Glory of St Dominic *for this chapel – his only ceiling painting – displays a mastery of colour, perspective and foreshortening. The artist had a profound influence on the young Tiepolo.*

The Nave
The vast interior is cross-vaulted, held by wooden tie-beams and supported by ten huge columns of Istrian stone blocks.

St George slaying the Dragon by Carpaccio, in the Scuola di San Giorgio degli Schiavoni

Scuola di San Giorgio degli Schiavoni ⑯

Calle Furlani. **Map** 8 E1. **℃** *(041) 522 88 28.* 🚆 *San Zaccaria.* ⏱ *Apr–Oct: 9:30am–12:30pm, 3:30–6:30pm Tue–Sun; Nov–Mar: 10am–12:30pm, 3–6pm Tue–Sun.* 🕙 *Sun pm, 1 Jan, 1 May, 25 Dec.* 🎟 🚫

WITHIN THIS surprisingly simple Scuola are some of the finest paintings of Vittore Carpaccio, commissioned by the Schiavoni community in Venice.

From the earliest days of the Republic, Venice forged trade links with the coastal region of Schiavonia (Dalmatia) across the Adriatic. By 1420 permanent Venetian rule was established there, and many of the Schiavoni came to live in Venice. By the mid 15th century the Slav colony in the city had grown considerably and the State gave permission for them to found their own confraternity *(see p127)*.

The Scuola was established in 1451. It is a delightful spot to admire Carpaccio's really exceptional works of art, and has changed very little since the rebuilding of the Scuola in 1551. The exquisite frieze, executed between 1502 and 1508, shows scenes from the lives of favourite saints: St George, St Tryphon and St Jerome. Each episode of the narrative cycle is remarkable for its vivid colouring, minutely observed detail and historic record of Venetian life. Outstanding among them are *St George Slaying the Dragon, St Jerome Leading the Tamed Lion to the Monastery*, and *The Vision of St Jerome*.

San Giovanni in Bragora ⑰

Campo Bandiera e Moro. **Map** 8 E2. **℃** *(041) 520 59 06.* 🚆 *Arsenale.* ⏱ *8:30–11am, 3–7pm Mon–Sat, 10–11am Sun.*

THE FOUNDATIONS of this simple church date back to ancient times but the existing building is essentially Gothic (1475–9). The intimate interior has major works of art which demonstrate the transition from Gothic to early Renaissance. Bartolomeo Vivarini's altarpiece, *Madonna and Child with Saints* (1478) is unmistakably Gothic. Contrasting with this is Cima da Conegliano's *Baptism of Christ* (1492–5) on the main altar. This large-scale narrative scene, in a realistic landscape, set a precedent for later Renaissance painters.

Museo Storico Navale ⑱

Campo San Biagio, Arsenale. **Map** 8 F3. **℃** *(041) 520 02 76.* 🚆 *Arsenale.* ⏱ *8:45am–1:30pm Mon–Sat.* 🕙 *public hols.* 🎟

IT WAS THE Austrians who, in 1815, first had the idea of assembling the remnants of the Venetian navy and creating a historical naval museum. They began with a series of models of vessels that had been produced in the 17th century by the Arsenale, and to these added all the naval paraphernalia they could obtain. The exhibits include friezes preserved from famous galleys of the past, a variety of maritime firearms and a replica of the Doge's ceremonial barge, the *Bucintoro*.

The collection has been housed in an ex-warehouse on the waterfront since 1958, and now traces Venetian and Italian naval history to the present day.

The first exhibits you see on entering are the World War II human torpedoes or "pigs". Torpedoes such as these helped sink HMS *Valiant* and HMS *Queen Elizabeth*: they were guided to their target by naval divers who jumped off just before impact.

The rest of the museum is divided into the Venetian navy, the Italian navy from 1860 to today, Adriatic vessels and the Swedish room. The museum is well laid out and there are very informative explanations in English.

Model of the *Bucintoro* in the Museo Storico Navale

Arsenale ⑲

Map 8 F1. 🚏 *Arsenale or Tana.*
Limited public access.

Heart of the city's maritime power, the Arsenale was founded in the 12th century and enlarged in the 14th to 16th centuries to become the greatest naval shipyard in the world. The word "arsenal" derives from the Arabic *darsina'a*, house of industry – which indeed it was.

At its height in the 16th century, a workforce of 16,000, the *arsenalotti*, were employed to construct, equip and repair the great Venetian galleys *(see pp44– 5)*. One of the first production lines in Europe, it was like a city within a city, with its own workshops, warehouses, factories, foundries and docks.

Entrance to the Arsenale, guarded by 16th-century towers

THE ASSEMBLY-LINE SYSTEM

The *arsenalotti*, master ship-builders of the 16th century

During the Arsenale's heyday, a Venetian galley could be constructed and fully equipped with remarkable speed and efficiency. From the early 16th century the hulls, which were built in the New Arsenal, were towed past a series of buildings in the Old Arsenal to be equipped in turn with rigging, ammunition and food supplies. By 1570, when Venice was faced with the Turkish threat to take Cyprus, the Arsenale proved capable of turning out an entire galley in 24 hours. Henry III of France witnessed the system's efficiency in 1574 when the *arsenalotti* completed a galley in the time it took for him to partake in a state feast.

Surrounded by crenellated walls, the site today is largely abandoned. The huge gateway and vast site are the only evidence of its former splendour. The gateway, in the form of a triumphal arch, was built in 1460 by Antonio Gambello and is often cited as Venice's first Renaissance construction.

The two lions guarding the entrance were pillaged from Piraeus (near Athens) by Admiral Francesco Morosini in 1687. A third lion, bald and sitting upright, bears runic inscriptions on his haunches, thought to have been carved by Scandinavian mercenaries who in 1040 fought for the Byzantine emperor against some Greek rebels.

By the 17th century, when the seeds of Venetian decline were well and truly sown, the number of *arsenalotti* plummeted to 1,000. Following the Fall of the Republic in 1797,

Napoleon destroyed the docks and stripped the *Bucintoro* (the Doge's ceremonial ship) of its precious ornament. Cannons and bronzes were melted down to contribute to victory monuments celebrating the French Revolution.

Today the area is under military administration and for the most part closed to the public. The bridge by the arched gateway affords partial views of the shipyard, but for a better view, take a trip on a *vaporetto* (No. 23 or 52) which takes you through the heart of the Arsenale Vecchio.

Some parts of the Arsenale are now being put to good use. The Corderia, the old rope factory, serves as a secondary exhibiton centre for the Biennale *(see p256)*. A research consortium developing marine and coastal technologies also operates from the Arsenale.

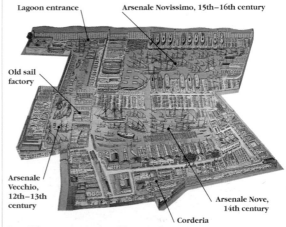

Lagoon entrance

Arsenale Novissimo, 15th–16th century

Old sail factory

Arsenale Vecchio, 12th–13th century

Arsenale Nove, 14th century

Corderia

Late 18th-century engraving of the Arsenale

Exploring Eastern Castello ⑳

THIS PEACEFUL STROLL takes you from the animated Castello quayside to the quieter eastern limits of the city. The focal point of the tour is the solitary island of San Pietro di Castello, site of the former cathedral of Venice. From here you head south to the island of Sant'Elena with its historic church and Venice's football stadium, and return via the public gardens along the scenic waterfront.

The calm and leafy Giardini Pubblici ⑯

(see p119). Then take the first on the left, marked Calle San Gioachin, cross a small bridge and turn left at the "crossroads". Once you are past Campo Ruga ⑤, take the second turning on the right

A tribute to the women fallen in World War II ⑱

Via Garibaldi

This broad, busy street ① was created by Napoleon in 1808 by filling in a canal. The first house on the right ② was the home of John Cabot and his son Sebastian, the Italian navigators who in 1497 found what they thought to be the coast of China (but in reality was the Labrador coast of Newfoundland). Near the end of the street, through a gate on the right, a bronze monument of Garibaldi ③ by Augusto Benvenuti (1885) marks the northern end of the Viale Garibaldi, which leads to the public gardens.

Returning to Via Garibaldi, take the left-hand embankment at the end of the street, pausing on the bridge ④ for distant views of the Arsenale

and cross the bridge over the broad Canale di San Pietro.

The island of San Pietro di Castello

The old church of San Pietro di Castello ⑥ and its free-standing, tilting campanile ⑦ overlook a grassy square. The island, once occupied by a fortress *(castello)*, was one of Venice's earliest settlements. The church, which was probably founded in the 7th century, became the cathedral of Venice and remained so until 1807 when San Marco took its place *(see p80)*. The existing church, built to a

Palladian design in the mid 16th century, has several notable features. These include the Lando Chapel, the Vendramin Chapel and the marble throne from an Arabic tomb-stone, originally said to have been the Seat of St Peter.

In the south of the square, Mauro Coducci's elegant stone campanile was built in 1482–8, and the cupola was added in 1670. Beside the church, the Palazzo Patriarcale (Bishop's

KEY

···   Walk route

🔆   View point

⛴   *Vaporetto* boarding point

The busy Via Garibaldi, with John Cabot's house on the far right ②

Palace) ⑧ was turned into barracks by Napoleon. The old cloisters are overgrown and strung with washing and fishing nets.

From the Bishop's Palace take the Calle drio il Campanile south from the square and turn left when you come to the canal. The first turning right takes you across the Ponte di Quintavalle ⑨, a wooden bridge with good views of brightly coloured boats anchored on either side of the waterway.

The island of San Pietro, with its curious leaning campanile ⑦

San Pietro to Sant'Elena

The large and semi-derelict building at the foot of the bridge is the ex-church and monastery of Sant'Anna ⑩. Take the first left off the *fondamenta*, cross Campiello Correr and then take Calle GB Tiepolo and cross the Secco Marina. Continue straight ahead and over the bridge for the Church of San Giuseppe ⑪. On the rare occasions it is open you can see Vincenzo Scamozzi's monument to Doge Marino Grimani

(1595–1605). Cross the square beyond the church and zigzag left, right and left again for Paludo San Antonio, an uninspiring modern street that has been reclaimed from marshland *(palude)*. At the far end cross the bridge over the Rio dei Giardini ⑫ and take the street ahead. A right turn along Viale 4 Novembre brings you down to the spacious gardens of Parco delle Rimembranze ⑬. At the southern end of the park, cut left at Calle Buccari ⑭, then right for the bridge over Rio di Sant'Elena. In front, the Church of Sant'Elena ⑮ is a pretty Gothic church founded in the 13th century. Retrace your steps over the bridge and turn left, following the waterfront back through the park.

Detail from Gothic façade of Sant'Elena ⑮

Giardini Pubblici and the Biennale Pavilions

At the far side of the park, the bridge across the Rio dei Giardini brings you to the public gardens and to the Biennale gate entrance ⑯. If it happens to be summer in an odd-numbered year, the gardens will be set up with the Biennale pavilions ⑰ at which 40 to 50 nations exhibit many examples of contemporary art *(see p256)*.

Riva dei Partigiani

Outside the public gardens on Riva dei Partigiani is a large bronze statue. Lying on the steps of the embankment, the monument can only be seen at low tide. Known as La Donna Partigiana, this is a memorial to all the women who were killed fighting in World War II ⑱.

TIPS FOR WALKERS

Starting point: The western end of Via Garibaldi.
Length: Just under 5 km (3 miles).
Getting there: Vaporetto No. 1 to Arsenale or No. 52 to Tana.
Stopping-off points: There are a handful of simple cafés and trattorias along the route, most of them on Via Garibaldi. The waterside Caffè Paradiso at the entrance to the Giardini Pubblici has excellent views. For good seafood, try the Hostaria Da Franz (see p241) along Fondamenta San Giuseppe (No. 754). The green shady parks are a welcome retreat from the bustle of the city.

Sant'Elena

0 metres   200
0 yards   200

SIGHTS AT A GLANCE

Churches
Angelo Raffaele **8**
Gesuati **14**
Santa Maria dei Carmini **6**
Santa Maria della Salute **19**
Santa Maria della Visitazione **13**
San Nicolò dei Mendicoli **7**
San Sebastiano **9**
San Trovaso **12**

Museums and Galleries
Accademia see pp130–33 **15**
Ca' Rezzonico **3**
Cini Collection **16**
Peggy Guggenheim
 Collection **17**

Historic Buildings
Dogana di Mare **20**
Scuola Grande dei Carmini **5**
Squero di San Trovaso **11**

Streets, Bridges and Squares
Campiello Barbáro **18**
Campo San Barnaba **1**
Campo Santa Margherita **4**
Ponte dei Pugni **2**
Zattere **10**

KEY

Street-by-Street map
See pp124–5

Vaporetto boarding point

Traghetto crossing

◁ **View across the Grand Canal
to Santa Maria della Salute**

DORSODURO

ORSODURO IS NAMED after the solid subsoil on which this area has been built up (the name means "hard backbone"). The western part, the island of Mendigola, was colonized centuries before the Rialto was established in AD 828 as the permanent seat of Venice. The settlement then spread eastwards, covering another six islands.

East of the Accademia, the Dorsoduro is a quiet and pretty neighbourhood with shaded squares, quiet canals and picturesque residences belonging to wealthy Venetians and foreigners. In the early 1900s the area was favoured by British expatriates who used to attend the Anglican church of St George in Campo San Vio. Among the area's attractions are the wide-embracing lagoon views,

Squero di San Trovaso, the gondola boatyard

both from the eastern tip near the Salute and from the Zattere across to the island of Giudecca. West of the Accademia, the *sestiere* is more vibrant, with the busy Campo Santa Margherita as its attractive focal point. Further west, the shabbier area around the beautiful church of San Nicolò dei Mendicoli was originally the home of fishermen and sailors. The Dorsoduro plays host to several major collections of art, notably the Accademia gallery and the Peggy Guggenheim Collection of 20th-century art. The churches are also rich repositories of paintings and sculpture: San Sebastiano has fine paintings by Paolo Veronese; the Scuola Grande dei Carmini and the church of the Gesuati have ceilings painted by Giambattista Tiepolo.

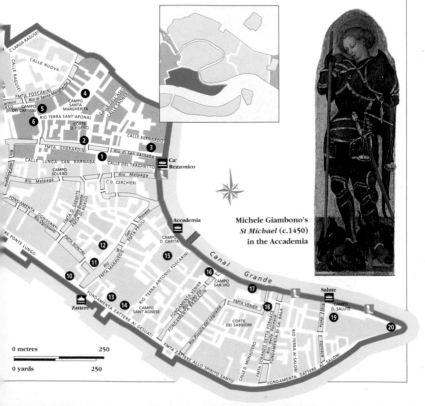

Michele Giambono's
St Michael (c.1450)
in the Accademia

0 metres 250
0 yards 250

Street-by-Street: Dorsoduro

BETWEEN THE IMPOSING palaces on the Grand Canal and the Campo Santa Margherita lies an almost silent neighbourhood of small squares and narrow alleys. The delightful Rio San Barnaba is best appreciated from the Ponte dei Pugni, near the barge selling fruit and vegetables. The Rio Terrà canal, though architecturally uninspiring, has a fascinating mask shop and some cafés that are lively at night-time. All roads seem to lead to Campo Santa Margherita, the heart of Dorsoduro. The square bustles with activity, particularly in the morning when the market stalls are functioning.

Reliefs on a house at Ponte Trovaso

★ Scuola Grande dei Carmini
Tiepolo painted nine ceiling panels for the Scuola in 1739–44. The central panel features the Virgin and St Simeon Stock ❺

Palazzo Zenobio has been an Armenian college since 1850. Occasionally visitors can see the sumptuous 18th-century ballroom.

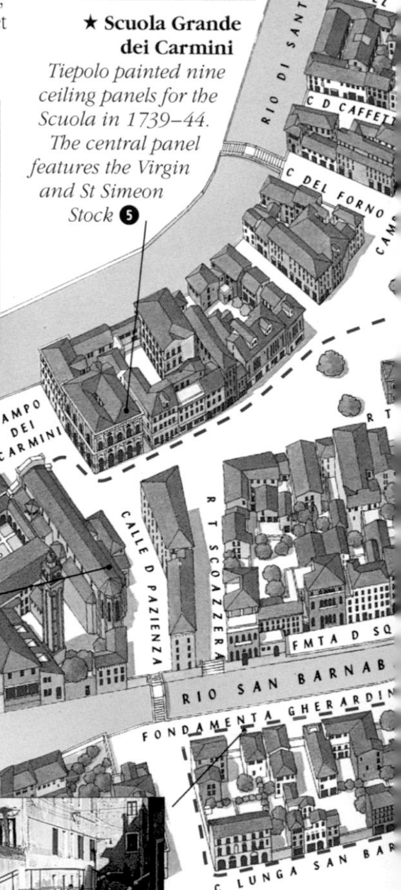

Santa Maria dei Carmini
The church's oldest feature is the Gothic side porch with fragments of decorative Byzantine reliefs ❻

KEY

— — — Suggested route

0 metres   50

0 yards   50

STAR SIGHTS

★ Scuola Grande dei Carmini

★ Ca' Rezzonico

★ San Barnaba

Fondamenta Gherardini runs beside the Rio San Barnaba, one of the prettiest canals in the *sestiere.*

Campo Santa Margherita
Open-air cafés are an integral part of the square. Causin sells particularly delicious Italian ice cream ❹

LOCATOR MAP
See Street Finder, map 6

Palazzo Giustinian is the 15th-century palace where Richard Wagner stayed while he was writing the second act of *Tristan and Isolde* in 1858.

Ca' Foscari, with its splendid setting, was chosen as the lodging place for Henry III of France in 1574.

Palazzo Nani is one of the fine palaces that lie on the great curve called the Volta del Canal.

Ca' Rezzonico

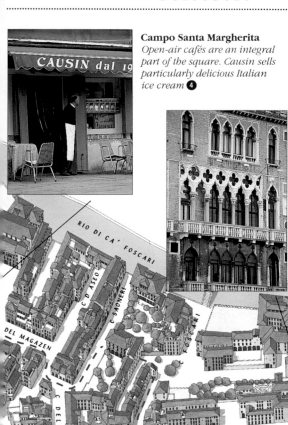

Ponte dei Pugni
Vicious fistfights used to take place on the top of this bridge ❷

★ **San Barnaba**
A floating barge crammed with crates of fruit and vegetables lends a colourful note to the area ❶

★ **Ca' Rezzonico**
The grand stairway has two putti, symbolizing winter and autumn ❸

Campo San Barnaba ❶

Map 6 D3. 🚤 Ca' Rezzonico.

T HE PARISH OF San Barnaba,
with its canalside square
at the centre, was known in
the 18th century as the home
of impoverished Venetian
patricians. These *barnabotti*
were attracted by the cheap
rents, and while some relied
on state support or begging,
others worked as bankers in
the State gambling house.

Today the square and canal,
with its laden vegetable barge,
are quietly appealing. The
church is fairly unremarkable,
apart from a Tiepolesque
ceiling and a *Holy Family*
attributed to Paolo Veronese.

Ponte dei Pugni ❷

Fondamenta Gherardini. **Map** 6 D3.
🚤 Ca' Rezzonico.

V ENICE HAS SEVERAL Ponti dei
Pugni ("bridges of fists"),
but this is the most famous.
Spanning the peaceful Rio San
Barnaba, the small bridge is
distinguished by two pairs of
footprints set in white stone
on top of the bridge. These
mark the starting positions for
the fights which traditionally
took place between rival
factions. Formerly there were
no balustrades and contenders
hurled each other straight into
the water. The battles became
so bloodthirsty that they were
banned in 1705.

**Boats and barges moored along
the Rio San Barnaba**

Tiepolo's *New World* fresco, part of a series in Ca' Rezzonico

Ca' Rezzonico ❸

Fondamenta Rezzonico 3136.
Map 6 E3. 📞 *(041) 241 01 00.*
🚤 Ca' Rezzonico. 🕐 *May–Oct:
10am–5pm; Nov–Apr: 10am–4pm
daily except Fri.* 🔴 *1 Jan, 1 May,
25 Dec.* 📷 🚫

T HIS RICHLY furnished
Baroque palace is one
of the most splendid in
Venice. It is also one of the
few palaces on the Grand
Canal, or indeed anywhere
in the city, which
opens its doors to
the public. Since
1934 it has housed
the museum of
18th-century
Venice, its rooms furnished
with frescoes, paint-
ings and period pieces
taken from other local
palaces or museums.

The building was
begun by Baldassare
Longhena (architect
of La Salute, *see p135*) in 1667,
but the funds of the Bon
family, who commissioned it,
ran dry before the second
floor was started. In 1712, long
after Longhena's death, the
unfinished palace was bought
by the Rezzonicos, a family of
merchants-turned-bankers
from Genoa. A large portion
of the Rezzonico fortune was
spent on the purchase, construction and decoration of
the palace. By 1758 it was in
a fit state for the Rezzonicos
to throw the first of the huge
banquets and celebratory
parties for which they later
became renowned.

In 1888 the palace was
bought by the poet Robert

*Allegory of Strength,
Andrea Brustolon*

Browning and his son, Pen,
who was married to an
American heiress. Browning
spoke of the "gaiety and
comfort of the enormous
rooms" but had little time to
enjoy them. In 1889 he died
of bronchitis.

The outstanding attraction in
the palace today is Giorgio
Massari's ballroom, which
occupies the entire breadth
of the building. It has been
beautifully restored and is
embellished with
gilded chandeliers,
carved furniture by
Andrea Brustolon
and a ceiling with
trompe l'oeil
frescoes. Three
rooms between the
ballroom and Grand
Canal side of the
palace have ceilings
with frescoes by
Giambattista Tiepolo
including, in the
Sala della Allegoria
Nuziale, his lively *Nuptial
Allegory* (1758).

Eighteenth-century paintings
occupy the *piano nobile*
(second floor). A whole room
is devoted to Pietro Longhi's
portrayals of everyday Venetian
life. Other paintings worthy of
note are Francesco Guardi's
Ridotto (1748) and *Nuns'
Parlour* (1768), and one of
the few Canalettos in Venice,
his *View of the Rio dei Mendicanti* (1725). Giandomenico
Tiepolo's fascinating series of
frescoes painted for his villa
at Zianigo (1770–1800) are
also to be found here. On the
floor above is a reconstructed
18th-century apothecary's
shop and a puppet theatre.

Campo Santa Margherita ❹

Map 6 D2. 🚤 *Ca' Rezzonico.*

THE SPRAWLING square of Santa Margherita, lined with houses from the 14th and 15th centuries, is the hub of western Dorsoduro. Market stalls, off-beat shops, and cafés attract a cross-section of the community. The fish stalls sell live eels and lobster, the *erborista* alternative medicine, and the bakers some of the tastiest loaves in Venice.

Santa Margherita, no longer a church, lies off the square at the northern end. Now an auditorium, it is owned by the university. Visitors can see sculptural fragments from the original 18th-century church, including gargoyles, on the truncated campanile in the square and on the house beside it. The Scuola dei Varotari (of the tanners), the isolated

A 15th-century carving of Santa Margherita and the dragon

building in the centre of the square, has a faded relief of the Madonna della Misericordia protecting the tanners.

Scuola Grande dei Carmini ❺

Campo Carmini. **Map** 5 C2. 🕿 *(041) 528 94 20.* 🚤 *Ca' Rezzonico.* ◯ *9am–noon, 3–6pm daily except Sun.* ● *1 May, 25 Dec.* 🎨 🚫

THE HEADQUARTERS of the Carmelite confraternity was built beside their church in 1663. In the 1740s Giambattista Tiepolo was commissioned to decorate the ceiling of the *salone* (hall) on the upper floor. These nine ceiling paintings so impressed the Carmelites that Tiepolo was promptly made an honorary member of the brotherhood.

The ceiling (which is best viewed with the mirrors that are supplied) shows *St Simeon Stock Receiving the Scapular of the Carmelite Order from the Virgin*. The scapular, two strips of cloth hung over the shoulders and tied by string, was widely believed at the time to protect the wearer from the pains of purgatory after death. The Carmelites honoured St Simeon Stock because he re-established the order in Europe after its expulsion from the Holy Land in the 13th century.

Santa Maria dei Carmini ❻

Campo Carmini. **Map** 5 C3. 🕿 *(041) 522 65 53.* 🚤 *Ca' Rezzonico or San Basilio.* ◯ *8am–noon, 3–7pm Mon–Sat, 8am–noon, 4:30–7pm Sun & public hols.*

KNOWN ALSO as Santa Maria del Carmelo, this church was built in the 14th century but has since undergone extensive alterations.

The most prominent external feature is the lofty campanile, whose perilous tilt was skilfully rectified in 1688. The interior is large, sombre and richly decorated. The arches of the nave are adorned with gilded

Scuola Grande dei Carmini

wooden statues, and a series of paintings illustrating the history of the Carmelite Order.

There are two interesting paintings in the church's side altars. Cima da Conegliano's *Adoration of the Shepherds* (c.1509) is in the second altar on the right (coins in the light meter are essential). In the second altar on the left is Lorenzo Lotto's *St Nicholas of Bari with Saints Lucy and John the Baptist* (c.1529). This painting demonstrates the artist's religious devotion, personal sensitivity and his love of nature. On the right-hand side of this highly detailed, almost Dutch-style landscape, there is a tiny depiction of St George killing the dragon.

SCUOLE

The *scuole* were peculiarly Venetian institutions. Founded mainly in the 13th century, they were lay confraternities existing for the charitable benefit of the neediest groups of society, the professions or resident ethnic minorities (such as the Scuola dei Schiavoni, *see p118*). Some became extremely rich, spending large sums on buildings and paintings, often to the disadvantage of their declared beneficiaries.

Upper Hall of the Scuola Grande dei Carmini

Nave of San Nicolò dei Mendicoli, one of the oldest churches in Venice

San Nicolò dei Mendicoli **7**

Campo San Nicolò. **Map** 5 A3.
((041) 275 03 82. 🚤 San Basilio.
🕐 10am–noon, 4–6pm daily.
🔵 Sun am.

CONTRASTING WITH the remote and rundown area which surrounds it, this church remains one of the most charming and delightful in Venice. Originally constructed in the 12th century, it has been rebuilt extensively over the years; the little porch on the north flank is 15th century.

Thanks to the Venice in Peril Fund, in the 1970s the church underwent one of the most comprehensive restoration programmes since the floods of 1966 (see p50). The floor, which was 30 cm (1 ft) below the level of the canals, was rebuilt and raised slightly to prevent further damage, the roofs and lower walls were reconstructed, and paintings and statues restored. The interior is richly embellished, particularly the nave with its 16th-century gilded wood statues. On the upper walls is a series of paintings of the life of Christ by Alvise dal Friso and other pupils of Veronese.

Angelo Raffaele **8**

Campo Angelo Raffaele. **Map** 5 B3.
((041) 522 85 48. 🚤 San Basilio.
🕐 8am–noon, 4–6pm Mon–Sat,
8am–noon, 5–6pm Sun & public hols.

THE SAVING GRACE of this dilapidated 17th-century church is the series of panel paintings on the organ balustrade. These were executed in 1749 by Antonio Guardi, brother of the more famous Francesco. They tell the tale of Tobias, the blind prophet cured by the archangel Raphael, after whom the church is named.

San Sebastiano **9**

Campo San Sebastiano. **Map** 5 C3.
🚤 San Basilio. 🕐 10am–5:30pm
Mon–Sat, 3–5:30pm Sun & public
hols. 🈂

THIS 16th-century church has one of the most colourful and homogeneous interiors of Venice. This is thanks to the artist Veronese who, from 1555 to 1560 and again in the 1570s, was commissioned to decorate the sacristy ceiling, the nave ceiling, the frieze, the east end of the choir, the high altar, the doors of the organ panels and the chancel – in that order. The paintings, which are typical of Veronese, are rich and radiant, with sumptuous costumes and colours. Among the finest of his works are the three ceiling paintings which tell the story of Esther, Queen of Xerxes I of Persia, who brought about the deliverance of the Jewish people. Appropriately, the artist is buried in San Sebastiano, alongside the organ.

Zattere **10**

Map 5 C4. 🚤 Zattere or San Basilio.

STRETCHING ALONG the southern part of the sestiere, the Zattere is the long quayside looking across to the island of Giudecca. From the 11th to 15th centuries, the city held the salt monopoly for the region, and the quays' name may derive from the

**San Sebastiano, viewed
from the bridge of the
same name**

Café tables laid out along the Zattere

floating rafts *(zattere)* where cargo was offloaded. On a sunny day it is a pleasure to sit at a waterside café here, looking across to the Church of the Redentore *(see p154)* or watching the waterbuses as they cross back and forth between the shores.

Squero di San Trovaso ⓫

Rio San Trovaso. **Map** 6 D4.
Zattere. *No public access.*

THIS IS ONE of the few surviving gondola workshops in Venice *(see pp28–9)* and the most picturesque. Its Tyrolean look dates from the days when craftsmen came down from the Cadore area of the Dolomites *(see p215).*

It is not open to the public, but from the far side of the Rio San Trovaso you can often watch the upturned gondolas being given their scraping and tarring treatment. You may see a new one under construction, but nowadays only around ten are made each year.

San Trovaso ⓬

Campo San Trovaso. **Map** 6 D4.
(041) 522 21 33. Zattere or Accademia. 8–11am, 3–5pm Mon–Sat.

THE CHURCH OF Santi Gervasio e Protasio, which in the eccentric Venetian dialect is slurred to San Trovaso, was built in 1590. Unusually it has two identical façades, one overlooking a canal, the other a quiet square. The church stood on neutral ground between the parishes of the rival factions of the Castellani and Nicolotti families, and tradition has it that this necessitated a separate entrance for each party.

The interior houses some late paintings by Jacopo Tintoretto, and there are two notable works of art worth seeking out. Michele Giambono's 15th-century Gothic painting, *St Chrysogonus on Horseback*, is situated in the chapel on the right of the chancel, and exquisite marble reliefs of angels with instruments decorate the altar of the Clary chapel opposite.

Santa Maria della Visitazione ⓭

Fondamenta delle Zattere. **Map** 6 E4.
(041) 522 40 77. Zattere. 8am–noon, 3–7pm daily.

SITUATED BESIDE the Gesuati, this Renaissance church was built between 1494 and 1524 by the Order of the Gesuati. After a period of closure and renovation, mass is once again held here. Inside the church is a fine wooden ceiling painted by 16th-century Umbrian and Tuscan artists. The exterior *bocca di leone* to the right of the façade is one of several "lion's mouth" denunciation boxes surviving from the rule of the Council of Ten *(see p42)*; this one was used to complain about the state of the streets.

Gesuati ⓮

Fondamenta delle Zattere. **Map** 6 E4.
(041) 523 06 25. Zattere. 8am–noon, 5–6pm daily.

NOT TO BE CONFUSED with the Gesuiti in northern Venice *(see p142)*, this church was built by the Dominicans, who took possession of the site in the 17th century when the Gesuati Order was suppressed. Work began in 1726 and the stately façade reflects that of Palladio's great Redentore church across the Giudecca. It is the most conspicuous landmark of the long Zattere quayside. Unlike the Redentore, the interior of the church is richly decorated. Tiepolo's frescoed ceiling, *The Life of St Dominic* (1737–39) demonstrates the artist's mastery of light and colour. Equally impressive (and far easier to see) is his *Virgin with Saints* (1740), situated in the first chapel on the right. The church also boasts two altar paintings by Sebastiano Ricci and Giambattista Piazzetta.

Gesuati façade statue

Squero di San Trovaso, where gondolas are given a facelift

Accademia ⓯

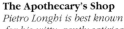

Exterior detail of the Accademia

THE LARGEST COLLECTION of Venetian art in existence, the Gallerie dell'Accademia, is housed in three former religious buildings. The basis of the collection was the Accademia di Belle Arti, founded in 1750 by the painter Giovanni Battista Piazzetta. In 1807 Napoleon moved the academy to these premises, and the collection was greatly enlarged by works of art from churches and monasteries he suppressed.

Ceiling Sketch
Tiepolo's The Translation of the Holy House to Loreto *(c.1742) was a sketch for the ceiling of the Scalzi church (see p145).*

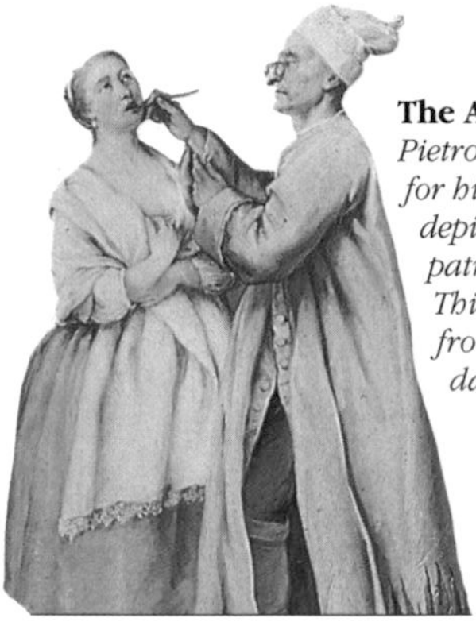

The Apothecary's Shop
Pietro Longhi is best known for his witty, gently satirical depictions of domestic patrician life in Venice. This detail comes from a painting dated c.1752.

KEY TO FLOORPLAN

- ☐ Byzantine and International Gothic
- ☐ Early Renaissance
- ☐ High Renaissance
- ☐ Baroque, genre and landscapes
- ☐ Ceremonial paintings
- ☐ Temporary exhibitions
- ☐ Non-exhibition space

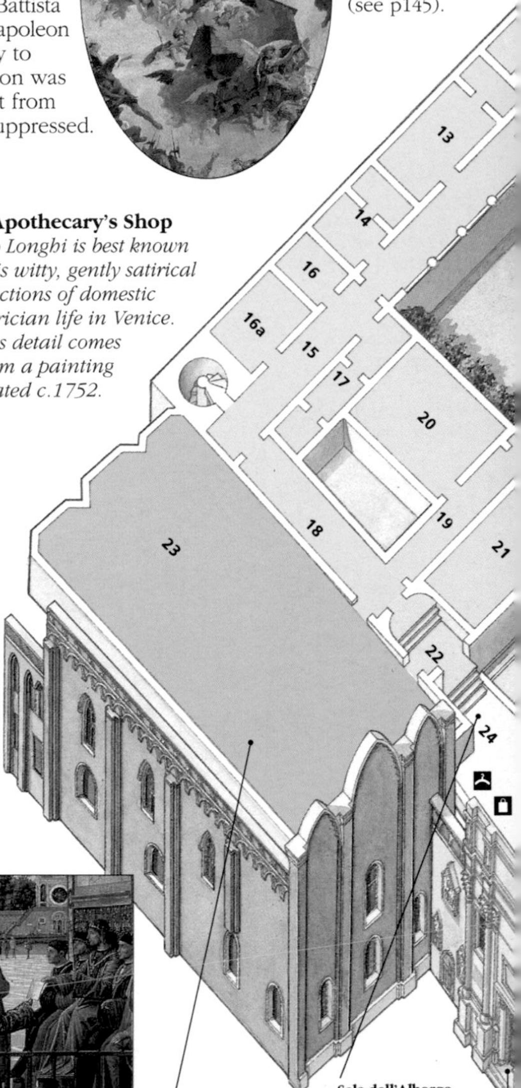

★ **Cycle of St Ursula** *(1495–1500) (detail)*
The Arrival of the English Ambassadors *is one of Vittore Carpaccio's eight paintings chronicling the tragic story of St Ursula.*

The former Church of Santa Maria della Carità
was rebuilt by Bartolomeo Bon in the mid 15th century.

Sala dell'Albergo

Entrance

The inner courtyard was designed by Andrea Palladio.

VISITORS' CHECKLIST

Campo della Carità. **Map** 6 E3.
(041) 522 22 47. Accademia.
9am–10pm Tue–Sun, 9am–
2pm Mon. **Last admission** 30 min
before closing. 1 Jan, 1 May,
25 Dec. **Quadreria**
3:30–5:30pm Tue (book first).

The Stealing of St Mark
Jacopo Tintoretto's painting of 1562 shows the Christians of Alexandria abducting the body of St Mark, which was about to be burnt by the pagans.

11

10

6

5

9

8

4

3

7

2

Bookshop

★ The Tempest (c.1507)
In his enigmatic landscape, Giorgione was probably indulging his imagination rather than portraying a specific subject.

★ Coronation of the Virgin
Paolo Veneziano's polyptych (1325) has a central image of the Virgin surrounded by a panoply of religious scenes. This detail shows episodes from the Life of St Francis.

STAR PAINTINGS

★ Cycle of St Ursula
   by Carpaccio

★ Coronation of the
   Virgin by Veneziano

★ The Tempest by
   Giorgione

GALLERY GUIDE
Most of the paintings are housed on one floor divided into 24 rooms. Where the rooms are numbered they are given Roman numerals. Restoration work is ongoing, so be prepared for absent paintings or whole sections closed off. The paintings are dependent on natural light, so to see them at their best try to visit on a bright morning. Upstairs, a second gallery, called Quadreria, contains works by Italian artists including Bellini, Veronese and Tintoretto.

Exploring the Accademia's Collection

SPANNING FIVE CENTURIES, the fascinating collection of paintings in the Accademia provides a complete spectrum of the Venetian school, from the medieval Byzantine period through the Renaissance to the Baroque and Rococo *(see pp26–7)*. The order is more or less chronological, with the exception of the final rooms, which take you back to the Renaissance.

Portrait of a Gentleman (c.1525)
by Lorenzo Lotto (detail)

BYZANTINE AND INTERNATIONAL GOTHIC

ROOM 1 SHOWS the influence of Byzantine art on the early Venetian painters. Paolo Veneziano, the true founder of the Venetian school, displays a blend of both western and eastern influences in his sumptuous *Coronation of the Virgin* (1325). The linear rhythms are quite unmistakably Gothic, yet the overall effect and the glowing gold background are distinctly Byzantine.

In the same room, *Coronation of the Virgin* (1448) by Michele Giambono shows the influence of International Gothic style, which was brought to Venice by Gentile da Fabriano and Pisanello. This particular style was characterized by delicate naturalistic detail, as typified by the birds and animals in the foreground of Giambono's painting.

Coronation of the Virigin (c.1448)
by Michele Giambono

Florence and Rome. The Bellini family – Jacopo, the father, and his two sons Gentile and Giovanni – played a dominant role in the early Venetian Renaissance.

Central to Venetian art in the 15th century was the *Sacra Conversazione*, where the Madonna is portrayed in a unified composition with saints. Giovanni Bellini's altarpiece for San Giobbe (c.1487) in Room 2 is one of the finest examples. Giovanni, the younger Bellini, was profoundly influenced by the controlled rational style and mastery of perspective in the works of his brother-in-law, Andrea Mantegna, whose work *St George* (c.1460) is in Room 4. To Mantegna's rationality and harsh realism Giovanni added humanity. This is seen in his Madonna paintings (Rooms 4 and 5), which are masterpieces of warmth and harmony. Outstanding examples are *The Madonna and Child between St Catherine and St Mary Magdalene* (c.1490) in Room 4; *Madonna of the Little Trees* (c.1487) and *Madonna and Child with John the Baptist and a Saint* (c.1505) in Room 5. The inventive young artist

EARLY RENAISSANCE

THE RENAISSANCE came late to Venice, but by the second quarter of the 15th century it had transformed the city into an art centre rivalling those of

Giorgione was influenced by Bellini, but went way beyond his master in his development of the landscape to create mood. In the famous, atmospheric *Tempest* (c.1507) in Room 5, this treatment of the landscape and the use of the figures to intensify that mood was an innovation adopted in Venetian painting of the 16th century and beyond.

Out on a limb from the main 16th-century Venetian tradition was the enigmatic Lorenzo Lotto, best known for portraits conveying moods of psychological unrest. His melancholic *Portrait of a Gentleman* (c.1525) in Room 7 is a superb example. More in the Venetian tradition, Palma il Vecchio's sumptuously coloured *Sacra Conversazione* in Room 8, painted around the same time, shows the unmistakable influence of the early work of Titian.

HIGH RENAISSANCE

OCCUPYING an entire wall of Room 10, the monumental *Feast in the House of Levi* by Paolo Veronese (1573) was originally commissioned

Feast in the House of Levi (detail)

as *The Last Supper*. However, the hedonistic detail in the painting, such as the drunkard and the dwarfs, was not well received and Veronese found himself before the Inquisition. Ordered to eliminate the profane content of the picture, he simply changed the title.

Jacopo Tintoretto made his reputation with *The Miracle of the Slave* (1548), which is also in Room 10. The painting shows his mastery of the dramatic effects of light and movement. This was the first of a series of works painted for the Scuola Grande di San Marco *(see p114)*. In the next room, Veronese's use of rich colour is best admired in the *Mystical Marriage of St Catherine* (c.1575).

Healing of the Madman (c.1496) by Vittore Carpaccio

BAROQUE, GENRE AND LANDSCAPES

The Rape of Europa (1740–50) by Francesco Zuccarelli (detail)

VENICE SUFFERED from a lack of native Baroque painters, but a few non-Venetians kept the Venetian school alive in the 17th century. The most notable among these was the Genoese Bernardo Strozzi (1581–1644). The artist was a great admirer of the work of Veronese, as can be seen in his *Feast at the House of Simon* (1629) in Room 11. Also represented in this room is Giambattista Tiepolo, the greatest Venetian painter of the 18th century.

The long corridor (12) and the rooms which lead from it are largely devoted to light-hearted landscape and genre paintings from the 18th century. Among them are pastoral scenes by Francesco Zuccarelli, works by Marco Ricci, scenes of Venetian society by Pietro Longhi and a view of Venice by Canaletto (1763). This was the painter's entry for admission to the Accademia, and is a fine example of his sense of perspective.

CEREMONIAL PAINTINGS

ROOMS 20 and 21 return to the Renaissance, featuring two great cycles of paintings from the late 16th century. The detail in these large-scale anecdotal canvases provide a fascinating glimpse of the life, customs and appearance of Venice at the time. Room 20 houses *The Stories of the Cross* by Venice's leading artists, commissioned by the Scuola of San Giovanni Evangelista *(see p104)*. Each one depicts an episode of the relic of the Holy Cross, which the kingdom of Cyprus donated to the Scuola. In *The Procession in St Mark's Square* (1496) by Gentile Bellini, you can compare the square with how it looks today. Another,

Vittore Carpaccio's *Healing of the Madman* (1496), shows the Rialto bridge which collapsed in 1524.

The second series, minutely detailed *Scenes from the Legend of St Ursula* (1490s) by Carpaccio in Room 21, provides a brilliant kaleidoscope of life. Mixing reality and imagination, Carpaccio relates the episodes from the life of St Ursula using settings and costumes of 15th-century Venice.

SALA DELL'ALBERGO

WHEN THE Scuola della Carità became the site of the Academy of Art in the early 19th century, the Scuola's *albergo* (where students lodged) retained its original panelling and 15th-century ceiling. The huge *Presentation of the Virgin* (1538) is one of the surprisingly few Titians in the gallery, and was painted for this very room. The walls are also adorned with a grandiose triptych (1446) by Antonio Vivarini and Giovanni d'Alemagna.

Detail from Titian's *Presentation of the Virgin* (1538)

Cini Collection ⑯

Palazzo Cini, San Vio 864. **Map** 6 E4.
☎ *(041) 521 07 55*. 🚤 *Accademia*.
🕐 *Aug–Nov: 10am–6pm
Tue–Sun*. ⬤ *Dec–Jul*. 🎨

THE PALAZZO CINI belonged
to Count Vittorio Cini
(1884–1977), a collector and
patron of the arts. Between
1951 and 1956 he restored
San Giorgio Maggiore *(see
p95)* and created the Cini
Foundation as a memorial to
his son, who was killed in an
air crash in 1949.

The collection displayed here
includes china, ivories, books,
illuminated manuscripts,
miniatures, porcelain and
furniture, but the outstanding
works of art are the Tuscan
Renaissance paintings that
Cini collected. These include
works by or attributed to
Botticelli, Piero di Cosimo,
Piero della Francesca, Filippo
Lippi and Pontormo.

The Cini Collection has
been open to the public since
1984, but unfortunately, it is
only open for four months
of the year.

Madonna col Bambino (c.1437) by
Filippo Lippi, the Cini Collection

Peggy Guggenheim Collection ⑰

Palazzo Venier dei Leoni, San Gregorio
701. **Map** 6 F4. ☎ *(041) 520 62 88*.
🚤 *Accademia*. 🕐 *11am–6pm
Wed–Mon*. ⬤ *25 Dec*. 🎨 🚫

INTENDED AS A four-storey
palace, the 18th-century
Palazzo Venier dei Leoni in
fact never rose beyond the
ground floor – hence its nickname, *Il Palazzo Nonfinito*
(The Unfinished Palace). In
1949 the building was bought
as a home by the American
millionairess Peggy Guggenheim (1898–1979), a collector,
dealer and patron of the arts.
A perspicacious and high-
spirited woman, she befriended
and furthered the careers of
many innovative abstract and
surrealist artists. One was Max
Ernst, who was the second of
her husbands.

The collection consists of
200 paintings and sculptures,
representing almost every
modern art movement. The
dining room has notable

Interno Olandese II (c.1928) by
Joan Miró

Cubist works of art including
The Poet by Pablo Picasso. An
entire room is devoted to
Jackson Pollock, who was a
Guggenheim discovery. Other
artists represented are Miró, de
Chirico, Magritte, Kandinsky,
Mondrian and Malevich.

Sculpture is laid out in the
house and garden. One of the
most elegant works is
Constantin Brancusi's
Maiastra (1912). The most
provocative piece is Marino
Marini's *Angelo della Città*

(Angel of the Citadel, 1948), a
prominently displayed man
sitting on a horse, erect in all
respects. Embarrassed onlookers avert their gaze to enjoy
views of the Grand Canal.

The Guggenheim is
one of the most
visited sights of the
city. The light-filled
rooms and the large
modern canvases
provide a striking
contrast to the
Renaissance paint-
ings which are the
main attraction in
Venetian churches
and museums. A
bonus for English
speakers is the team
of assistants, who are
usually arts gradu-
ates from Britain.

There are plans
by the Guggen-
heim to acquire
the splendidly
located customs house at
Punta della Dogana. If ful-
filled, it will enable many
works currently in storage to
see the light of day.

Maiastra
**by Constantin
Brancusi**

Façade of the Palazzo Venier dei Leoni, the home of the Peggy Guggenheim Collection of modern art

Campiello Barbaro ⑱

Map 6 F4. 🚢 *Salute.*

AN ENCHANTING little square, the Campiello Barbaro is shaded by trees and flanked on one side by the wisteria-clad walls of Ca' Dario. It is hard to believe the stories of murder, bankruptcy and suicide that have befallen the owners of this Grand Canal palace. The most recent was Raul Gardini, one of Italy's best-known industrialists, who shot himself in 1992.

The ill-fated Ca' Dario, which backs on to Campiello Barbaro

Santa Maria della Salute ⑲

Campo della Salute. **Map** 7 A4.
📞 (041) 522 55 58. 🚢 *Salute.*
🕐 9am–noon, 3–5:30pm daily.

THE GREAT BAROQUE church of Santa Maria della Salute, standing at the entrance of the Grand Canal, is one of the most imposing architectural landmarks of Venice. Henry James likened the church to "some great lady on the threshold of her salon . . . with her domes and scrolls, her scalloped buttresses and statues forming a pompous crown and her wide steps disposed on the ground like the train of a robe". The church was built in thanks-

giving for the deliverance of the city from the plague of 1630, hence the name *Salute*, meaning health and salvation. Each November, in celebration, *(see p35)*, worshippers approach across a bridge of boats which span the mouth of the Grand Canal for the occasion. Baldassare Longhena started the church in 1630 at the age of 32, and worked on it for the rest of his life. It was not completed until 1687, some five years after his death.

The interior is comparatively sober. It consists of a large octagonal space below the cupola and six chapels radiating from the ambulatory. The large domed chancel and grandiose high altar dominate the view from the main door. The altar's sculptural group by Giusto Le Corte represents the Virgin and Child giving protection to Venice from the plague. The best paintings inside Santa Maria della Salute

The Baroque church of Santa Maria della Salute viewed from across the Grand Canal

are in the sacristy to the left of the altar: Titian's early altar-piece of *St Mark Enthroned with Saints Cosmos, Damian, Roch and Sebastian* (1511–12) and his dramatic ceiling paintings of *Cain and Abel, The Sacrifice of Abraham and Isaac* and *David and Goliath* (1540–49). The *Wedding at Cana* (1551) on the wall opposite the entrance is a major work by Jacopo Tintoretto.

Dogana di Mare ⑳

Map 7 A4. 🚢 *Salute.*

THIS EASTERN promontory of the Dorsoduro provides a panorama which embraces the Riva degli Schiavoni, the island of San Giorgio Maggiore and the eastern section of Giudecca. The *dogana di mare*, or sea customs post, was originally built in the 15th century to inspect the cargo of ships which were intending to enter Venice. The customs house you see today was constructed in the late 17th century and replaced a tower which originally guarded the entrance to the Grand Canal. On the corner tower of the house two bronze Atlases support a striking golden ball with a weathervane figure of Fortuna on the top.

Interior of the Salute showing the octagonal core of the church

SIGHTS AT A GLANCE

Churches
Gesuiti **7**
Madonna dell'Orto **1**
Santi Apostoli **10**
San Giobbe **14**
San Giovanni Crisostomo **9**
Santa Maria dei Miracoli **8**
San Marziale **4**
Scalzi **13**

Streets and Squares
Campo dei Mori **2**
Fondamente Nuove **5**
Fondamenta della Sensa **3**

Historic Buildings
Oratorio dei Crociferi **6**
Palazzo Labia **12**

Art Gallery
Ca' d'Oro p144 **11**

Historic Area
The Ghetto **15**

0 metres   250

0 yards   250

◁ **The façade of
Tintoretto's house in
Fondamenta dei Mori**

CANNAREGIO

THE CITY'S MOST northerly *sestiere*, Cannaregio, stretches in a large arc from the 20th-century railway station in the west to one of the oldest quarters of Venice in the east. The northern quays look out towards the islands in the lagoon, while to the south the *sestiere* is bounded by the upper sweep of the Grand Canal.

The name of the quarter derives either from the Italian *canne*, meaning canes or reeds, which grew here centuries ago, or perhaps from "Canal Regio" or Royal Canal – the former name of what is now the Canale di Cannaregio. This waterway was the main entry to Venice before the advent of the rail link with the mainland. Over a third

Hanukah lamp in the Ghetto

of the city's population lives in Cannaregio. For the most part it is an unspoilt area, divided by wide canals, crisscrossed by alleys and characterized by small stores, simple bars and the artisans' workshops.

One of the prettiest and most remote quarters is in the north, near the church of Madonna dell'Orto and around Campo dei Mori. Tourism is concentrated along two main thoroughfares: the Lista di Spagna and the wide Strada Nova, both on the well-worn route from the station to the Rialto. Just off this route lies the world's oldest ghetto. Though now largely abandoned by Venetian Jews, this is historically the most fascinating quarter of Cannaregio.

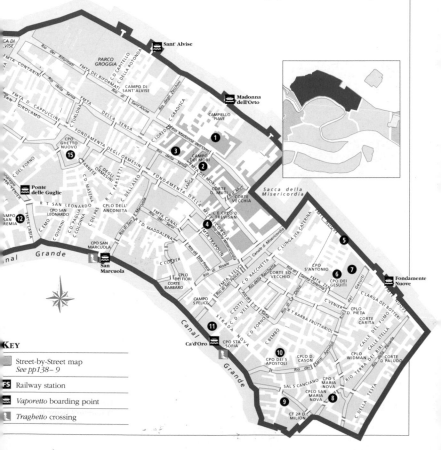

KEY

Street-by-Street map
See pp138–9

Railway station

Vaporetto boarding point

Traghetto crossing

Street-by-Street: Cannaregio

Channel marker in the lagoon

SURPRISINGLY FEW tourists find their way to this unspoilt quarter of northern Cannaregio. This is the more humble, peaceful side of Venice, where clean washing is strung over the water-ways and the streets are flanked by the softly crumbling façades of shuttered houses. Along the wide *fondamente*, the little shops and stores stock basic groceries and the bars are always crowded with local Venetians.

The quarter's cultural high-light is the lovely Gothic church of Madonna dell'Orto, Tintoretto's parish church.

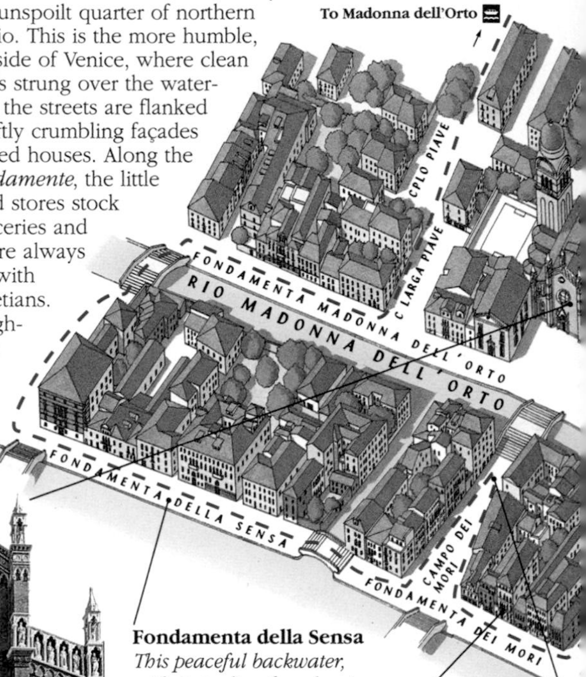

To Madonna dell'Orto

Fondamenta della Sensa
This peaceful backwater, with its peeling façades, is undisturbed by the rigours of tourism ❸

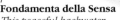

★ Campo dei Mori
This square is named after the stone statues of three Moors (Mori) which are carved on its walls ❷

★ Madonna dell'Orto
One of the finest Gothic churches in Venice, Madonna dell'Orto has a richly decorated façade and a wealth of works by Tintoretto ❶

Tintoretto lived with his family in this house, No. 3399 Fondamenta dei Mori, from 1574 until his death in 1594.

To Ca' d'Oro

KEY

 Suggested route

STAR SIGHTS

★ Madonna dell'Orto

★ Campo dei Mori

San Marziale
Ceiling paintings by Sebastiano Ricci (1700–25) and a bizarre Baroque altar adorn this Baroque church ❹

Fondamenta Gasparo Contarini is named after the cardinal, diplomat and scholar, who lived at Palazzo Contarini dal Zaffo *(see p68)* in the 16th century.

LOCATOR MAP
See Street Finder, maps 2, 3

Venetian oarsmen can often be seen practising their rowing technique on the quieter canals of Cannaregio.

La Sacca della Misericordia is a large man-made basin opening out into the lagoon, with views of the islands of San Michele and Murano.

Campo d'Abbazia, a peaceful open square with decorative herringbone floor tiles, is overlooked by the Scuola Vecchia della Misericordia and a deconsecrated church.

Fondamenta della Misericordia, named after the nearby *scuola*, was built in the Middle Ages.

0 metres   50
0 yards   50

The campanile of Madonna dell'Orto, crowned
by an onion-shaped cupola

Madonna dell'Orto ❶

Campo Madonna dell'Orto. **Map** 2 F2.
📞 *(041) 71 99 33.* 🚤 *Madonna
dell'Orto.* 🕐 *10:30am–5:30pm
Mon–Sat, 3–5:30pm Sun.* 📷

THIS LOVELY Gothic church is
frequently referred to as
the English Church in Venice
for it was British funds that
helped restore the building
after the 1966 floods *(see p50).*
The original church, founded
in the mid 14th century, was
dedicated to St Christopher,
patron saint of
travellers, to
protect the
boatmen who
ferried passengers
to the islands in the
northern lagoon.
The dedication was
changed and the
church reconstruct-
ed in the early 15th
century, following
the discovery, in a
nearby vegetable
garden *(orto),* of a
statue of the Virgin
Mary said to have
miraculous powers.
However, a 15th-
century statue of St
Christopher, newly
restored, still stands
above the portal.

The interior, faced
almost entirely in
brick, is large, light
and uncluttered.
The greatest trea-
sures are the works
of art by Tintoretto,
who was a parishioner of the
church. His tomb, which is
marked with a plaque, lies in
the chapel to the right of the
chancel. The most dramatic of
his works are the towering
paintings in the chancel
(1562–4). On the right wall is
The Last Judgment, whose
turbulent content caused John
Ruskin's wife Effie to flee the
church. In the painting *The
Adoration of the Golden Calf*
on the left wall, the figure
carrying the calf, fourth from
the left, is said to depict
Tintoretto himself.

Inside the chapel of San
Mauro you can see the
radically restored statue of the
Madonna which inspired the
reconstruction of the church.

To the right of the entrance
is Cima da Conegliano's
magnificent painting, *St John
the Baptist and Other Saints*
(c.1493). The vacant space
opposite belongs to Giovanni
Bellini's *Madonna with Child*
(c.1478) which was stolen for
the third time in 1993.

Campo dei Mori ❷

Map 2 F3. 🚤 *Madonna dell'Orto.*

ACCORDING TO popular
tradition, the "Mori" were
the three Mastelli brothers
who came from the Morea
(the Peloponnese). The brothers, who were silk merchants
by trade, took refuge in Venice
in 1112 and built the Palazzo
Mastelli, recognizable by its
camel bas relief, which once
backed on to the square. Their
weathered stone figures can
be seen embedded in the wall
of the *campo* on its eastern
side. The corner figure with
the makeshift rusty metal nose
(added in the 19th century) is
"Signor Antonio Rioba" who,
like the Roman Pasquino, was
the focus of malicious fun
and satire. A fourth oriental
merchant wearing a large
turban faces the Rio della
Sensa on the façade of
Tintoretto's house *(see p138).*

One of the stone Moors which
gave the Campo dei Mori its name

TINTORETTO (1518–94)

Jacopo
Robusti,
nicknamed
Tintoretto
because of
his father's
occupation of
silk dyer, was
born, lived and died
in Cannaregio. He left
Venice only once in his life.
A devout Christian, volatile
and unworldly, his was a
highly individual and theatrical style, conveyed by
vivid exaggeration of light
and movement, bold fore-
shortening and fiery, fluid
brushstrokes. His remar-
kably prolific output has
never been ascertained, but
scores of his works survive,
many still in the places for
which they were painted.
Examples of his canvases
can be seen in the church
of Madonna dell'Orto, the
Accademia *(see pp130–33),*
and the Doge's Palace *(see
pp84–9)* His crowning
achievement, however, was
the great series of works for
the Scuola Grande di San
Rocco *(see pp106–7).*

A local trattoria on a quiet quayside by the Rio della Sensa

Fondamenta della Sensa ❸

Map 2 E2. 🚏 *Madonna dell'Orto.*

WHEN THE MARSHY lands of Cannaregio were drained in the Middle Ages, three long, straight canals were created, running parallel to each other. The middle of these is the Rio della Sensa, which stretches from the Sacca di Sant'Alvise at its western end to the Canale della Misericordia in the east. The Fondamenta cuts through a quiet quarter of Cannaregio, where daily life goes on undisturbed by tourism. With its small grocery shops and simple local bars, the neighbourhood feels far removed from San Marco.

This is one of the poorer areas of the city, though the buildings are interspersed with fine (but neglected) palaces that once belonged to wealthy Venetians. Abbot Onorio Arrigoni lived at No. 3336 with his collection of antiques, and Palazzo Michiel (No. 3218) is an early Renaissance palace which became the French embassy.

San Marziale ❹

Campo San Marziale. **Map** 2 F3. 📞 *(041) 71 99 33.* 🚏 *San Marcuola.* ⏰ *4–6pm Mon–Sat.* ✝ *Mass 9:30am Sun.*

A BAROQUE CHURCH on medieval foundations, San Marziale was rebuilt between 1693 and 1721. The church is mainly visited for the ceiling frescoes by

Sebastiano Ricci, a painter of the decorative Rococo style. Executed between 1700 and 1705, relatively early in Ricci's career, these bold, foreshortened frescoes already combine the Venetian tradition with flamboyant Rococo flourishes. Sadly though, the vivid colours for which Ricci was known have been sullied by decades of grime. The central painting shows *The Glory of Saint Martial*, while the side paintings relate to the image of the Virgin.

Fondamente Nuove ❺

Map 3 B3. 🚏 *Fondamente Nuove.*

THE FONDAMENTE NUOVE or "New Quays" are actually over 400 years old. This chain of waterside streets borders

Altar of San Marziale showing a carving of the Virgin and Child

the northern lagoon for one kilometre (over half a mile), from the solitary Sacca della Misericordia to the Rio di Santa Giustina in Castello on the eastern side.

Before the construction of the quays in the 1580s, this was a desirable residential area where the air was said to be healthy and the houses had gardens sloping down to the lagoon.

One of the residents was Titian, who lived from 1531 to his death in 1576 in a now demolished house at Calle Larga dei Botteri No. 5182–3 (a plaque marks the site).

Today the quaysides are aesthetically uninspiring but they do provide splendid views of the northern lagoon and, on a clear day, the peaks of the Dolomites. The island most visible from the quays is San Michele in Isola (*see p151*), its dark stately cypress trees rising high above the cemetery walls.

Oratorio dei Crociferi ❻

Campo dei Gesuiti. **Map** 3 B3. 📞 *(041) 521 74 11.* 🚏 *Fondamente Nuove.* ⏰ *Apr–Oct: 10am–1pm Fri–Sun.*

FOUNDED IN THE 13th century as a hospital for returning Crusaders, the Oratorio dei Crociferi (built for the order of the Bearers of the Cross) was turned into a charitable institution for old people in the 15th century.

Between 1583 and 1591 the artist Palma il Giovane, commissioned by the Crociferi, decorated the chapel with a glowing cycle of paintings, depicting the crucial events in the history of this religious order. The paintings suffered terrible damage in the floods of 1966 (*see p50*), but thanks to funds from overseas, were successfully restored and the chapel reopened in 1984.

The inscriptions on the walls of some of the surrounding houses in the square are those of art and craft guilds, such as silk weavers and tailors, whose works formerly occupied the buildings.

The sumptuous ceiling frescoes of the Gesuiti church

Gesuiti ❼

Campo dei Gesuiti. **Map** 3 B4.
☎ (041) 528 65 79.
🚤 Fondamente Nuove.
🕐 10am–noon, 5–7pm daily.

T HE JESUITS' close links with the papacy provoked Venetian hostility during the 17th century, and for 50 years they were refused entry to the city. However in 1714 they were given permission to build this church in the north of Venice, on the site of a 12th-century church which had belonged to the Order of the Crociferi. Consecrated as Santa Maria Assunta, the church is always referred to simply as the Gesuiti; thus it is often confused with the Gesuati in Dorsoduro (see p129).

Domenico Rossi's imposing Baroque exterior gives only a hint of the opulence of the interior. The proliferation of green and white marble, carved in parts like great folds of fabric, gives the impression that the church is clothed in damask.

Titian's *Martyrdom of St Lawrence* (c.1555), above the first altar on the left, has been described by the art historian Hugh Honour as "the first successful nocturne in the history of art".

Santa Maria dei Miracoli ❽

Campo dei Miracoli. **Map** 3 B5.
☎ (041) 528 39 03. **🚤** Rialto.
🕐 10am–5:30pm Mon–Sat,
3–5:30pm Sun & public hols. **📷**

A N EXQUISITE masterpiece of the early Renaissance, the Miracoli is the favourite church of many Venetians and the one where they like to get married. Tucked away in a maze of alleys and waterways in eastern Cannaregio, it is small and somewhat elusive, with the opening hours dependent on the mood of the church custodian.

Often likened to a jewel box, the façade is decorated with various shades of marble, with fine bas-reliefs and sculpture. It was built in 1481–9 by the architect Pietro Lombardo and his sons to enshrine *The Virgin and Child* (1408), a painting believed to have miraculous powers. The picture, by Nicolò di Pietro,

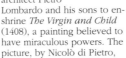

Decorative column, interior of Santa Maria dei Miracoli

can still be seen above the altar. The interior of the church, which ideally should be visited when pale shafts of sunlight are streaming in through the windows, is embellished by pink, white and grey marble and crowned by a barrel-vaulted ceiling (1528) which has 50 portraits of saints and prophets. The balustrade, between the nave and the chancel, is decorated by Tullio Lombardo's carved figures of St Francis, Archangel Gabriel, the Virgin and St Clare. The screen around the high altar and the medallions of the Evangelists in the cupola spandrels are also by Lombardo. Above the main door, the choir gallery was used by the nuns from the neighbouring convent, who entered the church through an overhead gallery. The Miracoli has recently undergone a major restoration programme, which was funded by the American Save Venice organization.

SANTA MARIA DEI MIRACOLI
The façade is a harmonious tapestry of decorated panels and multi-coloured polished stone.

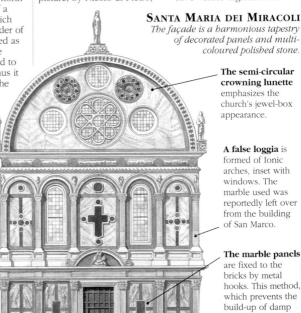

The semi-circular crowning lunette emphasizes the church's jewel-box appearance.

A false loggia is formed of Ionic arches, inset with windows. The marble used was reportedly left over from the building of San Marco.

The marble panels are fixed to the bricks by metal hooks. This method, which prevents the build-up of damp and salt water behind the panels, dates from the Renaissance.

San Giovanni Crisostomo, the last
work of Mauro Coducci

San Giovanni Crisostomo ⑨

Campo San Giovanni Crisostomo.
Map 3 B5. [(041) 522 71 55. ⬚
Rialto. ◯ 9am–9:45am, 10:30–
noon, 3:30–5pm Mon–Sat,
10:30am–noon, 3:30–5pm Sun.

THIS PRETTY little terracotta-
coloured church lies in a
bustling quarter close to the
Rialto. Built between 1479
and 1504, the church was the
last work of Mauro Coducci.
  The interior, which is built
on a Greek-cross plan, is dark
and intimate. Giovanni Bellini's
*St Jerome with Saints Christo-
pher and Augustine* (1513)
hangs above the first altar on
the right. Influenced by
Giorgione, this was probably
Bellini's last painting, executed
when he was in his eighties.
  Sebastiano del Piombo's *St
John Chrysostom and Six
Saints* (1509–11), which
hangs over the high altar, was
also influenced by Giorgione
– some believe he actually
painted the figures of St John
the Baptist and St Liberal.

Santi Apostoli ⑩

Campo Santi Apostoli. **Map** 3 B5.
[(041) 523 82 97. ⬚ Ca' d'Oro.
◯ 3–5pm Mon–Sat.

THE CAMPO Santi Apostoli is
a busy crossroads for
pedestrians en route to the
Rialto or the railway station.
Its church is unremarkable
architecturally and little

MARCO POLO

Born around 1254 in the
quarter of Cannaregio near
the Rialto, Marco Polo left
Venice at the age of 18 for
his four-year voyage to the
court of the Emperor Kublai
Khan. He impressed the
Mongol emperor and stayed
for some 20 years, working
as a travelling diplomat.
  Returning to Venice in
1295, he brought with him a
fortune in jewels and a host
of spellbinding stories about
the Khan's court.
  As a prisoner of war in
Genoa in 1298 he compiled
an account of his travels,
with the cooperation of an
inmate. Translated into
French, this was to become
Le Livre des merveilles.
Despite the fact that many
Italians disbelieved his won-
drous tales of the east, the
book was an instant success.

His nickname became Marco
Il Milione (of the million
lies); hence the name of the
two little courtyards where
the Polo family lived: Corte
Prima del Milion and Corte
Seconda del Milion.

Marco Polo leaving on his travels,
from a manuscript c.1338

remains of the 16th-century
building. A notable exception,
however, is the enchanting
late 15th-century Renaissance
Corner Chapel on the right of
the nave, believed to have
been designed by Mauro
Coducci. The chapel contains
The Communion of St Lucy by
Giambattista Tiepolo (1748),
the tomb of Marco Corner,
probably by Tullio Lombardo
(1511), and an inscription to
Corner's daughter, Caterina
Cornaro, Queen of Cyprus,
who was buried here before
she was moved to the Church
of San Salvatore (*see p94*).

Tomb of Doge Marco Corner in
Santi Apostoli (Corner Chapel)

Ca' d'Oro ⑪

See p144.

Palazzo Labia ⑫

Fondamenta Labia (entrance on
Campo S Geremia). **Map** 2 D4.
[(041) 524 28 12. ⬚ Ponte
Guglie. ◯ by appt only (visits
3–4pm Wed–Fri; phone to book on
morning of visit). ⬤ public hols.

THE LABIAS were a wealthy
family of merchants from
Catalonia who bought their
way into the Venetian patrici-
ate in 1646. Towards the end
of the century they built their
prestigious palace on the wide
Cannaregio Canal, close to its
junction with the Grand Canal.
In 1745–50 the ballroom was
frescoed by Giambattista
Tiepolo. The scenes are from
the life of Cleopatra but the
setting is Venice, and the
queen's attire is that of a
16th-century noble lady.
  Passed from one owner to
another the palace gradually
lost all trace of its former
grandeur and variously served
as a religious foundation, a
school and a doss-house.
Between 1964 and 1992 it
was owned by the Italian
broadcasting network, RAI,
who undertook its restoration.
  The frescoes can be seen
free of charge, but only by
making an appointment.

Ca' d'Oro ⓫

O NE OF THE GREAT showpieces of the Grand
Canal, the Ca' d'Oro (or House of Gold)
is the finest example of Venetian Gothic architecture in the city. The façade, with its finely
carved ogee windows, oriental pinnacles and
exotic marble tracery, has an unmistakable
flavour of the east. But this once gloriously
embellished *palazzo* suffered many changes
of fortune and there is now little inside to
remind you that this was once a 15th-century
palace. Since 1984 it has been home to the
Giorgio Franchetti Collection.

HISTORY

I N 1420 THE wealthy patrician,
Marino Contarini, commis-
sioned the building of what
he was determined would be
the most magnificent
palace in the city.
The decoration and
the intricate carving
were executed by a
team of Venetian
and Lombard crafts-
men, and he had
the façade adorned
in ultramarine, gold
leaf and vermilion.
  In the course of
the 16th century the house
was remodelled by a succession of owners, and by the
early 18th century was semi-
derelict. In 1846 the Russian
Prince Troubetzkoy bought it
for the famous ballerina Maria

Tullio Lombardo's
Double Portrait

Taglioni. Under her direction,
the Ca' d'Oro suffered barbaric
restoration. The open staircase
was ripped out, the wellhead
by Bartolomeo Bon (1427–8)
was sold and much of the
stonework removed. It was
finally rescued by
Baron Franchetti, a
patron of the arts,
who restored it to
its former glory
and bequeathed it
to the state in 1915.
Another restoration
programme was
put into action in
the 1970s and the
façade is once again
behind scaffolding. The pretty
paved courtyard, which can
only be glimpsed through a
gateway, contains Bon's
beautifully carved wellhead.
This was one of the pieces
retrieved by Franchetti.

FIRST FLOOR

P RIDE OF PLACE is given to
Andrea Mantegna's *St
Sebastian* (1506), the artist's
last painting and Franchetti's
favourite work of art. The
portego (gallery) opening on
to the Grand Canal is a showroom of sculpture. Among the
finest pieces are bronze reliefs
by the Paduan sculptor, Il
Riccio (1470–1532), Tullio
Lombardo's marble *Double
Portrait* (c.1493) and Sansovino's lunette of the Madonna
and Child (c.1530). Rooms to
the right of the *portego* have
some fine Renaissance
bronzes and, among the
paintings, an *Annunciation*
and *Death of the Virgin* (both
c.1504) by Vittore Carpaccio
and assistants. A room to the
left of the *portego* is devoted
to non-Venetian painting, and
includes Luca Signorelli's
Flagellation (c.1480).

SECOND FLOOR

T HE UPPER FLOOR, which is
often closed for lack of
personnel, houses paintings
by Venetian masters, including a *Venus* by Titian, two
Venetian views by Guardi, and
fresco fragments by Giorgione
and Titian. Other exhibits include tapestries and ceramics.

The Annunciation (1504) by Vittore Carpaccio and assistants

Scalzi ⓭

Fondamenta Scalzi. **Map** 1 C4.
📞 *(041) 71 51 15.* 🚉 *Ferrovia.*
🕐 *9:30am–noon, 3:30–7pm*
Mon–Sat, 3:30–5:30pm Sun.

B ESIDE THE modern railway
station *(see p58)* stands
the church of Santa Maria di
Nazareth, known as the Scalzi.
The *scalzi* were "barefooted"
Carmelite friars who came to
Venice during the 1670s and
commissioned their church to
be built on the Grand Canal.
Designed by Baldassare
Longhena, the huge Baroque
interior is an over-elaboration
of polychrome marble, gilded
woodwork and sculptures.

The 1934 ceiling painting, *The
Council of Ephesus* by Ettore
Tito, replaced Giambattista
Tiepolo's fresco of *The Translation of the Holy House to
Loreto* (1743–45), which was
almost entirely destroyed by
the Austrian bombardment of
24 October 1915.

San Giobbe ⓮

Campo San Giobbe. **Map** 1 C3. 📞
(041) 524 18 89. 🚉 *Ponte dei 3 Archi.*
🕐 *10am–noon, 3:15–6pm daily.*
If closed, ask at 620 by the church.

T HE CHURCH of San Giobbe
stands in a remote *campo*
full of cats. The early Gothic

structure of the church was
modified in the 1470s by
Pietro Lombardo who added
Renaissance elements such as
the saints over the portal. The
Martini chapel, second
on the left, is decorated
with Della Robbia-style
glazed terracotta.
The altarpieces by
Giovanni Bellini and
Vittore Carpaccio
were removed when
Napoleon suppressed
the monastery of San
Giobbe, and are now
in the Accademia
Gallery (*pp130–33*).

**Saint by Lombardo,
San Giobbe portal**

The Ghetto ⓯

Map 2 E3. 🚉 *Ponte Guglie.* **Museo
Ebraico** Campo del Ghetto Nuovo.
📞 *(041) 71 53 59.* 🚉 *Ponte Guglie.*
🕐 *10am–7pm (Oct–May: 10am–
4:30pm) Sun–Fri.* 🌑 *Jewish hols.* 📷

I N 1516 the Council of Ten
(see p42) decreed that all
Jews in Venice be confined to
an islet of Cannaregio. The
quarter was cut off by wide
canals and the two watergates
were manned by Christian
guards. The area was named
the Ghetto, after a foundry –
geto in Venetian – which
formerly occupied the site. The
name was subsequently
given to Jewish enclaves
throughout the world. By day
Jews were allowed out of the
Ghetto, but at all times they
were made to wear identifying
badges and caps. The only
occupations they could pursue
were trading in textiles,
money-lending and medicine.
    The rising number of Jews
forced the Ghetto to expand.

**Campo del Ghetto Nuovo, the
oldest part of the Ghetto**

The wrought iron bridge leading northwards out of the Ghetto

Buildings rose vertically (the
so-called skyscrapers of
Venice) and spread into the
Ghetto Vecchio (1541) and
the neighbouring Ghetto
Novissimo (1633).
By the mid 17th
century the Jewish
population num-
bered over 5,000.
    In 1797 Napoleon
pulled down the
gates, but under
the Austrians the
Jews were again
forced into confinement. It
was not until 1866 that they
were granted their freedom.
    Of the 600 Jews now in
Venice, only five families live
in the Ghetto. However, the
quarter has not lost its ethnic
character. There are kosher
food shops, a Jewish baker, a
Jewish library, and two synagogues where religious ceremonies still take place. There

**Flowers in front of the
Holocaust Memorial**

are also several shops on
the large, recently restored
Campo del Ghetto Nuovo,
which sell items such as glass
rabbis and Hanukah lamps.

Museo Ebraico
The small Jewish
Museum in the
Ghetto Nuovo
houses a collection
of artifacts from
the 17th–19th
centuries. A guided
tour of the quarter's
synagogues leaves from the
museum daily except Saturday,
every hour from 10:30am to
5:30pm (3:30pm in winter).
Led by English-speaking
guides, the tours give a fascinating glimpse into the past
life of the Ghetto. A short history of the quarter is followed
by a visit to the lavishly
decorated German, Spanish
and Levantine synagogues.

THE LAGOON ISLANDS

SHROUDED IN MYTH and super-stition, the lagoon was once the preserve of fishermen and hunters. But marauders in the 5th and 6th centuries AD drove mainland dwellers to the safety of the marshy lagoon *(see p41)*. Here, they conquered their watery environment, which was pro-tected from the open sea by thin sandbanks *(lidi)*, created from silt washed down by the rivers of the Po delta. In the 13th century the first *murazzi* were built – sea walls of angular stone which safeguard the

Image of the Madonna, Torcello

lidi from erosion. Experiments with tidal barriers continue in an effort to combat the ever-present threat of flooding *(see p51)*.

The thriving communities that once lived and traded here are long gone. Many of the islands, formerly used as sites for monas-teries, hospitals or powder fac-tories, are now abandoned, but each has a tale to tell. The leases of 13 islands are about to be auctioned, with the condition that the lease-holders take on full responsi-bility for restoration of the buildings.

SIGHTS AT A GLANCE

Burano **2**
Giudecca **6**
Lazzaretto Vecchio **12**
Lido **10**
Murano **4**
Poveglia **13**
San Clemente **11**

San Francesco del Deserto **3**
San Lazzaro degli Armeni **9**
San Michele **5**
San Servolo **7**
Santa Maria della Grazia **8**
Torcello pp152–3 **1**

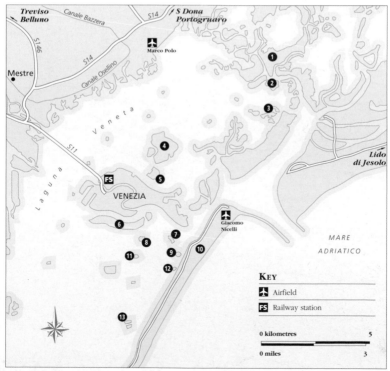

KEY

✈ Airfield

FS Railway station

0 kilometres   5

0 miles   3

◁ **The vivid façade of Casa Bepi in Burano**

Exploring the Lagoon

A TRIP TO THE LAGOON ISLANDS makes a welcome break from the densely packed streets of the city. Murano, celebrated for its glass, can be reached in a matter of minutes. Further north, Burano, the "lace island", and ancient Torcello are well worth the longer ride. The Lido, with its sandy beaches, is an easy journey from San Marco. Some of the lesser known islands are worth exploring too, but access can sometimes be difficult.

Murano
Some of Murano's canalside porticoes survive from medieval days **4**

Murano and San Michele are clearly visible from the northern quaysides of Venice.

San Michele
World-famous writers and artists are buried alongside Venetians on this island **5**

VENEZIA

San Giorgio in Alga had its monastery partially destroyed by fire in 1717. It was demolished in the 19th century.

SANTA MARIA DELLA GRAZIA **8**

SAN CLEMENTE **11**

Giudecca
Palladio's great church of the Redentore, on the waterfront, is the island's cultural highlight **6**

Sant'Angelo delle Polvere, recognizable by its towers, was formerly a powder factory.

SAN SPIRITO

Sacca Sessola, an artificial island, was the site of a hospital until 1980.

POVEGLIA **13**

Lido
Behind the crowded beaches and grand hotels, the Lido has some pleasantly peaceful waterways **10**

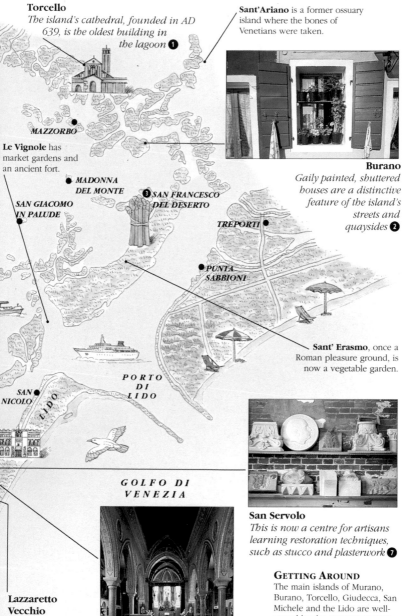

Torcello
The island's cathedral, founded in AD 639, is the oldest building in the lagoon ❶

Sant'Ariano is a former ossuary island where the bones of Venetians were taken.

MAZZORBO

Le Vignole has market gardens and an ancient fort.

● *MADONNA DEL MONTE*

❸ *SAN FRANCESCO DEL DESERTO*

SAN GIACOMO IN PALUDE

TREPORTI ●

Burano
Gaily painted, shuttered houses are a distinctive feature of the island's streets and quaysides ❷

● *PUNTA SABBIONI*

Sant' Erasmo, once a Roman pleasure ground, is now a vegetable garden.

PORTO DI LIDO

SAN NICOLO ●

LIDO

GOLFO DI VENEZIA

San Servolo
This is now a centre for artisans learning restoration techniques, such as stucco and plasterwork ❼

GETTING AROUND
The main islands of Murano, Burano, Torcello, Giudecca, San Michele and the Lido are well-served by the *vaporetto* system (*see pp274–5*). A few of the smaller islands have a limited public service; others can only be reached by water taxi or by paying a local with a boat.

Lazzaretto Vecchio
This tiny island with its varied past can be seen from the boat that runs from San Marco to the Lido ⓬

San Lazzaro degli Armeni
Visits to this green and pretty monastery island take in the church, library, museum and printing press ❾

KEY

	Major road
	Minor road

0 kilometres   2

0 miles   1

Torcello **❶**

See pp152–3.

**A stall selling lace and linen in
Burano's main street**

Burano **❷**

🚤 *No. 12 from Fondamente Nuove,
approx. 40–50 minutes (some go
direct, others via Torcello). No. 14
from San Zaccaria via the Lido and
Punta Sabbioni, approx. 1½ hours.*

B URANO IS THE MOST colourful
of the lagoon islands.
Lying in a lonely expanse of
the northern lagoon, it is distinguished from a distance by
the tall, dramatically tilted
tower of its church. In contrast
to the desolate Torcello, the
island is densely populated,
its waterways lined by brightly
painted houses.

A tour of the island's sights
will take an hour or so. The
street from the ferry stop takes
you to the main thoroughfare,
Via Baldassare Galuppi,
named after the Burano-born

composer (1706–85). The
street is lined with lace and
linen stalls and open-air
trattorias serving fresh fish.

🏛 **Scuola dei Merletti**
Piazza Baldassare Galuppi. 📞 *(041)
73 00 34.* ⬜ *Apr–Oct: 10am–5pm
Wed–Mon, Nov–Mar: 10am–4pm
Wed–Mon.* ⚫ *public hols.* 📷

The Buranese are fishermen
and lacemakers by trade. You
can still see the men scraping
their boats or mending nets,
but lacemakers are rare. In
the 16th century the local lace
was the most sought after in
Europe. It was so delicate it
became known as *punto in
aria* ("points in the air").
Foreign competition, coupled
with the Republic's decline,
led to a slump in the 18th
century in Burano's industry.
However, the need for a new
source of income led to a
revival of the skill in 1872 and
the founding of a lacemaking
school, the Scuola dei Merletti.

Today, authentic Burano
lace is hard to find. Genuine
pieces take weeks of painstak-
ing labour, and are expensive.
At the lacemaking school,
however, visitors can watch
Buranese women stitching
busily. Attached to the school
is a museum, displaying fine
antique lace.

Mazzorbo
Linked to Burano by a foot-
bridge, Mazzorbo is an island
of orchards and gardens.
Ferries en route to Burano
and Torcello pass through its
canal. The only surviving
church is the Romanesque-
Gothic Santa Caterina.

San Francesco del Deserto **❸**

Access, weather permitting, via
sándolo (rowing boat) from the quayside near the church in Burano. *Visits
to the island: 9–11am, 3–5pm Tue–
Sun.* **Monastery** 📞 *(041) 528 68 63.*

T HIS LITTLE OASIS of greenery,
inhabited by nine friars,
lies just south of Burano.
There is no *vaporetto* service
and to get there you must
bargain with the boatmen on
Burano's quayside, who will
row you across the shallow
waters and await your return.

One of the multilingual friars
will give you a tour of the old
church and the enchanting
gardens, which have a tree
said to have sprouted from
the staff of St Francis of Assisi.

**A Buranese fisherman about to
haul in the day's catch**

Murano **❹**

🚤 *No. 52 from San Zaccaria; No. 12,
13 or 23 from Fondamente Nuove.*

L IKE THE CITY of Venice,
Murano comprises a cluster
of small islands, connected by
bridges. It has been the centre
of the glassmaking industry
since 1291, when the furnaces
and glass craftsmen were
moved here from the city,
prompted by the risk of fire
to the buildings and the dis-
agreeable effects of smoke.

🏛 **Museo Vetrario**
Palazzo Giustinian, Fondamenta
Giustinian. 📞 *(041) 73 95 86.*
⬜ *10am–5pm (10am–4pm winter).*
⚫ *Wed.* 📷

Historically Murano owes its
prosperity entirely to glass.
From the late 13th century,
when the population num-
bered over 30,000, Murano
enjoyed self-government,
minted its own coins and had
its own Golden Book *(see
p42)* listing members of the

The multicoloured Casa Bepi, in a small square off Burano's main street

aristocracy. In the 15th and 16th centuries it was the principal glass-producing centre in Europe. Murano's glass artisans were granted unprecedented privileges, but for those who left the island to found businesses elsewhere there were severe penalties – even death.

Although a few of Murano's *palazzi* bear testimony to its former splendour, and its basilica still survives, most tourists visit for glass alone. Some are enticed by offers of free trips from factory touts in San Marco, others go by excursion launch or independently on the public *vaporetti*.

Some of the factories are now derelict, but glass is still produced in vast quantities. Among the plethora of kitsch (including imports from the Far East) are some wonderful pieces, and it pays to seek out the top glass factories *(see p249)*. Many furnaces, however, close at the weekend.

The Museo Vetrario (glass museum) in the huge Palazzo Giustinian houses a splendid collection of antique pieces. The prize exhibit of the collection is the Barovier wedding cup (1470–80), with enamelwork decoration by Angelo Barovier. The section devoted to modern glass, in a separate building at Campo Manin 1c, is closed for restoration.

🔒 **Basilica dei Santi Maria e Donato**
Fondamenta Giustinian. 📞 (041) 73 90 56. ⏰ 9:15am–noon, 4–7pm.

The colonnaded exterior of Murano's Basilica dei Santi Maria e Donato

The island's architectural highlight is the Basilica dei Santi Maria e Donato, whose magnificent colonnaded apse is reflected in the waters of the San Donato canal. Despite some heavy-handed restoration undertaken in the 19th century, this 12th-century church still retains much of its original beauty. Visitors should note the Veneto-Byzantine columns and Gothic ship's keel roof. An enchantingly evocative mosaic portrait of the Madonna, seen standing alone against a gold background, decorates the apse.

The church's floor, or *pavimento*, dating from 1140, is equally beautiful. With its medieval mosaics of geometric figures, exotic birds, mythical creatures and inexplicable symbols, it incorporates fragments of ancient glass from the island's foundries into its imagery.

Diaghilev's tombstone

San Michele ⑤

🚤 *No. 23 or 52.*

STUDDED WITH dark cypresses and enclosed within high terracotta walls, the cemetery island of San Michele lies just across the water from Venice's Fondamente Nuove. The bodies of Venetians were traditionally buried in church graveyards in Venice. But for reasons of hygiene and space, San Michele and its neighbour were designated cemeteries in the 19th century.

The church of San Michele in Isola stands by the landing stage. Designed by Mauro Coducci (c.1469), it was the first church in Venice to be faced in white Istrian stone. The cemetery itself rambles over most of the island. With its carved tombstones and chapels it has a curious fascination. Some graves have suffered neglect, but most are well-tended and enlivened by a riot of flowers.

The most famous graves are those of foreigners: Ezra Pound (1885–1972), in the *Evangelisti* (Protestant) section, and Sergei Diaghilev (1872–1929) and Igor Stravinsky (1882–1971) in the *Greci* or Orthodox section. These bodies have been allowed to rest in peace. Others were dug up after about ten years to make way for new arrivals, and the bones taken to the ossuary island of Sant'Ariano. Today, however, because of increasing lack of space on San Michele, most bodies are buried on the mainland.

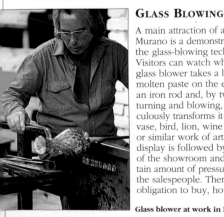

GLASS BLOWING

A main attraction of a trip to Murano is a demonstration of the glass-blowing technique. Visitors can watch while a glass blower takes a blob of molten paste on the end of an iron rod and, by twisting, turning and blowing, miraculously transforms it into a vase, bird, lion, wine goblet or similar work of art. The display is followed by a tour of the showroom and a certain amount of pressure from the salespeople. There is no obligation to buy, however.

Glass blower at work in Murano

Torcello ●

Established between the 5th and 6th centuries, Torcello grew into a thriving colony *(see p40)*, with palaces, churches and a population said to have reached 20,000. But with the rise of Venice the island went into decline. Today, the population is just 60 and all that remains of this once vigorous island is the Byzantine cathedral, the church of Santa Fosca and the memory of its former glory.

★ Apse Mosaic
The 13th-century Madonna, set against a gold background, is one of the most moving mosaics in Venice.

★ Domesday Mosaics
The huge and highly decorative mosaic of the Last Judgment covers the entire west wall.

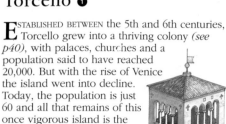

Pulpit
The present basilica dates from 1008, but includes many earlier features. The marble pulpit is made of fragments from the first, 7th-century church.

★ Iconostasis
The exquisite Byzantine marble panels of the rood screen are carved with peacocks, lions and flowers. This detailed relief shows two peacocks drinking from the fountain of life.

The Roman sarcophagus
below the altar is said to contain the relics of St Heliodorus.

Nave Columns
The finely carved capitals on the marble nave columns date from the 11th century.

VISITORS' CHECKLIST

🚤 No. 14 from San Zaccaria.
**Basilica di Santa Maria dell'
Assunta** 📞 (041) 73 00 84. 🕐
10am–12:30pm, 2–5pm daily. 📷
Campanile 🕐 daily. 📷 **Church
of Santa Fosca** 📞 (041) 73 00
84. 🕐 10am–12:30pm, 2–5pm
daily. **Museo dell'Estuario** 📞
(041) 73 07 61. 🕐 Apr–Sep:
10am–12:30pm, 2–5:30pm Tue–
Sun; Oct–Mar: 10:30am–12:30pm,
2–4pm Tue–Sun. ⬤ pub hols. 📷

Torcello's Last Canals
*Silted canals and malaria
hastened Torcello's decline.
One of the remaining
waterways runs from the
vaporetto stop to the basilica.*

Santa Fosca
*Built in the
11th and 12th
centuries on a
Greek-cross plan,
the church has
a lovely portico
and a serene
Byzantine
interior.*

The central dome
and cross sections are
supported by columns
of Greek marble with
fine Corinthian capitals.

Attila's Throne
*It was said that the 5th-
century king of the
Huns used this
marble seat as his
throne.*

To *vaporetto*
boarding point →

**Museo dell'
Estuario**
*Old church
treasures and
archaeological
fragments are
housed here.*

STAR FEATURES

★ **Apse Mosaic**

★ **Domesday Mosaics**

★ **Iconostasis**

Boats moored along the Ponte Lungo on the Giudecca

Giudecca ❻

🚤 No. 82 and 52 (to Zitelle only).

IN THE DAYS OF the Republic, the island of Giudecca was a pleasure ground of palaces and gardens. Today it is very much a suburb of the city, its dark narrow alleys flanked by apartments, its squares overgrown and its *palazzi* neglected. However, the long, wide quayside skirting the city side of the island makes a very pleasant promenade and provides stunning views of Venice across the water. The island was originally named Spinalunga (long spine) on account of its shape. The name Giudecca, once thought to have referred to the Jews, or *giudei*, who lived here in the 13th century, is more likely to have originated from the word *giudicati* meaning "the judged". This referred to troublesome aristocrats who, as early as the 9th century, were banished to the island.

The Hotel Cipriani *(see p231)*, among the most luxurious places to stay in Venice, is quietly and discreetly located at the tip of the island. In contrast, at the western end of the island looms the massive Neo-Gothic ruin of the Mulino Stucky. It was built in 1895 as a flour mill by the Swiss entrepreneur Giovanni Stucky, an unpopular employer who was murdered by one of his workers in 1910. The mill ceased functioning in 1954, and plans have recently been approved for its conversion into a hotel, apartments and a park.

🔒 Il Redentore
Campo Redentore. **(** (041) 523 14 15. 🚤 Redentore. ⏱ 10am–5:30pm Mon–Sat, 3–5:30pm Sun & public hols. 🖼

Giudecca's principal monument is Palladio's church of Il Redentore (the Redeemer). It was built in 1577–92 in thanksgiving for the end of the 1576 plague, which wiped out a third of the city's population. Every year since its creation, the doge and his entourage would visit the church, crossing from the Zattere on a bridge of boats. The Feast of the Redeemer is still celebrated on the third weekend in July *(see p34)*. The church of Il Redentore, styled on the architecture of ancient Rome, is a masterpiece of harmony and proportion. The Classical interior presents a marked contrast to the highly ornate and elaborate style of most Venetian churches. The main paintings, by Paolo Veronese and Alvise Vivarini, are in the sacristy to the right of the choir: apply to the sacristan for access. The most rewarding views of the Redentore are from Venice across the water. After dark, when the church is floodlit, it is a spectacular sight.

🔒 Le Zitelle
Fondamenta delle Zitelle. 🚤 Zitelle. ⏱ 10am for Sun mass only.

Palladio's church of Le Zitelle is now the site of Venice's most up-to-date congress centre. The church, though restored, is closed, apart from Sunday mass. The building adjoining the church was formerly a hostel for spinsters *(zitelle)*, who occupied themselves by making the fine Venetian *punto in aria* lace.

An artisan at work at the San Servolo training centre

San Servolo ❼

🚤 No. 20 from San Zaccaria. **Fondazione Europea pro Venetia Viva (** (041) 526 85 46. **Venice International University (** (041) 271 95 11.

HALF-WAY BETWEEN San Marco and the Lido is the island of San Servolo. Now a centre for teaching crafts and home to the Venice International University, it started life as one of the original monastery islands of Venice. Benedictine monks established a monastery here in the 8th century, and later added a hospital.

In 1725 the island became a lunatic asylum and a new hospital was built to house the patients. The Council of Ten *(see p42)* declared that this was to be strictly a shelter for "maniacs of noble family or comfortable circumstances". Poor maniacs were imprisoned or left to their own devices. In 1797 Napoleon scrubbed this discriminatory decree and the asylum became free to all.

Palladio's Redentore church, Giudecca

In 1980 this spartan island was taken over by the Fondazione Europea pro Venetia Viva (The European Centre for Training Craftsmen in the Conservation of the Architectural Heritage) and in 1996 Venice International University opened its doors here. Visits to the university can be arranged.

Santa Maria della Grazia ❽

No. 10 from San Zaccaria.

ORIGINALLY CALLED La Cavana or Cavanell, the island lies just a short distance away from San Giorgio Maggiore (see p95). Formerly a shelter for pilgrims on their journey to the Holy Land, it became a monastery island in the 15th century. Its name was changed when a church was constructed to enshrine a miraculous image of the Virgin, brought from Constantinople. The religious buildings, including a Gothic church with some fine paintings, were secularized under Napoleon. The island became a military zone under his rule, but the buildings were subsequently destroyed during the 1848 revolutionary uprising (see p48).

Today, Santa Maria della Grazia is occupied by a hospital for infectious diseases, but rumour has it that this is soon going to close.

San Lazzaro degli Armeni ❾

No. 20 from Riva degli Schiavoni. (041) 526 01 04. 3–5pm daily.

LYING JUST OFF the Lido (see p156), San Lazzaro degli Armeni is a small, very green monastery island, recognizable by the onion-shaped cupola of its white campanile. The buildings are surrounded by well-groomed gardens and dark groves of cypress trees. Since the 18th century it has been an Armenian monastery and centre of learning.

Early history

This small island served as an asylum in the 12th century and later became a hospital island for lepers, named after their patron saint, Lazarus. The lepers were then transferred to the Ospedale di San Lazzaro dei Mendicanti at Santi Giovanni e Paolo (see pp116–17). In 1717 an Armenian monk, Manug di Pietro, known as Mechitar ("the consoler"), was forced to flee his homeland, the Morea, when the Turks invaded. Venetian rulers gave him the island of San Lazzaro in the southern lagoon as a place of shelter. Here, he established a religious order. The Armenians rebuilt the island, setting up a monastery, church, library, study rooms, gardens and

Illuminated manuscript, San Lazzaro degli Armeni

Prince Nehmekhet's sarcophagus (c.1000 BC), San Lazzaro

orchards. The island became a place of study where monks taught (and still teach) young Armenians their culture.

The island today

Today, multilingual monks give visitors guided tours of the church, the art collection, the library and the museum, which houses Armenian, Greek, Indian and Egyptian artifacts. One of the most famous is an Egyptian sarcophagus complete with mummy, which is one of the best-preserved in the world. The most impressive exhibit is the printing hall where, over 200 years ago, a press produced works in 36 languages. A polyglot press is still in use, producing postcards, maps and prints for visitors.

Lord Byron

In 1816 the poet Byron would often row from Venice to absorb Armenian culture. Full of admiration for the monks, he wrote that the monastery "appears to unite all the advantages of the monastic institution without any of its vices . . . the virtues of the brethren . . . are well fitted to strike a man of the world with the conviction that 'there is another and a better', even in this life." The room where he studied, with mementoes, has been carefully preserved.

The garden and cloisters of San Lazzaro degli Armeni

The Lido, away from the crowds and glare of the beaches

Lido ⑩

🚏 Nos. 1, 82, 52, 6 and 14 to Santa Maria Elisabetta; No. 14 to San Nicolò; No. 17 from Tronchetto to San Nicolò.

THE LIDO is a slender sand-bank 12 km (8 miles) long which forms a natural barrier between Venice and the open sea. It is both a residential suburb of the city and – more importantly for tourists – the city's seaside resort. The only island in the lagoon with roads, it is linked to the main-land by car ferry. From Venice, the Lido is served by regular

The elegant bar of the Hôtel des Bains on the Lido

vaporetti. The fastest of these (Motonave No. 6) takes little more than ten minutes to reach its destination.

The Lido's main season runs from June to September, the most crowded months being July and August. In winter most hotels are closed.

The world's first lido

In the 19th century, before the Lido was developed, the island was a favourite haunt of Shelley, Byron and other literary figures. Byron swam from the Lido to Santa Chiara via the Grand Canal in under four hours.

Bathing establishments were gradually opened and by the turn of the century the Lido had become one of Europe's most fashionable seaside resorts, frequented by royalty, film stars and leading lights of the literati. They stayed in the grand hotels, swam in the sea or sat in deckchairs on the sands by the striped *cabanas*. Life in the Lido's heyday was brilliantly evoked in Thomas Mann's book *Death in Venice* (1912). The Hôtel des Bains, where the melancholic Von

Aschenbach stays, features in the novel and in Visconti's 1970 film. It is still a promi-nent landmark and an elegant place to stay (*see p231*).

The Lido is no longer the prestigious resort it was in the 1930s. Beaches are crowded, the streets busy and the ferries packed with daytrippers. Nevertheless the sands, sea and sporting facilities provide a welcome break from city culture. It is also the summer home for Venice's casino (*see p256*) and, when not over-crowded, the backwaters provide a green respite from the heat of Venice.

Exploring the island

The Lido can be covered by bus but a popular form of transport is the bicycle. You can hire one from the shop almost opposite the *vaporetto* stop at Santa Maria Elisabetta.

The east side of the island is fringed by sandy beaches. For passengers arriving by ferry at the main landing stage, these beaches are reached by bus, taxi or on foot along the Gran Viale Santa Maria Elisabetta. This is the main shopping street of the Lido. At the end of the Gran Viale you can turn left for the beaches of San Nicolò or right along the Lungomare G Marconi, which boasts the grandest hotels and the best beaches. The former control the latter in this area, and levy exorbitant charges (except to hotel residents) for the use of beach facilities.

Cabanas on the Lido beaches, hired out to wealthy Venetians

The long straight road parallel to the beach leads southwest to the village of Malamocco. There are some pleasant fish restaurants, but there is little evidence that this was once the 8th-century seat of the lagoon's government. Alberoni, at the southern end of the Lido, is the site of a golf course, a public beach and the landing stage for the ferry across to Pellestrina.

San Nicolò

The Lido's only quarter of cultural interest is San Nicolò in the north. Across the Porto di Lido, you can see the fortress of Sant'Andrea on the island of Le Vignole, built by Michele Sanmicheli between 1435 and 1449 to guard the main entrance of the lagoon. It was to the Porto di Lido that the doge was rowed annually to cast a ring into the sea in symbolic marriage each spring *(see p33)*. After the ceremony he would visit the nearby church and monastery of San Nicolò, founded in 1044 and rebuilt in the 16th century. The nearby Jewish cemetery, open to the public, dates from 1386.

The rest of this northern area is given over to an airfield. The aeroclub organizes flying lessons, parachuting or panoramic flights over Venice and the lagoon.

Aeroclub G Ancillotto

☎ *(041) 526 08 08.*

San Clemente ⓫

🚤 *No. 10 from San Zaccaria.*

FROM A REFUGE for pilgrims en route to the Holy Land, the island of San Clemente became a hermitage and site of a monastery. During the Republic it was the island where doges frequently met distinguished visitors, but from 1630 when the island was hit by the plague (said to have been brought by the Duke of Mantua) it served as a military depot. In the 19th century the island was turned into a lunatic asylum and most of the existing buildings date from that time.

INTERNATIONAL FILM FESTIVAL

Film fans flock to the Lido every year in late summer for the International Film Festival. The event was inaugurated in 1932 under the auspices of the Biennale *(see p256)* and was so successful that the Palazzo del Cinema was built four years later. During its history the festival has attracted big names in the film world; it has also been plagued by bureaucracy and political in-fighting. There are signs however that the event is making a comeback and the famous names are now returning to the Lido.

The event takes place over two weeks in late August/early September. Films are shown day and night either in the Palazzo del Cinema or the Astra Cinema. Tickets can be hard to come by, but you can normally spot the stars (along with the paparazzi) for the price of a drink on the terrace of the Excelsior Hotel. See also page 255.

Poster advertising the first Lido International Film Festival, 1932

Lazzaretto Vecchio ⓬

No public access.

THIS SMALL ISLAND which lies just west of the Lido has served variously as a hospice for pilgrims travelling to the Holy Land, a home for victims of the plague and an ammunitions depot. The island's church, whose venerated image of the Virgin was taken by the Carmelites to adorn their Scalzi church, sadly no longer exists. Nowadays the island is a home for stray dogs. In summer the casino boat, running from San Marco to the Lido, passes close by.

Poveglia ⓭

No public access.

FORMERLY CALLED Popilia on account of all its poplar trees, the island was once a thriving little community with its own government and monastery. Devastated during the war with Genoa in 1380, it fell into decline, and over the centuries became a refuge for plague victims, an isolation hospital and a home for the aged. Today the land is used for growing crops and vines. Its low hump and distinguishing tower, once part of the city's defence system, can be seen across the lagoon from Malamocco on the Lido.

San Clemente in the southern lagoon, seen through the evening mist

THE VENETO
AREA BY AREA

THE VENETO AT A GLANCE 160–161
THE VENETO PLAIN 162–185
VERONA AND LAKE GARDA 186–209
THE DOLOMITES 210–219

The Veneto at a Glance

THE VENETO'S SHEER VARIETY makes it one of Italy's most fascinating regions to explore. The cities of Verona, Padua and Vicenza are all noted for outstanding architecture, churches and museums. Villas in the rural hinterland are gorgeously frescoed with scenes from ancient mythology. The lagoon has busy fishing ports and beach resorts, while Lake Garda, with its glorious mountain scenery, historic castles and water sports, makes a perfect holiday playground. Northwards lie the majestic Dolomites, Italy's premier region for skiing, which attract visitors in the summer, too, with their alpine beauty and excellent hiking facilities.

Monti Lessini
Scores of scenic villages, such as Giazza (see p191), nestle in the vineyard-clad valleys of the Lessini mountains.

Verona
An ancient Roman stronghold, famous as the home of the lovers Romeo and Juliet, Verona today is a city of opera, theatre and art (see pp192–203).

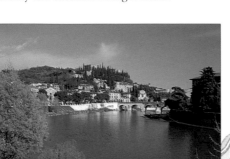

VERONA AND LAKE GARDA
Pages 186–209

Lake Garda
Most beautiful of all the Italian lakes, Garda is surrounded by Scaligeri castles such as the magnificent Sirmione (see p204).

Vicenza
Dominated by the architecture of Palladio, Vicenza (see pp168–73) is the model Renaissance city.

Dolomites
Erosion has sculpted the limestone peaks of the Dolomites into bizarre columns and spires, with alpine villages hidden in steep valleys (see p216).

Villa Barbaro
Veronese's lavish frescoes are the perfect complement to one of Palladio's grandest rural villas, surrounded by statue-filled formal gardens, grottoes and pools (see p24).

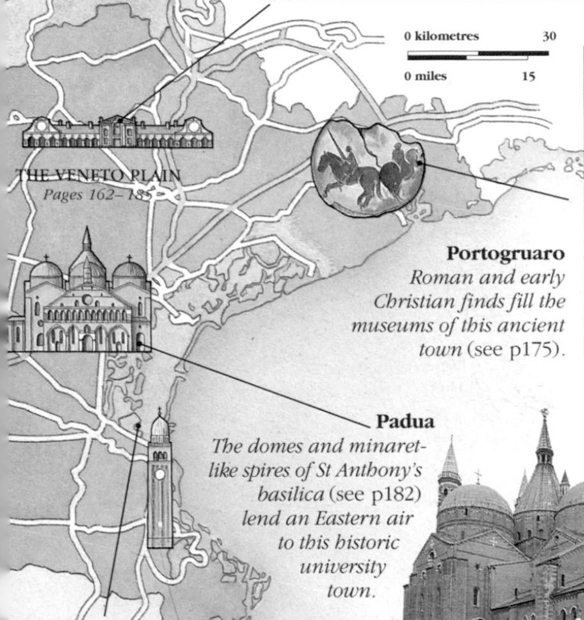

THE DOLOMITES
Pages 210–219

0 kilometres 30

0 miles 15

THE VENETO PLAIN
Pages 162–185

Portogruaro
Roman and early Christian finds fill the museums of this ancient town (see p175).

Padua
The domes and minaret-like spires of St Anthony's basilica (see p182) lend an Eastern air to this historic university town.

Chioggia
Flocks of wading birds frequent the wild marshland around Chioggia (see p185), the Venetian lagoon's principal fishing port.

THE VENETO PLAIN

T HE GREAT ARC OF LAND *that forms the Veneto Plain is one of tremendous contrast, and has much to offer the visitor. Its ancient cities are rich in history and their magnificent architecture is world renowned. The source of the region's wealth is manifest in the industrial landscapes around the towns, but these are never far from beautiful countryside, which includes the green Euganean Hills, calm lagoons and the undulating foothills of the Dolomites.*

The area known as the Veneto Plain sweeps round from the Po river delta in the southwest to the mountains that form the border between Italy and Slovenia. The whole region is crossed by a series of rivers, canals and waterways, all of which converge in the Adriatic sea.

The river-borne silt deposits that created the Venetian Lagoon cover the region, making the land fertile. The Romans established their frontier posts here, and these survive today as the great cities of Vicenza, Padua and Treviso. Their strategic position at the hub of the empire's road network enabled them to prosper under Roman rule, as they continued to do under the benign rule of the Venetian empire more than 1,000 years later.

Wealth from agriculture, commerce and the spoils of war paid for the beautification of these cities through the building of Renaissance palaces and public buildings, many of them designed by the region's great architect, Andrea Palladio. His villas can be seen all over the Veneto, symbols of the idyllic and leisured existence once enjoyed by the region's aristocrats.

The symbols of modern prosperity – factories and scarred landscapes – are encountered frequently, especially around the town of Mestre. Yet there are areas of extraordinary beauty as well. Petrarch *(see p184)*, the great medieval romantic poet, so loved the area that he made his home among the gently wooded Euganean Hills.

Fishing from a breakwater in the lagoon at Chioggia

◁ **Classical figure in the nymphaeum of the Villa Barbaro near Asolo**

Exploring the Veneto Plain

THE LANDSCAPE OF THE VENETO PLAIN is as flat as a board, but it is far from dull. Villagers in the small communities dotted throughout the region used to compete to build the tallest church tower, and these seemingly needle-thin landmarks soaring skywards draw the traveller on. Great stone castles, dating from the 14th century, rise on almost every promontory, each with a backdrop on clear days of the distant Alps.

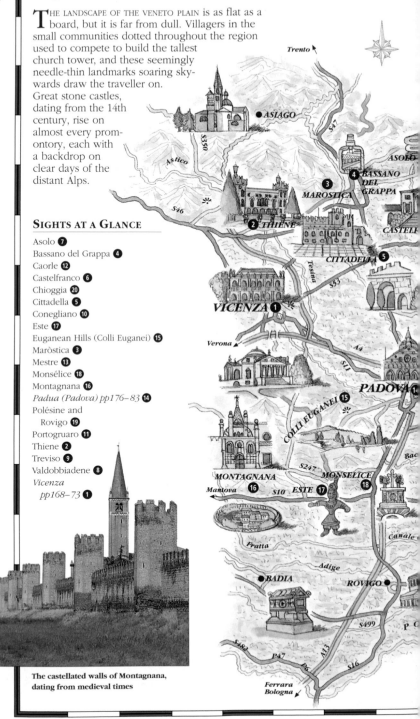

SIGHTS AT A GLANCE

Asolo **7**
Bassano del Grappa **4**
Caorle **12**
Castelfranco **6**
Chioggia **20**
Cittadella **5**
Conegliano **10**
Este **17**
Euganean Hills (Colli Euganei) **15**
Maròstica **3**
Mestre **13**
Monsélice **18**
Montagnana **16**
Padua (Padova) pp176–83 **14**
Polésine and
    Rovigo **19**
Portogruaro **11**
Thiene **2**
Treviso **9**
Valdobbiadene **8**
*Vicenza
    pp168–73* **1**

The castellated walls of Montagnana, dating from medieval times

GETTING AROUND

An extensive rail network and good bus services make this region easy to explore by public transport. Roads are heavily used, so avoid cities and *autostrade* during rush hours.

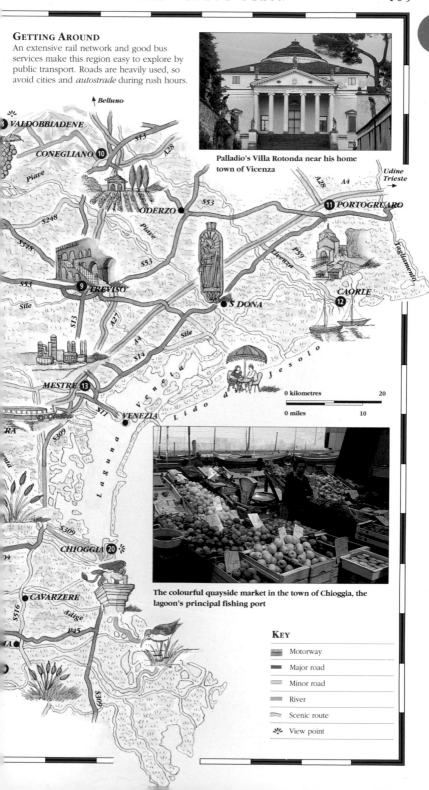

Palladio's Villa Rotonda near his home town of Vicenza

The colourful quayside market in the town of Chioggia, the lagoon's principal fishing port

KEY

	Motorway
	Major road
	Minor road
	River
	Scenic route
☀	View point

Vicenza ❶

See pp168–73.

Thiene ❷

Road map C3. 👥 20,000. 🚌
ℹ️ *Piazza Ferrarin 20. (0445) 36
95 44.* 😃 *Mon am.* **Shops closed
Wed pm.**

THIENE IS ONE of the area's
many textile towns, manu-
facturing jeans and sweatshirts
for sale all over Europe. Two
villas nearby are worth a visit.
The heavily fortified towers
and battlemented walls of the
Castello Porto-Colleoni are
offset by pretty Gothic windows. At the time it was built,
it stood in open countryside,
and the defences were a precaution against bandits and
raiders. Inside, 16th-century
frescoes by Giambattista Zelotti
add a lighter note and many
portraits of horses remind the
visitor that the villa's owners,
the Colleoni family, were employed by the Venetian cavalry.
　Zelotti also frescoed the
Villa Godi Malinverni, the
first villa designed by Palladio
(see pp24–5). The garden is
charming, and the frescoes
are magnificent. Inside are
works by Italian Impression-
ists and a lovely portrait by
Pietro Annigoni (1910–88)
called *La Strega* (the Sorceress).

🏛 **Castello Porto-Colleoni**
Corso Garibaldi 2. 📞 *(0445) 36 60 15.*
⭕ *21 Mar–30 Nov: Sun; Mon–Sat for
groups only by appt.* 🈲 🈳 *Sun pm.*
🏛 **Villa Godi Malinverni**
Via Palladio 44. 📞 *(0445) 86 05 61.*
⭕ *Tue, Sat & Sun afternoons.* 🈲

The human chess game in the town square of Maròstica

Maròstica ❸

Road map C3. 👥 7,000. 🚌
ℹ️ *Piazza Castello 1. (0424) 721 27.*
😃 *Tue am.*

MARÒSTICA is an almost perfect medieval fortified
town, surrounded by walls
built in 1370 by the Scaligeri
(see p207). The rampart walk
from the **Castello Inferiore**
(lower castle), now the town
hall, to the **Castello Superiore**
(upper castle) has fine views.
　The lower castle exhibits
costumes worn by participants
in the town's human chess
tournament, the *Partita a
Scacchi*, held every other September *(see p35).* Up to 500
people participate in this colourful re-enactment of a game
first played here in 1454.

🏛 **Castello Inferiore**
Piazza Castello 1. ⭕ *daily.*
● *Easter, 25 Dec.* 🈲

Bassano del Grappa ❹

Road map C3. 👥 38,770. 🚉 🚌
ℹ️ *Largo Corona d'Italia 35. (0424)
52 43 51.* 😃 *Tue, Thu & Sat am.*

THIS PEACEFUL TOWN, which
stands at the foot of Monte
Grappa, is synonymous with
Italy's favourite after-dinner
drink. The crystal clear grappa
is not named after the town, although the liquor is produced
here. The name is a corruption
of *graspa*, the Italian term for
the lees that are left after wine
production and used in distil-
ling grappa. Information on
the process is given at the
Museo degli Alpini, reached
by crossing the graceful Ponte
degli Alpini bridge. Designed
in 1569 by Palladio, it is built
of timber to allow it to flex
when hit by spring meltwaters.
　Bassano is also famous for
majolica wares *(see p252)* on
display at **Palazzo Sturm**.
The locally born artist Jacopo
Bassano (1510–92) and sculptor Antonio Canova (1757–
1822) are celebrated in the
Museo Civico.

🏛 **Museo degli Alpini**
Via Anagarano 2. 📞 *(0424) 50 36
62.* ⭕ *Tue–Sun.*
🏛 **Palazzo Sturm**
Via Ferracina. 📞 *(0424) 5249 33.*
⭕ *Apr–Oct: Tue–Sun; Nov–Mar:
Fri–Sun.* 🈲
🏛 **Museo Civico**
Piazza Garibaldi. 📞 *(0424) 52 22 35.*
⭕ *Tue–Sun.* 🈲

The Ponte degli Alpini at Bassano del Grappa

Cittadella 5

Road map C3. 18,000. FS
Via Marconi 3. (049) 597 06 27.
Mon am.

THIS ATTRACTIVE TOWN is the twin of Castelfranco. Each was fortified and Cittadella still preserves its 13th-century moated walls. These are interrupted by four gates and by 16 towers. The Torre di Malta near the southern gate was used as a torture chamber by Ezzelino de Romano, who ruled in the mid 13th century. Far more pleasant to contemplate is the *Supper at Emmaus* painting in the **Duomo**, a masterpiece by local Renaissance artist, Bassano.

Fresco from the Villa Emo at Fanzolo, near Castelfranco

Castelfranco 6

Road map D3. 30,000.
Via Francesco M Preti 39. (0423) 49 50 00. Tue & Fri am.

FORTIFIED IN 1199 by rulers of Treviso, as a defence against the neighbouring Paduans, the historic core of this town lies within well-preserved walls. **Casa di Giorgione**, claimed to be the birthplace of artist Giorgione (1478–1511), houses a museum devoted to the life of the man who created such moody and mysterious works as *The Tempest (see p131)*. One of his few directly attributable works is *The Madonna and Child with Saints Liberal and Francis* (1504) displayed in the **Duomo**. This entrancing picture was commissioned by Tuzio Costanza to stand above the tomb of his son, Matteo, killed in battle in 1504.

The pretty town of Asolo in the foothills of the Dolomites

At Fanzolo, 8 km (5 miles) northeast of Castelfranco, is the **Villa Emo**, designed in 1564 by Palladio. Here, Zelotti's sumptuous frescoes reveal the love lives of Greek deities.

Casa di Giorgione
Piazzetta del Duomo. (0423) 49 12 40. Tue–Sun. public hols.
Villa Emo
Fanzolo di Vedelago. (0423) 47 64 14. 5, irregular service. Apr–Oct: daily pm & Sun am; Nov–Mar: Sat & Sun pm. 25 Dec.

Asolo 7

Road map D3. 2,000.
Piazza d'Annunzio 2. (0423) 52 90 46. Sat. **Shops closed** Mon am & Wed pm.

ASOLO IS beautifully sited among the cypress-clad foothills of the Dolomites. Queen Caterina Cornaro (1454–1510) once ruled this tiny walled town *(see p43)*, and the poet Cardinal Pietro Bembo coined the verb *asolare* to describe the bittersweet life of enforced idleness she endured. Among others who have fallen in love with the narrow streets and grand houses was poet Robert Browning, who named a volume of poems *Asolanda* (1889) after the town.

Just 10 km (6 miles) east of Asolo is the **Villa Barbaro** at Masèr *(see pp24–5)*, while 10 km (6 miles) north is the village of Passagno, birthplace of Antonio Canova. Canova's remains lie inside the huge temple-like church which he designed himself. Nearby is the family home, the **Casa di Canova**. The Gypsoteca here houses the plaster casts and clay models for many of Canova's sculptures.

Villa Barbaro
Masèr. (0423) 92 30 04. Tue, Sat, Sun & hols pm. winter: Tue.
Casa di Canova
Piazza Canova. (0423) 54 43 23. Tue–Sun. 1 Jan, Easter, Christmas.

Valdobbiadene 8

Road map D3. 10,700. FS
Viale Vittoria 13. (0423) 97 21 25. Mon. **Shops closed** Mon pm.

VALDOBBIADENE, surrounded by beautiful vineyard-planted hills, is a major centre for the sparkling white wine called Cartizze. To the east, the Strada del Vino Bianco (white wine route) stretches 34 km (21 miles) to the town of Conegliano *(see p175)*, passing vineyards offering wine to try and to buy.

ENVIRONS: About 30 km (18 miles) northeast is Follina, where the church of **San Pietro di Foletto** has remarkable Romanesque frescoes. These include a depiction of Christ surrounded by tools connected with various trades.

Vines near Valdobbiadene

Street-by-Street: Vicenza ➊

Detail on No. 21 Contrà Porti

VICENZA IS KNOWN as the city of Andrea Palladio (1508–80), a man who started out as a humble stone-mason and became the most influential architect of his time. As you walk around the city it is fascinating to study the evolution of his distinctive style. In the centre is the monumental basilica he adapted to serve as the town hall while all around are the palaces he built for Vicenza's wealthy citizens.

Loggia del Capitaniato
This covered arcade was designed by Palladio in 1571.

Contrà Porti has some of the most elegant *palazzi* in Vicenza.

Palazzo Valmarana
Palladio's impressive building of 1566 was originally intended to be three times larger. It was not completed until 1680, 100 years after the architect's death.

Duomo
Vicenza's cathedral was rebuilt after bomb damage during World War II left only the façade and choir intact.

KEY

‒ ‒ ‒ Suggested route

STAR SIGHTS

★ **Piazza dei Signori**

★ **Casa Pigafetta**

CORSO ANDREA PALLADIO

VIA BATTISTI

CONTRÀ LAMPERTICO

CONTRÀ P.

PIAZZA DEL DUOMO

CONTRÀ CA

CONTRÀ MUSCHER

CONTRÀ GARIBALDI

CONTRÀ SAN ANTONIO

0 metres   150
0 yards   150

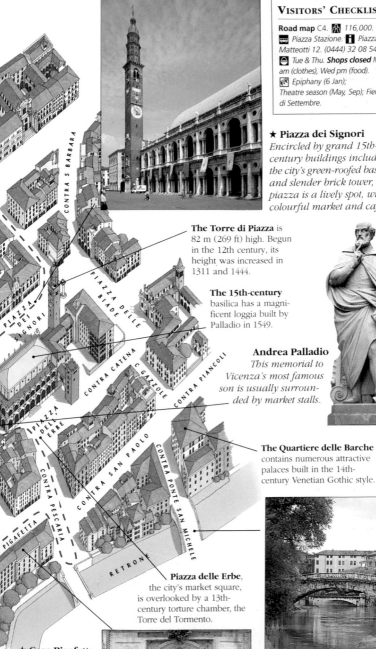

VISITORS' CHECKLIST

Road map C4. ⌂ *116,000.* FS
▭ *Piazza Stazione.* ⓘ *Piazza
Matteotti 12. (0444) 32 08 54.*
⊖ *Tue & Thu.* **Shops closed** *Mon
am (clothes), Wed pm (food).*
◈ *Epiphany (6 Jan);
Theatre season (May, Sep); Fiera
di Settembre.*

★ **Piazza dei Signori**
*Encircled by grand 15th-
century buildings including
the city's green-roofed basilica
and slender brick tower, the
piazza is a lively spot, with a
colourful market and cafés.*

The Torre di Piazza is
82 m (269 ft) high. Begun
in the 12th century, its
height was increased in
1311 and 1444.

The 15th-century
basilica has a magni-
ficent loggia built by
Palladio in 1549.

Andrea Palladio
*This memorial to
Vicenza's most famous
son is usually surroun-
ded by market stalls.*

The Quartiere delle Barche
contains numerous attractive
palaces built in the 14th-
century Venetian Gothic style.

Piazza delle Erbe,
the city's market square,
is overlooked by a 13th-
century torture chamber, the
Torre del Tormento.

Ponte San Michele
*This elegant stone bridge,
built in 1620, provides lovely
views of the surrounding town.*

★ **Casa Pigafetta**
*This striking house
was the birthplace
of Antonio Pigafetta,
who in 1519 set
sail round the world
with Magellan.*

Exploring Vicenza

VICENZA, THE GREAT PALLADIAN CITY, is celebrated the world over for its architecture. It is also one of the wealthiest cities in the Veneto, with much to offer the visitor, from Roman and Renaissance monuments to elegant shops selling all manner of fine goods.

Statues gazing down from their pillars in the Piazza dei Signori

Piazza dei Signori

At the heart of Vicenza, this square is dominated by the startling bulk of the Palazzo della Ragione, often referred to as the "basilica". Its green, copper-clad roof is shaped like an upturned boat with a balustrade that bristles with the statues of Greek and Roman gods. The colonnades were designed by Palladio in 1549 to support the city's 15th-century town hall, which had begun to subside. This was his first public commission, and his solution ensured the survival of the building.

The astonishingly slender Torre di Piazza alongside has stood since the 12th century. Opposite is the elegant café, the Gran Caffè Garibaldi, which is next to Palladio's Loggia del Capitaniato (1571). The Loggia's upper rooms contain the city's council chamber.

Contrà Porti

Contrà (an abbreviation of contrada, or district) is the Vicenza dialect word for street. On the western side is a series of pretty Gothic buildings with painted windows and ornate balconies, including Palazzo Porto-Colleoni (No. 19). These houses reflect the architecture of Venice, a

reminder that Vicenza was part of the Venetian empire.

Several fine Palladian *palazzi* stand on this street. The Palazzo Thiene (No. 12) of 1545–50, the Palazzo Porto Barbarano (No. 11) of 1570, and the Palazzo Iseppo da Porto (No. 21) of 1552 all illustrate the sheer variety of Palladio's style – Classical elements are common to all three, but each is unique. The Palazzo Thiene reveals some intriguing details of Palladio's methods: though the building appears to be of stone, close inspection reveals that it is built of cheap lightweight brick, cleverly rendered to look like masonry.

Casa Pigafetta

Contrà Pigafetta. *No public access*. This highly decorated Spanish Gothic building of 1481 has clover-leaf balconies, gryphon brackets and Moorish windows. The owner, Antonio Pigafetta, sailed round the world with Magellan in 1519–22, being one of only 20 men who survived the voyage.

Museo Civico

Piazza Matteotti. *(0444) 32 13 48.* ◯ *Tue–Sun.*

Vicenza's excellent Museo Civico is housed in Palladio's Palazzo Chiericati, built in 1550. Inside is a fresco by Giulio Carpione of a naked charioteer, representing the Sun, who appears to fly over the ceiling of the entrance hall. The upstairs rooms hold many excellent pictures. Among the Gothic altarpieces from Vicenza's churches is Hans Memling's *Crucifixion* (1468–70), the central panel of a triptych whose side panels are now in New York.

In the later rooms are newly cleaned works by the local artist, Bartolomeo Montagna (c.1450–1523), including his remarkable *Pala di San Bartolo Madonna* and *Madonna with Saints*.

Santa Corona

This impressive Gothic church was built in 1261 to house a thorn from Christ's Crown of Thorns, donated by Louis IX of France. In the Porto Chapel is the tomb of Luigi da Porto (died 1529), author of the novel *Giulietta e Romeo*, upon which Shakespeare based his famous play. Notable paintings

Carpione's ceiling fresco in the large entrance hall of the Museo Civico

include Giovanni Bellini's *Baptism of Christ* (c.1500–5) and Paolo Veronese's *Adoration of the Magi* (1573). In the cloister the Museo Naturalistico-Archeologico exhibits natural history and archaeology.

🔒 San Lorenzo
The portal of this church is a magnificent example of Gothic stone carving, richly decorated with the figures of the Virgin and Child, and St Francis and St Clare. Sadly the frescoes inside are damaged, but there are fine tombs. The lovely cloister, north of the church, is a flower-filled haven of calm.

The elegant Villa Rotonda, most famous of all Palladio's works

The beautiful cloister of the church of San Lorenzo

🔒 Monte Berico
Basilica di Monte Berico. ⬤ *daily.*
Monte Berico is the green, cypress-clad hill to the south of Vicenza to which wealthy Vicenzans once escaped in the heat of summer to enjoy the cooler air and bucolic charms of their agricultural estates. Today, shady *portici*, or colonnades, run alongside the wide avenue linking central Vicenza to the basilica on top of the hill. The *portici* have numerous shrines along the route, built for the benefit of pilgrims climbing to the domed basilica. The basilica itself was built in the 15th century and enlarged in the 18th, and is dedicated to the Virgin who appeared on this spot during the 1426–8 plague to announce that Vicenza would be spared.
Coachloads of pilgrims still travel to the lovely Baroque church, where Bartolomeo Montagna's

moving *Pietà* fresco (1572) makes an impact amid the ornate confectionery of the interior. The other attractions that are worth visiting include a good fossil collection in the cloister, and Veronese's fine painting, *The Supper of St Gregory the Great* (1572). This is located in the refectory; if you would like to see the painting you will have to ask. The large canvas was cut to ribbons by bayonet-wielding soldiers during the revolutionary outbursts of 1848 – a picture on the wall next to the work shows how it was painstakingly restored.

♨ Villa Valmarana
Via dei Nani 12. 📞 *(0444) 54 39 76.* ⬤ *mid Mar–end Oct.* ⬤ *Mon.* 📷
The wall alongside the Villa Valmarana (which was built in 1688 by Antonio Muttoni) is topped by the figures of dwarfs which give the building its alternative name – *ai Nani* (of the Dwarfs). Inside, the walls are

The Baroque hilltop church, the Basilica di Monte Berico

covered with gravity-defying frescoes by Giambattista Tiepolo, in which the fleshy and pneumatic gods of Mount Olympus float about on clouds watching scenes from the epics of Homer and Virgil. In the separate Foresteria (guest house), the frescoes with themes of peasant life and the seasons, painted by Tiepolo's son, Giandomenico, are equally decorative but more earthily realistic.
The villa can be reached by a short and enjoyable walk from the basilica on Monte Berico. Head downhill along Via M d'Azeglio to the high-walled convent on the right where the road ends, then take the Via San Bastiano. You will reach the villa after some ten minutes.

♨ Villa Rotonda
Via della Rotonda 25. 📞 *(0444) 32 17 93.* **Villa** ⬤ *15 Mar–15 Oct: Wed.* 📷 **Garden** ⬤ *all year: Tue–Sun.* 📷
With its regular, symmetrical forms, this is the epitome of Palladio's architecture, and the most famous of all his villas. The design, a dome on top of a cube, is simple yet aesthetically satisfying, as is the contrast between the green lawns, crisp white walls and terracotta roof tiles. Built between 1550 and 1552, it has inspired lookalikes in cities as far away as Delhi, London and St Petersburg. Fans of *Don Giovanni* will enjoy spotting locations used in Joseph Losey's 1979 film. To reach the Villa Rotonda, follow the path that passes the Villa Valmarana.

Vicenza: Teatro Olimpico

Europe's oldest surviving indoor theatre, the Teatro Olimpico is an elegant and remarkable structure, largely made of wood and plaster and painted to look like marble. Fashionable architect Andrea Palladio *(see pp24–5)* began work on the design in 1579, but he died the following year without finishing it. His pupil, Vincenzo Scamozzi, took over the project and completed the theatre in time for its ambitious opening performance of Sophocles's tragic drama, *Oedipus Rex*, on 3 March 1585.

Bacchantes
Euripides' Greek tragedy is still performed using Scamozzi's versatile scenery.

Main ticket office

★ **Odeon Frescoes**
The gods of Mount Olympus, after which the theatre is named, decorate the Odeon, a room used for music recitals.

Anteodeon
Oil lamps from the original stage set are now displayed in the theatre's Anteodeon, whose frescoes (1595) depict the theatre's opening performance.

★ **Stage Set**
Scamozzi's scenery represents the Greek city of Thebes. The streets are cleverly painted in perspective and rise at a steep angle to give the illusion of great length.

STAR FEATURES

★ **Stage Set by Vincenzo Scamozzi**

★ **Odeon Frescoes**

Courtyard Sculptures
The courtyard of the former castle is decorated with sculpture donated by members of the Olympic Academy, the learned body that built the theatre.

VISITORS' CHECKLIST

Piazza Matteotti. (0444) 32 37 81. to Piazza Matteotti. 9am–12:15pm, 2:15–4:45pm Mon–Sat, 9am–12:15pm (summer: 2:15–6:45pm also) Sun. Regular theatre performances. No general visits during shows.

Armoury Gateway
This stone gateway, with its military-style carvings, leads from Piazza Matteotti into the picturesque theatre courtyard.

The auditorium was designed by Palladio to resemble the outdoor theatres of ancient Greece and Rome, such as the arena at Verona *(see p195)*, with a semi-circle of "stone" benches (actually made of wood) and a ceiling painted to portray the sky.

Costume Designs for Sofonisba
Ancient Greek vases inspired the costumes for this tragedy (1562) by Palladio's patron, GG Trissino.

Façade Statues
The toga-clad figures are portraits of sponsors who paid for the theatre's construction.

The medieval town of Treviso, built around ancient canals

Treviso **❾**

Road map D3. 🏛 *81,655.* 🚌 **FS**
🛈 *Piazzetta Monte di Pietà 8. (0422)
54 76 32.* 🛒 *Tue & Sat am.*

FULL OF attractive balconied houses overlooking willow-fringed canals, Treviso is a rewarding city for visitors. Comparisons are often made with Venice, but Treviso has its own distinctive character. A good place to explore the architecture is the main street, Calmaggiore, which links the cathedral with the rebuilt 13th-century town hall, the Palazzo dei Trecento. The tradition of painting the exterior of the houses dates back to the medieval period, and this form of decoration, applied to brick and timber, compensated for the lack of suitable building stone. The bustling fish market also dates back to medieval times. It is held on an island in the middle of Treviso's river Sile so that the remains of the day's trading can be flushed away instantly.

⛪ Duomo
Treviso's cathedral, founded in the 12th century, was reconstructed in the 15th, 16th and 18th centuries. Inside is Titian's *Annunciation* (1570), but it is upstaged by the striking *Adoration of the Magi* fresco (1520) of Titian's arch rival, Il Pordenone. Other memorable works are *The Adoration of the Shepherds* fresco by Paris Bordone, and the monument to Bishop Zanetti (1501) by Pietro Lombardo and his sons.

🏛 Museo Civico
Borgo Cavour 24. 📞 *(0422) 51 337.*
🛑 *Tue–Sun.* ⬤ *public hols.* 🎫
The Museo Civico houses an archaeology collection and a picture gallery. The best works are in Room 11 – Lorenzo Lotto's *Portrait of a Dominican* (1526), Titian's *Portrait of Sperone Speroni* (1544) and Bassano's *Crucifixion*. The famous 14th-century frescoes depicting the life of St Ursula, by Tomaso da Modena, have been rehoused in the church of Santa Caterina (for admission ask at the Museo Civico).

⛪ San Nicolò
Nestling near the 16th-century town wall is the bulky Dominican church of San Nicolò, full of tombs and frescoes. The piers of the nave bear vivid portraits of saints by Tomaso da Modena who also painted the humorous pictures of monks (1352) on the chapter house walls, which include the first ever depiction of spectacles in art. A magnificent tomb (1500) by Antonio Rizzo is framed by a fresco of page boys (c.1500) by Lorenzo Lotto.

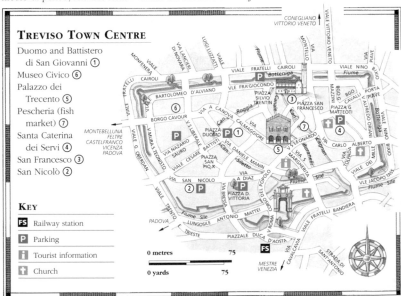

TREVISO TOWN CENTRE

Duomo and Battistero
  di San Giovanni ①
Museo Civico ⑥
Palazzo dei
  Trecento ⑤
Pescheria (fish
  market) ⑦
Santa Caterina
  dei Servi ④
San Francesco ③
San Nicolò ②

KEY
FS Railway station
P Parking
🛈 Tourist information
✝ Church

0 metres   75
0 yards   75

Conegliano ⑩

Road map D3. 🏛 *35,300*. 🚌
🅸 *Via Colombo 45. (0438) 21 230.*
🅰 *Fri.* **Shops closed** *Mon am.*

Conegliano lies between the Prosecco-producing vine-yards and those which produce fine red wine *(see pp238–9)*. Wine makers from both areas learn their craft at Conegliano's renowned wine school. The town's winding and arcaded main street, Via XX Settembre, is lined by 15th- to 18th-century *palazzi*, some decorated with external frescoes, some in Venetian Gothic style. The **Duomo** contains the town's one great work of art, a gorgeous altarpiece by Cima da Conegliano (1460–1518) showing the *Virgin and Child with Saints* (1493). This was commissioned by the religious brotherhood whose frescoed headquarters, the Scuola di Santa Maria dei Buttati, stands beside the Duomo.

Reproductions of Cima's famous paintings are displayed in the **Casa di Cima**, the artist's birthplace. His detailed landscapes were based on the hills around the town; they can still be viewed from the gardens surrounding the **Castelvecchio** (old castle). A small museum of local history is housed in the castle.

🏠 Casa di Cima
Via Cima. 🅲 *(0438) 21 660.*
🅾 *daily (phone to arrange).* 📷
♦ Castelvecchio
Piazzale Castelvecchio. 🅲 *(0438) 228 71.* 🅾 *Tue–Sun (Nov: Sun only).* 📷

A mythical statue on the theatre in Conegliano's Via XX Settembre

The foundations of Roman buildings in Concordia, near Portogruaro

Portogruaro ⑪

Road map E3. 🏛 *26,000*. 🚌 🄵🅂
🅸 *Via Martiri 19–21. (0421) 722 35.*
🅰 *Thu.* **Shops closed** *Mon.*

Situated on the main road linking Venice to Trieste, Portogruaro is the medieval successor to the Roman town of Concordia Sagittaria. Finds from Concordia, including statues, mosaics, tomb inscriptions and building materials, are displayed in the town's **Museo Concordiese**. To see where these were unearthed, visit the modern village of Concordia, 2 km (1 mile) south of Portogruaro, where the footings of ruined Roman buildings can be seen all around the church and baptistry.

🏛 Museo Concordiese
Via Seminaro 22. 🅲 *(0421) 726 74.*
🅾 *daily.* ● *1 Jan, 1 May, Christmas.*

Caorle ⑫

Road map E3. 🏛 *11,700*. 🚌
🅸 *Calle delle Liburniche 11. (0421) 810 85.* 🅰 *Sat am.*

Like Venice, Caorle was built among the swamps of the Venetian lagoon by refugees fleeing the Goths in the 5th century. Today it is a fishing village and a busy beach resort perched on the edge of a huge expanse of purpose-built lagoons, carefully managed to encourage fish to enter and spawn. The young are then fed and farmed.

The area is also of great interest to naturalists for the abundant bird life of the reed-fringed waters. The town's 11th-century **Duomo** is worth a visit for its Pala d'Oro, a gilded altarpiece made up of 12th- and 13th-century Byzantine panel reliefs.

Local fishermen at work in the village of Caorle

Mestre ⑬

Road map D4. 🏛 *183,650*. 🚌
🅸 *Rotatoria Villa Bona Sud, Marghera. (041) 93 77 64.* 🅰 *Wed & Fri am.*

Mestre, the industrial off-spring of Venice, is often favoured by visitors as a cheap base for exploring the region, and there are some good restaurants here. Flying into Venice's Marco Polo airport *(see pp270–71)*, you cannot miss the factories and oil terminals that surround Mestre and its neighbour, Marghera, vital to the region's economy.

Street-by-Street: Padua ⑭

THE CITY CENTRE of Padua (Padova) is one of the liveliest in northern Italy, thanks to a large student population and to the two street markets, one specializing in fruit and the other in vegetables. These take place every day except Sunday around the vast Palazzo della Ragione, the town's medieval law court and council chamber. The colonnades round the exterior of the *palazzo* shelter numerous bars, restaurants and shops selling meat, game, cheeses and wine.

Palazzo del Capitanio
Built between 1599 and 1605 for the head of the city's militia, the tower incorporates an astronomical clock made in 1344.

Piazza dei Signori
is bordered by attractive arcades which house small speciality shops, interesting cafés and old-fashioned wine bars.

Corte Capitaniato, a 14th-century arts faculty (open for concerts), contains frescoes which include a rare portrait of Petrarch.

Loggia della Gran Guardia
Now used as a conference centre, this fine Renaissance building, dating from 1523, once housed the Council of Nobles.

PIAZZA CAPITANIATO

VIA SAN CLEMENTE

PIAZZA DEI SIGNORI

VIA MONTE DI PIETA

VIA MANIN

PIAZZA DEL DUOMO

VIA VANDELLI

VIA GRITTI

VIA SONCIN

The Palazzo del Monte di Pietà has 16th-century arcades and statues enclosing a medieval building.

★ **Duomo and Baptistry**
The 12th-century baptistry of the Duomo contains one of the most complete medieval fresco cycles to survive in Italy, painted by Giusto de' Menabuoi in 1378 and now restored.

KEY

– – –	Suggested route

0 metres   75

0 yards   75

★ **Caffè Pedrocchi**
Built like a Classical temple, the Caffè Pedrocchi has been a famous meeting place for students and intellectuals since it opened in 1831.

Palazzi Communali
This complex, which houses the city's council offices, has a 13th-century defensive tower.

The Palazzo della Ragione, the "Palace of Reason" was, in medieval times, the city court of justice. Its interior is covered with magnificent astrological frescoes.

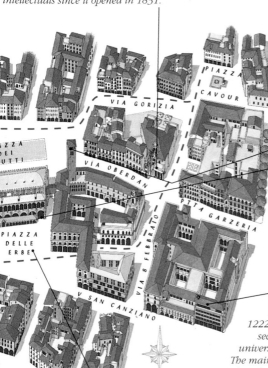

Padua University
Founded in 1222, this is the second oldest university in Italy. The main building dates back to the 16th century.

★ **Piazza delle Erbe**
There are good views on to the market place from Palladio's 15th-century loggia, which runs alongside the Palazzo della Ragione.

STAR SIGHTS

★ **Duomo and Baptistry**

★ **Caffè Pedrocchi**

★ **Piazza delle Erbe**

Exploring Padua

PADUA IS AN OLD UNIVERSITY TOWN with an illustrious academic history. Rich in art and architecture, it has two particularly outstanding sights. The first is the Scrovegni Chapel *(see pp180–81),* situated in the north of the city, which is renowned for Giotto's lyrical frescoes. Close to the railway station, it forms part of the Eremitani museums complex. The second is the Basilica di Sant'Antonio, one of Italy's most popular pilgrim shrines, which forms the focal point for a number of sights in the south of the city *(see p182).*

Sundial on the façade of the Palazzo della Ragione

Detail from the Egyptian room, upper floor of the Caffè Pedrocchi

🏛 Caffè Pedrocchi

Via VIII Febbraio 2. ⬤ *for restoration.*
Grand cafés have long played an important role in the intellectual life of northern Italy, and many knotty philosophical problems have been thrashed out over the tables of the Caffè Pedrocchi since its doors first opened in 1831. Politics superseded philosophy when it became a centre of the Risorgimento movement, dedicated to liberating Italy from Austrian rule; it was the scene of uprisings in 1848, for which several student leaders were executed. Later it became famous as the café that never closed its doors. Althoug currently closed for restoration, its popularity is likely to remain undiminished when it reopens and people will still come to talk, read, play cards or watch the world go by as they eat or drink.

The upstairs rooms, decorated in florid medieval, Moorish, Egyptian, Greek and other styles, are used for lectures, concerts and exhibitions.

🏛 Palazzo del Bo (University)

Via VIII Febbraio 2. ☎ (049) 827 33 00.
⬤ *Tue am, Wed & Fri pm, Thu.* 🈲 ✓
Named after a tavern called *Il Bo* (the ox), the historic main university building is mostly used today for graduation

ceremonies. Originally it housed the medical faculty, renowned throughout Europe. Among its famous teachers and students was Gabriele Fallopio (1523–62), after whom the Fallopian tubes are named.

Elena Lucrezia Corner Piscopia became the first woman graduate in 1678 – long before women were allowed to study at many of Europe's other universities. Her statue stands on the staircase leading to the upper gallery of the 16th-century courtyard.

Visitors on the guided tour are shown the pulpit Galileo used when he taught here from 1592 until 1610. They also see the anatomy theatre, built in 1594, the world's oldest surviving medical lecture theatre.

🏛 Palazzo della Ragione

Piazza delle Erbe. ☎ (049) 820 50 06.
⬤ *Tue–Sun.* ⬤ *1 Jan, 1 May, 25 Dec.* 🈲 ♿
The "Palace of Reason", also known as the "Salone" by locals, was built to serve as Padua's law court and council chamber in 1218. The vast main hall was originally frescoed by the celebrated artist Giotto, but fire destroyed his work in 1420. The frescoes that survive today are by the relatively unknown Nicola Miretto, though their astrological theme is fascinating.

The Salone is breathtaking in its sheer size. It is Europe's biggest undivided medieval hall, 80 m (260 ft) long, 27 m (90 ft) wide and 27 m (90 ft) high. The scale is reinforced by the wooden horse displayed at one end – a massive beast, copied from Donatello's Gattamelata statue *(see p183)* in 1466 and originally made to be pulled in procession during Paduan festivities.

The walls are covered in Miretto's frescoes (1420–25), a total of 333 panels depicting the months of the year with appropriate gods, zodiacal signs and seasonal activities.

Also within the *palazzo* is the Stone of Shame, on which bankrupts were exposed to ridicule before they were sent into exile.

The 16th-century galleried anatomy theatre in the Palazzo del Bo

Eremitani Museums

THIS MAJOR MUSEUM COMPLEX occupies a group of 14th-century monastic buildings attached to the church of the Eremitani, a reclusive Augustinian order. The admission ticket includes entry to the Scrovegni Chapel *(see pp180–81)*, which stands on the same site, overlooking the city's Roman amphitheatre, and to the Archaeology Museum, the Bottacin Museum of coins and medals, and the Medieval and Modern Art Museum, all of which are housed around the cloisters.

The tomb of the Volumni family in the archaeological collection

EREMITANI CHURCH

ALONGSIDE the museum complex is the Eremitani church (1276–1306), with its magnificent roof and wall tombs. Interred here is Marco Benavides (1489–1582), a professor of law at the city university, whose mausoleum was designed by Ammannati, a Renaissance architect from Florence. Sadly missing from the church are Andrea Mantegna's celebrated frescoes of the lives of St James and St Christopher (1454–7), which were destroyed during a bombing raid in 1944. Two scenes from this magnificent work survive in the Ovetari Chapel, south of the sanctuary. *The Martyrdom of St James* was reconstructed from salvaged fragments, and *The Martyrdom of St Christopher* was removed carefully and stored elsewhere before the bombing. Otherwise only photographs on the walls remain to hint at the quality of the lost works.

THE MUSEUMS

THE HIGHLIGHT of the rich archaeological collection is the temple-like tomb of the Volumni family, dating from the 1st century AD. Among several other Roman tombstones from the Veneto region is one to the young dancer, Claudia Toreuma – sadly, a fairly dull inscribed column rather than a portrait. The collection also includes some fine mosaics, along with several impressive life-size statues depicting muscular Roman deities and toga-clad dignitaries. For most visitors the Renaissance bronzes are

Angels in Armour **(15th century) by Guariento in the Art Museum**

likely to be the most appealing feature of the museum, especially the comical *Drinking Satyr* by Il Riccio (1470–1532).

Coin collectors should make a point of visiting the Bottacin Museum. Among the exhibits there is an almost complete set of Venetian coinage and some very rare examples of Roman medallions.

The massive Medieval and Modern Art Museum is in the process of being organized and will eventually cover the entire history of Venetian art, with paintings from Giotto to the present day. Part of the museum that has already been completed looks at Giotto and his influence on local art, using the Crucifix from the Scrovegni Chapel as its centrepiece. The Crucifix is flanked by an army of angels (late 15th century) painted in gorgeous colours by the artist Guariento. Another 15th-century painting worth a look is *Portrait of a Young Senator* by Giovanni Bellini.

Early 14th-century crucifix on loan from the Scrovegni Chapel

VISITORS' CHECKLIST

Piazza Eremitani.
((049) 820 45 50.
○ Feb–Oct: 9am–7pm
Tue–Sun; Nov–Jan: 9am–6pm
Tue–Sun. **Only chapel open**
Mon. ● public hols.

Padua: Scrovegni Chapel

Enrico Scrovegni built this chapel in 1303, hoping thereby to spare his dead father, a usurer, from the eternal damnation wished upon him by the poet Dante in his *Inferno*. The chapel is filled with harmonious frescoes of scenes from the life of Christ, painted by Giotto between 1303 and 1305. As works of great narrative force, they exerted a powerful influence on the development of European art.

The Nativity
The naturalism of the Virgin's pose marks a departure from Byzantine stylization, as does the use of natural blue for the sky, in place of celestial gold

Expulsion of the Merchants
Christ's physical rage, the cowering merchant and the child hiding his face are all typical of Giotto's style.

The Coretti
Giotto painted the two panels known as the Coretti as an exercise in perspective, creating the illusion of an arch with a room beyond.

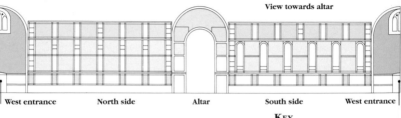

View towards altar

West entrance　　North side　　Altar　　South side　　West entrance

Gallery Guide

It is best to book your visit to the chapel in advance. Long queues often build up at the entrance owing to strict limits on the number of visitors allowed in at any one time. The duration of visits is also timed. If you haven't booked it is best to visit early in the day, before the coach tours arrive, or towards the end of the day. If there is a long queue, try visiting the rest of the Eremitani complex first and return to the chapel later. On entry the custodian will offer you a board, printed in several languages, with a basic numbered key.

Key

☐ Episodes of Joachim and Anna

☐ Episodes from the Life of Mary

☐ Episodes from the Life and Death of Christ

☐ The Virtues and Vices

☐ The Last Judgment

The Last Judgment
*This scene fills the entire
west wall of the chapel.
Its formal composition
is closer to the
Byzantine tradition
than some of the other
frescoes, with parts
probably painted by
assistants. A model of
the chapel is shown,
being offered to the
Virgin by Scrovegni.*

View towards entrance

Mary is Presented at the Temple
*Giotto sets many scenes against an
architectural background, using the
laws of perspective to give a sense of
three dimensions.*

Injustice
*The Virtues and
Vices are
painted in
monochrome.
Here Injustice is
symbolized by
scenes of war,
murder and
robbery.*

Lament over the Dead Christ
*Giotto's figures express their grief
in different ways, some huddled,
some gesturing wildly.*

GIOTTO

The great Florentine artist Giotto
(1266–1337) is regarded as the
father of Western art. His work,
with its sense of pictorial space,
naturalism and narrative drama,
marks a decisive break with the
Byzantine tradition of the preceding 1,000 years. He is the first
Italian master whose name has
passed into posterity, and although
he was regarded in his lifetime as a
great artist, few of the works attributed
to him are fully documented. Some may have been
painted by others, but his authorship of the frescoes
in the Scrovegni Chapel need not be doubted.

The lofty interior of Padua's
16th-century duomo

🔒 Duomo and Baptistry
Padua's duomo was commissioned from Michelangelo in 1552, but his designs were sketchy and much altered during the course of the building work. Of the earlier 4th-century cathedral which stood on the site, the domed Romanesque baptistry still survives, with its vibrant frescoes painted by Giusto de' Menabuoi (c.1376). The frescoes cover biblical stories, such as the Creation, the Miracles, Passion, Crucifixion and Resurrection of Christ, and the Last Judgment.

🔒 Basilica di Sant'Antonio
This exotic church, with its minaret-like spires and Byzantine domes, is also known as Il Santo. It was begun in 1232 to house the remains of St Anthony of Padua, a preacher who modelled himself on St Francis of Assisi. Although he was a simple man who rejected worldly wealth, the citizens of Padua built one of the most lavish churches in Christendom to serve as his shrine.

The exotic outline reflects the influence of Byzantine architecture; a cone-shaped central dome is surrounded by a further seven domes, rising above a façade that combines Gothic with Romanesque elements. The interior is more conventional, however. Visitors are kept away from the high altar, which features Donatello's magnificent reliefs (1444–5) on the miracles of St Anthony, and his statues of the Crucifixion, the Virgin and several Paduan saints. Access is permitted to the tomb of St Anthony in the north transept, which is hung with offerings and photographs of people who have survived car crashes or serious illness thanks to the saint's

The Basilica di Sant'Antonio and Donatello's statue of Gattamelata

The Brenta Canal

THE RIVER BRENTA, between Padua and the Venetian Lagoon, was canalized in the 16th century. Flowing for a total of 36 km (22 miles), its potential as a transport route was quickly realized, and fine villas were built along its length. Today, these elegant buildings can still be admired, and three open their doors to the public: the Villa Foscari at Malcontenta, the Villa Widmann-Foscari at Mira, and the Villa Pisani at Stra. All three can be visited on an 8½-hour guided tour from Padua, travelling to Venice (or from Venice to Padua) along the river on board the Burchiello motor launch.

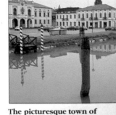

The picturesque town of
Mira on the Brenta Canal

Fiessa d'Artico •   S11

← PADOVA

KEY

▬▬	Tour route
= =	Roads
🚤	Boat stops

Villa Pisani ①
This 18th-century villa features an extravagant frescoed ceiling by Tiepolo.

assistance. The walls around
the shrine are decorated with
large marble reliefs depicting
St Anthony's life, carved in
1505–77 by various artists, including Jacopo Sansovino and
Tullio Lombardo. These are
rather cold by comparison with
the lively *Crucifixion* fresco
(1380s) by Altichiero da Zevio
in the opposite transept. This is
a pageant-like painting, full of
everyday scenes from medieval
life and masterly depictions of
people, animals and plants.

One of four stone bridges spanning the canal around Prato della Valle

⛩ Statue of Gattamelata
Near the entrance to the
basilica stands one of the
great Renaissance works. This
gritty portrait of the mercenary
soldier Gattamelata (whose
name means "Honey Cat") was
created in 1443–52, honour-
ing a man who in his life did
great service to the Venetian
Republic. Donatello won fame
for the monument, the first
equestrian statue made of this
size since Roman times.

⛩ Scuola del Santo and Oratorio di San Giorgio
Piazza del Santo. ☎ (049) 875 52 35.
Scuola ☐ *daily.* ● *1 Jan, 25 Dec.*
Oratorio ● *for restoration.*
These two linked buildings
contain five excellent frescoes,
including the earliest docu-

mented paintings by Titian.
These comprise two scenes
from the life of St Anthony in
the Scuola del Santo, executed
in 1511. The delightful saints'
lives and scenes from the life
of Christ in the San Giorgio
oratory are the work of two
artists, Altichiero da Zevio
and Jacopo Avenzo, who
painted them in 1378–84.

❧ Orto Botanico
Via Orto Botanico 15. ☎ (049) 65
66 14. ☐ *Apr–Oct: 9am–1pm,
3–6pm daily; Nov–Mar: 9am–1pm
Mon–Sat.* 🖼 &
Founded in 1545, Padua's
botanical garden is the oldest
in Europe, and it retains much
of its original appearance; one
of the palm trees dates to 1585.
Originally intended for the
cultivation of medicinal plants,

the pathways now spill over
with exotic foliage, shaded by
ancient trees. The gardens were
used to cultivate the first lilacs
(1565), sunflowers (1568) and
potatoes (1590) grown in Italy.

⛩ Prato della Valle
The Prato (field) claims to be
the largest public square in
Italy, and its elliptical shape
reflects the form of the Roman
theatre that stood on the site.
St Anthony of Padua used
to preach sermons to huge
crowds here, but subsequent
neglect saw the area turn into
a malaria-ridden swamp. The
land was drained in 1767 to
create the canal that now
encircles the Prato. Four stone
bridges cross the picturesque
channel, which is lined on
both sides by statues of 78
eminent citizens of Padua.

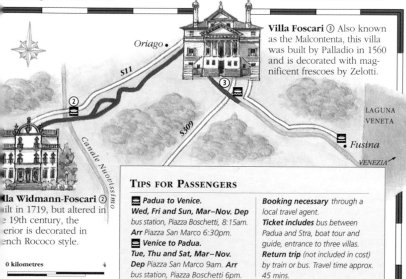

Villa Foscari ③ Also known
as the Malcontenta, this villa
was built by Palladio in 1560
and is decorated with magnificent frescoes by Zelotti.

Oriago

S11

③

LAGUNA
VENETA

Canale Nuovissimo

S309

🚏 *Fusina*

VENEZIA

②

la Widmann-Foscari ②
ilt in 1719, but altered in
e 19th century, the
erior is decorated in
ench Rococo style.

0 kilometres — 4

0 miles — 2

TIPS FOR PASSENGERS
🚌 **Padua to Venice.**
Wed, Fri and Sun, Mar–Nov. Dep
bus station, Piazza Boschetti, 8:15am.
Arr *Piazza San Marco 6:30pm.*
🚌 **Venice to Padua.**
Tue, Thu and Sat, Mar–Nov.
Dep *Piazza San Marco 9am.* **Arr**
bus station, Piazza Boschetti 6pm.

Booking necessary *through a
local travel agent.*
Ticket includes *bus between
Padua and Stra, boat tour and
guide, entrance to three villas.*
Return trip *(not included in cost)
by train or bus. Travel time approx.
45 mins.*

The Euganean Hills, formed by ancient volcanic activity

Euganean Hills ⑮

Road map C4. 🚶 *10,000.*
ℹ️ *Viale Stazione 60, Montegrotto Terme.* ☎ *(049) 79 33 84.*

T HE CONICAL Euganean Hills, remnants of long-extinct volcanoes, rise abruptly out of the surrounding plain. Hot springs bubble up out of the ground at Abano Terme and Montegrotto Terme where scores of establishments offer thermal treatments, ranging from mud baths to immersion in the hot sulphurated waters. Spa cures such as this date back to Roman times, and you can see extensive remains of the Roman baths and theatre at Montegrotto.

🏠 Abbazia di Praglia

Via Abbazia di Praglia, Bresseo di Teòlo. ☎ *(049) 990 00 10.*
🕐 *Tue–Sun pm.*
The Benedictine monastery at Praglia, 6 km (4 miles) west of Abano Terme, is a peaceful haven in the tree-clad hills. Here the monks grow herbs commercially and restore ancient books. They also lead guided tours of the dignified Renaissance church (1490–1548), which is renowned for its beautiful cloister.

🏛 Casa di Petrarca

Via Valleselle 4, Arquà Petrarca.
☎ *(0429) 71 82 94.* 🕐 *Tue–Sun.*
📷
The picturesque town of Arquà Petrarca, on the southern edge of the Euganean hills, was once simply Arquà. Its name changed in 1868 to honour the medieval poet, Francesco Petrarca, known in English as

Petrarch (1303–74), who lived here in his old age. He had often sung the praises of the well-tended landscape of olive groves and vineyards, and spent the last few years of his life living in a house frescoed with scenes from his lyrical poems. Though the house has since been altered, it still contains the poet's desk and chair, his bookshelves and his mummified cat, while the setting is as beautiful as ever. Petrarch is buried in a simple sarcophagus located in the piazza in front of the church.

🏛 Villa Barbarigo

Valsanzibio. ☎ *(049) 913 00 42 .*
🕐 *Feb–Nov.* 📷
To the north of Arquà is the Villa Barbarigo at Valsanzibio, the only one of scores of villas, built by wealthy Paduans, regularly open to the public. The villa itself is of a simple design compared with the Baroque garden. Planted from 1669, it is full of variety, with fountains, statues and lakes.

The house of the poet Petrarch in the town of Arquà Petrarca

Montagnana ⑯

Road map C4. 🚶 *10,000.* 🚌 📷
ℹ️ *Piazza Trieste 3. (0429) 813 20.*
📅 *Thu. **Shops closed** Mon am & Wed pm.*

M EDIEVAL brick walls encircle this town, extending for 1,895 m (2,105 yd), pierced by four gateways and defended by 24 towers. Entering through the eastern Padua Gate, it is impossible to miss Palladio's **Villa Pisani** (c.1560), with its façade featuring the original owner's name (Federico Pisani) in bold letters below the pediment. Just inside the castellated Padua Gate is the town's archaeological museum. The Gothic–Renaissance **Duomo** contains Paolo Veronese's *Transfiguration* (1555).

Antique market in Montagnana

Este ⑰

Road map C4. 🚶 *17,600.* 🚌
📷 ℹ️ *Piazza Maggiore 9A. (0429) 36 35.* 📅 *Wed & Sat am. **Shops closed** Mon & Wed am.*

E XCAVATIONS at Este have un-covered impressive remains of the ancient Ateste people, who flourished from the 9th century BC until they were conquered by the Romans in the 4th century BC. The arch-aeological finds, including funerary urns, figurines, bronze vases and jewellery, are on display in the excellent **Museo Nazionale Atestino**, set with-in the walls of the town's 14th-century castle. The mus-eum also displays examples of Roman and medieval art, and pieces of local pottery, famous since the Renaissance period, and still produced.

🏛 **Museo Atestino**

Palazzo Mocenigo. █ *(0429) 20 85.* ⬤ *daily.* ⬤ *1 Jan, 1 May, 25 Dec.* 📷

Monsélice ⓲

Road map C4. 🏘 *17,000.* FS ➡
ℹ *Via Roma 1. (0429) 78 30 26.*
🛒 *Mon.* **Shops closed** *Mon am, Wed pm.*

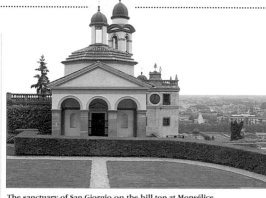

The sanctuary of San Giorgio on the hill top at Monsélice

T HE TOWN of Monsélice stands around the foot of a hill quarried extensively on its western flank for rich deposits of crystalline minerals. The castle-topped hill is now a nature reserve and nesting site for rare birds of prey. The hilltop is therefore out of bounds, but you can climb up Via del Santuario as far as **San Giorgio**, to see its exquisite inlaid marble work.

Returning to the lower town, note the 13th-century cathedral and the statue-filled Baroque gardens of the Villa Nani that can be glimpsed through the villa gates. Nearby is **Ca' Marcello**, a 14th-century castle with wonderful period furnishings, fine frescoes and tapestries, and suits of armour on display.

Marble inlay detail from San Giorgio

🏰 **Ca' Marcello**

Via del Santuario. █ *(0429) 729 31.* ⬤ *Apr–mid-Nov: Tue–Sun.* 📷 🎫

Polésine and Rovigo ⓳

Road map C5. ➡ ℹ *Via J. Dunant 10, Rovigo. (0425) 36 14 81.*

P OLESINE is the flat expanse of fertile agricultural land, crisscrossed by canals and subject to flooding, that lies between the river Adige and the Po. The Po delta has a wealth of fascinating birdlife, with visitors such as egrets, herons, curlews and bitterns.

The most scenic areas are around Scardovari and Porto Tolle, on the south side of the Po. Companies in Porto Tolle offer canoe and bicycle hire and half-day boat cruises.

The modern city of Rovigo has one outstanding monument, the splendid octagonal church called **La Rotonda** (1594–1602), decorated with paintings and statues in niches.

ENVIRONS: Ancient Adria, 22 km (14 miles) east of Rovigo, was founded as a Greek port, but a deliberate programme of land reclamation and silt deposition has now left Adria dry, apart from a 24-km (15-mile) canal. The exhibits in the **Museo Archeologico** explain the town's changing fortunes and the fascinating display items include a complete iron chariot dating from the 4th century BC.

🏛 **Museo Archeologico**

Via Badini 59, Adria. █ *(0426) 216 12.* ⬤ *daily.* ⬤ *1 Jan, 1 May, 25 Dec.* 📷

Chioggia ⓴

Road map D4. 🏘 *56,000.* ➡ FS
🚢 ℹ *Lungomare Adriatico 101. (041) 40 10 68.* 🛒 *Thu.*

C HIOGGIA is the principal fishing port on the lagoon and the bustling, colourful **fish market** is a good reason to come here early in the day (open every morning except Monday). Many visitors enjoy the gritty character of the port area, with its smells, its vibrantly coloured boats and the tangle of nets and tackle. The town also has numerous inexpensive restaurants which serve fresh fish in almost every variety. Eel, crab and cuttlefish are the local specialities. There is a beach area at Sottomarina, on the western part of the island. Worth seeking out for a special visit is Carpaccio's *St Paul* (1520), the artist's last known work, which is permanently housed in the church of **San Domenico**.

Net mending in the traditional way, Chioggia

VERONA AND LAKE GARDA

VERONA IS ONE OF NORTHERN ITALY'S *most alluring cities, its noble palaces, quiet cloisters and ancient streets every bit as romantic as you would expect of Romeo and Juliet's city. On the doorstep are the well-known vineyards of Soave, Bardolino and Valpolicella, set against the rugged slopes of the Little Dolomites. To the west lie the beautiful shores of Lake Garda, a mere 30 minutes' drive from Verona by car, but a world away in atmosphere.*

Set within the curves of the river Adige, Verona has been a prosperous and cosmopolitan city since the Romans colonized it in 89 BC. It stands astride two important trade routes – the Serenissima, connecting the great port cities of Venice and Genoa, and the Brenner Pass, used by commercial travellers crossing the Alps from northern Europe. This helps to explain the Germanic influence in Verona's magnificent San Zeno church, or the realism of the paintings in the Castelvecchio museum, owing more to Dürer than to Raphael.

Verona's passion and panache, however, is purely Italian. Stylish shops and cafés sit amid the impressive remains of Roman monuments. The massive Arena amphitheatre fills with crowds of 20,000 or more, who thrill to opera beneath the stars. All over the city, art galleries and theatres testify to a crowded calendar of cultural activities.

Italy's largest lake, Lake Garda, is renowned for its beautiful scenery. The broad southern end of the lake, with its waterfront promenades, is very popular with Italian and German visitors. Those in search of peace can escape to the heights of the Monte Baldo mountain range, rising above the eastern shore. The ridge marks the western edge of the mountainous region north of Verona. Here is the great plateau of Monti Lessini, with its little river valleys that fan out southwards to join the river Adige.

Giardino Giusti in Verona, one of Italy's finest Renaissance gardens

◁ The pretty cobbled streets of Sirmione

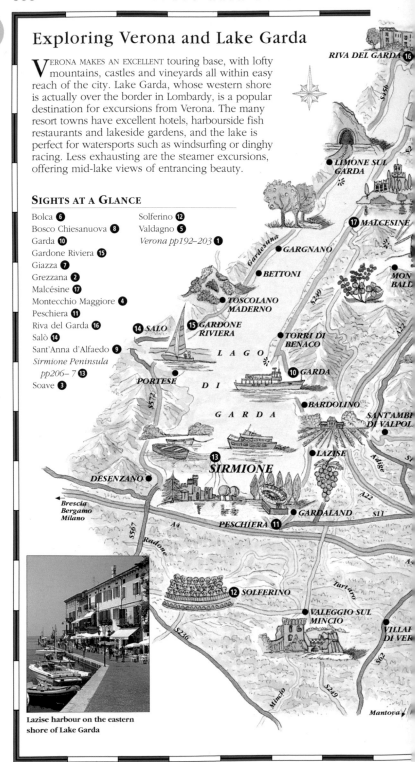

Exploring Verona and Lake Garda

Verona makes an excellent touring base, with lofty mountains, castles and vineyards all within easy reach of the city. Lake Garda, whose western shore is actually over the border in Lombardy, is a popular destination for excursions from Verona. The many resort towns have excellent hotels, harbourside fish restaurants and lakeside gardens, and the lake is perfect for watersports such as windsurfing or dinghy racing. Less exhausting are the steamer excursions, offering mid-lake views of entrancing beauty.

SIGHTS AT A GLANCE

Bolca **6**
Bosco Chiesanuova **8**
Garda **10**
Gardone Riviera **15**
Giazza **7**
Grezzana **2**
Malcésine **17**
Montecchio Maggiore **4**
Peschiera **11**
Riva del Garda **16**
Salò **14**
Sant'Anna d'Alfaedo **9**
Sirmione Peninsula pp206–7 **13**
Soave **3**

Solferino **12**
Valdagno **5**
Verona pp192–203 **1**

RIVA DEL GARDA **16**

LIMONE SUL GARDA

17 MALCESINE

GARGNANO

BETTONI

MON BALD

TOSCOLANO MADERNO

14 SALO

15 GARDONE RIVIERA

TORRI DI BENACO

L A G O

PORTESE

D I

10 GARDA

BARDOLINO

SANT'AMBI DI VALPOL

G A R D A

DESENZANO

13
SIRMIONE

LAZISE

GARDALAND

PESCHIERA **11**

Brescia
Bergamo
Milano

12 SOLFERINO

VALEGGIO SUL MINCIO

VILLAF DI VER

Mantova

Lazise harbour on the eastern shore of Lake Garda

GETTING AROUND

The roads around Verona are heavily used by commercial vehicles and commuter traffic, so expect delays, especially during morning and evening rush hours. Motorways are faster, but are among the oldest in Italy, only two lanes wide and subject to frequent roadworks. There is a good east–west rail service, linking Verona to the southern shores of Lake Garda, but for north–south travel, to the mountains and around the lake, buses are the only public transport option. For ferries across Lake Garda, see p204.

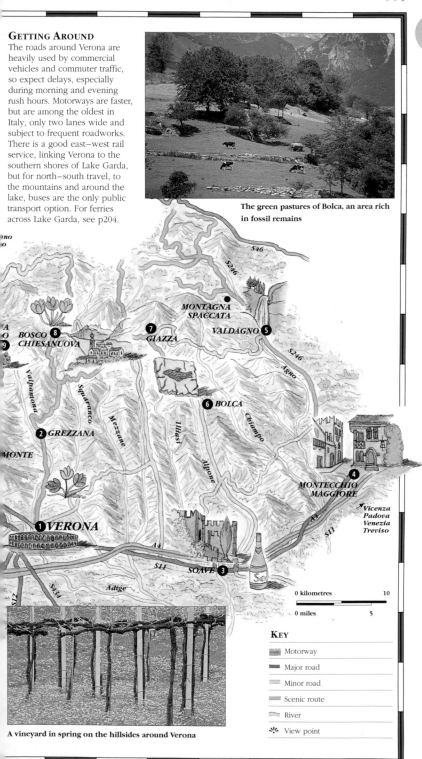

The green pastures of Bolca, an area rich in fossil remains

A vineyard in spring on the hillsides around Verona

KEY

▬	Motorway
▬	Major road
▬	Minor road
▬	Scenic route
▭	River
❊	View point

0 kilometres   10

0 miles   5

The 14th-century Castello Romeo, on a hill overlooking Montecchio

Verona ❶

See pp192–203.

Grezzana ❷

Road map B4. 🚹 *9,680.* 🚌
ℹ *Via Marconi, 14.* 🏛 *1st Wed and 3rd Fri each month.*

IN GREZZANA itself, seek out the 13th-century church of Santa Maria which, though frequently rebuilt, retains its robustly carved Romanesque font and its campanile of gold, white and pink limestone.

ENVIRONS: Grezzana is in the foothills of the scenic Piccole Dolomiti or Little Dolomites. Close to the town, at nearby Cuzzano, is the 17th-century Baroque **Villa Allegri-Arvedi**. To the south, in Santa Maria in Stelle, is a Roman nymphaeum (a shrine to the nymphs who guard the fresh-water spring) next to the church (known as the Pantheon).

🏛 **Villa Allegri-Arvedi**
Cuzzano di Grezzana.
📞 *(045) 90 70 45.*
🕐 *for groups only (book by phone).* 📷 ♿

Soave ❸

Road map B4. 🚹 *6,820.* 🚌
ℹ *Piazza Antenna 2. (045) 768 06 48.* 🏛 *Tue.*

SOAVE IS a heavily fortified town ringed by 14th-century walls. Its name is familiar all over Europe because of the light and dry white wine that is produced and exported from here in great quantity. Visitors will see few vineyards around the town, since these are mainly located in the hills to the north, but evidence of the industry can be seen in the gleaming factories on the outskirts, where the Garganega grapes are crushed and the fermented wine bottled. Cafés and wine cellars in the town centre provide plenty of opportunity for sampling the local wine.

The city walls rise up the hill to the dramatically sited **Rocca Scaligeri**, an ancient castle enlarged in the 14th century by the Scaligeri rulers of Verona and furnished in period style.

🏰 **Rocca Scaligeri**
Via Castello Scaligero.
📞 *(045) 768 00 36.* 🕐 *Tue–Sun.* 📷

Rocca Scaligeri, the ancient castle in Soave

Montecchio Maggiore ❹

Road map C4. 🚹 *20,000.* 🚌
ℹ *Via Leonardo da Vinci 50, Alta di Montecchio. (0444) 69 65 46.*
🏛 *Fri am, Sat pm.*

VISITORS TO industrialized Montecchio Maggiore come principally to see the two 14th-century castles on the hill above the town. In popular legend these are known as the **Castello di Romeo** and the **Castello di Giulietta**. There is no evidence that they belonged to Verona's rival Capulet and Montague families *(see p199)*, but they look romantic, and provide lovely views over the vineyard-clad hills to the north.

♣ **Castello di Romeo**
Via Castelli 4 Martiri. 📞 *(0444) 49 12 95.* 🕐 *Sun pm.*
♣ **Castello di Giulietta**
Via Castelli 4 Martiri. 📞 *(0444) 49 12 95.* 🕐 *Wed pm, Thu–Mon am & pm.*

The dramatic gorge of Montagna Spaccata, north of Valdagno

Valdagno ❺

Road map C3. 🚹 *28,000.* 🚌
ℹ *Viale Trento. (0445) 40 11 90.*
🏛 *Tue am, Fri am.*

A SCENIC DRIVE of 20 km (12 miles) from Montecchio Maggiore leads to Valdagno, a town of woollen mills and 18th-century houses. Just northwest is the Montagna Spaccata, its rocky bulk split by a dramatic 100-m (330-ft) deep gorge and waterfall.

Fossilized plant remains found in the rocks near Bolca

Bolca ⑥

Road map B3. 👥 *500.* 🚌
Shops closed *Mon am (clothes), Wed pm (food).*

PRETTY BOLCA sits at the centre of the Monti Lessini plateau, looking down the valley of the river Alpone and surrounded by fossil-bearing hills. The most spectacular finds have been transferred to Verona's Museo Civico di Scienze Naturali *(see p203)*, but the local **Museo di Fossili** still has an impressive collection of fish, plants and reptiles preserved in the local basalt stone. A circular walk of 3 km (2 miles) from the town (details available from the museum) takes in the quarries where the fossils were found.

🏛 **Museo di Fossili**
Via San Giovanni Battista.
📞 *(045) 656 50 88.* ⬜ *daily.* 📷

Giazza ⑦

Road map B3. 👥 *220.* 🚌
🛈 *Via Zagaro 24. (045) 784 71 60.*
Shops closed *Mon am (clothes), Wed pm (food).*

THE SMALL TOWN of Giazza has an almost Alpine appearance. Its **Museo Etnografico** covers the history of the Tredici Comuni (the Thirteen Communes). In reality there are far more than 13 little hamlets dotted about the plateau, many of them settled by Bavarian farmers who migrated from the German side of the Alps in the 13th century. Cimbro,

their German-influenced dialect, has now all but died, but other traditions survive. For example, their huge mountain horns, *tromboni*, are still part of local festivities.

🏛 **Museo Etnografico**
Via dei Boschi, 62. 📞 *(045) 784 70 50.* ⬜ *daily in summer; Sat & Sun in winter.* 📷 ♿

Bosco Chiesanuova ⑧

Road map B3. 👥 *2,985.* 🚉 🚌
🛈 *Piazza della Chiesa 34. (045) 705 00 88.* 🚌 *Sun.*

ONE OF THE principal ski resorts of the region, Bosco Chiesanuova is well supplied with hotels, ski lifts and cross-country routes. To the east, near Camposilvano, is the **Valle delle Sfingi** (valley of the sphinxes), so called because of its large and impressive rock formations.

Sant'Anna d'Alfaedo ⑨

Road map B3. 👥 *2,458.* 🚌 🛈 *in Bosco Chiesanuova.* 🚌 *Wed am.*

DISTINCTIVELY Alpine in character, Sant'Anna d'Alfaedo is noted for the stone tiles used to roof local houses. The hamlet of Fosse, immediately to the north, is a popular base for walking excursions up the **Corno d'Aquilio** (1,546 m/5,070 ft), a mountain which boasts one of the world's deepest potholes, the **Spluga della Preta**, 850 m (2,790 ft) deep.

More accessible is another natural wonder, the **Ponte di Veia**, just south of Sant'Anna, a great stone arch bridging the valley. Prehistoric finds have been excavated from the caves at either end. This spectacular natural bridge is one of the largest of its kind in the world.

The town of Giazza, spectacularly situated on the Monti Lessini plateau

Verona ❶

Dragon carving on Duomo façade

V ERONA IS A VIBRANT and self-
confident city, the second biggest
in the Veneto region (after Venice)
and one of the most prosperous in
northern Italy. Its ancient centre
boasts many magnificent Roman
remains, second only to those of
Rome itself, and *palazzi* built of *rosso di Verona*, the
local pink-tinged limestone, by the city's medieval
rulers. Verona has two main focal points, the massive
1st-century AD Arena and the Piazza Erbe
with its colourful market, separated by a
maze of narrow lanes lined with some of
Italy's most elegant boutiques.

Verona as seen from the Museo Archeologico

Verona's rulers

In 1263 the Scaligeri
began their 127-year
rule of Verona. They
used ruthless tactics
in their rise to
power, earning
nicknames like
Mastino (Mastiff)
and Cangrande
(Big Dog), but
once in power
the Scaligeri family
brought peace to a
city racked by civil
strife and inter-family
rivalry. They proved
to be relatively just and
cultured rulers – the poet
Dante was welcomed to
their court in 1301–4, and
he dedicated his *Paradise*,
final part of the epic *Divine
Comedy*, to Cangrande I.

Verona fell to the Visconti
of Milan in 1387, and a succession of outsiders – Venice,
France and Austria – followed
before the Veneto was united
with Italy in 1866.

Fruit and vegetable stall in a side street of old Verona

KEY

▦	Street-by-Street map *See pp196–7*
▫	Pedestrian area
FS	Railway station
P	Parking
✚	Tourist information
✚	Church

♣ Castelvecchio

Corso Castelvecchio 2. **[** (045) 59 44 34. ☐ Tue–Sun. 🗺 🕭

This spectacular castle, built by Cangrande II between 1355 and 1375, has been transformed into one of the Veneto's finest art galleries. Various parts of the medieval structure have been linked together using aerial walkways and corridors, designed to give striking views of the building itself, as well as the exhibits within. Arranged chronologically, these are excellent and varied.

The first section contains a wealth of late Roman and early Christian material – 7th-century silver plate that shows armoured knights in combat, 5th-century brooches and glass painted with a portrait of Christ the Shepherd in gold. The martyrdom scenes depicted on the carved marble sarcophagus of Saints Sergius and Bacchus (1179) are gruesomely realistic.

The following section, which is devoted to medieval and early Renaissance art, vividly demonstrates the influence of northern art on local painters, suggesting strong links with Verona's neighbours across the Alps. Here, instead of the serene saints and virgins of Tuscan art, the emphasis is on brutal realism. This is summed up in the 14th-century *Crucifixion with Saints*, which depicts the tortured musculature of Christ and the racked faces of the mourners in painful detail. Far more lyrical is a beautiful 15th-century painting by Stefano da Verona called *The Madonna of the Rose Garden*. This contains many allusions to popular medieval fables, including the figure of Fortune with her wheel. In the painting the Virgin sits in a pretty garden alive with decorative birds and angels gathering rosebuds.

Other Madonnas from the 15th century, attributed to Giovanni Bellini, are displayed among the late Renaissance works upstairs. Jewellery, suits of armour, swords and shield bosses feature next, some dating back to the 6th and 7th centuries when Verona

Cangrande I's horse in ceremonial garb

was under attack from Teutonic invaders from beyond the Alpine range.

After the armour room, take the walkway that leads out along the river flank of the castle, with its dizzying views of the swirling waters of the river Adige and the Ponte Scaligero (*see p194*). Next, turning a corner, one finds Cangrande I, his equestrian statue dramatically displayed out of doors on a plinth. This 14th-century statue once graced Cangrande's tomb (*see p198*), and is remounted here. It is possible to study every detail of the horse and rider draped in their ceremonial garb. Despite Cangrande's cherubic cheeks and inane grin, his face is remarkably forceful and compelling.

Beyond lie some of the museum's celebrated paintings, notably Paolo Veronese's *Deposition* (1565) and a portrait attributed by some to Titian, by others to Lorenzo Lotto.

SIGHTS AT A GLANCE

Arco dei Gavi ④
Arena ⑦
Castelvecchio ③
Duomo ⑫
Giardino Giusti ⑱
Museo Archeologico ⑯
Museo Civico di Scienze Naturali ⑲
Museo Lapidario Maffeiano ⑤
Piazza Erbe ⑨
Piazza dei Signori ⑧
Ponte Scaligero ②
Sant'Anastasia ⑪
San Fermo Maggiore ⑥
San Giorgio in Braida ⑬
Santa Maria Antica ⑩
Santa Maria in Organo ⑰
Santo Stefano ⑭
San Zeno Maggiore ①
Teatro Romano ⑮

0 metres   500
0 yards   500

Courtyard of Castelvecchio

Around the Arena

MOST VISITORS TO Verona first arrive at Piazza Brà, a large, irregularly shaped square with a public garden. On the north side is an archway known as the Portoni della Brà. Dominating the eastern side of the piazza is the Roman Arena, Verona's most important monument, still in use today for operatic performances. The piazza is ringed with 19th-century buildings that resemble ancient temples and historical landmarks.

Ponte Scaligero, part of the old defence system of Castelvecchio

♦ Ponte Scaligero

This medieval bridge was built by Cangrande II between 1354 and 1376. The people of Verona love to stroll across it to ponder the river Adige in all its moods, or to admire summer sunsets and distant views of the Alps. Such is their affection for the bridge that it was rebuilt after the retreating Germans blew it up in 1945, an operation that involved dredging the river to salvage the medieval masonry. The bridge leads from Castelvecchio *(see p193)* to the Arsenal on the north bank of the Adige, built by the Austrians between 1840 and 1861 and now fronted by public gardens. Looking back from the gardens it is possible to see how the river was used as a natural moat to defend the castle, with the bridge providing the inhabitants with an escape route.

♦ Arco dei Gavi and Corso Cavour

Dwarfed by the massive brick walls of Castelvecchio, the monumental scale of this Roman triumphal arch is now hard to appreciate. Originally the arch straddled the main Roman road into the city, today's Corso Cavour. But French troops who were occupying Castelvecchio in 1805 damaged the monument so much that a decision was made to move it to its present, less conspicuous position just off the Corso in 1933.

Continuing up Corso Cavour, there are some fine medieval and Renaissance palaces to admire (especially Nos. 10, 11 and 19) before the Roman town gate, the **Porta dei Borsari**, is reached. The gate dates from the 1st century BC, but looking at the pedimented windows and niches it is not difficult to see what influenced the city's Renaissance architects.

The Roman Arco dei Gavi, 1st century AD

🏛 Museo Lapidario Maffeiano

Piazza Brà 28. ☎ *(045) 59 00 87.* ◯ *Tue–Sun.* 🔲
This "museum of stone" displays all kinds of architectural fragments hinting at the last splendour of the Roman city. There are numerous carved funerary monuments, and a large part of the collection consists of Greek inscriptions collected by the museum's 18th-century founder, Scipione Maffei.

♦ San Fermo Maggiore

San Fermo Maggiore consists of not one but two churches. This can best be appreciated from the outside, where the eastern end is a jumble of rounded Romanesque arches below with pointed Gothic arches rising above. The lower church, now rather dank because of frequent flooding, dates from 1065, but the upper church of 1313 is more impressive. It has a splendid ship's keel roof, masses of medieval fresco work and some monumental tombs. Frescoes from the 14th century, just inside the main door, are by Stefano de Zevico. They show the fate meted out to four Franciscan missionaries who journeyed to India in the mid 14th century. Nearby is the Brenzoni mausoleum (1439) by Giovanni di Bartolo with Pisanello's *Annunciation* fresco (1426) above. In the south aisle is an unusually ornate pulpit of 1396 with saints in canopied niches above, surrounded by frescoes of the Evangelists and Doctors of the Church.

The apse of the lower church of San Fermo Maggiore

The Arena

Verona's amphitheatre, completed around AD 30, is the third largest in the world, after Rome's Colosseum and the amphitheatre at Capua, near Naples. Originally, the Arena could hold almost the entire population of Roman Verona, and visitors came from across the Veneto to watch mock battles and gladiatorial combats. Since then, the Arena has been used for public executions, fairs, theatre performances, bullfighting and opera.

VISITORS' CHECKLIST

Piazza Brà, Verona.
(045) 800 32 04.
Tue–Sun 9am–7pm, **last adm:** 6:30pm. Mon, 25 & 26 Dec. Access via arcades 5 and 7. Classical concerts and operas (see pp256–7).

Interior
The interior has survived virtually intact, maintained by the Arena Conservators since 1580.

The façade of the Arena seen from Piazza Brà

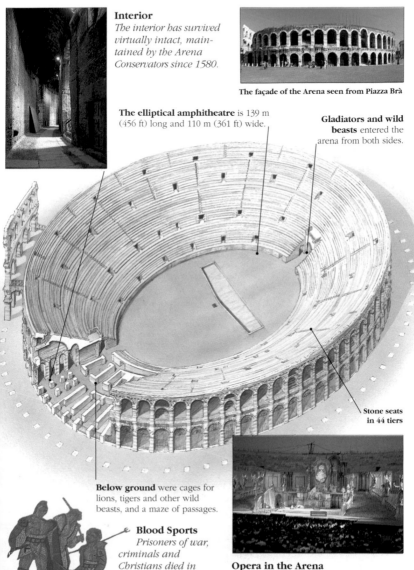

The elliptical amphitheatre is 139 m (456 ft) long and 110 m (361 ft) wide.

Gladiators and wild beasts entered the arena from both sides.

Stone seats in 44 tiers

Below ground were cages for lions, tigers and other wild beasts, and a maze of passages.

Blood Sports
Prisoners of war, criminals and Christians died in their thousands in the name of entertainment.

Opera in the Arena
Today, performances of Verdi's Aida *and other popular operas can attract a capacity crowd of 25,000.*

Street-by-Street: Verona

SINCE THE DAYS OF THE ROMAN EMPIRE, the Piazza Erbe has been the centre of Verona's commercial and administrative life. Built on the site of the ancient Roman forum, it is an enjoyably chaotic square, bustling with life. Shoppers browse in the colourful market at stalls sheltered from the sun by wide-brimmed umbrellas. The massive towers and *palazzi* of the Scaligeri rulers of Verona have retained their medieval feel, even though they have been altered and adapted many times.

★ Piazza dei Signori
This square is bordered by individual Scaligeri palazzi *linked by Renaissance arcades and carved stone archways.*

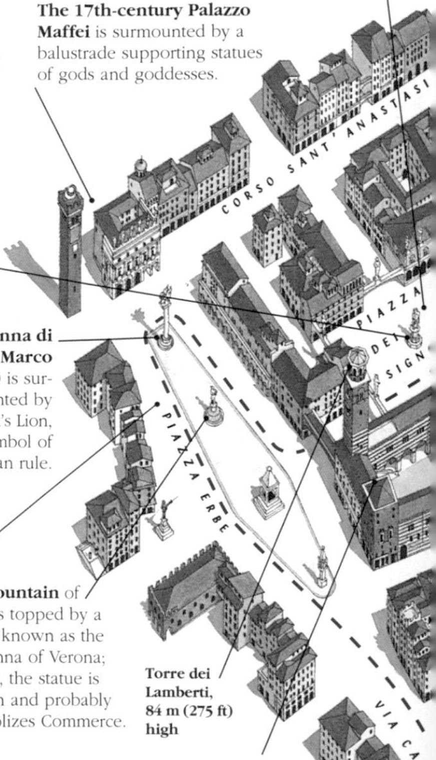

Statue of Dante
Dante, the medieval poet, stayed in Verona as a guest of the Scaligeri during his period in exile from his native Florence. His statue (1865) looks down on Piazza dei Signori.

The 17th-century Palazzo Maffei is surmounted by a balustrade supporting statues of gods and goddesses.

CORSO SANT'ANASTASIA

PIAZZA DEI SIGN

Colonna di San Marco (1528) is surmounted by St Mark's Lion, the symbol of Venetian rule.

PIAZZA ERBE

The fountain of 1368 is topped by a figure known as the Madonna of Verona; in fact, the statue is Roman and probably symbolizes Commerce.

Torre dei Lamberti, 84 m (275 ft) high

VIA CAP

Piazza Erbe
Verona's medieval herb market is now lined with art galleries, up-market boutiques and inviting pavement cafés.

Palazzo della Ragione
The medieval Palace of Reason features an elegant Renaissance staircase. It leads from the exterior court-yard into the magistrates' rooms on the upper floor.

Via Sottoriva is lined with arcaded medieval houses and typifies the heart of the old city.

Sant'Anastasia
Carved hunchbacks (gobbi), crafted in 1495, form the unusual supports for the holy water stoups in this church.

★ **Scaligeri Tombs**
In this masterpiece of 14th-century Gothic funerary art, soldier saints stand guard around the tombs, a reminder of the military prowess of Verona's powerful medieval rulers.

Santa Maria Antica is a little Romanesque church which dates back to the 7th century. The canopied tomb of Cangrande I rises above the entrance.

Ponte Nuovo
The "new bridge" (1540) spans the river Adige, linking the hills on the east bank of the city with Verona's historic centre.

0 metres	100
0 yards	100

KEY

- - - Suggested route

STAR SIGHTS

★ **Piazza dei Signori**

★ **Scaligeri Tombs**

Casa di Giulietta
The House of Juliet looks the part, with its marble balcony and romantic setting, although there is no evidence linking this house with the romantic legend.

Central Verona

THE STREETS OF THIS ANCIENT city centre owe their grid-like layout to the order and precision of the Romans. At the heart is the lively Piazza Erbe, where crowds shop in the ancient market place. The fine *palazzi*, churches and monuments date mostly from the medieval period.

An elegant café in the spacious Piazza dei Signori

🏛 Piazza Erbe

Piazza Erbe is named after the city's old herb market. Today's stalls, shaded by huge umbrellas, sell everything from lunchtime snacks of herb-flavoured roast suckling pig in bread rolls to fresh-picked fruit or delicious wild mushrooms.

The **Venetian lion** that stands on top of a column to the north of the square marks Verona's absorption in 1405 into the Venetian empire. The statue-topped building that completes the north end of Piazza Erbe is the baroque **Palazzo Maffei** (1668), now converted to shops and luxury apartments. An assortment of boutiques and cafés line the edge of the square.

The **fountain** that splashes away quietly in the middle of the piazza is often overlooked amid the competing attractions of the market's colourful stalls. Yet the statue at the fountain's centre dates from Roman times, a reminder that this long piazza has been in almost continuous use as a market place for 2,000 years.

🏛 Piazza dei Signori

In the centre of Piazza dei Signori is a 19th-century **statue of Dante**, who surveys

Stonework detail, Piazza dei Signori

the surrounding buildings with an appraising eye. His gaze is fixed on the grim **Palazzo del Capitano**, home of Verona's military commander, and the equally intimidating **Palazzo della Ragione**, the palace of Reason, or law court, both built in the 14th century. The Palazzo della Ragione is not quite so grim within. The courtyard has a handsome external stone staircase, added in 1446–50. Fine views of the Alps can be had by climbing the 84-m (275-ft) **Torre dei Lamberti**, which rises from the western side of the courtyard.

Behind the statue of Dante is the pretty Renaissance **Loggia del Consiglio**, or council chamber, with its frescoed upper façade (1493) and statues of Roman worthies born in Verona. These include Catullus the poet, Pliny the natural historian and Vitruvius the architectural theorist.

The piazza is linked to Piazza Erbe by the Arco della Costa, or the arch of the rib, whose name refers to the whale rib hung beneath it, put up here as a curiosity in the distant past.

🔒 Santa Maria Antica

This tiny Romanesque church is almost swamped by the bizarre Scaligeri tombs built up against its entrance wall. Because Santa Maria Antica was their parish church, the Scaligeri rulers of Verona chose to be buried here, and their tombs speak of their military prowess *(see p207)*.

Over the entrance to the church is the impressive tomb of Cangrande I, or Big Dog (died 1329), topped by his equestrian statue. This statue is a copy; the original is now in the Castelvecchio *(see p193)*. The other Scaligeri tombs are next to the church, surrounded by an intricate wrought-iron fence featuring the ladder motif of the family's original name (*della Scala*, meaning "of the steps"). Towering above the fence are the spire-topped tombs of Mastino II, or Mastiff (died 1351) and Cansignorio, meaning Noble Dog (died 1375).

The fountain in Piazza Erbe, erected in the 14th century

These two tombs are splendidly decorated with Gothic pinnacles, bristling like lances. In their craftsmanship and design there is nothing else in European funerary architecture quite like these spiky, thrusting monuments.

Plainer tombs nearer the church wall mark the resting place of other members of the Scaligeri family – Mastino (died 1277) who founded the Scaligeri dynasty, having been elected mayor of Verona in 1260, and two who did not have dog-based names: Bartolomeo (died 1304) and Giovanni (died 1359).

🔒 Sant'Anastasia

A huge and lofty church, Sant'Anastasia was begun in 1290 and built to hold the massive congregations who came to listen to the rousing sermons typically preached by members of the fundamentalist Dominican order. The most interesting aspect of the church is its Gothic portal, with its faded 15th-century frescoes and carved scenes

The lofty, Romanesque interior of Sant'Anastasia

The façade of the Duomo, Santa Maria Matricolare

from the life of St Peter Martyr, and in the two holy water stoups inside. These are supported on delightfully realistic figures of beggars in ragged clothing, known as *i gobbi*, the hunchbacks (the one on the left carved in 1495, the other a century later).

Off the north aisle is the sacristy, home to Antonio Pisanello's fresco, *St George and the Princess* (1433–38). Despite being badly damaged, the fresco still conveys something of the aristocratic grace of the Princess of Trebizond, with her noble brow and her ermine-fringed cloak, as St George prepares to mount his horse in pursuit of the dragon.

🔒 Duomo

Visitors to Verona's cathedral (begun in 1139) pass through a magnificent Romanesque portal carved by Nicolò, one of the two master masons who carved the façade of San Zeno *(see pp200–201)*. Here

he sculpted the swordbearing figures of Oliver and Roland, knights whose exploits in the service of Charlemagne were celebrated in medieval poetry. Alongside them stand saints and evangelists with bold staring eyes and flowing beards. To the south there is a second Romanesque portal carved with Jonah and the Whale (removed for restoration) and comically grotesque caryatids (load-bearing figures).

The highlight of the interior is Titian's *Assumption* (1535–40) in the first chapel on the left. Further down on the left is the entrance to the Romanesque cloister which contains excavated remains of earlier churches on the site. It also leads to the baptistry, known as San Giovanni in Fonte (St John of the Spring). This 8th-century church, built from Roman masonry, features a massive marble font carved in 1200 with scenes from the life of Christ.

ROMEO AND JULIET

The tragic story of Romeo and Juliet, written by Luigi da Porto of Vicenza in the 1520s, inspired countless poems, films, ballets and dramas. At the **Casa di Giulietta** (Juliet's house), No. 27 Via Cappello, Romeo is said to have climbed to Juliet's balcony: in reality this is a restored 13th-century inn. Crowds throng here, but few visit the run-down house dubbed the **Casa di Romeo** in Via delle Arche Scaligeri. More rewarding for visitors is the so-called **Tomba di Giulietta**, displayed in a crypt below the cloister of San Francesco al Corso on Via del Pontiere. The plain and empty stone sarcophagus is not especially riveting in itself, but the setting is atmospheric.

The lovers *Romeo and Juliet* from a 19th-century illustration

Verona: San Zeno Maggiore

Stone façade detail

BUILT BETWEEN 1123 and 1135 to house the shrine of Verona's patron saint, San Zeno is northern Italy's most ornate Romanesque church. The façade is embellished with marble reliefs of biblical scenes, matched in vitality by bronze door panels showing the miracles of San Zeno. Beneath an impressive rose window, a graceful porch canopy rests on two slim columns. A brick campanile soars to the south, while a squat tower to the north is said to cover the tomb of King Pepin of Italy (777–810).

Nave Ceiling
The nave has a magnificent example of a ship's keel ceiling, so called because it resembles the inside of an upturned boat. This ceiling was constructed in 1386 when the apse was rebuilt.

Striped brickwork is typical of Romanesque buildings in Verona. Courses of local pink brick are alternated with ivory-coloured tufa.

Altarpiece
Andrea Mantegna's three-part altarpiece (1457–59) depicts the Virgin and Child with various saints. The painting served as an inspiration to local artists.

★ Cloister
North of the church the fine, airy cloister (1123) has rounded Romanesque arches on one side and pointed Gothic arches on the other.

STAR FEATURES

★ West Doors

★ Cloister

★ Crypt

BRONZE DOOR PANELS

The 48 bronze panels of the west doors are primitive but forceful in their depiction of biblical stories and scenes from the life of San Zeno. Those on the left date from 1030 and survive from an earlier church on the site; those on the right were made 100 years later. Huge staring eyes and Ottoman-style hats, armour and architecture feature prominently, and the meaning of some scenes is not known – the woman suckling two crocodiles, for example.

| **Descent into limbo** | **Christ in Glory** | **Human head** |

VISITORS' CHECKLIST

Piazza San Zeno. ☎ (045) 800 61 20. 🚌 31, 32, 33 from Castelvecchio. ◐ 8:30am–6:30pm Mon–Sat, Sun pm. ✝ Sun & after 6pm Mon–Sat. ◐ during services. 📷 ♿

Nave and Main Altar
The nave of the church is modelled on an ancient Roman basilica, the Hall of Justice. The main altar is situated in the raised sanctuary where the judge's throne would have stood.

The campanile, started in 1045, reached its present height of 72 m (236 ft) in 1178.

Rood Screen
Marble statues of Christ and the Apostles, dating from 1250, are ranged along the sanctuary rood screen.

The rose window
symbolizes the Wheel of Fortune: figures around the rim show the rise and fall of human fortunes.

Marble side panels, carved in 1140, depict events from the life of Christ to the left of the doors, and scenes from the Book of Genesis to the right.

★ West Doors
Each of the wooden doors has 24 bronze plates joined by bronze masks, nailed on to the wood to look like solid metal. A bas relief above the doors depicts San Zeno vanquishing the devil.

★ Crypt
The vaulted crypt contains the tomb of San Zeno, appointed first bishop of Verona in AD 362, who died in AD 380.

Across the Ponte Romano

THE PONTE ROMANO, or Roman Bridge, links Verona's city centre to the eastern bank of the river Adige. This up-market residential district is dotted with fine palaces, gardens and churches, and offers good views back on to the towers and domes of the medieval city.

View from the Teatro Romano across the river Adige

♪ Teatro Romano

Rigaste Redentore 2. 【 (045) 800 03 60. ☐ Tue–Sun. 🎫

When this theatre was built in the 1st century BC the plays performed would have included satirical dramas by such writers as Terence and Plautus. The tradition continues with open-air perform-ances at the annual Shakespeare festival.

The theatre is built into a bank above the river Adige, and the views over the city must have been every bit as entrancing to the Roman theatregoers as the events being enacted on stage. Certainly it is for the views that the theatre is best visited today, since little survives of the original stage area, though the semi-circular seating area remains largely intact.

In the foreground of the view is one of three Roman bridges that brought traffic into the city. This is the only one to have survived, although it had to be painstakingly reconstructed after World War II. In common with all the city's bridges it was blown up in 1945 by retreating German soldiers who were attempting to delay the advance of Allied troops. Of the five arches, the two nearest to the theatre are least altered.

⛁ Museo Archeologico

Rigaste Redentore 2. 【 (045) 800 03 60. ☐ Tue–Sun. 🎫

A lift carries visitors from the Teatro Romano up through the cliffs to the monastery above. This is now converted into an archaeological museum in which panoramic views over the city vie for attention with the range of exhibits. The first part of the museum displays well-restored mosaics, one of which depicts the kind of gory gladia-torial combat that once went on in Verona's amphi-theatre (see p195). Such barbaric performances, seen as a legitimate way of disposing of crimi-nals and prisoners of war, finally came to an end in the early 5th century following a decree from the Christian Emperor Honorius.

In the little mon-astic cells to the side of this room, visitors can see a bronze bust of the first Roman emper-or, the young Augustus Caesar (63 BC–AD 14), who succeeded in

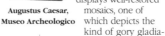

Augustus Caesar, Museo Archeologico

outmanoeuvring his oppo-nents, including Mark Antony and Cleopatra, to become the sole ruler of the Roman world in 31 BC. The subject of the female bust in the adjoining cell is unknown. Next comes the tiny cloister, littered with mosaics and ancient masonry fragments, and an extensive warren of ancient rooms which are used to display pottery, glass, inscriptions and tombstones. Labelling stops after a while and visi-tors are left to puzzle out the age and nature of exhibits for themselves.

⛪ Santo Stefano

This is one of the city's oldest churches; the original, long-demolished building was constructed in the 6th century. It served as Verona's cathedral until the 12th century when the new Duomo was built (see p199) on the opposite bank of the Adige. Visitors to Santo Stefano are afforded a striking view of the Duomo across the river, taking in the Romanesque apse and the bishop's palace alongside. Santo Stefano itself was rebuilt at the same time by Lombard architects and given its octa-gonal red brick campanile, but the original apse survives.

Inside the church there is a Byzantine-influenced arrange-ment of a stone bishop's seat and bench, and a gallery with 8th-century carved capitals. The apse (which is often locked) is even older, dating back to the original 6th-century building. In the crypt there are fragments of 13th-century frescoes and a 14th-century statue of St Peter.

Towering above the church to the east is Castel San Pietro, strikingly fronted by flame-shaped cypress trees. The present castle was built in 1854 under Austrian rule, but it stands on the ruins of an earlier castle which was built by the Visconti of Milan when the Milanese captured Verona in 1387.

Figure of St Peter, Santo Stefano

🔒 San Giorgio in Braida

San Giorgio is a rare example in Verona of a domed Renaissance church. It was begun in 1477 by Michele Sanmicheli, an architect best known for his military works. Sanmicheli also designed the classically inspired altar, which is topped by Paolo Veronese's *Martyrdom of St George* (1566). This celebrated painting is outshone by the calm and serene *Virgin Enthroned between St Zeno and St Lawrence* (1526) by Girolamo dai Libri. This work has a beautifully detailed background landscape and a lemon tree growing behind the Virgin's throne.

Marquetry cockerel in Santa Maria in Organo

🔒 Santa Maria in Organo

Some of the finest inlaid woodwork to be seen in Italy is in this church. The artist was Fra Giovanni da Verona, an architect and craftsman who worked for nearly 25 years, from 1477 to 1501, on these stunning examples of illusionistic marquetry. The seat backs in the choir and cupboard fronts in the sacristy are full of entertaining detail. By clever interpretation of perspective, Fra Giovanni gave depth to flat landscapes, depicted city views glimpsed through an open window, and created "cupboard interiors" stacked with books, musical instruments, or bowls of fruit. Most charming of all are the little animal pictures – look out for the rabbit on the lectern and the owl and the cockerel in the sacristy.

Fossilized fish from Verona's natural history museum

🏛 Museo Civico di Storia Naturali

Lungadige Porta Vittoria 9.
📞 (045) 807 94 00. ⭘ daily
exc Fri. 📷

Verona's natural history museum contains an outstanding collection of fossils which can be enjoyed on a purely aesthetic level without any knowledge of palaeontology. Whole fish, trees, fern leaves and dragonflies are captured in extraordinary detail. The fossils were found in rock in the foothills of the Little Dolomites north of the city during quarrying for building stone *(see* Bolca, *p191).*

Human prehistory is represented by finds from ancient settlements round Lake Garda, and there are reconstructions of original lake villages. On the upper floor, cases full of stuffed birds, animals and fish provide an extensive account of today's living world, making this a good museum for visiting with children or on rainy days.

🌿 Giardino Giusti

Via Giardino Giusti 2. 📞 (045) 803 40 29. ⭘ daily. 📷 ♿

Hidden among the dusty façades of the Via Giardino Giusti is the entrance to one of Italy's finest Renaissance gardens. They were laid out in 1580 and, as with other gardens of the period, artifice and nature are deliberately juxtaposed. The formal lower garden of clipped box hedges, gravel walks and potted plants is contrasted with an upper area of wilder natural woodland, the two parts linked by stone terracing.

Past visitors have included the English traveller Thomas Coryate who, writing in 1611, called this garden "a second paradise". The diarist John Evelyn, visiting 50 years later, thought it the finest garden in Europe. Today the garden makes an excellent spot for a quiet picnic.

Italianate topiary and statuary in the Giardino Giusti

Around Lake Garda

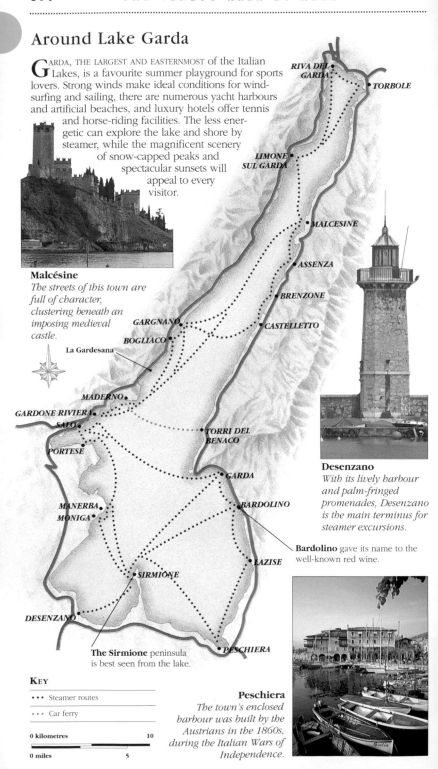

Garda, THE LARGEST AND EASTERNMOST of the Italian Lakes, is a favourite summer playground for sports lovers. Strong winds make ideal conditions for windsurfing and sailing, there are numerous yacht harbours and artificial beaches, and luxury hotels offer tennis and horse-riding facilities. The less energetic can explore the lake and shore by steamer, while the magnificent scenery of snow-capped peaks and spectacular sunsets will appeal to every visitor.

Malcésine
The streets of this town are full of character, clustering beneath an imposing medieval castle.

Desenzano
With its lively harbour and palm-fringed promenades, Desenzano is the main terminus for steamer excursions.

Bardolino gave its name to the well-known red wine.

The Sirmione peninsula is best seen from the lake.

KEY

••• Steamer routes

••• Car ferry

0 kilometres   10

0 miles   5

Peschiera
The town's enclosed harbour was built by the Austrians in the 1860s, during the Italian Wars of Independence.

LA GARDESANA

This is the name given to the 143-km (89-mile) perimeter road that hugs the lake shore. For much of its route the road is cut through solid rock, sometimes following a narrow ledge in the cliff face, sometimes passing through tunnels (around 80 in total). The switchback route offers spectacular views at every turn, particularly at Gargnano, and there are numerous viewing points. Places of interest along La Gardesana include the splendid 18th-century gardens of Palazzo Bettoni at Bagliaco and the castle at Riva del Garda.

The scenic road to Limone

LAKE TRIPS

Lake Garda's ferries are still called steamers, even though they are diesel-powered today. The major towns around the southern rim of the lake all have jetties where you can buy a ticket and board the boat for a leisurely cruise. From the water you can see gardens and villas that are otherwise hidden from view. A trip from one end of the lake to the other takes approximately two hours 20 minutes. There is also a regular hydrofoil service around the lake, and catamarans operate around the southern end.

The hydrofoil operating out of Desenzano harbour

Lake Garda steamer at dusk near Peschiera

Garda ⑩

Road map A3. 🏠 *3,400.* 🚌 🛈 *Lungolago Regina Adelaide 3 (045) 725 51 94.* 🕒 *Fri.* **Shops closed** *Wed pm.*

NUMEROUS PAVEMENT cafés brighten the streets and fill the air with conversation around the central Palazzo dei Capitani, which was built in the 15th century for the use of the Venetian militia. The small town museum has exhibits relating to prehistoric rock engravings found at Punta San Vigilio, 2 km (1 mile) west of the town.

Peschiera ⑪

Road map A4. 🏠 *8,800.* 🚌 🛈 *Piazza Municipio. (045) 755 16 73.* 🕒 *Mon am.* **Shops closed** *Wed in winter.*

AT PESCHIERA the River Mincio flows out of Lake Garda to join the River Po. The fortress at the entrance was built by Austrians in the 19th century. Named Fortezza del Quadrilatero because of its square shape, it replaced a 15th-century stronghold.

ENVIRONS: Just outside the town is **Gardaland**, a theme park with a replica of the ancient Egyptian Valley of the Kings. Another attraction for children is the **Parco Faunistico**, a zoo with a safari park and models of dinosaurs.

🌿 **Gardaland**
Loc. Ronchi, 37014 Castelnuovo del Garda. 📞 *(045) 644 97 77 or 644 95 55.* 🕒 *Apr–Sep.* 🖼

🌿 **Parco Faunistico**
Nr. Bussolengo. 📞 *(045) 717 00 80.* 🕒 *mid-Mar–Oct: 9:30am–6pm daily; Nov–mid-Mar: Sat & Sun.* 🖼

Solferino ⑫

Road map A4. 🏠 *2,118.* 🚌 🛈 *Via Francese. (0376) 85 40 68.* 🕒 *Sat pm.* **Shops closed** *Mon pm.*

THE BATTLE of Solferino (1859) left 40,000 Italian and Austrian troops dead and injured, abandoned without medical care or burial. Shocked by such neglect, a Swiss man named Henri Dunant began a campaign for better treatment. The result was the first Geneva Convention, signed in 1863, and the establishment of the International Red Cross. In the town of Solferino there is a war museum and an ossuary chapel, lined with bones from the battlefield. There is also a memorial to Dunant built by the Red Cross with donations from member nations.

The ossuary chapel at Solferino, lined with skulls

Sirmione Peninsula ⑬

CHARMING SIRMIONE is a finger of land extending into the southern end of Lake Garda,
connected to the mainland by a bridge. The
Roman poet Catullus (born in 848 BC) owned
a villa here: the ruins of the Grotte di Catullo
lie among ancient olive trees at the northern
tip. The Rocca Scaligeri castle stands guard at
the base of the peninsula, and beyond, the
narrow streets of the
village give way to
peaceful lakeside walks
and elegant spa hotels.

View Towards the Grotto
*The high central tower commands
views over the castle and the whole
of the Sirmione peninsula.*

★ Rocca Scaligeri
*The castle was built in
the 13th century by the
Scaligeri of Verona. It is
cleverly designed to trap
shipborne invaders,
leaving them vulnerable
to missiles dropped from
the castle walls.*

**The main keep
tower** was used
for bombarding
attackers trapped
below.

The moat, originally a
complex defence system,
is today home to carp.

**Piazza
Castello**

Sirmione Old Town
*Narrow stone-paved streets
are packed with shops
selling crafts and souvenirs.*

**Visiting the
Peninsula**
*Cars must be parked
before entering
Sirmione, leaving
the medieval streets
for pedestrians.*

STAR FEATURES

★ **Rocca Scaligeri**

★ **Grotte di Catullo**

VISITORS' CHECKLIST

Road map A4. 🚌 🚢 ℹ️ *Viale Marconi 2. (030) 91 61 14.* **Rocca Scaligeri and Castle Museum** 📞 (030) 91 64 68. 🕐 Apr–Sep: 9am–6pm daily. Oct–Mar: 9am–1pm Tue–Sun. 🚫🎫 **Grotte di Catullo** 📞 (030) 91 61 57. 🕐 8:30am–7pm (4pm in winter) Tue–Sat, 9am–6pm (4pm in winter) Sun & public hols. ⬤ Mon. 🎫

Lakeside Walk
Following the eastern shores of the peninsula, this pretty walk links the village to the Grotte di Catullo.

San Pietro
Founded in AD 765, on Sirmione's highest point, this church contains a 12th-century fresco of Christ in Majesty.

★ Grotte di Catullo
This complex of villas, baths and shops, built as a resort for wealthy Romans from the 1st century BC, lies ruined here. Finds are displayed in the Antiquarium building.

The inner harbour provided a haven for fishermen during lake storms and an anchorage for the castle fleet.

The drawbridge is heavily fortified, linking the castle to the mainland and offering an escape route to its inhabitants.

THE SCALIGERI

The Rocca Scaligeri is one of many castles built throughout the Verona and Lake Garda region by the Scaligeri family *(see p192)*. During the turbulent 13th and 14th centuries, powerful military rulers fought each other incessantly in pursuit of riches and power. Despite the autocratic nature of their rule, the Scaligeri brought a period of peace and prosperity to the region, fending off attacks by the predatory Visconti family who ruled neighbouring Lombardy.

The Scaligeri ruler, Cangrande I

Salò ⑭

Road map A3. 🏘 *10,000.* 🚉
ℹ *Lungolago Zanardelli.* 🚌 *Sat.*

LOCALS PREFER to associate this elegant town with Gaspare da Salò (1540–1609), the inventor of the violin, rather than with Mussolini, the World War II dictator. Mussolini set up the so-called Salò Republic in 1943 and ruled northern Italy from here until 1945, when he was shot by the Italian resistance.

Happier memories are evoked by Salò's buildings, including the cathedral with its unusual wooden altarpiece (1510) by Paolo Veneziano. The main appeal of the town derives from its waterfront buildings, painted in pastel shades, and the lake views. Salò marks the start of the Riviera Bresciana, where the shore is lined with luxurious villas and grand hotels set in semi-tropical gardens.

Gardone Riviera ⑮

Road map A3. 🏘 *2,500.* 🚉
ℹ *Corso Repubblica 37.* 🚌 *Wed.*

GARDONE'S MOST appealing feature is the terraced public park which cascades down the hillside, planted with noble and exotic trees. Equally exotic are the Mediterranean and African plants in the **Hruska Botanical**

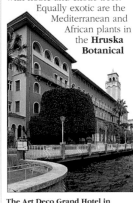

The Art Deco Grand Hotel in Gardone Riviera

Gardens, founded in 1910, which benefit from the town's mild winter climate. Gardone has long been a popular resort – the magnificent 19th-century **Villa Alba** (now a congress centre) was built for the Austrian emperor to escape the bitter winters of his own country. The Art Deco **Grand Hotel** on the waterfront was built for lesser beings.

High above the town is the **Villa il Vittoriale**, built for the poet, Gabriele d'Annunzio. His Art Deco villa has blacked-out windows (he professed to loathe the world) and is full of curiosities, including a coffin-shaped bed. The garden has a landlocked warship, the prow raised high over Lake Garda.

🌺 **Hruska Botanical Gardens**
Via Roma. ◯ *daily Mar–Oct.*
♿

🏛 **Villa il Vittoriale**
Via Vittoriale 12. 📞 *(0365) 201 30.*
◯ *Tue–Sun.* ● *1 Apr.* ♿

Valpolicella Wine Tour

THIS CIRCULAR TOUR takes in the beautiful, remarkably varied scenery of the wine district that lies between Verona and Lake Garda. On the shores of Lake Garda itself, deep and fertile glacial soils provide sustenance for the grapes that are used to make Bardolino, a wine that is meant to be drunk young *(see pp238– 9)*. Inland, the rolling foothills of the Lessini mountains shelter hamlets where lives and working rhythms are tuned to the needs of the vines. These particular vines are grown to produce the equally famed Valpolicella, a red wine that varies from light and fruity to full-bodied.

TIPS FOR DRIVERS

Starting point: Verona.
Length: 45 km (28 miles).
Approximate driving time: 3 hours.
Stopping-off points: The main village of the Valpolicella region, San Pietro in Cariano, has cafés and restaurants.

Affi ④
This wine-producing village is surrounded by vineyards planted in the sheltered basin of the Adige Valley.

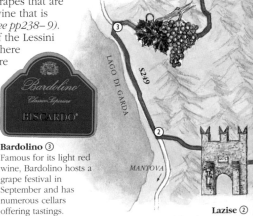

Bardolino ③
Famous for its light red wine, Bardolino hosts a grape festival in September and has numerous cellars offering tastings.

Lazise ②
Lazise has long been the chief port of Garda's eastern shore, its picturesque harbour and medieval church guarded by a 14th-century castle.

KEY

━━━ Tour route
═══ Other roads

Looking across Lake Garda from Riva del Garda

Riva del Garda ⑯

Road map B3. 🏠 *13,600.* 🚌
🛈 *Giardini di Porta Orientale 8.
(0464) 55 44 44.* 🛥 *2nd & 4th Wed
in summer.* **Shops closed** *Mon, Sat
pm in winter.*

L IVELY RIVA'S waterfront is
overlooked by the moated
Rocca di Riva, a former
Scaliger fortress. Inside is a

good museum, with exhibits
from the region's prehistoric
lake villages, built by driving
huge piles far out into the
lake bed to support house
platforms. Today, windsurfers
use the lake because of the
consistent offshore winds.

⚓ **Rocca di Riva**
Piazza Cesare Battista. 📞 *(0464) 57
38 69.* ◯ *Tue–Sun.* 🎟 &

Malcésine ⑰

Road map B3. 🏠 *3,500.* 🚌
🛈 *Via Capitanato 6. (045) 740 05
55.* 🛥 *Sat.*

G ERMAN VISITORS who come
to Malcésine trace the
journey taken by the poet
Goethe in 1788. His travels
were full of mishaps, and at
Malcésine he was accused of
spying and locked up.

From Malcésine, visitors can
take the **cable car** up to the
flat summit of Monte Baldo
(1,745 m/5,725 ft). The
journey takes 15 minutes, and
on a clear day it is possible to
see the distant peaks of the
Dolomites and the Gruppo di
Brenta range. Footpaths for
walkers are signposted at the
top. The lower slopes are
designated nature reserves; a
good place to see the local
flora is the **Riserva Naturale
Gardesana Orientale**, just to
the north of Malcésine.

Sant'Ambrogio di Valpolicella ⑤
Apart from red wine, this village
is a source of the pink stone
used for Verona's palaces.

Gargagnago ⑥
The Alighieri wine estate
is owned by a direct
descendant of the
medieval poet Dante, and
set around a 14th-century
villa built by Dante's son.

Cloisters of San Giorgio in Valpolicella

Pedemonte ⑦
The Villa Santa Sofia wine
estate operates out of a
theatrical villa designed by
Palladio, but never
completed.

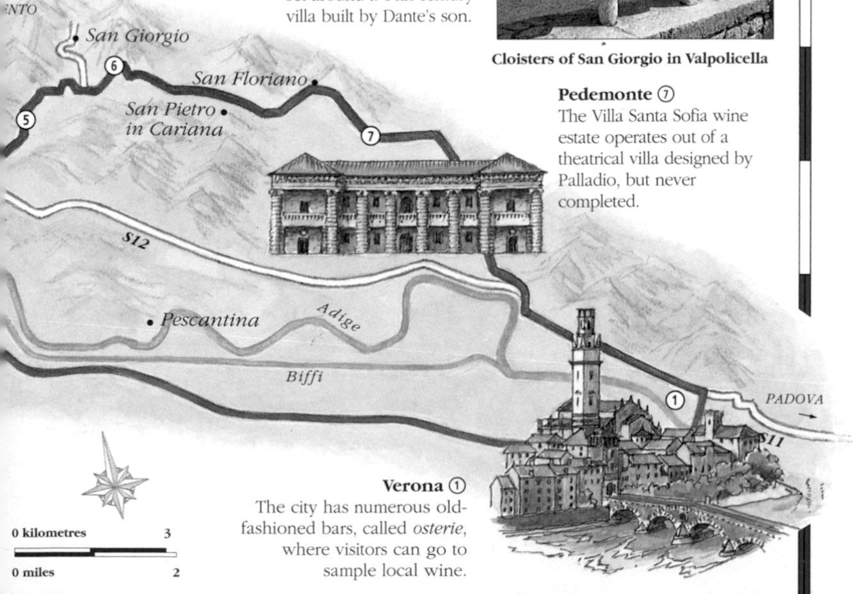

San Giorgio
⑥
San Floriano
*San Pietro
in Cariana*
⑤
⑦
S12
Pescantina
Adige
Biffi
PADOVA
①
S11

Verona ①
The city has numerous old-
fashioned bars, called *osterie*,
where visitors can go to
sample local wine.

0 kilometres   3

0 miles   2

THE DOLOMITES

T HE NAME OF THE DOLOMITES *conjures up a vision of spectacular mountains, as noble and awe-inspiring as the Alps. To the south of the region lie the cities of Feltre, Belluno and Vittorio Veneto. To the north is the renowned ski resort of Cortina d'Ampezzo. In between, travellers will encounter no more cities – just ravishing views, unfolding endlessly, and pretty hamlets tucked into remarkably lush and sunny south-facing valleys.*

The Dolomites cover a substantial portion of the Veneto's land mass, and it is easy to forget, when visiting the cities of the flat Veneto plain, that behind them lies this range of mountains rising to heights of 2,000 m (6,500 ft) and more. Catering for an urban population hungry for fresh air and freedom, the towns and villages of the Dolomites have striven to balance the needs of tourism and nature.

Italian is the region's principal language, although German is also widely spoken, reflecting the region's strong historic links with the Austrian Tyrol. Once ruled by the Hapsburgs, certain areas of the region only became part of Italy in 1918, after the break up of the Austro-Hungarian empire at the end of World War I. Some of that war's fiercest fighting took place in the Dolomites, as both sides tried to wrest control of the strategic valley passes linking Italy and Austria-Hungary.

Striking war memorials in many villages and towns provide a sad reminder of that time.

Today the region is renowned for its winter sports facilities. International cross-country ski competitions were held in Cortina d'Ampezzo as early as 1902, and in 1956 the town hosted the Winter Olympics. Today, Cortina is considered to be Italy's most exclusive resort, the winter playground of film stars and royalty.

Outdoor café in the old town of Feltre

◁ Pleasure boats on Lake Misurina, looking towards the peaks of the Sorapiss

Exploring the Dolomites

Titian's
statue, Pieve
di Cadore

THE ENVIRONMENT of the Dolomites is completely
different from the industrialized Veneto plain.
Huge areas are designated nature reserves,
while others, accessible by chair lifts, allow
visitors to enjoy the views and appetite-
sharpening treks in the mountain meadows.
Refuges, dotted along the high trails, offer
dormitory accommodation and
refreshments, while hamlets
have comfortable hotels.
Snow covers the peaks
from October to May,
and it is possible to ski all
year round on Marmolada,
at 3,343 m (10,970 ft) the
highest peak in the Dolomites.

Mountain chalet near the stadium at
Cortina d'Ampezzo

SIGHTS AT A GLANCE

Belluno ⑤
Cortina d'Ampezzo ①
Dolomites (Dolomiti)
    pp216–17 ④
Feltre ⑦
Misurina ②
Pieve di Cadore ③
Valzoldana ⑥
Vittorio Veneto ⑧

0 kilometres   10

0 miles   5

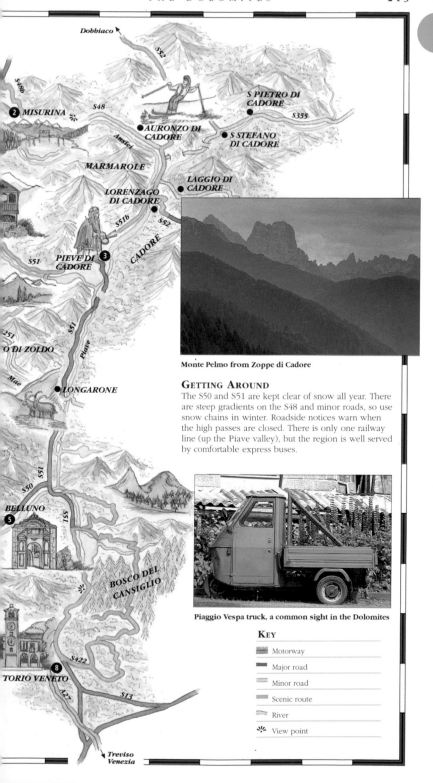

Dobbiaco

S52

S48b

2 MISURINA

S48

● AURONZO DI CADORE

S PIETRO DI CADORE

S355

● S STEFANO DI CADORE

Ansiei

MARMAROLE

LAGGIO DI ● CADORE

LORENZAGO DI CADORE

S51b

S52

S51

PIEVE DI CADORE 3

CADORE

S51

S51

251

Piave

O DI ZOLDO

Mae

● LONGARONE

Monte Pelmo from Zoppe di Cadore

GETTING AROUND

The S50 and S51 are kept clear of snow all year. There are steep gradients on the S48 and minor roads, so use snow chains in winter. Roadside notices warn when the high passes are closed. There is only one railway line (up the Piave valley), but the region is well served by comfortable express buses.

S51

S50

BELLUNO 5

S51

BOSCO DEL CANSIGLIO

Piaggio Vespa truck, a common sight in the Dolomites

S422

8

TORIO VENETO

427

S13

KEY

	Motorway
	Major road
	Minor road
	Scenic route
	River
※	View point

Treviso Venezia

Cortina d'Ampezzo **1**

Road map D1. **7,000.**
Piazzetta San Francesco 8. (0436)
3231. Tue, Fri.

ITALY'S TOP SKI RESORT, much
favoured by the smart set
from Turin and Milan, is well
supplied with restaurants and
bars. The reason for its popularity is the dramatic scenery,
which adds an extra dimension
to the pleasure of speeding
down the
slopes.

Skiers at Cortina

Strolling along the Corso Italia in Cortina d'Ampezzo

Wherever you look, crags and
spires rise skyward, thrusting
their weather-sculpted shapes
above the trees.

As a consequence of the
resort hosting the 1956 Winter
Olympics, Cortina has better
than normal sports facilities.
If you want something more
adventurous than downhill or
cross-country skiing, there is
a ski jump and a bobsleigh
run to test your nerve. The

Olympic ice stadium regularly
holds skating discotheques,
and there are several good
swimming pools, tennis courts
and riding facilities.

During the summer months,
Cortina becomes an excellent
base for walkers. Information
on trails and guided walks is
available from the tourist
office or, during the summer,
from the Club Alpino Italiano
next door (*see p224*).

The Dolomite Road

THE STRADA DELLE DOLOMITI, or Dolomite Road, is one of
the most beautiful routes anywhere in the Alps, and is a
magnificent feat of highway construction. It starts in the
Trentino-Alto Adige region at Bolzano and enters the
Veneto region at the Passo del Pordoi, at 2,239 m (7,346 ft)
the most scenic of all the Dolomite passes. From here the
route follows the winding S48 for another 35 km (22 miles)
east to the resort of Cortina d'Ampezzo.

There are plenty of stopping places along the route
where you can enjoy spectacular views. In many of the ski
resorts, cable cars will carry you up to alpine refuges
(some with cafés attached) that are open from mid June to
mid September. These refuges mark the
start of a series of signposted walks.

TIPS FOR DRIVERS

Starting point: Passo del Pordoi.
Length (within the Veneto):
35 km (22 miles).
Approximate driving time:
Two hours, but allow a full day to
include the return journey and
time to stop and enjoy the
stunning scenery.
Stopping-off points: The small
towns of Pieve di Livinallongo and
Andraz have good cafés and
restaurants.

Passo del Pordoi ①
To the south is the Gran Vernal
at 3,210 m (10,530 ft); to the
north the Gruppo di Sella rise
to 3,152 m
(10,340 ft).

← BOLZANO

KEY

Tour route	
Other roads	
View point	

0 kilometres · · · · · · · · · 5

0 miles · · · · · · · · · 2

Arabba ②
Arabba is a pleasant resort
with a funicular railway to
the Col Burz (1,943 m/
6,370 ft) to the north.

Misurina ❷

Road map D1. 🏃 81. 🚌
ℹ️ *Via Misurina. (0435) 390 16
(summer and Christmas only).*

S MALLER AND QUIETER than
Cortina, Misurina nestles by
the exquisite Lake Misurina.
The lake's mirror-like surface
reflects the peaks of Monte
Cristallo, Cima di Cadini and
Tre Cime (Three Peaks) di

**One of the creeks flowing into
Lake Misurina**

Lavaredo. Take the
road that climbs
northeast for 8 km
(5 miles) to the
Auronzo mountain
refuge for a stunning
view of the peaks
(2,999 m/9,840 ft).

Pieve di Cadore ❸

Road map D1. 🏃 4,000. 🚌
ℹ️ *Tai di Cadore, Piazza Venezia 20.
(0435) 316 45.*

F OR CENTURIES the Cadore
forests supplied Venice with
its timber. The main town of
this vast mountainous region
is Pieve di Cadore, primarily
known as the birthplace of
Titian. The humble **Casa di
Tiziano** can be visited, and
the nearby **Museo Archeologico** has exhibits of finds
from the pre-Roman era.
   Principally, though, this is a
base for touring the scenic
delights of the region. North

Titian's house at Pieve di Cadore

of Pieve the valley narrows to
a dramatic ravine, and the
road north to Comelica and
Sesto is noted for its alpine
scenery and its traditional
balconied houses. Continuing
northeast, you can follow the
Piave river to its source, 8 km
(5 miles) north of Sappada.

⚱ Casa di Tiziano
Via Arsenale 4. 📞 (0435) 322 62.
🕐 Jun–Sep: Tue–Sun. 🈂️

🏛 Museo Archeologico
Romano e Preromano
Palazzo della Magnifica Comunità
Cadorina, Piazza Tiziano 2.
📞 (0435) 322 62. 🕐 Jun–Sep:
Tue–Sun. 🈂️

Falzarego ⑤
War memorials record the
fighting that took place
here in 1914–18 on the
frontier between Austria
and Italy.

Cortina d'Ampezzo ⑥
Descending to Cortina,
the view is dominated
by the irregularly
shaped Cinque Torri
(Five Towers).

BELLUNO

Andraz ④
The ruined Castello
di Andraz, sitting
on its rocky out-
crop, was built in
the 14th century to
prevent banditry
and to control the
approach to the
Passo di Falzarego.

Pieve di Livinallongo ③
The chief town of the scenic Cordevole
valley, Pieve offers spectacular views of
dolomitic peaks and cliffs.

**Visitors at the summit of the
Passo di Falzarego**

The Dolomites ❹

IT WAS DR DEODAT DOLOMIEU who, in 1789, first analysed the composition of the mountain range named after him. The Dolomites, formed of mineralized coral laid down beneath the sea during the Triassic era, were uplifted when the European and African continental plates collided 60 million years ago. Unlike the glacier-eroded saddles and ridges of the main body of the Alps, the gleaming white rocks have been sculpted by ice, sun and rain into the characteristic cliffs, spires and "organ pipes" that we see today; an inspiring sight, especially when dawn sunlight turns the rock rose pink.

Outdoor Activities
Chair-lifts provide access to ski-runs, footpaths and picnic sites, for a closer encounter with the grandeur of the peaks.

Small rural communities live by dairy farming and forestry.

At Lake Misurina and other artificial and natural leisure lakes, the outflow is used to supply hydro-electric power.

Climbers and Hikers
Much of the countryside is accessible only on foot, but the Dolomites have an extensive network of waymarked paths for hikers, and mountain huts (rifugi) *for overnight stops.*

Onion Domes
Church towers in the Dolomites are often capped by onion-shaped domes, a legacy of Austro-Hungarian rule in the region (see p46).

Monte Piana
Reminders of World War I battles still scar the Dolomites. Monte Piana, on the Austro-Italian front, saw much bitter fighting.

Traditional Farms

Large timber barns are used for sheltering animals and storing winter fodder and fuel. Overhanging roof eaves take rain and snow away from the house.

Marked routes now guide walkers along tracks created over several centuries by shepherds and cowherds.

Forests of larch, spruce, pine and fir provide commercial timber, firewood and shelter for wildlife.

THE LANDSCAPE OF THE DOLOMITES

The deep-sided river valleys between the Dolomites' craggy peaks shelter isolated villages which have traditionally survived from forestry and keeping livestock. Tourism has had a major impact on these small communities, some of which have become large resorts. Extensive areas of the Dolomites are now protected by law from development and are accessible only on foot.

NATURE IN THE DOLOMITES

Forests and meadows support an astonishing richness of wildlife. Alpine plants, in flower between June and September, have evolved their miniature form to survive the harsh winds.

The Flora

Gentian *seeds are used to make a bitter local liqueur.*

The red mountain lily *thrives on sunbaked slopes.*

Potentilla *roots were once used to produce red dye.*

Saponaria, *a type of soapwort, covers rocks and scree.*

The Fauna

The ptarmigan's *plumage changes from mottled brown in summer to snow white in winter. This bird feeds on mountain berries and young plant shoots.*

The chamois, *a shy mountain antelope prized for its soft, pliant skin, is protected in the national parks, where hunting is forbidden.*

Roe deer *are very common, because their natural predators – wolves and lynx – have died out. Their voracious appetite for tree saplings has become a problem for foresters.*

Belluno ❺

Road map D2. 🏠 35,800. 🚉 🚌
ℹ️ Piazza dei Martiri 27/E. (0437) 94
00 83. 🛒 Sat. **Shops closed** Mon
am & Wed pm.

Façade and entrance to Palazzo Rettori in Belluno

PᴵᴄᴛᴜʀᴇsQᴜᴇ ʙᴇʟʟᴜɴᴏ, capital of Belluno province, serves as a bridge between the two very different parts of the Veneto, with the flat plains to the south and the Dolomite peaks to the north. Both are encapsulated in the picture-postcard views to be seen from the 12th-century **Porta Ruga** at the southern end of Via Mezzaterra, the main street of the old town. Even more spectacular are the views from the campanile of the 16th-century **Duomo** which was designed by Tullio Lombardo, but rebuilt twice after damage by earthquakes.

The nearby baptistry contains a font cover with the figure of John the Baptist carved by Andrea Brustolon (1662–1732), whose elaborate furnishings decorate Ca' Rezzonico in Venice (see p126). Brustolon's works also grace the churches of **San Pietro** (altars and angels) and **Santo Stefano** (candelabra and a

Exterior fresco, Zoppe di Cadore

Crucifix). On the same square is the **Torre Civica** (12th-century), all that survives of the medieval castle, and the city's most elegant building, the Renaissance **Palazzo dei Rettori** (1491), once home to Belluno's Venetian rulers.

The **Museo Civico** is worth visiting for the archaeological exhibits, and the paintings by Bartolomeo Montagna (1450–1523) and Sebastiano Ricci (1659–1734). Just to the right of the museum is the town's finest square, the **Piazza del Mercato**, which features arcaded Renaissance palaces and a fountain built in 1410.

South of the town are the ski resorts of the Alpe del Nevegal. It is worth taking the chair lift in the summer to the Rifugio Brigata Alpina Cadore (1,600 m/5,250 ft) which has superb views and a botanical garden specializing in alpine plants.

🏛 Museo Civico

Via Duomo 16. 🔔 (0437) 94 43 36.
🕐 mid-Apr–mid-Oct: Tue–Sun;
mid-Oct–mid-Apr: Mon–Sat.

Valzoldana ❻

Road map D1. 🚌 from Longarone.
ℹ️ Via Roma 10, Forno di Zoldo
(0437) 78 73 49.

Tʜᴇ ᴡᴏᴏᴅᴇᴅ Zoldo valley is a popular destination for walking holidays. Its main resort town is Forno di Zoldo and the surrounding villages are noted for their Tyrolean-style alpine chalets and hay-lofts. Examples built in wood

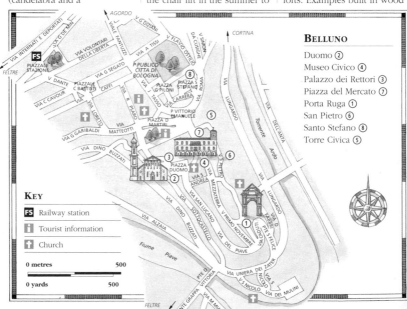

BELLUNO

Duomo ②
Museo Civico ④
Palazzo dei Rettori ③
Piazza del Mercato ⑦
Porta Ruga ①
San Pietro ⑥
Santo Stefano ⑧
Torre Civica ⑤

KEY

🚉 Railway station
ℹ️ Tourist information
✝ Church

0 metres 500
0 yards 500

on stone foundations can be seen at Fornesighe, 2 km (1 mile) northeast of Forno di Zoldo, and on the slopes of Monte Penna at Zoppe di Cadore, 8 km (5 miles) north.

If you have the time, do a circular tour of the area. Drive north on the S251, via Zoldo Alto to Selva di Cadore, then west via Colle di Santa Lucia (a favourite viewpoint for keen photographers). From here take the S203 south through the lakeside resort of Alleghe. The route passes through wonderful scenery with woodland, flower-filled meadows and pretty mountain hamlets which complement the splendour of the rocky crags.

The southernmost town of the area is Agordo, nestling in the Cordevole Valley. From here, a spectacularly scenic route follows the S34 northeast to the Passo Duran (1,605 m/5,270 ft), descending to Dont, close to your starting point. Wayside shrines mark the route and it is worth stopping on your way down to visit village shops selling local woodcarving. Take care when driving along this narrow and winding road.

Selva di Cadore from Colle di Santa Lucia, northwest of Valzoldana

A Renaissance *palazzo* on Via Luzzo in Feltre

Feltre ❼

Road map D2. 👥 19,600. 🚆 🚌
ℹ️ *Piazzetta Trento e Trieste 9. (0439) 2540.* 🛍️ *Tue & Fri am.* **Shops closed** *Mon am, Wed pm.*

FELTRE OWES its venerable good looks to the vengeful Holy Roman Emperor, Maximilian I. He sacked the town twice, in 1509 and in 1510, at the outbreak of the war against Venice waged by the League of Cambrai (*see p44*). Despite the destruction of its buildings and the murder of most of its citizens, Feltre remained stoutly loyal to Venice, and

Venice repaid the debt by rebuilding the town after the war. Thus the main street of the old town, Via Mezzaterra, is lined with arcaded early 16th-century houses, most with steeply pitched roofs to keep snow from settling.

Follow the steep main street to the striking Piazza Maggiore, where you can see the remains of Feltre's medieval castle, the church of **San Rocco** and a fountain by Tullio Lombardo (1520).

On the eastern side of the square, Via L Luzzo is lined with beautiful Renaissance palaces, one of which houses the **Museo Civico**. This displays paintings by the local artist Lorenzo Luzzo, who was known as Il Morto da Feltre (The Dead Man of Feltre), a nickname given to him by his contemporaries because of the deathly pallor of his skin.

🏛 Museo Civico
Palazzo Villabruna, Via L Luzzo 23.
📞 *(0439) 88 52 42.* 🕐 *Tue–Sun.*
⛔ *public hols.*

Vittorio Veneto old town and river

Vittorio Veneto ❽

Road map D2. 👥 30,000. 🚆 🚌
ℹ️ *Piazza del Popolo 18. (0438) 572 43.* **Shops closed** *Tue (some Wed pm).* 🛍️ *Mon.*

TWO SEPARATE TOWNS, Ceneda and Serravalle, were merged and renamed Vittorio Veneto in 1866 to honour the unification of Italy under King Vittorio Emanuele II. The town later gave its name to the last decisive battle fought in Italy in World War I. The **Museo della Battaglia** in the Ceneda quarter, the commercial heart of the town, commemorates this. Serravalle is more picturesque, with many fine 15th-century *palazzi*, and pretty arcaded streets. Franco Zeffirelli shot scenes for his film *Romeo and Juliet* in this town that sits at the base of the rocky Meschio gorge. To the east, via Anzano, the S422 climbs up to the Bosco del Cansiglio, a wooded plateau.

🏛 Museo della Battaglia
Piazza Giovanni Paolo I.
📞 *(0438) 576 95.* 🕐 *Tue–Sun.* 📷

TRAVELLERS'
NEEDS

WHERE TO STAY 222-233
RESTAURANTS, CAFÉS AND BARS 234-247
SHOPS AND MARKETS 248-253
ENTERTAINMENT IN THE VENETO 254-257

WHERE TO STAY

VENICE'S PERENNIAL attraction to romantics and art lovers means it has an astonishing number of hotels for its size, many of them in former *palazzi*. On the mainland, ancient cities

Sign for a small hotel

abound with hotels and *pensioni*, often housed in magnificent old buildings and extravagantly decorated. Those in the smaller towns are often run by families who take pride in their reputation.

Lake Garda is a long-established resort area with many hotels to choose from, and the mountainous north of the region is an all-year-round holiday area with accommodation of all types. Here you can find self-catering in a small farmhouse at very reasonable cost, and there are also numerous idyllically situated and well-equipped campsites. Budget options in the cities include self-catering flats, hostels and dormitory accommodation, and the mountains offer simple refuges for enthusiastic walkers. For more information on hotels in Venice and the Veneto see the listings on pages 228–33.

WHERE TO LOOK

UNLIKE MOST other cities, Venice has hardly any "undesirable" addresses. You will pay considerably more for a hotel in the immediate vicinity of the Piazza San Marco, but in such a compact city even apparently outlying areas such as Cannaregio or Santa Croce *(see pp14–15)* are never far from places of interest. Addresses in Venice are immensely confusing *(see p277)* but a map reference for each hotel is given in the listings. The maps referred to are to be found on pages 282–9 (Venice) and pages 12–13 (the Veneto).

Most visitors feel it is worth splashing out for a few nights' stay in Venice itself, despite the cost, though an increasing number stay in Verona or

Outside the Hotel Marconi *(see p229)* on the busy Riva del Vin

Hotel Europa e Regina *(see p229)* overlooking the Grand Canal

Padua and "commute" into Venice by train. Do not be tempted by the relatively low prices of the Mestre hotels, unless you are prepared to stay in a sprawling industrial town. Remember, too, that if you are travelling by car you will have to pay stiff parking charges at the Piazzale Roma car park or one of its satellites for the duration of your stay in Venice *(see pp278–279)*.

Many of the hotels in minor inland towns of the Veneto cater primarily for business travellers, but if you plan to explore the region you will find some lovely villa hotels in the countryside. Padua and Verona have a number of hotels, but those in Verona are fully booked for months ahead in the summer opera season, so forward planning is essential. Further north there is more choice. The

region is an all-year-round holiday area with accommodation of all types. Here you can find self-catering in a small farmhouse at very reasonable cost, and there are also numerous idyllically hotels are geared to holiday-makers, with lovely gardens, swimming pools and sports facilities. But bear in mind that Italians as well as foreign tourists flock to the lakes and mountains, so it is always advisable to plan your trip and book in advance.

HOTEL PRICES

HOTEL CHARGES were de-regulated in 1994, so that hotels are free to charge what they feel the market will bear rather than being tied to the tariffs determined by their star rating. Venice is an expensive place to stay and nowadays can hardly be said to have a "low season" with the benefits of lower or negotiable prices. You will be unlikely to find a basic double room for less than L100,000. Occasionally you can find some cheaper rooms from November to February, when the weather is often superb. But remember that many hotels close out of season. Some re-open for Carnival – and raise their prices accordingly.

July and August are the most expensive months at the resorts along Lake Garda. In the Dolomites winter, when skiers flock to the area, is the high season and the hotels may close during the summer.

Single room rates are higher than individual rates for two people sharing a double room. Prices include tax.

HIDDEN EXTRAS

IF YOU ARE TRAVELLING on a budget, try to avoid hotels with inclusive breakfast as this is rarely good value for money. You are expected to tip at least L1,000 for room service and about L2,000 for bellboys, even if service is included in the price of the room. Laundry services are usually expensive, as are drinks from the minibar and telephone calls from hotel rooms. Check all the rates when you make the booking. Some small hotels in Venice, and most in holiday areas like Lake Garda, may expect you to take full- or half-board during the high season.

HOTEL GRADINGS AND FACILITIES

ITALIAN HOTELS are classified by a rating system from one to five stars. However, each province sets its own

level for grading, so standards for each category may vary from one area to another. Some hotels may not have a restaurant, but those which do sometimes welcome non-residents who wish to eat.

Air-conditioning is rare in old buildings. Although the thick stone walls provide good insulation against the summer's heat, if you cannot tolerate high temperatures it is well worth choosing air-conditioned accommodation in Venice during the hottest months. Under Italian law, central heating remains off, whatever the temperature outside, until 1 November. This is something that is worth remembering if you plan a late-October trip.

Children are welcome everywhere but smaller hotels have limited facilities. Venice is not an ideal destination for children. If you want to take them with you, it is better to choose a hotel on the Lido where they will have access to the beach and also probably a garden.

WHAT TO EXPECT

HOTELS ARE obliged by law to register you with the police, so they will ask for your passport when you arrive. They may need to keep it for a few hours, but make sure you take it back, because you will need identification to change money or

Hotel Excelsior
(see p231)

Hotel Do Pozzi *(see p229)*

traveller's cheques. Italian hotel rooms are not "cosy": carpets are rare, the storage space is usually very limited and luxuries such as tea-making facilities are un-known, even in four- and five-star establishments. The decor may be simple and Italian taste can be rather different from what you are used to. However, hotel staff will be friendly and charming, and the standard of cleanliness is high. The bathrooms are, almost without exception, spotlessly clean, even when they are shared. Less expensive hotels are unlikely to have bathtubs; showers are considered more hygienic and more economical on water. Rooms without a bathroom usually have a washbasin and towels are provided.

Breakfast is very light – a cup of coffee and a brioche (a plain or cream- or jam-filled pastry), though hotels generally include fruit juice, bread rolls and jam as well. It is always cheaper to have breakfast in a bar.

With the exception of Venice, where the only sounds are water-borne or human, Italian towns can be very noisy. If you are a light sleeper, ask for a room that is away from the street, or come equipped with earplugs to deaden traffic sounds and church bells.

Check-out time is usually noon in four- and five-star hotels and between ten and noon in small establishments. If you stay longer you will be asked to pay for an extra day.

The elegant Villa Cortine Palace on the Sirmione peninsula *(see p232)*

BOOKING AND PAYING

BOOK AT LEAST two months in advance if you want to stay in a particular hotel in the high season; some people book as far as six months or a year ahead in Venice itself. The local tourist office will have listings of all the hotels in the area, and they will be able to advise you on the best hotels in each star category. Hotels above the L100,000 price bracket usually take credit cards, but check which cards are accepted when you make your reservation – Italy is still very much a cash country. You can generally pay the deposit by credit card, or send a Eurocheque or international money order.

Under Italian law, a booking is valid as soon as the deposit is paid and confirmation is received. As in restaurants, you are required by law to keep your hotel receipts until you leave the country.

DISABLED TRAVELLERS

FACILITIES FOR the disabled are limited throughout Italy, and Venice poses its own particular problems. A list of tour operators that

The conveniently located Hotel La Fenice *(see p229)*

specialize in holidays for the disabled can be obtained from the **Italian State Tourist Office**. For further advice for the disabled, see p261.

HOTELS IN HISTORIC BUILDINGS

MANY OF Venice's hotels are housed in buildings of historical or artistic interest, for example in Gothic *palazzi*. Some of the best are included in the listings here. In the Veneto region there are some attractive villa hotels and a

number of these are included in the guide produced by **Relais and Châteaux**.

SELF-CATERING

SELF-CATERING flats in Venice proper are hard to come by, owing to the insatiable demand for property in the city. **International Chapters** handle some holiday lets within the city, as do **Tailor Made Tours** and **Vacanze in Italia**. Alternatively you could try one of the Venetian agents, such as **Sant'Angelo**

DIRECTORY

TOURIST OFFICE

Italian State Tourist Office (ENIT)
1 Princes Street
London W1R 8AY.
📞 0171-408 1254.

HISTORIC HOTELS

Relais & Châteaux
Grosvenor Gardens House,
35–37 Grosvenor
Gardens, London
SW1W 0BS.
📞 0171-491 2516.

SELF-CATERING AGENCIES

Agriturist Ufficio Regionale
Via C Monteverdi 15
Venezia Mestre 30170.
📞 (041) 98 74 00.

Gruppo Italia
Calle della Toletta,
Dorsoduro 1215.
Map 6 D3.
📞 (041) 528 82 00.

International Chapters
47–51 St John's Wood
High St, London
NW8 7NJ.
📞 0171-722 9560.

Sant'Angelo
Campo Sant'Angelo
San Marco 3818.
Map 6 F2.
📞 (041) 522 15 05.

Tailor Made Tours
22 Church Rise
London SE23 2UD.
📞 0181-291 9736.

Vacanze in Italia
Manor Court Yard, Bignor,
near Pulborough,

West Sussex RH20 1QD.
📞 0181-291 9736.

BUDGET ACCOMMODATION

Associazione Italiana Alberghi per la Gioventù
Via Cavour 44
00184 Rome.
📞 (06) 487 11 52.

Foresteria Valdese
Campo Santa Maria
Formosa,
Castello 5170.
Map 7 C1.
📞 (041) 528 67 97.

Istituto Ciliota
Calle delle Muneghe
San Marco 2976.
Map 6 F2.
📞 (041) 520 48 88.
*Accommodation available
Jun–Sep only.*

Ostello Venezia
Fondamenta delle Zitelle
Giudecca 86.
Map 7 B5.
📞 (041) 523 82 11.

CAMPSITES AND MOUNTAIN REFUGES

Club Alpino Italiano
Via Fonseca Pimental 7
20127 Milan.
📞 (02) 26 14 13 78.

Marina di Venezia
Via Montello 6
Punta Sabbioni.
📞 (041) 96 61 46.

San Nicolò
Riviera San Nicolò 65
Lido. 📞 (041) 526 74 15.

Touring Club Italiano
Corso Italia 10, 20122
Milan. 📞 (02) 852 61.

or **Gruppo Italia**, although they may prefer to deal with longer rentals.

Under the **Agriturismo** scheme there is plenty of self-catering accommodation in the Veneto, usually on working farms. There is an Agriturist office in each region, which will give further information, although you may have to book with the owner. This type of accommodation ranges from simple conversions to luxurious and spacious villas with swimming pools. Prices reflect these variations, and they also fluctuate according to the time of year. Low-season prices for four people start at about L1 million per week.

Detail on the Hotel Danieli

BUDGET ACCOMMODATION

ONE- OR two-star budget hotels charging from L40,000 to L80,000 per person per night are generally small, family-run places. These used to be known as *pensioni*, but the term is no longer used very much officially. However, many places retain the name and the personal character that has made them so popular. They rarely offer breakfast and have very few rooms with private bathrooms. You should not expect particularly high standards of service. A variation on these *pensioni* are *affittacamare*, or rented rooms, are even

smaller establishments, and they also offer excellent value for money.

Accommodation in hostels and dormitories is sometimes available at convents and religious institutions, and it is often possible to arrange it through the local tourist offices. The **Associazione Italiana Alberghi per la Gioventù** (Italian Youth Hostel Association) in Rome has lists of youth hostels throughout the whole of Italy. The main youth hostel in Venice is the beautifully situated **Ostello Venezia** on the Giudecca. Book well ahead for if you want to stay in July or August.

Lists and booking forms for youth hostels are available through the Italian Tourist Board worldwide, or from local offices. The Venice office also produces a simple typed list of all kinds of hostel accommodation in Venice itself.

CAMPSITES AND MOUNTAIN REFUGES

THERE ARE good campsites throughout the region, concentrated mainly on the mainland to the north of Venice, on the shores of Lake Garda and in the northern mountains. A list of campsites and mountain refuges can be obtained from **ENIT** or local tourist offices. Most huts in

the mountain districts are owned by the **Club Alpino Italiano**, based in Milan, who can provide full information. The **Touring Club Italiano** publishes annually a list of campsites: *Campeggi e Villaggi Turistici in Italia.*

A suitcase boat transporting visitors' luggage to a hotel

USING THE LISTINGS

Hotels on pages 229–33 are listed according to area and price category. The symbols summarize the facilities available at each hotel.

🛁 all rooms have bath and/or shower unless otherwise indicated
1️⃣ single-rate rooms available
🔣 rooms for more than two people available, or an extra bed can be put in a double room
📺 television in all rooms
🎛 air-conditioning in all rooms
🏊 swimming pool in the hotel
♿ wheelchair access
🛗 lift
🅿 parking available
🍴 restaurant
💳 credit cards accepted
⬤ closed out of season *(see p223)*

Price categories for a standard double room per night, including tax and service:
Ⓛ under L100,000
ⓁⓁ L100,000–L160,000
ⓁⓁⓁ L160,000–L240,000
ⓁⓁⓁⓁ L240,000–L340,000
ⓁⓁⓁⓁⓁ over L340,000

Garden terrace of the Hôtel des Bains on the Lido *(see p231)*

Venice's Best Hotels

Hotels in Venice range from the luxurious and renowned, which are mainly clustered along the Grand Canal, to simple, family-run places in the quieter parts of the city. Wherever you stay, you will be within easy reach of the main attractions, with restaurants and shops close at hand. All the hotels shown on this map have something special to recommend them, whether it is the waterside position, a garden or a quiet location away from the crowds. Always book well in advance, and remember that many Venetian hotels are shut at some stage in winter. The hotels shown here are the best in their particular style or price range.

Zecchini
One of the most attractive hotels on the busy Lista di Spagna, the Zecchini is good value. (See p230.)

Cannaregio

Al Sole
Situated beside a tranquil canal, this Gothic palazzo is away from the main tourist haunts, but within easy reach by foot or water of all the sights. (See p229.)

San Polo and Santa Croce

Dorsoduro

| 0 metres | 500 |
| 0 yards | 500 |

Agli Alboretti
This charming hotel in a central location has attractive rooms and a garden courtyard. (See p230.)

Gritti Palace
One of Venice's most famous hotels, the Gritti offers rooms and service of impeccable standard in an historic palazzo on the Grand Canal. (See p229.)

Giorgione
This high-class, spacious hotel, with its excellent facilities, offers every modern comfort at lower prices than others of similar calibre. (See p231.)

Marconi
This efficiently run hotel, housed in an old palazzo, has views of the Grand Canal and the Rialto Bridge. (See p229.)

Castello

n Marco

La Residenza
This family-run hotel offers good value for money and is away from the crowds. It has frescoed public rooms and antiques, but the bedrooms are more simple. (See p230.)

Flora
A flower-filled garden is just one of the attractions of this delightful hotel. (See p229.)

Londra Palace
Tchaikovsky once stayed in this grand palazzo with its views to San Giorgio Maggiore. Today's guests appreciate the welcoming bar and restaurant. (See p230.)

Hotels in Venice

THIS CHART is a quick reference to recommended hotels in Venice and the lagoon. They are listed within each *sestiere* in price order. More details for these and for hotels in the Veneto are given on the following pages. For information on other types of accommodation, see pages 224–5.

		Number of Rooms	All Rooms with Bath/Shower	Air Conditioning	Restaurant	Attractive View	Garden/Terrace	Open All Year	Easy Access
San Marco *(see p229)*									
Ai Do Mori	ⓁⓁ	11				■		■	●
Al Gambero	ⓁⓁⓁ	30		●		■		■	●
Do Pozzi	ⓁⓁⓁⓁ	30	●			■	●	■	●
Flora	ⓁⓁⓁⓁ	44	●	■			●	■	●
La Fenice et des Artistes	ⓁⓁⓁⓁ	68	●	■				■	
Santo Stefano	ⓁⓁⓁⓁ	11	●	■					●
San Moisè	ⓁⓁⓁⓁ	16	●	■		■		■	
Cavalletto e Doge Orseolo	ⓁⓁⓁⓁⓁ	96	●	■	●			■	●
Europa e Regina	ⓁⓁⓁⓁⓁ	192	●	■	●	■	●	■	●
Gritti Palace	ⓁⓁⓁⓁⓁ	93	●	■	●	■		■	●
Monaco and Grand Canal	ⓁⓁⓁⓁⓁ	74	●	■	●	■	●	■	●
San Polo and Santa Croce *(see pp229–30)*									
Alex	ⓁⓁ	11						■	
Falier	ⓁⓁⓁ	19	●					■	
Al Sole	ⓁⓁⓁⓁ	80	●	■	●		●	■	
Locanda Sturion	ⓁⓁⓁⓁ	11	●			■		■	
Marconi	ⓁⓁⓁⓁ	26	●	■		■			●
Castello *(see p230)*									
La Residenza	ⓁⓁⓁ	16	●			■			●
Paganelli	ⓁⓁⓁ	22	●			■	●		●
Pensione Wildner	ⓁⓁⓁⓁ	16	●		●	■	●		●
Danieli	ⓁⓁⓁⓁⓁ	233	●	■	●	■	●	■	●
Londra Palace	ⓁⓁⓁⓁⓁ	53	●	■	●	■		■	●
Dorsoduro *(see p230)*									
Montin	Ⓛ	10			●		●	●	
Agli Alboretti	ⓁⓁⓁ	25	●	■	●	■	●	■	●
Messner	ⓁⓁⓁ	34	●	■	●		●	■	
Pensione La Calcina	ⓁⓁⓁ	40				■			●
Pensione Seguso	ⓁⓁⓁ	40			●	■	●		
Pausania	ⓁⓁⓁⓁ	26	●	■			●		
Pensione Accademia Villa Maravegie	ⓁⓁⓁⓁ	27				■	●	■	
Cannaregio *(see pp230–31)*									
Zecchini	ⓁⓁⓁ	27	●					■	●
Abbazia	ⓁⓁⓁⓁ	36	●				●	■	●
Giorgione	ⓁⓁⓁⓁ	70	●	■			●	■	●
Continental	ⓁⓁⓁⓁⓁ	93	●	■	●	■	●	■	●
The Lagoon Islands *(see p231)*									
Villa Parco (Lido)	ⓁⓁⓁⓁ	23	●	■	●		●		
Cipriani (Giudecca)	ⓁⓁⓁⓁⓁ	105	●	■	●	■	●		●
Excelsior Palace (Lido)	ⓁⓁⓁⓁⓁ	197	●	■	●	■	●		●
Hôtel des Bains (Lido)	ⓁⓁⓁⓁⓁ	191	●	■	●	■	●		●
Quattro Fontane (Lido)	ⓁⓁⓁⓁⓁ	59		■	●		●		

VENICE

SAN MARCO

Ai Do Mori

Calle Larga San Marco, San Marco 658. **Map** 7 B2. ((041) 520 48 17. **Rooms:** 11. 🛏 3. Ⓛ Ⓛ

This friendly little hotel has only a few rooms with their own bath, but it is clean and characterful, and offers extremely good value.

Al Gambero

Calle dei Fabbri, San Marco 4687. **Map** 7 A2. ((041) 522 43 84. **Rooms:** 30. 🛏 4. ① ¶¶ 🎍 Ⓛ Ⓛ Ⓛ

Recently modernized, the Al Gambero has simple rooms, many of them singles, and several with a canal view. It is situated a stone's throw from the Piazza on one of Venice's main shopping streets.

Do Pozzi

Corte Do Pozzi, San Marco 2373. **Map** 7 A3. ((041) 520 78 55. FAX 522 94 13. **Rooms:** 30. 🛏 ① 🎍 🎍 Ⓛ Ⓛ Ⓛ Ⓛ

The Do Pozzi (see p223) boasts a charming setting in a peaceful green courtyard. Its rooms are quiet, despite its proximity to the tourist-filled Piazza San Marco. The hotel also has a very attractive and welcoming reception area.

Flora

Calle Larga XXII Marzo, San Marco 2283/a. **Map** 7 A3. ((041) 520 58 44. FAX 522 82 17. **Rooms:** 44. 🛏 ① 🎍 🎍 🎍 Ⓛ Ⓛ Ⓛ Ⓛ

This quiet hotel in a secluded alley is only a few minutes from the Piazza (see p227). Some rooms are small, although all have their own bathroom. In summer it is possible to enjoy a leisurely breakfast in the fragrant flower-filled garden.

La Fenice et des Artistes

Campiello Fenice, San Marco 1936. **Map** 7 A3. ((041) 523 23 33. FAX 520 37 21. **Rooms:** 68. 🛏 ① 🎍 🎍 🎍 Ⓛ Ⓛ Ⓛ Ⓛ

A pretty hotel, furnished with antiques. On fine days you can sit outside for breakfast, or later in the day enjoy a quiet drink from the bar (see p224).

Santo Stefano

Campo Santo Stefano, San Marco 2957. **Map** 6 F3. ((041) 520 01 66. FAX 522 44 60. **Rooms:** 11. 🛏 ① 🎍 🎍 🎍 Ⓛ Ⓛ Ⓛ Ⓛ

The Campo Santo Stefano is one of Venice's most characteristic quarters, and the rooms in this tall, narrow hotel offer a bird's-eye view of the surrounding area. The furnishings are traditionally Venetian, but some of the rooms are rather cramped.

San Moisè

Piscina San Moisè, San Marco 2058. **Map** 7 A3. ((041) 520 37 55. FAX 521 06 70. **Rooms:** 16. 🛏 ① 🎍 🎍 🎍 Ⓛ Ⓛ Ⓛ Ⓛ

The San Moisè is a wonderfully quiet but central hotel on a placid back canal. The rooms differ considerably in size, but are in the traditional Venetian style and furnished with antiques.

Cavalletto e Doge Orseolo

Calle Cavalletto, San Marco 1107. **Map** 7 B2. ((041) 520 09 55. FAX 523 81 84. **Rooms:** 96. 🛏 ① 🎍 🎍 🎍 ¶¶ 🎍 Ⓛ Ⓛ Ⓛ Ⓛ Ⓛ

This excellent hotel has been welcoming visitors for more than 200 years. The rooms are bright and cheerful, with extras ranging from minibars to window boxes. The hotel also has a bar and pleasant restaurant.

Europa e Regina

Calle Larga XXII Marzo, San Marco 2159. **Map** 7 A3. ((041) 520 04 77. FAX 523 15 33. **Rooms:** 192. 🛏 ① 🎍 🎍 🎍 🎍 ¶¶ 🎍 *Private launch service. Access to private beach.* 🎍 Ⓛ Ⓛ Ⓛ Ⓛ

The Europa (see p222) offers the best value of all the deluxe hotels. The rooms are large and many of them have views across the Grand Canal. The magnificent public rooms are sumptuously ornate and gilded, in typical Venetian style, and for those who like to eat and drink al fresco there is a garden courtyard and canalside terrace with breathtaking views.

Gritti Palace

Santa Maria del Giglio, San Marco 2467. **Map** 7 A3. ((041) 79 46 11. FAX 520 09 42. **Rooms:** 93. 🛏 ① 🎍 🎍 🎍 🎍 ¶¶ 🎍 *Private launch service. Access to private beach.* 🎍 Ⓛ Ⓛ Ⓛ Ⓛ

This renowned deluxe hotel overlooking the Grand Canal is situated in the fine 15th-century palazzo that once belonged to the Gritti family (see p226). The hotel is elegant, sumptuous and old-fashioned in the best sense, with superb rooms and meticulous service. The iconic writer Ernest Hemingway was a guest here during his stay in Venice.

Monaco and Grand Canal

Calle Vallaresso, San Marco 1325. **Map** 7 B3. ((041) 520 02 11. FAX 520 05 01. **Rooms:** 74. 🛏 ① 🎍 ① 🎍 🎍 ¶¶ 🎍 Ⓛ Ⓛ Ⓛ Ⓛ Ⓛ

Housed in an 18th-century palazzo, this elegant hotel looks across the Grand Canal to the Salute. The public rooms have an intimate feeling and the bedrooms are decorated with lovely furniture and pretty fabrics. The restaurant on the terrace beside the Grand Canal is one of the best in Venice.

SAN POLO AND SANTA CROCE

Alex

Rio Terrà Frari, San Polo 2606. **Map** 6 E1. ((041) 523 13 41. **Rooms:** 11. 🛏 2. ① Ⓛ Ⓛ

It is some time since the rooms of this family-run hotel were over-hauled, but the excellent value and good position near the Frari compensate for any shabbiness.

Falier

Salizzada San Pantalon 130, Santa Croce 30135. **Map** 5 C1. ((041) 71 08 82. FAX 20 65 54. **Rooms:** 19. 🛏 ① 🎍 Ⓛ Ⓛ Ⓛ

Away from the majority of the Venice hotels and on the edge of the student district, the Falier has recently been refurbished.

Al Sole

Fondamenta Minotta, Santa Croce 136. **Map** 5 C1. ((041) 71 08 44. FAX 71 43 98. **Rooms:** 80. 🛏 ① 🎍 🎍 ¶¶ 🎍 Ⓛ Ⓛ Ⓛ Ⓛ

Although this is not the most attractive part of Venice, the Al Sole is in a pretty corner. This 14th-century building offers guests marble-floored reception areas and pleasant rooms. There is a shady courtyard where you can have a drink. You may have to accept half-board in the busy season.

Locanda Sturion

Calle del Storione, San Polo 679. **Map** 7 A1. ((041) 523 62 43. FAX 52 28 37 80. **Rooms:** 11. 🛏 ① 🎍 🎍 Ⓛ Ⓛ Ⓛ Ⓛ

Situated just a few yards from the Grand Canal and close to the Rialto, the Sturion's central location has long been part of its appeal. The rooms have recently undergone transformation, making this friendly hotel an attractive base offering exceptional value.

For key to symbols see p225

Marconi

Riva del Vin, San Polo 729. **Map** 7 A1.
█ *(041) 522 20 68.* **FAX** *522 97 00.*
Rooms: 26. ▣ ① TV ▤ ▨
Ⓛ Ⓛ Ⓛ Ⓛ

Those in search of Venetian opulence will appreciate the reception areas of the Marconi, which was once a 16th-century *palazzo (see p227)..* The bedrooms are less grand but some overlook the Grand Canal. The Marconi is well situated beside the Rialto Bridge.

CASTELLO

La Residenza

Campo Bandiera e Moro, Castello 3608.
Map 8 E2. █ *(041) 528 53 15.* **FAX** *523 88 59.* **Rooms:** 16. ▣ ① ▨
Ⓛ Ⓛ Ⓛ

The Residenza was once a 14th-century *palazzo (see p227).* Although the bedrooms are basic, the frescoed ceilings and antique furniture in the public rooms are quite delightfully elegant.

Paganelli

Riva degli Schiavoni, Castello 4182.
Map 8 D2. █ *(041) 522 43 24.* **FAX** *523 92 67.* **Rooms:** 22. ▣ ①
▨ Ⓛ Ⓛ Ⓛ

The cosy and old-fashioned rooms in the Paganelli provide views of St Mark's Basin that would cost three times as much at other hotels along the Riva. Rooms in the *dipendenza* (annexe) on San Zaccaria do not have the view, although they are quieter.

Pensione Wildner

Riva degli Schiavoni, Castello 4161.
Map 8 D2. █ *(041) 522 74 63.* **FAX** *526 56 15.* **Rooms:** 16. ▣ ①
TV ▤ ⑪ ▨ Ⓛ Ⓛ Ⓛ Ⓛ

Another family-run hotel on the Riva, the Pensione Wildner offers simple yet immaculate bedrooms with stunning views across to San Giorgio Maggiore. It has a small bar if you prefer not to sit at the tables outside, among the crowds on the busy Riva. In high season you may have to take half-board.

Danieli

Riva degli Schiavoni, Castello 4196.
Map 7 C2. █ *(041) 522 64 80.* **FAX** *520 02 08.* **Rooms:** 233. ▣ ①
▦ TV ▤ ⑪ *Access to private beach.* ▨ Ⓛ Ⓛ Ⓛ Ⓛ Ⓛ

One of Venice's top hotels, the Danieli is the epitome of luxury. It was the palace of the Dandolo family and has strong literary and musical connections *(see p113).*

The reception rooms are splendid, lit by resplendent Venetian glass chandeliers, and the service is impeccable. There are two wings, one built in the 1940s, and an older section, obviously the first choice for guests.

Londra Palace

Riva degli Schiavoni, Castello 4171.
Map 8 D2. █ *(041) 520 05 33.*
FAX *522 50 32.* **Rooms:** 53. ▣ ①
TV ▤ ▣ ⑪ ▨ Ⓛ Ⓛ Ⓛ Ⓛ Ⓛ

On the long Riva where hotels are cheek by jowl, the monument to King Vittorio Emanuele is a useful landmark outside this statuesque stone-faced hotel *(see p227).* It was once two palaces and had elegant public rooms, a good restaurant and a delightful bar. The rooms are traditional in style and extremely comfortable, though some of the singles are rather small. It was here that Tchaikovsky composed his Fourth Symphony.

DORSODURO

Montin

Fondamenta Eremite, Dorsoduro 1147. **Map** 6 D3. █ *(041) 522 71 51.* **FAX** *520 02 55.* **Rooms:** 10. ▣ 7.
① ⑪ ▨ Ⓛ

These ten rooms above one of Venice's best-known restaurants are full of charm and character, despite the lack of private bathrooms. It is essential to book.

Agli Alboretti

Rio Terrà Antonio Foscarini, Dorsoduro 884. **Map** 6 E4. █ *(041) 523 00 58.* **FAX** *521 01 58.* **Rooms:** 25. ▣ ①
▦ ▤ ⑪ ▨ ● *Jan.* Ⓛ Ⓛ Ⓛ

Attractively situated near the Accademia, this hotel has modern, elegant rooms, although they are rather on the small side. The cosy reception area is wood-panelled and there is a garden where you can recuperate after a hard day's sightseeing *(see p226).* The Agli Alboretti is a great favourite with English and American visitors.

Messner

Rio Terrà dei Catecumeni, Dorsoduro 216. **Map** 6 F4. █ *(041) 522 74 43.* **FAX** *522 72 66.* **Rooms:** 34. ▣ 30.
① ▦ ⑪ ▨ Ⓛ Ⓛ Ⓛ

This hotel was renovated a few seasons ago; the rooms are modern and a good size. There is a nice bar and a peaceful courtyard. Families with children are particularly welcome.

Pensione La Calcina

Zattere ai Gesuati, Dorsoduro 780.
Map 6 E4. █ *(041) 520 64 66.* **FAX** *522 70 45.* **Rooms:** 40. ▣ 20. ①
▨ Ⓛ Ⓛ Ⓛ

This simply furnished and airy *pensione,* convenient for the Accademia, is very popular. All the rooms are comfortable and a few have the bonus of splendid views across the Giudecca canal.

Pensione Seguso

Zattere ai Gesuati, Dorsoduro 779.
Map 6 E4. █ *(041) 528 68 58.*
FAX *522 23 40.* **Rooms:** 40. ▣ 28.
① ▦ ▣ ⑪ ▨ ● *winter.* Ⓛ Ⓛ Ⓛ

The rooms of this pleasant *pensione* are traditionally furnished and the reception areas crammed with antiques and books. Nearly all the rooms look out on to water, either the Giudecca canal, or the Rio San Vio. You need to book well ahead, and you may find that in high season half-board is compulsory.

Pausania

Rio di San Barnaba, Dorsoduro 2824.
Map 6 D3. █ *(041) 522 20 83.* **FAX** *(041) 52 22 989.* **Rooms:** 26. ▣ ①
▦ TV ▨ Ⓛ Ⓛ Ⓛ Ⓛ

This small, welcoming hotel offers a peaceful escape from the agitation of city life. Most of the bedrooms are situated around a picturesque and secluded garden. With reasonable prices and friendly staff, this is a pleasant place to stay during the busy summer months.

Pensione Accademia Villa Maravegie

Fondamenta Bollani, Dorsoduro 1058–1060. **Map** 6 E3. █ *(041) 521 01 88.* **FAX** *523 91 52.* **Rooms:** 27. ▣ 26. ① ▤ ▨ Ⓛ Ⓛ Ⓛ Ⓛ

Visitors return again and again to this elegant 17th-century villa which was once the Russian Embassy. The rooms are mainly furnished with antiques and some are small, but the garden makes up for these minor inconveniences. Book well ahead.

CANNAREGIO

Zecchini

Lista di Spagna, Cannaregio 152. **Map** 2 D4. █ *(041) 71 56 11.* **FAX** *71 50 66.* **Rooms:** 27. ▣ 23. ▨ Ⓛ Ⓛ Ⓛ

The Zecchini occupies two floors of an attractive building and is reached via a flight of stairs *(see p226).* The rooms overlook one of Venice's busiest streets, so it can be a bit noisy. The price, and luxuriousness, of the rooms varies considerably.

Abbazia

Calle Priuli, Cannaregio 66/68.
Map 1 C4. **(** *(041) 71 73 33.*
FAX *71 79 49.* **Rooms:** 36. 🚹 1
📋 🅂 ⑩⑩⑩⑩

Quietly situated just off the lively Lista di Spagna, the Abbazia is probably the best hotel in the station area. The rooms are large and comfortable and there is a garden in which you can relax with a drink from the bar.

Giorgione

Santi Apostoli, Cannaregio 4587.
Map 3 B5. **(** *(041) 522 58 10.*
FAX *523 90 92.* **Rooms:** 70. 🚹 1
🎴 📺 🔃 🅂 ⑩⑩⑩⑩

This is a modern, recently refurbished hotel housed in a delightful colour-washed building. The Giorgione has a spacious reception area and bar *(see p 227)*, and a delightful garden. It is conveniently situated for the Rialto area.

Continental

Lista di Spagna, Cannaregio 166.
Map 2 D4. **(** *(041) 71 51 22.*
FAX *524 24 32.* **Rooms:** 93. 🚹 1
🎴 📺 📋 🔃 🍴 🅂 ⑩⑩⑩⑩

The Continental is a large, well equipped hotel in the busy station area. It has modern rooms, some of which overlook the Grand Canal. Other rooms look out over the adjacent, tree-shaded *campo* and these are usually quieter.

THE LAGOON ISLANDS

Villa Parco

Via Rodi 1, Lido di Venezia.
(*(041) 526 00 15.* **FAX** *526 76 20.*
Rooms: 23. 🚹 1 🎴 📋 🍴 🅂
⑩⑩⑩

With the sea just a few minutes away and set in its own gardens, this family-run hotel is an ideal place to stay if you are holidaying with children. The modern rooms are pleasant and the hotel is quietly situated in a residential area near the summer casino. Parking is available for guests who arrive with their own cars.

Cipriani

Giudecca 10. **Map** 7 C5. **(** *(041)*
520 77 44. **FAX** *520 39 30.* **Rooms:**
105. 🚹 1 🎴 📺 📋 🅂 ♿ 🔃
🍴 *Private launch service.* 🅂
● *Nov–Mar.* ⑩⑩⑩⑩⑩

Set in gardens occupying the entire eastern tip of the Giudecca, the Cipriani has been one of the world's great hotels since it opened

in 1963. Guests enjoy luxurious surroundings and perfect service. The bedrooms and suites are furnished with taste and opulence, and each one has been decorated in a different style. The renowned restaurant has splendid terraces which are delightful for dining.

Excelsior Palace

Lungomare Marconi 41, Lido di Venezia. **(** *(041) 526 02 01.*
FAX *526 72 76.* **Rooms:** 197. 🚹 1
🎴 📺 📋 🔃 🍴 *Private launch service. Private beach.* 🅂 ● *mid-Feb–mid-Mar.* ⑩⑩⑩⑩⑩

When it opened in 1907, the Excelsior was the largest luxury resort hotel in the world *(see pp48–9)*. The exterior is flamboyantly Moorish – even the beach *cabanas* are styled like Arabian tents. The interior, offering every service and comfort, is equally splendid, though it may not appeal to all tastes. The hotel is at its liveliest during the annual Film Festival *(see p255)* – the Palazzo del Cinema and the summer home of the casino are only a few minutes' walk away.

Hôtel des Bains

Lungomare Marconi 17, Lido di Venezia. **(** *(041) 526 59 21.*
FAX *526 01 13.* **Rooms:** 191. 🚹 1
🎴 📺 📋 🔃 🍴 *Private launch service. Private beach.* 🅂 ● *winter.*
⑩⑩⑩⑩

Film fans will recognize the des Bains as the location for Luchino Visconti's *Death in Venice*, set in the hotel where Thomas Mann wrote the original novel. Built in the early 1900s, its reception rooms have an Art Deco elegance, and there is a verandah for dining *(see p225)*. The bedrooms are spacious. Across the road the hotel's private beach is equipped with bathing huts with a view looking out over the Adriatic.

Quattro Fontane

Via Quattro Fontane 16, Lido di Venezia. **(** *(041) 526 02 27.* **FAX** *526 07 26.* **Rooms:** 59. 🚹 1 📺 📋
🍴 🅂 ● *mid-Nov–mid-Apr.*
⑩⑩⑩⑩

This is the nicest of the smaller hotels on the Lido. It is set in pretty gardens and has its own tennis court for the use of guests. The reception rooms and bedrooms are all furnished with antiques and the green and white gabled exterior gives the hotel a distinctive alpine look. On warm summer days you can enjoy a meal out of doors in the tranquil creeper-clad courtyard. The Quattro Fontane is only a few minutes from the sea.

THE VENETO PLAIN

ASOLO

Villa Cipriani

Road map D3. Via Canova 298, 31011. **(** *(0423) 95 21 66.* **FAX** *95 20 95.* **Rooms:** 31. 🚹 1 🎴 📺 📋
♿ 🔃 📋 🍴 🅂 ⑩⑩⑩⑩⑩

Situated in the gentle foothills of the mountains, Asolo is a good base for exploring a wide area. This superbly comfortable hotel is housed in a 16th-century villa where Robert Browning once lived. The standards are very high here, and the beautiful garden, with its excellent view, is a major attraction.

BASSANO AREA

Victoria

Road map C3. Viale Diaz 33, 36061 Bassano del Grappa . **(** *(0424) 50 36 20.* **FAX** *50 31 30.* **Rooms:** 23. 🚹
1 🎴 📺 📋 🅂

The Victoria is just outside the old city walls and well placed for sightseeing in Bassano. The rooms are comfortable and there is a garden, where you can enjoy a quiet drink.

Belvedere

Road map C3. Piazzale G Giardino 14, 36061 Bassano del Grappa.
(*(0424) 52 98 45.* **FAX** *52 98 47.*
Rooms: 91. 🚹 1 🎴 📺 📋 ♿
🔃 📋 🍴 🅂 ⑩⑩⑩

One of Bassano's main squares, just outside the old centre, is the setting for the town's most lavishly appointed hotel. This is a large and busy establishment at the top of the orbital road, which can be noisy, but it has comfortable rooms and a high level of service.

CHIOGGIA

Grande Italia

Road map D4. Piazza Vigo 1, 30015.
(*(041) 40 05 15.* **FAX** *40 01 85.*
Rooms: 43. 🚹 1 🎴 🔃 📋 🅂
♿ No access. ⑩⑩⑩

The Grande Italia stands right at the head of Chioggia's main street and is well situated for the boats running to Venice via Pellestrina and the Lido. A solid, unpretentious and old-fashioned hotel, it offers comfortable rooms at low prices.

For key to symbols see p225

CONEGLIANO

Canon d'Oro

Road map D3. Via XX Settembre 129, 31015 . (*(0438) 342 46.* **Rooms:** *35.* 🛏 1 ♨ TV 🍴 📶 P 🅿 L L

This three-star hotel offers solid comfort and a warm welcome in an old building. The location, on the main street of Conegliano, is ideal for exploring the historic town centre. There is a garden in which to relax, and you can sample a glass of Prosecco in the friendly bar.

PADUA

Grande Italia

Road map D4. Corso del Popolo 81, 35131. (*(049) 876 11 11.* **Rooms:** *60.* 🛏 TV 🍴 L L

Situated close to most of the city's main sights, this hotel is a very good value choice. The decor and furniture are slightly shabby, but the rooms are comfortable. Quieter rooms, located at the back of the hotel, are available.

Leon Bianco

Road map D4. Piazzetta Pedrocchi 12, 35122. (*(049) 875 08 14.* **FAX** *875 61 84.* **Rooms:** *22.* 🛏 1 ♨ TV 🍴 📶 P 🅿 L L

It is essential to book ahead to make sure of a room at this central hotel, overlooking the Caffè Pedrocchi *(see p178).* The rooms are on the small side but it is friendly and welcoming.

Augustus Terme

Road map C4. Viale Stazione 150, 35036 Montegrotto Terme.
(*(049) 79 32 00.* **FAX** *79 35 18.*
Rooms: *130.* 🛏 1 ♨ TV 🍴 ♒ 📶 P 🍴 🅿 ● *5 Jan–28 Feb, 20 Nov–20 Dec.* L L L

The spa town of Montegrotto Terme has a number of modern hotels and makes a useful last-minute stopping point for drivers with no pre-booked accommodation. The Augustus Terme is one of the best hotels here: big, comfortable and functional, with a pretty garden and tennis court. You can also sample the thermal hot springs.

Donatello

Road map D4. Via del Santo 102, 35123. (*(049) 875 06 34.*
FAX *(049) 875 08 29.* **Rooms:** *49.* 🛏 1 ♨ TV 🍴 📶 P 🍴 🅿 ● *mid-Dec–mid-Jan.* L L L

Named after the sculptor of the great equestrian statue on the piazza outside, the Donatello is opposite the Basilica di Sant' Antonio *(see p182).* The old shell encloses a modern hotel whose bedrooms are large and comfortable, if lacking in character.

TREVISO

Beccherie

Road map D3. Piazza Ancillotto 10, 31100. (*(0422) 54 08 71.* **Rooms:** *14.* 🛏 1 TV 🍴 🅿 L L

This is by far the best of Treviso's budget hotels: clean, comfortable and welcoming, and situated right in the middle of the historic town centre. The hotel restaurant offers an excellent range of local dishes.

VALDOBBIADENE

Diana

Road map D3. Via Roma 49, 31049. (*(0423) 97 62 22.* **FAX** *97 22 37.*
Rooms: *54.* 🛏 1 ♨ TV 🍴 📶 P 🍴 L L

Lying at the northern end of the Strada del Vino Prosecco, the attractive town of Valdobbiadene stands on the slopes of the Venetian pre-Alps overlooking the Piave valley. The Diana has good facilities and comfortable rooms.

VICENZA

Casa San Raffaele

Road map C4. Viale X Giugno 10, 36100 Santa Monte Berico.
(*(0444) 54 57 67.* **FAX** *54 22 59.*
Rooms: *24.* 🛏 1 ♨ 📶 P 🅿 L

This tranquil hotel lies on the slopes of Monte Berico, with its lovely views over the city. It takes about half an hour to walk into town, but the good rooms make it by far the best choice among the less expensive hotels.

Campo Marzio

Road map C4. Viale Roma 27, 36100. (*(0444) 54 57 00.*
FAX *32 04 95.* **Rooms:** *35.* 🛏 1 TV 🍴 P 🍴 🅿 L L L

This stylish, modern hotel, with good facilities, is near the city centre. It is set in a peaceful area not far from the cathedral.

VERONA AND LAKE GARDA

LAKE GARDA SOUTH

Peschiera

Road map A4. Via Parini 4, 37010 Peschiera del Garda. (*(045) 755 05 26.* **FAX** *755 04 44.* **Rooms:** *30.* 🛏 ♨ ♒ 📶 P 🍴 🅿 ● *Nov–Mar.* L L

Just five minutes' drive off the A4 motorway at the southern end of Lake Garda, the little town of Peschiera makes a good overnight stopping place. The Peschiera is a modern building in a traditional style set in its own grounds, with lofty, cool bedrooms and friendly staff. The proprietors will collect train travellers from the station.

Villa Cortine Palace

Road map A4. Via Grotte 12, 25019 Sirmione del Garda. (*(030) 990 58 90.* **FAX** *91 63 90.* **Rooms:** *49.* 🛏 ♨ TV 🍴 📶 P 🍴 🅿 ● *25 Oct–2 Apr.* L L L L L *half-board only.*

The fabulous grounds of this tranquil hotel *(see p223)* cover a third of the Sirmione peninsula *(see pp206–7).* The huge frescoed rooms of this Classical villa are furnished with antiques, while the bedrooms, standard of comfort, food and service are all you would expect from a hotel of this calibre.

LAKE GARDA WEST

Hotel du Lac

Road map A3. Via Colletta 21, 25084 Gargnano. (*(0365) 711 07.*
FAX *725 94.* **Rooms:** *12.* 🛏 ♨ TV P 🍴 🅿 ● *mid-Oct–end Mar.*

The dining room of this pretty, stuccoed old building overhangs the water and many bedrooms have balconies facing the lake. This family-run hotel makes a good base for exploring the western shore of Lake Garda.

Capo Reamol

Road map B3. Via IV Novembre 92, 25010 Limone sul Garda. (*(0365) 95 40 40.* **FAX** *95 42 62.* **Rooms:** *48.* 🛏 1 ♨ TV 🍴 📶 P 🍴 🅿 *Oct–Apr.* L L L L

This hotel has a stunning location below the main road and right on the lake's edge. All the spacious bedrooms have their own terrace and good meals are served in the waterside dining room. The hotel's facilities are excellent for families, and include a private beach and jetty, a gym, sauna and jacuzzi and good sunbathing terraces.

Lido Palace

Road map B3. Viale Carducci 10, 38066 Riva del Garda. ((0464) 55 26 64. FAX 55 19 57. **Rooms:** 63. 🛏 TV 🔃 🕭 🐧 P 🍴 🖉 ● Nov–15 Mar. ⑛⑛⑛⑛

A spacious country villa houses this immaculately maintained hotel, standing in its own grounds on the outskirts of Riva. Try to book one of the high-ceilinged rooms on the first floor; the upper floors are more cramped. There is a tennis court for visitors' and the lake offers water-sports facilities.

LAKE GARDA EAST

Bisesti

Road map A3. Corso Italia 34, 37016 Garda. ((045) 725 57 66. FAX 725 59 27. **Rooms:** 90. 🛏 1 🔃 🐧 P 🍴 🖉 ● Oct–Mar. ⑛⑛

Conveniently placed near the centre of town and only five minutes' walk from Lake Garda, the Bisesti is a well-equipped modern holiday hotel set in its own grounds and with access to a private beach. Many of the rooms have a balcony and the dining room overlooks the garden.

Kriss Internazionale

Road map A3. Lungolago Cipriani 3, 37011 Bardolino. (045) 621 24 33. FAX 721 02 42. **Rooms:** 33. 🛏 1 🔃 TV 🔃 🐧 P 🍴 🖉 Dec–Feb. ⑛⑛

Attractively situated on a small promontory jutting into the lake, this modern hotel caters specifically for holiday-makers. Rooms have balconies and lake views, there is a garden, and the hotel has a private beach. The hotel will provide transport from the bus station for those travellers who arrive without a car.

Sailing Center Hotel

Road map B3. Località Molini Campagnola 3, 37018 Malcésine. ((045) 740 00 55. FAX 740 03 92. **Rooms:** 32. 🛏 🔃 TV 🔃 P 🍴 🖉 ● Oct–Mar. ⑛⑛⑛

Far from the crowds, sited on land jutting into the lake, this modern hotel just outside the main town of Malcésine makes a good base for families for a short stay. The rooms are cool and pleasant, and there is a tennis court and private beach for residents.

Locanda San Vigilio

Road map A3. San Vigilio, 37016 Garda. ((045) 725 66 88. FAX (045) 725 65 51. **Rooms:** 7. 🛏 TV 🔃 P 🍴 🖉 ● Nov–Mar. ⑛⑛⑛⑛

One of the loveliest and most exclusive hotels on Lake Garda, the Locanda lives up to every expectation of comfort, good taste and impeccable service. There is a private beach and a walled garden.

VERONA

Il Torcolo

Road map B4. Vicolo Listone 3, 37100. ((045) 800 75 12. FAX 800 40 58. **Rooms:** 19. 🛏 1 🔃 TV 🔃 P 🖉 ● mid–end Jan. ⑛⑛

An extremely popular hotel within a stone's throw of the Arena, the Torcola has some pretty, traditional rooms, and others which are more modern. With its charming interior, breakfast terrace and friendly owners, the hotel is always busy.

Colomba d'Oro

Road map B4. Via Carlo Cattaneo 10, 37100. ((045) 59 53 00. FAX 59 49 74. **Rooms:** 49. 🛏 1 TV 🔃 🐧 P ⑛⑛⑛⑛

An old stone building on a quiet pedestrian street near the Arena houses this central hotel. Rooms are rather plain, but the parking is a bonus and there are good restaurants in the neighbourhood.

Giulietta e Romeo

Road map B4. Vicolo Tre Marchetti 3, 37100. ((045) 800 35 54. FAX 801 08 62. **Rooms:** 30. 🛏 1 🔃 🕭 🐧 🖉 ⑛⑛⑛

This hotel is situated on a quiet street near the Arena. The spacious bedrooms are comfortable, with modern furnishings. Breakfast is served in the bar and there are some good restaurants nearby.

Due Torri Hotel Baglioni

Road map B4. Piazza Sant' Anastasia 4, 37100. ((045) 59 50 44. FAX 800 41 30. **Rooms:** 91. 🛏 1 🔃 TV 🔃 🐧 P 🍴 🖉 ⑛⑛⑛⑛⑛

One of the oldest and perhaps most eccentric Italian hotels, the Due Torri is right in the heart of medieval Verona. The huge bedrooms are each decorated in the style of a different era, with contemporary furnishings, and there are plenty of painted ceilings and frescoed walls. Staying here is an unforgettable experience.

THE DOLOMITES

BELLUNO

Astor

Road map D2. Piazza dei Martiri 26/e, 32100. ((0437) 94 20 94. FAX 94 24 93. **Rooms:** 32. 🛏 1 🔃 TV 🐧 🖉 ⑛⑛

This centrally situated hotel is a good choice when visiting the region's main town. The Astor's rooms are comfortable and well designed, and offer very good value. In winter it is popular with skiers and there is a lively atmosphere in the bar.

CORTINA D'AMPEZZO

Corona

Road map D1. Via Val di Sotto 12, 32043. ((0436) 3251. FAX (0436) 86 73 39. **Rooms:** 38. 🛏 1 🔃 TV 🐧 🍴 🖉 ● mid–Apr–mid–Jun, mid–Sep–mid–Dec. ⑛⑛⑛ half-board only.

Among upmarket Cortina's many stylish hotels, the Corona has much to offer. The bedrooms are pretty and comfortable, the bar and restaurant well-appointed, and there is also a relaxing garden.

Menardi

Road map D1. Via Majon 110, 32043. ((0436) 2400. FAX (0436) 86 21 83. **Rooms:** 53. 🛏 1 🔃 TV 🐧 P 🍴 🖉 ● mid–Apr–mid–Jun, mid–Sep–mid–Dec ⑛⑛⑛

The Menardi family have run this hotel on the outskirts of Cortina since 1900. Originally built as a farmhouse, it is furnished with antiques and has a welcoming and homely atmosphere.

SAN VITO DI CADORE

Hotel Ladinia

Road map D1. Via Ladinia 14, 32046. ((0436) 890450. FAX 992 11. **Rooms:** 46. 🛏 🔃 🐧 P 🍴 🖉 ● Easter–May, Oct–Christmas. ⑛⑛⑛

In the scenic Ampezzo valley, the Hotel Ladinia is in a tiny resort village 11 km (7 miles) south of Cortina. Popular in summer as well as during the skiing season, the Ladinia is geared to holiday-makers. There is a tennis court; and you can have a drink in the bar, or outside in the garden.

For key to symbols see p225

RESTAURANTS, CAFÉS AND BARS

RESTAURANTS IN VENICE and the Veneto serve predominantly Italian food from the region, with the emphasis in Venice very much on fish. Wherever you go, you will find the cooking simple, with dishes that make full use of the traditional local ingredients.

Most Venetians eat lunch *(pranzo)* around 12:30pm and dinner *(cena)* from 8pm, though restaurants start serving dinner earlier to cater for the many foreign visitors.

Egyptian detail, Caffè Pedrocchi

Restaurants may be closed for several weeks during the winter and also for two to three weeks during the staff summer holidays. Closing dates are included in the listings, but avoid disappointment by asking your hotel to phone first to confirm that the restaurant is open. Finding restaurants can be confusing in Venice, so use the map references provided. The restaurants listed on pages 240–45 are some of the best across all price ranges.

El Gato restaurant, Chioggia, famous for its fish *(see p242)*

TYPES OF RESTAURANTS

ITALIAN EATING PLACES have a bewildering variety of names, and the differences between them are very subtle. A *trattoria*, an *osteria* and a *ristorante* are pretty similar in terms of price, cooking and ambience, though originally *ristoranti* were a little smarter, while *trattorie* were more homely concerns. Nowadays, these distinctions are blurred so names can be misleading. A *birreria* and a *spaghetteria* are more down-market eating places that sell beer, pasta dishes and snacks; you will mainly find these outside Venice itself. A good *pizzeria* will use wood-fired ovens for the pizza; if this is the case it will normally be open only in the evenings.

If you do not want to eat a full meal at lunchtime you can always stop in a bar or café for a snack. For further information on light meals see page 246.

OPENING TIMES AND CLOSING DAYS

OPENING TIMES are virtually the same throughout Venice and the Veneto: from noon to 2:30pm for lunch, and from 7:30pm to 10:30pm for dinner. Under Italian law all restaurants close one day a week and some close for an additional evening as well; closing days are staggered so there is always somewhere open in the area. Individual restaurants' closing days are given in the listings.

The main bar of the historic Caffè Pedrocchi *(see p178)*

VEGETARIAN FOOD

ITALIANS FIND it difficult to understand vegetarianism, but if you eat fish you should have no difficulty eating well. If not, there is still a variety of meatless dishes since many starters *(antipasti)*, soups and pasta sauces are vegetable-based. Salads and vegetables are always good, and most places will be happy to serve an omelette *(frittata)* or a selection of cheese.

FIXED-PRICE MENUS

IN THE DAYS when Italy was building its tourist industry all restaurants had to supply a fixed-price menu. This has largely fallen into abeyance, particularly outside the main tourist centres. Restaurants may often have the so-called *menu turistico* pinned up in the street, but not on offer inside. Such menus, if you do find them, are usually boring and offer no opportunity to sample the wonderful variety of the local cuisine. If money is tight it is far better to have a good pasta dish and some salad, which is acceptable in all but the grandest places.

The *menu gastronomico* is a fixed-price menu consisting of six or seven courses, which allows you to sample the full range of a chef's specialities.

HOW MUCH TO PAY

TRANSPORT CHARGES can add as much as 30 per cent to the price of basic commodities coming into Venice, which partly explains the high cost of eating. In cheaper eating places and *pizzerie* you can have a two-course meal with half a litre of wine for around L20,000–30,000. Three-course meals average about L35,000–50,000, and in up-market restaurants you can easily pay L100,000–140,000. In the Veneto, prices are lower, except for stylish restaurants in Verona and along Lake Garda during the summer.

Nearly all restaurants have a cover charge *(pane e coperto)*, usually L2,000–5,000. Many also add a 10 per cent service charge *(servizio)* to the bill *(il conto)*, so always establish whether or not this is the case. Where leaving a tip is a matter of your own discretion, 12–15 per cent is acceptable.

Restaurants are obliged by law to give you a receipt *(una ricevuta fiscale)*. Scraps of paper with an illegible scrawl are illegal, and you are within your rights to ask for a proper bill. The preferred form of payment is cash, but many restaurants will accept payment by major credit cards. Check which cards are accepted when booking.

MAKING RESERVATIONS

WHATEVER the price range, Venice's best restaurants are always busy, so it is best to reserve a table, especially if you are making a long boat trip to get there. If restaurants do not accept bookings, try to arrive early to avoid queuing.

DRESS CODE

ITALIANS LIKE to dress up to dine, though, with rare exceptions, this does not mean that men have to wear a tie, and only occasionally will you feel under-dressed without a jacket. Smart casual clothes are the general rule for men, though ladies in evening attire will not look at all out of place.

Eating under the loggia of Treviso's Palazzo dei Trecento *(see p174)*

READING THE MENU

BOTH LUNCH and dinner in a restaurant follow the same pattern and usually start with an *antipasto*, or hors d'oeuvres (seafood, olives, beef carpaccio, ham, salami), followed by the *primo* (soup, rice or pasta). The main course, or *secondo*, will be fish or meat, either served alone or accompanied by vegetables *(contorni)* or a salad *(insalata)*. These are never included in the price of the main course.

To finish, there will probably be a choice of fruit *(frutta)*, a pudding *(dolce)* or cheese *(formaggio)*, or a combination of all three. Coffee – Italians always have an *espresso*, never a *cappuccino* – is ordered and served right at the end of the meal, often with a *digestivo*. In cheaper restaurants, the menu *(il menu)* may be chalked up or the waiter may simply recite the day's special dishes at your table.

A short break at Carnival

CHOICE OF WINE

HOUSE WINES will usually be local *(see pp238–9)*. Cheaper restaurants will have a limited wine list, but at the top of the scale there should be a wide range of Italian and local wines and a selection of foreign vintages.

CHILDREN

CHILDREN ARE welcome in restaurants, particularly in simple, family-run ones. Smart places may be less welcoming, particularly in the evenings. Special facilities such as high chairs are not commonly provided. Most restaurants will prepare a half-portion *(mezza porzione)* if requested, and some charge less for these smaller helpings.

SMOKING

ITALIANS STILL smoke more than most Europeans. Virtually no restaurants set aside space for non-smokers.

WHEELCHAIR ACCESS

VERY FEW RESTAURANTS make special provision for wheelchairs, though a word when booking should ensure a conveniently situated table and assistance on arrival.

USING THE LISTINGS
Key to the symbols in the listings on pp240–45.

🍴 fixed-priced menu
👔 jacket and tie required
🪑 tables outside
🗔 air conditioning
🍷 good wine list
★ highly recommended
💳 credit cards accepted.
Check which cards are accepted when booking.

Price categories for a three-course meal for one including a half-bottle of house wine, cover charge, tax and service.
Ⓛ under L25,000
ⓁⓁ L25,000–L50,000
ⓁⓁⓁ L50,000–L75,000
ⓁⓁⓁⓁ L75,000–L100,000
ⓁⓁⓁⓁⓁ over L100,000

What to Eat in Venice and the Veneto

TRADITIONAL VENETIAN specialities rely on the freshest of seasonal produce, meat and cheese from the mainland, and a huge variety of fish and seafood. Pasta is eaten here, as all over Italy, but more typical is polenta, made from maize flour, and also the many types of risotto. The mainland produces some renowned salamis. In the mountainous north, game and wild mushrooms provide the basis for some wonderful dishes, while Lake Garda is noted for *coregone*, a firm pink-fleshed fish rather like trout. The long red radicchio from Treviso is famous all over Italy, while Bassano del Grappa and Sant'Erasmo provide wonderful asparagus.

Young globe artichoke

Baccalà Mantecata
This is dried salted cod, mixed to a paste with olive oil, parsley and garlic.

Fiori di Zucchini
Courgette flowers stuffed with fish mousse, fried in a light batter, are a seasonal dish.

Small squid   Spider crab

Lobster   Mussels   Prawns

Antipasto di Frutti di Mare
The seafood selection is dressed with olive oil and lemon juice. It may include exotic shellfish rarely found outside the Lagoon.

Risotto alle Seppie
Cuttlefish ink colours the rice in this traditional risotto.

Carpaccio
Wafer-thin slices of raw beef dressed with oil are served here with rocket and parmesan cheese.

Risi e Bisi
Made with fresh peas and flavoured with bacon, this risotto is soft and liquid.

Brodo di Pesce
Fish soup, a classic Venetian dish, is sometimes flavoured with saffron.

Zuppa di Cozze
This is a delicious way of cooking mussels, with white wine, garlic and parsley.

Spaghetti alle Vongole
Fresh clams are served with spaghetti in a piquant sauce made with hot chilli peppers.

Grilled polenta

Home-made tomato sauce

Grated parmesan cheese

Polenta
Made from maize, polenta may be yellow or a more delicate white.

Sardine in Saor
A traditional Venetian way of serving fish is with a sweet and sour sauce.

Anguille in Umido
These eels are cooked in a light tomato sauce with white wine and garlic.

Fegato alla Veneziana
Tender calf's liver is lightly cooked on a bed of onions in this traditional speciality.

Faraona con la Peverada
The sauce for this succulent guinea fowl is based on an ancient Arabian recipe.

Insalata Mista
Wild young leaves of many shapes and colours make up this summer salad.

Radicchio alla Griglia
These red endive leaves from Treviso are grilled over a hot fire.

Mozzarella

Pecorino

Gelati
In summer, ice cream is made with fresh seasonal fruits.

Gorgonzola

Parmesan

Tiramisù
This dessert is made with coffee-soaked sponge cake and mascarpone cheese.

Cheeses
Local cheeses such as asiago, fontina and montasio may be included on the cheese board.

Amaretti
Small almond biscuits are served with coffee.

What to Drink in Venice and the Veneto

ITALY HAS BEEN MAKING WINE for over 3,000 years, and production in the Veneto reflects this, with the largest output in Italy of superior DOC wines. The area produces an abundance of different wines, which include not only well-known names such as Soave, Valpolicella and Bardolino, but many others which are also excellent value for money. Although Italians tend to drink lighter wines with their food, the area is also noted for some excellent strong wines. Italy's famous *digestivo*, grappa, originated in this corner of the country, and meals are often preceded by an *aperitivo* or a glass of sparkling local Prosecco.

Grapes drying in Valpolicella

RED WINE

RED WINES IN THE VENETO are produced mainly near Bardolino and Valpolicella between Verona and Lake Garda *(see pp208–9)*. Made predominantly from the Corvina grape, they are usually light and fruity, but quality can vary so it is worth looking for reliable names.

Valpolicella comes in several forms. In addition to the normal easy-drinking wine, it is available as a *ripasso*, boosted in colour and strength by macerating the skins of the grapes before pressing. Recioto della Valpolicella is very different, a rich, sweet wine made from selected air-dried grapes. Some Reciotos undergo further fermentation to remove the sweetness, producing the strong, dry Recioto Amarone. These are some of the strongest naturally alcoholic wines in the world and are delicious but expensive.

Excellent red wines are also made by producers such as Venegazzù and Maculan from the Cabernet Sauvignon and Merlot grapes.

Red Venegazzù   Masi's ripasso

Bardolino wine is light, fruity and garnet-red in colour.

Amarone is full-bodied, rich, full of fruit and very alcoholic.

READING WINE LABELS

ITALIAN WINES are classified by four quality levels. Starting at the top, DOCG status *(Denominazione di Origine Controllata e Garantita)* has been awarded to a small number of Italian growing areas, none of which are in the Veneto. Most quality wines – more than 250 in the whole of Italy – are in the DOC category (as above but without the "guarantee") and these can be relied on as good value, quality wines. IGT *(Indicazione Geografica Tipica)* is a category new to Italy, corresponding to the popular French Vin de Pays. The final classification is *vino da tavola*, or table wine, but due to the inflexible Italian wine laws many superb wines appear in this category.

No vintage recommendations are given in the chart because almost all Veneto wines are made for young drinking.

WINE TYPE	RECOMMENDED PRODUCERS
WHITE WINE	
Soave	Anselmi, Bertani, Col Baraca (Masi), Boscaini, CS di Soave, Masi, Pieropan, Scamperle, Tedeschi, Zenato, Zonin
Bianco di Custoza	Cavalchina, Le Tende, Le Vigne di San Pietro, Pezzini, San Leone, Tedeschi, Zenato
Breganze di Breganze	Maculan
Gambellara	CS di Gambellara, Zonin
RED WINE	
Bardolino	Alighieri, Bertani, Bolla, Boscaini, Guerrieri-Rizzardi, Masi, Tedeschi
Valpolicella	Alighieri, Allegrini, Bertani, Bolla, Boscaini, Guerrieri-Rizzardi, Masi, Tedeschi, Zenato
Ripasso Valpolicella (non-DOC)	Serègo Alighieri, Jago (Bolla), Le Cane (Boscaini), Le Sassine (Le Ragose), Campo Fiorin (Masi), Capitel San Rocco (Tedeschi)
Recioto and Recioto Amarone della Valpolicella	Serègo Alighieri, Allegrini, Masi, Quintarelli, Le Ragose, Tedeschi

WHITE WINE

Bianco di Custoza

White Recioto

THE VENETO produces more white wine than red, and most of the region's whites are from vineyards around the hilltop town of Soave *(see p190)*. These wines can be dull, but increasing numbers of producers are trying to raise Soave's image. Bianco di Custoza, a creamy, richer tasting "super Soave" from the eastern shores of Lake Garda, is well worth trying. Breganze is a name to look out for, with Maculan a leader in making fresh, clean, inexpensive wines and world-class dessert wines. Gambellara is made mainly from Soave's Garganega grape and is seldom of poor quality. Venegazzù is another producer you can trust for good quality white wines.

APERITIFS AND OTHER DRINKS

ITALIAN APERITIFS tend to be wine-based, bitter, herb-flavoured drinks such as Martini and Campari. Less familiar are the herbal Punt e Mes, Cynar (made from artichokes), and the vivid orange Aperol, which is good mixed with white wine and soda. Crodino is a popular non-alcoholic choice.

For settling the stomach after a good meal there are *amari* (bitters) and *digestivi*. Montenegro and Ramazzotti are well worth trying, and grappa, distilled from wine lees *(see Bassano del Grappa p166)*, is another favourite. A local speciality, Trevisana, is mixed with an extract of the long red radicchio from Treviso. Italian brandy can be rather oily, but Vecchia Romagna is a reliable name.

Grappa

Crodino

SOFT DRINKS

ITALIAN BOTTLED fruit juices are good, and come in delicious flavours such as pear, apricot and peach. Many bars will squeeze you a *spremuta* of fresh orange *(arancia)* or grapefruit *(pompelmo)* juice on the spot. A *frullato* is an ice-cold mix of milk and fresh fruit.

Spremuta di arancia

Pieropan is a top quality producer of Soave. The single-vineyard wines from here are superb.

White vino da tavola wines range from pale and dry to sweet and golden coloured.

Venegazzù's Pinot Grigio wine is dry and goes well with Venetian seafood.

Puiatti's white Ribolla wine is fruity but dry. It is made in neighbouring Friuli.

PROSECCO

The Veneto's own sparkling wine, Prosecco is perfect as either a refreshing light *aperitivo* or with a meal. It originates in Conegliano *(see p175)*, the home of Italy's greatest wine school, and comes in both *secco* (dry) or *amabile* (medium-sweet) forms, and as *frizzante* or *spumante* (semi and fully sparkling). An excellent accompaniment to both fruit and seafood, it is also the traditional base for Bellini, a delicious *aperitivo* of wine mixed with fresh white peach juice *(see p92)*. This drink has bred several variants, such as Mimosa (with orange) and Tiziano (with red grape juice).

Prosecco   **Bellini cocktail**

COFFEE

COFFEE IS AN ESSENTIAL part of Italian life. Milky *cappuccino* with chocolate powder is drunk at breakfast time, and tiny cups of strong black *espresso* throughout the day. If you like your coffee with milk, choose a *caffè con latte*, or with just a dash of milk, *caffè macchiato*. Black coffee that is not too strong is *caffè lungo*; a *doppio* has an extra kick and a *corretto* has a good measure of alcohol.

Espresso   **Cappuccino**

VENICE

SAN MARCO

Al Conte Pescaor

Piscina San Zulian, San Marco 544.
Map 7 B1. 📞 *(041) 522 14 83.*
🌑 *Sun.* 🍽 Ⓛ Ⓛ Ⓛ

It is worth seeking out this little
restaurant for its superb fish.
Despite its position, the clientele
are mainly local, which guarantees
the quality of the food.

Al Graspo de Ua

Calle Bombaseri, San Marco 5094.
Map 7 A1. 📞 *(041) 520 01 50.*
🌑 *Mon.* 🖥 🍽 📶 🍷 Ⓛ Ⓛ Ⓛ

Housed in three small rooms that
were once part of the old sacristy
of the church of San Bartolomeo,
the food here is Venetian with a
difference. Worth sampling are the
antipasto of prawns, artichokes
and rocket, while main courses
include fillet of John Dory.

Le Bistrot de Venise

Calle del Fabbri, San Marco 2159.
Map 7 B2. 📞 *(041) 523 66 51.*
📶 🖥 🍽 ★ 🍷 Ⓛ Ⓛ Ⓛ

This excellent restaurant serves
traditional Venetian cuisine. It also
has a very good wine list. A meeting place for local artists and poets,
the restaurant holds cultural events
in the afternoons and has a cabaret
and live music in the evenings.

Antico Martini

Campo San Fantin, San Marco 1980.
Map 7 A2. 📞 *(041) 522 41 21.*
🌑 *Tue, Wed lunch.* 📶 🖥 🍽 ★
🍷 Ⓛ Ⓛ Ⓛ

The terrace of this smart restaurant
used to overlook the Fenice theatre,
and dining inside has its advantages
too – meals are served until 1am.
The cooking is based on regional
specialities; breast of duck with
black truffles is recommended.
Puddings include an iced mousse
with raspberry sauce. The wine list
features more than 300 labels.

Da Arturo

Calle degli Assassini, San Marco 3656.
Map 7 A2. 📞 *(041) 528 69 74.*
🌑 *Sun. Ann hol Aug.* 🖥 🍽
Ⓛ Ⓛ Ⓛ

This high-quality, wood-panelled
restaurant is unique in Venice in
that it serves no fish or seafood
dishes. Interesting antipasti include
aubergines *"in saor"* (a vinegary
sweet and sour sauce), and there
are red wines of great distinction.
Vegetarians are catered for.

Do Forni

Calle dei Specchieri. San Marco 468.
Map 7 B2. 📞 *(041) 523 21 48.*
🖥 🍽 🍷 Ⓛ Ⓛ Ⓛ

A large "show business" establishment, the Do Forni has two dining
rooms furnished in contrasting
styles; one rustic but smart and the
other more elegant. The mixed
grilled fish is a house speciality
which should not be missed.

Harry's Bar

Calle Vallaresso, San Marco 1323.
Map 7 B3. 📞 *(041) 528 57 77.*
🖥 🍷 Ⓛ Ⓛ Ⓛ Ⓛ

People eat at Harry's Bar because
of its fame. The food is expensive,
but can certainly be good. Prawns
with oil and lemon, baked
tagliolini with prosciutto and
carpaccio alla Cipriani (raw
marinated beef) are among the
more interesting dishes. The wine
list is good and the cocktails are
justifiably world renowned.

Hotel Gritti

Campo Santa Maria del Giglio, San
Marco 2467. **Map** 6 F3.
📞 *(041) 79 46 11.* 📶 🖥 🍽
★ Ⓛ Ⓛ Ⓛ Ⓛ

The dining room of this famous
hotel is in the Venetian Gothic
building. The terrace overlooks the
Grand Canal and the church of
Santa Maria della Salute. Classic
dishes include baby prawns with
radicchio, *pasta e fagioli* (pasta
and beans), saffron risotto with
chicken livers and fried scampi.

La Caravella

Calle Larga XXII Marzo, San Marco
2396. **Map** 7 A3. 📞 *(041) 520 89 01.*
🖥 🍽 ★ 🍷 Ⓛ Ⓛ Ⓛ Ⓛ

One of two restaurants in the
Hotel Saturnia, the Caravella is
decorated to resemble the interior
of a 16th-century Venetian galley.
The food is outstanding, with a
range of imaginative dishes that
includes a smooth lobster soup,
bigoli and scampi in champagne.

Tiepolo dell'Europa e Regina

Calle Larga XXII Marzo, San Marco
2159. **Map** 7 A3. 📞 *(041) 520 04 77.*
📶 🖥 🍽 ★ 🍷 Ⓛ Ⓛ Ⓛ Ⓛ

This beautiful hotel restaurant is in
a 16th-century palace on the Grand
Canal and has a waterside terrace
where guests can eat outdoors in
summer. The food lives up to the
setting, featuring dishes such as
seafood salad, porcini mushrooms
with parmesan cheese, *fegato alla
veneziana*, raspberry crêpes and
tiramisù. The wine list is excellent.

SAN POLO AND SANTA CROCE

Antica Bessetta

Calle Savio, San Polo 1395. **Map** 2 E5.
📞 *(041) 72 16 87.* 🌑 *Tue, Wed
lunch.* Ⓛ Ⓛ Ⓛ

This simple family-run restaurant
offers real Venetian home-cooking,
including *risi e bisi* (fresh spring
pea risotto) in season, home-made
pasta and good scampi.

Trattoria alla Madonna

Calle della Madonna, San Polo 594.
Map 7 A1. 📞 *(041) 522 38 24.*
🌑 *Wed.* 🖥 ★ 🍷 Ⓛ Ⓛ Ⓛ

This big, lively fish restaurant is a
perennial favourite with Venetians
and tourists alike. The seafood
risotto and fish soup are excellent,
and the fried and grilled main fish
courses all highly recommended.

Antica Trattoria Poste Vecie

Rialto Pescheria, San Polo 1608.
Map 3 A5. 📞 *(041) 72 18 22.*
🌑 *Tue.* 📶 ★ 🍷 Ⓛ Ⓛ Ⓛ

This stylish restaurant, situated
near the fish market, claims to be
the oldest in Venice. It offers
dishes such as home-made ravioli
and tagliolini, baked turbot and
brill, and there is an impressive
pudding trolley.

Da Fiore

Calle dello Scalater 2202a, San Polo
1608. **Map** 6 D2. 📞 *(041) 72 13 08.*
🌑 *Sun & Mon.* 🖥 🍽 🍷
Ⓛ Ⓛ Ⓛ

The excellent fish specialities on
offer at Da Fiore include a wonderful seafood antipasto, grilled fish
and *fritto misto* (mixed seafood in
batter). The restaurant has a good
wine list, but the house white is
also well worth a try.

CASTELLO

Hostaria da Franz

Fondamenta San Giuseppe, Castello
754. **Map** 8 D1. 📞 *(041) 522 08 61.*
🌑 *Tue.* 📶 🖥 🍽 ★ 🍷 Ⓛ Ⓛ Ⓛ

Situated behind the Public
Gardens, the Gasparini's restaurant
with its canalside terrace serves
some of the best seafood in
Venice. Try the gnocchi with
prawns and spinach, marinated
prawns and peppers, or fried fish
with polenta.

Corte Sconta

Calle del Pestrin, Castello 3886.
Map 8 E2. [C] *(041) 522 70 24.*
● *Sun & Mon.* 🚻 🔒 ★ 🍽
ⓁⓁⓁ

The Proietto family have built
up this restaurant from a simple
eating house to one of the city's
top dining spots. It is rather
difficult to find, but worth the
effort for the superb fish dishes
and home-made pasta, served in
the pretty garden in summer.

Les Deux Lions del Hotel Londra Palace

Riva degli Schiavoni, Castello 4171.
Map 8 D1. [C] *(041) 520 05 33.* 🚻
🗐 🍽 ⓁⓁⓁⓁ

A hotel restaurant with a good reputation, Les Deux Lions has a terrace
right on the Riva. The cooking is
Italian and French; the *entrecôte
béarnaise* is recommended, as is
the casseroled Verona chicken. The
desserts are good; the chocolate
gateau made with plain, milk and
white chocolate tops the list.

Arcimboldo

Calle dei Furlani, Castello 3219. **Map**
8 D1. [C] *(041) 528 65 69.* ● *Tue in
winter.* 🗐 🔒 🍽 ⓁⓁⓁⓁ

This restaurant takes its name from
16th-century painter Arcimboldo,
who used vegetables and fruit to
create portraits of people. It offers
equally diverse interpretations on
the Venetian culinary theme. Try
sea-bass with tomatoes or marinated
salmon with citrus fruit and herbs.

Danieli Terrace

Riva degli Schiavoni, Castello 4191.
Map 8 D2. [C] *(041) 522 64 80.* 🚻
🗐 🔒 ★ 🍽 ⓁⓁⓁⓁ

The panorama over St Mark's Basin
from this stylish hotel restaurant is
magnificent, and the food and
service are just what you would
expect from an establishment of
this calibre. The risotti are very
good and the excellent wine list
features solely Italian wines.

DORSODURO

Da Silvio

Calle San Pantalon, Dorsoduro.
Map 6 D2. [C] *(041) 520 58 33.*
● *Sat lunch & Sun.* 🚻 Ⓛ

It is a pleasure to find a genuine
neighbourhood restaurant in
Venice, and this one has a lovely
garden for summer eating. The
menu has no surprises, but the
food is all fresh and home-made.

Taverna San Trovaso

Fondamenta Priuli, Dorsoduro 1016.
Map 6 E3. [C] *(041) 520 37 03.*
● *Mon.* 🗐 🍽 ⓁⓁ

This cheerful, bustling restaurant
on two floors is between the
Accademia and the Zattere. The
cooking is straightforward and
they also serve pizzas.

Locanda Montin

Fondamenta Eremite, Dorsoduro 1147.
Map 6 D3. [C] *(041) 522 71 51.* ●
Tue eve & Wed. 🚻 ★ 🍽 ⓁⓁⓁ

This famous restaurant, with its
artistic and literary connnections,
can be variable in quality and
service, but the garden is a delight
and the atmosphere lively. It also
contains a commercial art gallery.

Agli Alboretti

Rio Terrà Sant'Agnese, Dorsoduro 882.
Map 6 E4. [C] *(041) 523 00 58.*
● *Wed & Thu lunch.* 🗐 🔒 🍽
ⓁⓁⓁⓁ

Named after the trees outside, Agli
Alboretti is welcoming inside and
refreshing in summer, when you
can eat outside under the pergola.
The cooking has innovative
touches – try saffron risotto with
scampi and mussels, monkfish
tails or veal with cherries.

Ai Gondolieri

San Vio, Dorsoduro 366. **Map** 6 F4.
[C] *(041) 528 63 96.* ● *Tue.* 🗐 🔒
★ 🍽 ⓁⓁⓁⓁ

Housed in a genuine old inn, sym-
pathetically restored, this restaurant
is owned by Giovanni Trevisan,
whose wife Marisa does the cooking. She is a dedicated regional
cook and her specialities include
some excellent vegetable dishes
such as the long red radicchio from
Treviso and *sformati* of wild leaves.

Linea d'Ombra

Zattere ai Saloni, Dorsoduro 19. **Map**
7 A4. [C] *(041) 520 47 20.* ● *Wed
& Sun pm.* 🚻 🗐 🔒 🍽 ⓁⓁⓁⓁ

Situated at the end of the Zattere,
the Linea comes into its own in
summer, when you can dine on
the terrace and enjoy breathtaking
views across to the Giudecca. The
food includes several hard-to-find
Venetian dishes such as *baccalà
mantecato* and *sarde in saor*.

CANNAREGIO

Vini Da Gigio

Fondamenta San Felice, Cannaregio
3628/a. **Map** 3 A4. [C] *(041) 528
51 40.* ● *Mon.* 🔒 🍽 ⓁⓁ

Traditional Venetian food with a
modern twist is prepared in this
cosy but elegant restaurant. The
risotto with nettles and prawns is
excellent, and puddings include
crema fritta alla veneziana.

Ostaria al Bacco

Fondamenta delle Cappuccine,
Cannaregio 3054. **Map** 2 D2. [C] *(041)
71 74 93.* ● *Mon.* 🚻 🍽 ⓁⓁ

The emphasis is on fish in this rustic
restaurant with its pretty shaded
courtyard. First courses include
spaghetti with black cuttlefish sauce
and *frittura di pesce* (lightly fried
local fish). *Baccalà*, the classic dried
salted cod dish, is also on the menu.

Fiaschetteria Toscana

San Crisostomo, Cannaregio 5719.
Map 3 B5. [C] *(041) 528 52 81.*
● *Tue.* 🚻 🗐 🔒 🍽 ⓁⓁⓁⓁ

This restaurant, run by the Busatto
family, offers many Venetian
dishes as well as Scottish beef.
The warm salad of lagoon fish is
a delicious antipasto, and main
dishes include eels and turbot with
black butter and capers.

THE LAGOON ISLANDS

Antica Trattoria alla Maddalena

Mazzorbo. [C] *(041) 73 01 51.*
● *Thu.* 🚻 🍽 ⓁⓁ

Close beside the *vaporetto* stop on
Mazzorbo, this modest restaurant
originally was, and still is, the local
bar and eating house. However,
visitors flock here to dine in tran-
quillity and savour the famous wild
duck with fettuccine or polenta.

Do Mori

Eufemia, Giudecca 588. [C] *(041) 522
54 52.* ● *Sun.* ★ 🍽 ⓁⓁ

This rustic-style restaurant, right on
the Giudecca waterfront, is run by
the ex-chef from Harry's Bar, and
it shows – though the prices are
very attractive. The cooking is
homely Venetian, with good
antipasti, home-made pasta and
several fine fish dishes. Puddings
are home made and good.

Ai Pescatori

Via Galuppi 371, Burano. [C] *(041) 73
06 50.* ● *Wed.* 🚻 🗐 🔒 ★ 🍽
ⓁⓁⓁ

Recently renovated, Ai Pescatori is
still a welcoming restaurant where
you can eat outside in summer. Interesting dishes include lobster and
tagliolini with cuttlefish. In winter
the menu is known for its game
dishes. The wine list is extensive.

Harry's Dolci

Eufemia,Giudecca 773. **Map** 5 C5.
📞 *(041) 522 48 44.* ☐ *Apr–Oct.*
● *Tue.* 🏠 🍴 ★ 🅿 Ⓛ Ⓛ Ⓛ

What started as a bar and tearoom is now a restaurant serving many of the specialities of the main establishment *(see p240)*. You can enjoy *pasta e fagioli* (pasta and beans), *carpaccio* (marinated raw beef in slivers) and liver, preceded by a genuine Bellini and followed by the delicious house chocolate cake. They also sell the range of Cipriani foodstuffs.

Da Romano

Piazza Galuppi 221, Burano.
📞 *(041) 73 00 30.* ● *Tue.* 🏠 🍴
🅿 Ⓛ Ⓛ Ⓛ Ⓛ

Founded in the 1930s, this pretty restaurant with its shady terrace on Burano's main street is now run by the original owner's son. It serves excellent fish at lower prices than you would find in Venice.

Osteria al Ponte del Diavolo

Torcello. 📞 *(041) 73 04 01.* ● *Wed.*
🏠 ★ 🅿 Ⓛ Ⓛ Ⓛ

The Osteria gets its name from the graceful bridge across Torcello's now neglected main canal. It was set up by a breakaway trio of staff from Cipriani, so the traditional fish-based menu is good. The large terrace, makes this an attractive spot to stop for lunch.

Hotel Cipriani

Giudecca 10. **Map** 7 C5.
📞 *(041) 520 77 44.* 🏠 🍴 🅿
★ 🅿 Ⓛ Ⓛ Ⓛ Ⓛ

The setting and style alone almost justify the high prices of the Hotel Cipriani. The mirror-lined dining room reflects the lagoon and the summer terrace is an oasis of calm. The food is creative and the wine list good. Sample the antipasti buffet before moving on to the other specialities, which include a fish "surprise" in pastry.

Locanda Cipriani

Piazza Santa Fosca 29, Torcello.
📞 *(041) 73 01 50.* ● *Tue. Ann hol Jan.* 🏠 🍴 🅿 Ⓛ Ⓛ Ⓛ Ⓛ Ⓛ

The most far-flung of the Cipriani establishments was transformed from a fisherman's inn in the 1930s. Dishes include *fritto misto*, and risotto made with fresh greens from the Locanda's picturesque kitchen garden. Lunch here makes a good outing, and the restaurant's launch will collect you from Piazza San Marco.

THE VENETO PLAIN

ASIAGO

Ristorante Casa Rossa

Road map C3. Via Kaberlaba 19, 36012. 📞 *(0424) 46 20 17.*
● *Thu.* 🏠 🍴 ★ 🅿 Ⓛ Ⓛ

Situated in the hills of the Sette Comuni (Seven Communities), this simple restaurant is noted for its regional cooking. Try the savoury cake with wild salad leaves, the duck breast and the wild berry tart. You can eat outside in the garden.

ASOLO

Villa Cipriani

Road map D3. Via Canova 298, 31011. 📞 *(0423) 95 21 66.* 🍴 🏠 🍴 🅿 ★ 🅿 Ⓛ Ⓛ Ⓛ Ⓛ

This 16th-century villa houses one of the grand hotels of the Veneto *(see p231)*. The restaurant serves innovative and creative food, using local ingredients in such dishes as pappardelle (broad flat pasta) with scampi, tomatoes and basil, and veal medallions with asparagus and artichoke hearts.

BRENTA CANAL

Alla Posta

Road map D4. Via Ca' Tron 33, Dolo. 📞 *(041) 41 07 40.* ● *Mon. Ann hol 1–15 Jan, 1 week Jul.* 🍽 🏠 🍴 🅿 🅿 Ⓛ Ⓛ Ⓛ

The Modena family run this superb fish restaurant, which is housed in an old Venetian staging posthouse. The anchovy and potato tart is particularly good.

CASTELFRANCO

Barbesin

Road map D3. Via Montebelluna 41. 📞 *(0423) 49 04 46.* ● *Wed eve and Thu. Ann hol 1–15 Jan, 7–21 Aug.* 🍽 🍴 🅿 🅿 Ⓛ Ⓛ

This restaurant is very good value. It serves a variety of regional specialities, including risotto of porcini mushrooms and duck breast with rosemary.

CHIOGGIA

El Gato

Road map D4. Campo San Andrea 653, 30015. 📞 *(041) 40 18 06.*
● *Mon & Tue lunch. Ann hol Jan–15 Feb.* 🏠 🍴 🅿 ★ 🅿 Ⓛ Ⓛ Ⓛ

Classic cooking in a restrained setting makes this restaurant special. As you would expect in a fishing port, the emphasis is on seafood. The cuttlefish is cooked in the traditional Chioggian way and served with polenta.

CONEGLIANO

Al Salisa

Road map D3. Via XX Settembre 2, 31015. 📞 *(0438) 242 88.* ● *Tue eve & Wed. Ann hol Aug.* 🍴 🏠 🅿
★ 🅿 Ⓛ Ⓛ

This elegant little restaurant in an old house has a pretty veranda where you can eat outside on warm summer evenings. Among the interesting dishes here are home-made fettuccine with a sauce of radicchio and chicken livers, and turbot cooked wrapped in spinach. Try the superlative cold zabaglione for pudding.

EUGANEAN HILLS

Trattoria da Piero Ceschi

Road map C4. Piazza Trento 16, 35042 Este. 📞 *(0429) 28 55.*
● *Thu. Ann hol Jul.* Ⓛ Ⓛ

Located right in the historic centre of Este, this friendly little restaurant serves local prosciutto and genuine porchetta, a whole roast suckling pig with herbs and spices. Pietro, the owner, chef and head waiter, personally selects his excellent wine list from local producers.

La Montanella

Road map C4. Via Costa 33, 35032 Arquà Petrarca. 📞 *(0429) 71 82 00.*
● *Tue eve & Wed. Ann hol 7–14 Jan, 10–20 Aug.* 🍽 🏠 🅿 🅿
🅿 Ⓛ Ⓛ Ⓛ

Petrarch spent the last years of his life at Arquà Petrarca, the prettiest of the Euganean spa towns *(see p184)*. Eating at La Montanella is a pleasure, with a menu that includes asparagus tortelloni and guinea-fowl among its treats.

MESTRE

Dall'Amelia

Road map D4. Via Miranesi 113, 30171 Mestre. (*(041) 91 39 51.*) *Wed.* ¶❶ 🖥 🍷 🍴 Ⓛ Ⓛ Ⓛ Ⓛ

This restaurant is considered to be one of the finest specializing in classic Venetian cooking. A separate area for those eating fried fish is indicative of the standard here. Specialities include tagliolini with fresh tomatoes and anchovies, and porcini mushrooms with rocket, as well as a wide choice of fish and mouth-watering puddings. The wine list is exceptional.

Ristorante Marco Polo

Road map C4. Via Forte Marghera, 30173 Mestre. (*(041) 98 98 55.*) *Sun. Ann hol Aug.* ¶❶ 🖥 🍷 Ⓛ Ⓛ Ⓛ Ⓛ

Familiar dishes are given a personal interpretation here. John Dory with wild fennel, and swordfish with capers are good choices, while meat-eaters will enjoy the veal with porcini mushrooms.

ODERZO

Gambrinus Parco

Road map E3. Località Gambrinus 22, 31020 San Polo di Piave. (*(0422) 85 50 43.*) *Mon (exc public hols). Ann hol 7–31 Jan.* ¶❶ 🖥 🍷 ★ 🍴 Ⓛ Ⓛ Ⓛ

This restaurant is faithful to the regional culinary tradition. Two outstanding fish dishes are the freshwater prawns alla Gambrinus and the sturgeon cooked with coarse salt.

PADUA

Osteria L'Anfora

Road map D4. Via dei Soncin 13, 35122. (*(049) 65 66 29.*) *Sun.* 🍷 🍴 Ⓛ

This enticing restaurant serves traditional Venetian cuisine enlivened by influences originally brought to Venice by Renaissance merchants.

Boccadoro

Road map D4. Via della Resistenza 49, 35100 Noventa Padovana. (*(049) 62 50 29.*) *Tue eve & Wed. Ann hol 2–12 Jan, 4–27 Aug.* ¶❶ 🖥 🍷 🍴 Ⓛ Ⓛ

Good Paduan food is served in this family-run restaurant. There is an excellent radicchio soup and the goose is worth sampling.

La Braseria

Road map D4. Via N Tommaseo 48, 35100. (*(049) 876 09 07.*) *Sun. Ann hol 1 week Aug.* 🍴 Ⓛ Ⓛ

This is a friendly restaurant where you can enjoy straightforward cooking. The penne with porcini mushrooms and the smoked ham called *speck* are recommended.

Belle Parti El Toulà

Road map D4. Via Belle Parti 11, 35100. (*(049) 875 18 22.*) *Sun. Ann hol 3 weeks Aug.* 🖥 🍷 🍴 Ⓛ Ⓛ Ⓛ

This comfortable, distinguished restaurant is housed in a 16th-century *palazzo*. The vegetable recipes, such as the aubergine *sformato*, are particularly good.

San Clemente

Road map C4. Corso Vittorio Emanuele II 142, 35123. (*(049) 880 31 80.* **FAX** *(049) 880 30 15.*) *Sun & Mon lunch. Ann hol Aug.* ¶❶ 🖬 🖥 🍷 ★ 🍴 Ⓛ Ⓛ Ⓛ Ⓛ

San Clemente occupies a villa attributed to Palladio, and stands in a tranquil garden. The excellent food and service match the impressive ambience, and dishes such as pigeon with stuffed pear and chicken ravioli are unusual and good. The wine list includes some fabulous Tuscan Brunello wines. If you want lunch it is advisable to ring beforehand.

PORTOGRUARO

Alla Botte

Road map E3. Viale Pordenone 46, 30026. (*(0421) 76 01 22.*) *Sun in winter.* ¶❶ 🍴 🖥 ★ 🍴 Ⓛ Ⓛ

This cosy hotel restaurant serves good local food, and the menu usually includes some dishes from neighbouring Friuli. The gnocchi flavoured with nettles are well worth trying.

Duilio

Road map E3. Via Strada Nuova 19, 30021 Caorle. (*(0421) 810 87.*) *Mon in winter.* 🍴 🖬 🍷 ★ 🍴 Ⓛ Ⓛ

In this roomy restaurant fish-based regional recipes are given an imaginative modern slant. Turbot is gently poached in champagne or used as a filling for the lightest of savoury pancakes.

ROVIGO

Tre Pini

Road map C5. Viale Porta Po 68, 45100. (*(0425) 42 11 11.*) *Sun.* 🖬 🍷 🍴 Ⓛ Ⓛ

The three pines which give the restaurant its name are in the garden of this pretty villa. Specialities of the chef include a delicious onion tart, eels cooked with herbs, and wild duck.

TREVISO

Agnoletti

Road map D3. Via della Vittoria 190, Giavera del Montello. (*(0422) 77 60 09.*) *Mon & Tue. Ann hol 6–30 Jan.* 🖬 Ⓛ Ⓛ

A pretty hillside location north of Treviso and a lovely garden make this restaurant well worth a visit. Seasonal antipasti and the gnocchi are recommended.

Osteria dalla Pasina

Road map D3. Via Peschiere 15, Dosson di Casier. (*(0422) 38 21 12.*) *Mon eve, Tue & Sat lunch. Ann hol 1 week Christmas, 3 weeks Aug.* ¶❶ 🖥 🍷 🍴 Ⓛ Ⓛ

This *osteria* offers tasty dishes which make the most of seasonal produce. The risotto with scampi and asparagus makes a good prelude to tender rabbit cooked with herbs and there are deliciously light mousses and sorbets for pudding.

Toni del Spin

Road map D3. Via Inferiore 7, 31100. (*(0422) 54 38 29.*) *Sun all day & Mon lunch. Ann hol 3 weeks Aug.* 🖥 🍷 🍴 Ⓛ Ⓛ

A homely restaurant offering good value, Toni's serves hearty regional fare. Typical house specialities include *pasta e fagioli*, baked tripe and a rich tiramisù.

Ristorante alle Beccherie

Road map D3. Piazza Ancillotto 10, 31100. (*(0422) 54 08 71.*) *Sun eve & Mon. Ann hol 15–30 Jul.* 🖬 🖥 🍷 🍴 Ⓛ Ⓛ Ⓛ

The Beccherie is one of Treviso's oldest restaurants, housed in a lovely old Venetian-style building with period furniture and discreet service. The guinea fowl with pepper sauce, served with a good risotto of radicchio, is delicious.

Ristorante Enoteca Marchi

Road map D3. Via Castellana 177, Montebelluna. **(** *(0423) 238 75.* ● *Tue pm & Wed. Ann hol 5–20 Aug.* **¶⓿𝄢 𝄬 🗐 🖃 ★ 🖾 ⓁⓁⓁ**

This restaurant is worth patronizing for the wines alone – there are over 500 Italian and foreign wines. Try the spaghetti with radicchio and pomegranate, and the lamb cooked in Prosecco.

VICENZA

Al Torresan

Road map C3. Via Zabarella 1, 36042 Breganze. **(** *(0445) 87 32 60.* ● *Thu. Ann hol end Jul–15 Aug.* **𝄬 🗐**

In the autumn locals flock here to enjoy the wild mushroom dishes. The cooking is hearty and is complemented by the local wines.

Antica Trattoria Tre Visi

Road map C4. Corso Palladio 25, 36100. **(** *(0444) 32 48 68.* ● *Sun eve & Mon. Ann hol Jul, 26 Dec–2 Jan.* **🗐 🖃 🖾 ⓁⓁ**

Housed in an old inn dating from the 1500s, this restaurant is right in the historic town centre. Diners can see into the busy kitchen, where Luigi cooks good Vicentine dishes.

Taverna Aeolia

Road map C4. Piazza C.Da Schio 1, 36023 Costozza di Longare. **(** *(0444) 55 50 36.* ● *Tue. Ann hol 1–15 Nov.* **¶⓿𝄢 𝄬 🗐 🖃 🖾 ⓁⓁ**

Luca Chemello, chef-patron at this elegant villa, does wonderful things in the kitchen to complement the charm of the frescoed dining room. Tortellini with artichokes and lamb cooked with sesame seeds are two of his delicious specialities.

Leoncino

Road map C4. Via Tavernelle 72, 36077 Altavilla Vicentina. **(** *(0444) 57 20 32.* ● *Sun & Mon. Ann hol 27 Dec–10 Jan, Aug.* **𝄢 🖃 🖾 ⓁⓁⓁ**

This rustic restaurant just outside Vicenza is run by the Tecchio family. Good local dishes include the famous *bolliti misti* (boiled meats) served with a delicious herby sauce sharpened with capers.

Ristorante Storione

Road map C4. Strada Pasubio 64, 36100. **(** *(0444) 56 62 44.* ● *Sun.* **🖳 𝄢 🗐 🖃 🖾 ⓁⓁⓁ**

The Zorzo family run this charming restaurant with its pretty garden. Sturgeon *(storione)* is among the many fish specialities. Parents are encouraged to bring children.

Cinzia e Valerio

Road map C4. Piazzetta Porta Padova 65/67, 36100. **(** *(0444) 50 52 13.* ● *Sun eve & Mon. Ann hol 26 Dec–5 Jan, 3 weeks Aug .* **¶⓿ 🗐 🖃 ★ 🖾 ⓁⓁⓁ**

This stylish restaurant within the old city walls serves nothing but fish. Featured on the menu are marinated raw salmon, prawn risotto, delicate fillets of sole and lobster, mussels and clams.

VERONA AND LAKE GARDA

LAKE GARDA SOUTH

Antica Locanda Mincio

Road map A4. Via Michelangelo 12, 37067 Valeggio sul Mincio. **(** *(045) 795 00 59.* ● *Wed eve & Thu. Ann hol 3 weeks Nov, 2 weeks Feb.* **𝄢 🗐**

The Locanda was once a staging post and is now a delightful dining spot with frescoed walls and open fireplaces. The "rustic" hors d'oeuvres are a good choice for a starter, and many of the main courses have a regional emphasis.

Esplanade

Road map A4. Via Lario 10, 25015 Desenzano del Garda. **(** *(030) 914 33 61.* ● *Wed.* **¶⓿ 𝄢 🖃 ★ 🖾 ⓁⓁⓁ**

This is a waterside restaurant where you can find imaginative food with firmly regional roots. Courgette flowers are stuffed with scampi, there is a light lake-fish terrine and main courses include lamb with onions, potatoes and a rosemary sauce. The extensive wine list has some interesting dessert wines.

Trattoria Vecchia Lugana

Road map A4. Piazzale Vecchia Lugana 1, 25019 Lugana di Sirmione. **(** *(030) 91 90 12.* ● *Mon eve & Tue. Ann hol 6 Jan–15 Feb.* **¶⓿ 𝄢 🖃 ★ 🖾 ⓁⓁⓁ**

Meat is cooked on the old open fire in the kitchen of this charming restaurant. You can sample a good range of local dishes, including lake fish and tender young kid served with polenta. The wine list is strong on Garda labels.

LAKE GARDA WEST

Alla Campagnola

Road map A3. Via Brunati 11, 25087 Salò. **(** *(0365) 221 53.* ● *Mon & Tues lunch. Ann hol 2 weeks Jan.* **¶⓿ 𝄢 🖃 🖾 ⓁⓁ**

At this mother-and-son establishment Elisa Dal Bom has revived some interesting traditional recipes. She serves an array of vegetables as an antipasto, and pasta stuffed with pumpkin or aubergine.

Capriccio

Road map A3. Piazza San Bernardo 6, Frazione Montinelle, 25080 Manerba del Garda. **(** *(0365) 55 11 24.* ● *Tue in winter. Ann hol Jan–Feb.* **¶⓿ 𝄢 🗐 🖃 🖾 ⓁⓁ**

The terrace here has a fine view over the lake and hills and the menu offers a good choice of fish. Local olive oil is extensively used. Puddings include a delicate muscat-grape jelly with a peach sauce.

Villa Fiordaliso

Road map A3. Corso Zanardelli 132, 25083 Gardone Riviera. **(** *(0365) 201 58.* ● *Mon & Tue lunch. Ann hol Jan–Feb.* **¶⓿ 𝄢 🖃 ★ 🖾 ⓁⓁⓁ**

This stylish restaurant is housed in the villa that was the love-nest of Mussolini and Clara Petacci. In summer you can eat in the garden, which sweeps down to the lake, and enjoy creative cuisine from the best local ingredients.

La Tortuga

Road map A3. Porticciolo di Gargnano, 25084 Gargnano del Garda. **(** *(0365) 712 51.* ● *Mon eve & Tue. Ann hol Jan–Feb.* **¶⓿ 🗐 𝄬 ★ 🖾 ⓁⓁⓁⓁ**

La Tortuga has a charming lakeside location and light, imaginative cuisine. Lake fish is cooked with care; try the *coregone,* served with tomatoes and capers.

LAKE GARDA EAST

Locanda San Vigilio Regina

Road map A3. Località San Vigilio, 37016 Garda. **(** *(045) 725 66 88.* ● *Ann hol Nov–Mar.* **¶⓿ 🖳 *eve.* 𝄢 🖃 ★ 🖾 ⓁⓁⓁⓁ**

This restaurant forms part of one of the loveliest hotels on Lake Garda. You can start with a selection from the antipasto buffet and then choose from the quite astounding range of fish dishes.

VERONA

Al Bersagliere

Road map B4. Dietro Pallone 1, 37100. [(045) 800 48 24. ● Sun. Ann hol 15–30 Jun. 📠 🖪 ★ 🖪 ⓁⓁ

An old wood-lined dining room makes a pleasant setting for some traditional Veronese cooking: game in season, mixed boiled meats, and polenta with wild mushrooms.

Bottega del Vino

Road map B4. Via Scudo di Francia 3, 37100. [(045) 800 45 35. ● Tue. 🖫 🖪 🖪 ⓁⓁ

A haunt of local wine-producers, the Bottega has more than 800 wines on its list. The food is good, with several specialities, including a good selection of antipasti.

Ciccarelli

Road map B4. Via Mantovana 171, 37100. [(045) 95 39 86. ● Fri eve & Sat. Ann hol 25 Jul–25 Aug. 🖫 ★ 🖪 ⓁⓁ

Ten minutes' drive from Verona, Ciccarelli's has been renowned for over 40 years. There are excellent grilled, roast and boiled meats, home-made pasta, and superb *crème caramel all'amaretto*.

Baba-jaga

Road map B4. Via Cabalao 11, 37030 Montecchia di Crosara. [(045) 745 02 22. ● Sun eve & Mon. Ann hol Jan, last 2 weeks Aug. 📠 🖫 🖪 🖪 ⓁⓁⓁ

This is a good choice in the Soave wine-producing area. The lengthy menu includes black truffle risotto, linguine with sturgeon, leeks and tomatoes, and fillet of sea bass.

El Cantinon

Road map B4. Via S Rochetto 11, 37100. [(045) 59 52 91. ● Wed. 🖫 🖪 🖪 🖪 ⓁⓁⓁ

Wine-lovers will find a huge range of excellent Italian and foreign wines. Two sample dishes are fillet of pork with porcini mushrooms, and fresh goat's cheese with leeks and scampi. Service in the wood-beamed dining room is excellent.

Arche

Road map B4. Via Arche Scaligere 6, 37100. [(045) 800 74 15. ● Sun & Mon lunch. 🖾 🖫 🖪 ★ 🖪 ⓁⓁⓁⓁ

The Arche has long enjoyed a good reputation. The accent is on fish and dishes include a seafood soup with lentils and a wonderful warm lobster salad with basil and rocket.

Il Desco

Road map B4. Via dietro San Sebastiano 5/7, 37100. [(045) 59 53 58. ● Sun. Ann hol 1–7 Jan, 15–30 Jun. 🖾 🖫 🖪 ★ 🖪 ⓁⓁⓁⓁ

There is harmony and attention to detail in every aspect of this lovely restaurant in a 16th-century *palazzo*. It is recognized as one of Italy's best. The imaginative menu is full of temptations: potato cake with truffles, lobster risotto, leeks and glazed onions, and a delicious range of puddings.

THE DOLOMITES

BELLUNO

Antica Locanda al Cappello

Road map D2. Piazza Papa Luciani 20, 32026 Mel. [(0437) 75 36 51. ● Tue eve, Wed exc Aug & Christmas. Ann hol 1–20 Jul. 🖫 📠 🖪 ★ 🖪 ⓁⓁ

Antique furniture complements the frescoed rooms of this stylish restaurant, which is situated on a beautiful late-Renaissance piazza. The chef prepares a selection of interesting dishes, which include poppy-seed gnocchi and ravioli stuffed with radicchio. Game is often on the menu, too.

Locanda San Lorenzo

Road map D2. Via IV Novembre 79, 32015 Puos d'Alpago. [(0437) 45 40 48. ● Wed exc Jul & Aug. 🖾 🖫 🖪 ★ 🖪 ⓁⓁⓁ

Trout, rabbit, duck and pigeon are served at this hotel restaurant in a hillside village above the lake of Santa Croce. The Dal Farra brothers are the chefs and take justifiable pride in their regional cooking with a modern slant.

Ristorante El Zoco

Road map D2. Via Cademai 18, 32100. [(0436) 86 00 41. ● Mon in low season. Ann hol Easter–May, Nov. 🖫 📠 🖪 ★ 🖪 ⓁⓁⓁ

Game, particularly chamois meat, features in the culinary repertoire here. The vegetable dishes are of a high standard, especially the *sformato* of Trevisan radicchio and the grilled wild mushrooms.

Dolada

Road map D2. Via Dolada 21, 32010 Pieve d'Alpago. [(0437) 47 91 41. ● Mon, Tue lunch exc Jul & Aug. Ann hol 10 Jan–5 Feb. 🖫 📠 🖪 ★ 🖪 ⓁⓁⓁⓁ

An obscure village on the slopes of Monte Dolada is home to one of Italy's great restaurants. Enzo and Rossana de Pra's reputation is well-founded, and the cooking is deft and sure. Chicken breast with truffle oil, salmon mousse, and contrefilet of beef with thyme are served with imaginative vegetables and superb wines.

CADORE AREA

Dal Cavalier

Road map E1. Località Cima Gogna, 32041 Auronzo di Cadore. [(0435) 98 34. ● Wed exc Jul, Aug & Christmas. 🖾 🖫 📠 🖪 🖪 ★ 🖪 ⓁⓁ

The Munerin family run this mountain restaurant, which has period furniture and a large collection of copper pots. Good dishes include braised venison with wild mushrooms. The wine list is very strong on hard-to-find regional wines.

Al Capriolo

Road map D1. Via Nazionale 108, 32040 Vodo di Cadore. [(0435) 48 92 07. ● Dec–Apr, Jul–Sep. ● Tue exc Jul & Aug. 🖫 📠 🖫 🖪 ★ 🖪 ⓁⓁ

You will find good game, including venison and elk, at this restaurant which is situated in stunning surroundings in the heart of the Dolomites. As a bonus, truffles are used for flavouring.

CORTINA D'AMPEZZO

El Toulà

Road map D1. Via Ronco 123, 32043. [(0436) 33 39. ● Mon. Ann hol Easter–mid-Jul, mid-Sep–mid-Dec. 🖫 📠 🖫 🖪 ★ 🖪 ⓁⓁⓁⓁ

You can eat on the terrace of this rustic but chic restaurant, which was originally a hay barn. The food is sophisticated and good, and includes dishes such as basil crêpes, veal, duck, and a range of delicious puddings.

For key to symbols see p235

Bars and Cafés in Venice

MANY BARS IN Venice draw their trade from tourists and are busy throughout the day, as visitors ease their aching feet and consult their guide-books. Custom is swelled mid-morning and around lunchtime as the Venetians drop in for a drink or snack and to use the telephone. Cafés range from basic one-room bars patronized by local workmen, to opulent coffee houses in old-world style, such as **Caffè Quadri** and **Caffè Florian**. Even the humblest establishment provides a continuous range of refreshments and you can enjoy anything from a morning coffee or lunchtime beer, to an aperitif or a final brandy before bed. Bars also serve snacks throughout their opening hours: freshly baked morning pastries and lunchtime sandwiches, rolls, cakes, biscuits and sometimes home-made ice cream. Wine bars often have a wide range of traditional Venetian snacks, and so make good places to stop for lunch.

BARS

ITALIANS WILL OFTEN stop for breakfast in a bar on their way to work. This normally consists of a *cappuccino* (milky coffee) and a *brioche* (a plain, jam- or cream-filled pastry). **Pasticceria Dal Mas**, on the main route from the station to the Rialto, is much favoured by early morning commuters.

A wide range of alcoholic drinks is on offer, and you can ask for a glass of wine or beer on tap. Beer from the keg is called *birra alla spina* and comes in three different sizes: *piccola, media* and *grande*. Italian and imported bottled beers are also available, though the latter can be expensive. All bars serve glasses of mineral water and it is acceptable to request a glass of tap water *(acqua del rubinetto)*, which will be free. Most bars also serve delicious freshly squeezed fruit juices *(una spremuta)* and milk-shakes made with fruit *(un frullato)*. Italian bottled juices are good and are available in delicious flavours such as apricot and pear.

All bars serve a range of sandwiches *(tramezzini)* and filled rolls *(panini)*, and often have toasted sandwiches and pizzas as well. Some double as cake-shops *(pasticceria)*, and these have a tempting range of calorie-filled delights on display to eat in or take away. If you are near the Accademia, seek out the tiny **Pasticceria Vio** for wonderful cakes, or for an expensive treat, go to **Harry's Dolci** on the Giudecca *(see p241)*.

Bear in mind that sitting down to drink in a bar or café can cost a lot more than standing at the bar, as there is a table charge, which can be high. This rises proportionally as you draw nearer San Marco. Some bars, particularly in the less tourist-frequented areas, have a stand-up counter only. All have a lavatory *(il bagno* or *il gabinetto)*, though you may have to ask at the desk for the key. It is also worth noting that bars and cafés tend to shut earlier here than in other parts of Italy, particularly in winter.

The normal procedure is to choose what you want to eat or drink, then ask for it and pay at the cashdesk. You will be given a receipt *(lo scontrino)* which you present at the bar. If they are busy, a L100 coin will usually speed things up. If you decide to sit down, either inside or at an outside table, your order will be taken by a waiter who will bring the bill when he delivers the drinks. You should expect to pay double or more for this, but you can stretch your drink out for as long as you like.

WINE BARS

THERE IS AN OLD tradition in Venice called *cichetti e l'ombra*, meaning "a little bite and the shade". The little bite ranges from a slice of bread and *prosciutto crudo* (raw cured ham), meatballs or fried vegetables, to sardines and *baccalà* (salt cod). The shade is a glass of wine, so called because the gondoliers used to snatch a glass in the shade away from the glare of the sun on the water. Wine bars serving these snacks and a range of wines are numerous and heavily populated by locals. Many, such as **Do Mori**, are in the crowded alleys off the Rialto, but one of the nicest is the **Cantina del Vino già Schiavi** near the Ponte San Trovaso.

CAFÉS AND ICE CREAM PARLOURS

COFFEE HOUSES have played their part in the history of the Veneto – notably Padua's Caffè Pedrocchi *(see p178)* – and a visit to Venice would not be complete without a drink at the historic **Caffè Florian** or **Caffè Quadri**. It is a hard decision whether to take a table outside and watch the crowds or to experience the elegant charm of the interior rooms, with their atmosphere of past eras. The prices are sky-high, but you can take your time and be entertained by the resident orchestras.

Harry's Bar *(see p92)*, is another world-famous bar and café. In summer it is crammed with foreigners and the prices are always high, but for a treat, sip a Bellini, a mixture of Prosecco and fresh white peach juice, in the place where it was invented.

The cafés along the Zattere, with their lovely views across the Giudecca Canal, make good places to pause, and the prices are much lower. Many Venetian squares have cafés with tables outside. There are several in the Campo Santo Stefano, or try **Bar Colleoni** in Campo Santi Giovanni e Paolo (San Zanipolo). **Il Caffè** is the nicest in Campo Santa Margherita.

Venetian ice cream is definitely among the best in Italy, with ice cream shops *(gelaterie)* serving a wide selection of seasonal flavours, some unique to Venice. The Venetians eat ice cream all year round, often instead of pudding or as the finale to the evening stroll, or *passeggiata*. It comes as either a cone *(un cono)* or a cup *(una coppa)* and it is normal to have at least three flavours. **Paolin** on Campo Santo Stefano is one of the best ice cream shops. You could also try **Il Doge**, which is in Campo Santa Margherita, and **Nico** on the Zattere, where you will find *gianduiotto*, a rich chocolate-based Venetian speciality. Make certain you buy ice cream made on the premises, *artigianato* or *produzione propria*, and experiment with what is clearly seasonal; the high-summer fruit ices such as melon, peach and apricot are refreshing and mouthwatering.

DIRECTORY

SAN MARCO

Bar Gelateria Paolin
Campo Santo Stefano
San Marco 2962.
Map 6 F3.

Caffè Florian
Piazza San Marco,
San Marco 56/59.
Map 7 B2.

Caffè Quadri
Piazza San Marco
San Marco 120–24.
Map 7 B2.

Harry's Bar
Calle Vallaresso,
San Marco 1323.
Map 7 B3.

Hostaria da Zorzi
Calle dei Fuseri
San Marco 4359.
Map 7 A2.

Osteria Terrà Assassini
Rio Terrà degli Assassini
San Marco 3695.
Map 7 A2.

Rosa Salva
Merceria San Salvador
San Marco 951.
Map 7 B1.

Vino Vino
Ponte delle Veste,
San Marco 2007.
Map 7 A3.

SAN POLO AND SANTA CROCE

Bar Dogale
Campo dei Frari, San
Polo 3012. **Map** 6 E1.

Do Mori
Calle Do Mori
San Polo 429. **Map** 3 A5.

Do Spade
Sottoportega delle Do
Spade, San Polo 860.
Map 3 A5.

Soto Sopra
Calle San Pantalon
San Polo 3740.
Map 6 D2.

CASTELLO

Bar Colleoni
Campo Santi Giovanni e
Paolo, Castello 6811.
Map 3 C5.

Bar Gelateria Riviera
Ponte de la Pietà
Riva degli Schiavoni 4153.
Map 8 D2.

Bar Mio
Via Garibaldi
Castello 1820.
Map 8 F3.

Bar Orologio
Campo Santa Maria
Formosa, Castello 6130.
Map 7 C1.

Caffè al Cavallo
Campo Santi Giovanni e
Paolo, Castello 6823.
Map 3 C5.

La Boutique del Gelato
Campo San Lio,
Castello 5727.
Map 7 B1.

Snack & Sweet
Salizzada San Lio
Castello 5689.
Map 7 B1.

DORSODURO

Ai do Draghi
Calle della Chiesa
Dorsoduro 3665.
Map 6 F4.

Ai Pugni
Fondamenta Gherardini
Dorsoduro 2836.
Map 6 D3.

Bar Cucciolo
Zattere ai Gesuati
Dorsoduro 782.
Map 6 E4.

Bar Gelateria Causin
Campo Santa Margherita
Dorsoduro 2996.
Map 6 D2.

Bar Gelateria Il Doge
Campo Santa Margherita
Dorsoduro 3058A.
Map 6 D2.

Bar Gelateria Nico
Zattere ai Gesuati
Dorsoduro 922.
Map 6 D4.

Bar Pasticceria Vio
Rio Terrà della Toletta
Dorsoduro 1192.
Map 6 D3.

Cantina del Vino già Schiavi
Ponte San Trovaso
Dorsoduro 992.
Map 6 E4.

Il Caffè
Campo Santa Margherita
Dorsoduro 2963.
Map 6 D3.

CANNAREGIO

Alla Bomba
Calle dell'Oca,
Cannaregio 4297.
Map 3 A5.

Bar Algiubagio
Fondamenta Case Nuove
Cannaregio 5039.
Map 1 C2.

Bar Gelateria Solda
Campo Santi Apostoli
Cannaregio 4440.
Map 3 B5.

Caffè Pasqualigo
Salizzada Santa Fosca
Cannaregio 2288.
Map 2 F4.

Enoteca Boldrin
San Canciano
Cannaregio 5550.
Map 3 B5.

Il Gelatone
Rio Terrà Maddalena,
Cannaregio 2063.
Map 2 F3.

Osteria da Alberto
Calle Larga Giacinto
Gallina,
Cannaregio 5401.
Map 3 C5.

Pasticceria Dal Mas
Lista di Spagna,
Cannaregio 150/A.
Map 2 D4.

THE LAGOON ISLANDS

Bar della Maddalena
Mazzorbo.

Bar Ice
Campo San Donato
Murano.
Map 4 F2.

Bar La Palanca
Fondamenta Santa
Eufemia, Giudecca 448.
Map 6 D5.

Bar Palmisano
Via Baldassare Galuppi,
Burano.

Bar Trono di Attila
Torcello.

Harry's Dolci
Fondamenta San Biagio
Giudecca 773.
Map 6 D5.

Lo Spuntino
Via Baldassare Galuppi
Burano.

SHOPS AND MARKETS

T HE NARROW STREETS of Venice are lined with beautifully arranged windows that cannot fail to tempt shoppers, and the city has the additional bonus of being truly pedestrianized. Few cities of similar size have such a wide variety of goods to browse through as you explore the fascinating and diverse neighbourhoods. There is still a strong

Piece of traditional Murano glass

artisan tradition in Venice, and alongside glass and lace you will find high-quality fashion and leather goods, antiques and jewellery. In the Veneto, which is one of Italy's most prosperous regions, every town boasts a wide range of shops, and many have seasonal speciality markets. In country areas you can buy wine and olive oil direct from the producers.

Display of jewellery in a shop window in the Frezzeria

WHEN TO SHOP

G ENERALLY, SHOPS open around 9 or 9:30am and close for lunch at 12:30 or 1pm, with the exception of food shops and markets, which are in business from 8am. In the afternoon stores are open from 3:30pm to 7:30pm in winter, and 4pm to 8pm in summer. In Venice, many stores aimed directly at tourists are open all day and even on Sundays, as are big out-of-town supermarkets and hypermarkets – useful if you are self-catering in the region.

Monday is usually the traditional closing day in northern Italy though, again, this does not apply to all shops in Venice itself. The smaller towns in the Veneto often have very variable opening hours, with perhaps food shops closing on Mondays but ironmongers and clothes shops closing on Wednesdays. Shops and markets in the Veneto are

often closed for two or three weeks during the national holiday time in August.

The best time for finding bargains is during the January and July sales: look out for window signs with the words *saldi* or *sconti*.

WHERE TO SHOP IN VENICE

T HE GLITTERING Mercerie *(see p95)*, which runs from Piazza San Marco to the Rialto, has been the main shopping street since the Middle Ages and, together with the parallel Calle dei Fabbri, is still a honey pot for the crowds. West of San Marco, the zigzagging Frezzeria is full of interesting and unusual shops. The main route from the Piazza to the Accademia Bridge is lined with up-market speciality stores, while the streets north of Campo Santo Stefano *(see p93)* are another excellent trawling ground for quality souvenirs and gifts.

Across the Grand Canal, the narrow streets from the Rialto southwest towards Campo San Polo *(see p101)* are lined with a wide variety of less

expensive stores, while near the station the bustling Lista di Spagna and the route along the Strada Nova towards the Rialto cater for the everyday needs of ordinary Venetians.

The islands of Murano and Burano *(see pp150 – 51)* are *the* places to buy traditional glass and lace.

HOW TO PAY

M AJOR CREDIT cards and Eurocheques are usually accepted in the main stores for larger purchases, but cash is preferred for small items, and smaller shops will want cash. Traveller's cheques are also accepted, though the rate that you will get is less favourable than at a bank.

By law, shopkeepers should give you a receipt *(ricevuta fiscale)*, which you should keep until you are some distance away from the store (legally this is 600 m). If a purchased item is defective, most shops will change the article or give you a credit note, as long as you show the till receipt. Cash refunds are not usually given.

VAT EXEMPTION

V ISITORS FROM non-European Union countries can reclaim the 19 per cent sales tax (IVA) on goods exceeding L300,000 from the same shop. Ask for an invoice when you buy the goods and inform the shop that you intend to reclaim the tax. The invoice must be stamped at customs as you leave Italy. The shop will reimburse the tax in lire, once they have received the stamped invoice.

A colourful display of T-shirts with the "Venezia" logo

Designer clothes shop in Treviso

FASHION AND ACCESSORIES

I N VENICE, the big names in fashion are all found near San Marco. **Armani**, **Laura Biagiotti**, **Missoni** and **Valentino** all have stylish shops just off the Piazza. For really innovative and outrageous designs visit **Fiorella** in Campo Santo Stefano. **La Pantofola**, in the Calle della Mandola, sells a range of good value leather shoes and a wide variety of traditional Venetian slippers in a stunning range of colourful velours. For a genuine gondolier's shirt, take a look at what's on offer in **Emilio Ceccato**.

FABRICS AND INTERIOR DESIGN

V ENICE HAS long been famed for sumptuous brocades, fine silks and figured velvets. **Trois** sells silks by the metre, including the gossamer-fine pleated silks invented by Fortuny for his Delphos dresses *(see p94)*, and **Valli** has wonderful designer silks and other fabrics in its shop in the Mercerie. The famous house of **Rubelli** has a shop on Campo San Gallo. Here you will find a variety of rich brocades and velvets. **Color Casa**, in San Polo, has equally lovely textiles at slightly lower prices, and **Jesurum**, not far from the Bridge of Sighs, is the place to go for beautiful fine linens. They also sell seductive lingerie. The Lido's

Gran Viale has a number of stylish shops that are devoted to modern interior design and which sell beautiful objects for the home.

MASKS AND COSTUMES

Y OU CAN BUY cheap, mass-produced masks all over the city, but a genuine one is a good souvenir, and you will be spoilt for choice. **Laboratorio Artigiano Maschere** in Castello revived traditional mask-making and their designs are absolutely stunning. Near Campo San Polo **Tragicomica** sells costumes and masks, as well as Commedia dell'Arte figures. You will find these at **Il Prato** on the Frezzeria too, where they also make string puppets. Dorsoduro has several workshops; **Mondonovo**, just off Campo Santa Margherita, has a marvellous selection of masks and costumes.

A typical Venetian mask

In the weeks leading up to Carnival, maskmakers are, of course, extremely busy, but at other times of the year many workshops welcome visitors and are pleased to show you their craft *(see p31)*.

GLASS

T HE BEST PLACE to buy glass is on the island of Murano, where it has been made since the 13th century *(see p151)*. All the main manufacturers have their furnaces and showrooms here, catering to mainstream taste. Some manufacturers also have showrooms in Venice itself.

On Murano, **Seguso** and **Barovier e Toso** make glass to traditional designs with good simple lines. You will find similarly attractive pieces in Venice at **Paolo Rossi**, where they specialize in reproductions of antique glass. **Pauly** and **Venini** both have shops near San Marco; they represent the top end of the market and some of their designs are very pleasing.

JEWELLERY

V ENICE'S SMARTEST jewellers are **Missiaglia** and **Nardi**, both in the arcades of Piazza San Marco. Shops on the Rialto Bridge sell cheaper designs, and this is a good place to find bracelets and chains, whose price is determined by the weight of the gold. For inexpensive, pretty Venetian glass earrings, necklaces and bracelets try **FGB** in Campo Santa Maria Zobenigo.

Wide range of fruit and vegetables for sale in the Rialto market

A typical general food store in the San Marco area

DEPARTMENT STORES

DEPARTMENT STORES are not as common in Italy as in many other countries. The main chain store in Venice is Coin, which sells everything from umbrellas to tableware. Standa and Upim are cheaper supermarket-style options. You will find branches of these in other towns in the Veneto.

Treasure trove in one of the art shops on Murano

BOOKS AND GIFTS

THE BEST GENERAL bookshop in Venice is **Goldoni**, in Calle dei Fabbri, which also sells maps. **Filippi Editori Venezia** stocks facsimile editions of old books and books about Venice. **Fantoni**

is a specialist art bookshop, and English books are sold at **Libreria Serenissima**.

Hand-made marbled and dragged paper are typically Venetian, and these are used as book covers and made up into writing desk equipment. The **Legatoria Piazzesi** sells hand-blocked papers and stationery items. **Paolo Olbi** constantly adds to their wide range of papers, while **Alberto Valese-Ebru** uses a distinctive marbling technique on fabrics as well as paper.

The San Barnaba area has several art and craft shops where you can buy unusual gifts and souvenirs. **Signor Blum** on the Campo San Barnaba has charming carved and painted wooden objects and toys. Another carver, **Livio de Marchi**, makes large whimsical wooden ornaments. **La Bottega dell'Arte** sells interesting paper objects, as well as masks. For unusual soaps and other toiletries browse in **Il Melograno**, a lovely herbalist in Campo Santa Margherita.

MARKETS AND FOOD SHOPS

ONE OF THE delights of Venice is a morning spent exploring the food markets and shops around the Rialto. Fruit and vegetable stalls sprawl to the west of the bridge and the Pescheria, or

fish market, lies right beside the Grand Canal *(see p100)*. The neighbouring streets are full of unusual and excellent food shops. Olive oil, vinegar and dried pasta, which comes in multifarious colours, shapes and flavours, are all good choices if you are looking for food to take home. **Aliani (Casa del Parmigiano)** is a superlative cheese shop right by the vegetable market, where you can also buy a selection of fresh pasta, salamis and ready-made dishes for a picnic.

Round the corner, on Ruga dei Spezieri, the **Drogheria Mascari** has a fine range of coffees, teas, dried fruits, seeds and nuts. **Pasticceria Marchini** is Venice's best pasticceria, selling traditional Venetian sweetmeats as well as cakes and biscuits.

Viale Santa Maria Elisabetta, the main shopping street of the Lido

DIRECTORY

FASHION AND ACCESSORIES

Emilio Ceccato
Sottoportico di Rialto
San Polo 16/17.
Map 7 A1.
(041) 522 27 00.

Emporio Armani
Calle dei Fabbri, San
Marco 989. **Map** 7 B2.
(041) 523 78 08.

Fiorella
Campo Santo Stefano
San Marco 2806.
Map 6 F3.
(041) 520 92 28.

Laura Biagiotti
Calle Larga XXII Marzo
San Marco 2400–2401.
Map 7 A3.
(041) 520 34 01.

Missoni
Calle Vallaresso, San
Marco 1312. **Map** 7 B3.
(041) 520 57 33.

La Pantofola
Calle della Mandola, San
Marco 3718. **Map** 6 F2.
(041) 522 21 50.

Valentino
Salizzada San Moisè, San
Marco 1473. **Map** 7 A3.
(041) 520 57 33.

FABRICS AND INTERIOR DESIGN

Annelie
Calle Lunga San Barnaba
Dorsoduro 2748.
Map 6 D3.
(041) 520 32 77.

Color Casa
Calle della Madonneta
San Polo 1990.
Map 6 F1.
(041) 523 60 71.

Jesurum
Mercerie del Capitello
San Marco 4857.
Map 7 B2.
(041) 520 61 77.

Rubelli
Campo San Gallo, San
Marco 1089.
Map 7 B2.
(041) 523 61 10.

Trois
Campo San Maurizio,
San Marco 2666.
Map 6 F3.
(041) 522 29 05.

Valli
Merceria San Zulian
San Marco 783.
Map 7 B1.
(041) 522 57 18.

MASKS AND COSTUMES

Balo Coloc
Calle Lunga,
San Croce 2134.
Map 2 F5.
(041) 524 05 51.

Laboratorio Artigiano Maschere
Barbaria delle Tole
Castello 6657.
Map 4 D5.
(041) 522 31 10.

Mondonovo
Rio Terrà Canal
Dorsoduro 3063.
Map 6 D3.
(041) 528 73 44.

Il Prato
Frezzeria, San Marco 1770.
Map 7 A2.
(041) 520 33 75.

Tragicomica
Calle dei Nomboli,
San Polo 2800.
Map 6 F1.
(041) 72 11 02.

GLASS

Barovier e Toso
Fondamenta Vetrai 28
Murano. **Map** 4 E3.
(041) 73 90 49.

Paolo Rossi
Campo San Zaccaria, San
Marco 4685. **Map** 8 C2.
(041) 523 00 90.

Pauly
Calle Larga, Ponte dei
Consorzi, San Marco.
Map 7 C2.
(041) 520 98 99.

Seguso
Ponte Vivarini 143
Murano.
Map 4 E2.
(041) 73 94 23.

Venini
Piazzetta dei Leoncini
San Marco 314. **Map** 7 B2.
(041) 522 40 45.

JEWELLERY

FGB
Campo Santa Maria
Zobenigo, San Marco 2514.
Map 7 C1.
(041) 523 65 56.

Missiaglia
Procuratie Vecchie, San
Marco 125. **Map** 7 B2.
(041) 522 44 64.

Nardi
Procuratie Nuove, Piazza
San Marco, San Marco
69–71. **Map** 7 B2.
(041) 522 57 33.

BOOKS AND GIFTS

Alberto Valese-Ebru
Campiello Santo Stefano
San Marco 3471.
Map 6 F3.
(041) 523 88 30.

Cartoleria Accademia
Rio Terrà Carità, Dorsoduro
1044. **Map** 6 E3.
(041) 520 70 86.

Cartoleria Testolini
Fondamenta Orseolo
San Marco 1744.
Map 7 A2.
(041) 522 30 85.

Erborista Il Melograno
Campo Santa Margherita
Dorsoduro 2999.
Map 6 D2.
(041) 528 51 17.

Fantoni
Salizzada San Luca
San Marco 4119.
Map 7 A2.
(041) 522 07 00.

Filippi Editori Venezia
Calle Casselleria, Castello
5284. **Map** 7 C1.
(041) 523 69 16.

Goldoni
Calle dei Fabbri
San Marco 4742.
Map 7 A1.
(041) 522 23 84.

La Bottega dell'Arte
Ponte San Barnaba
Dorsoduro 2806.
Map 6 D3.

Legatoria Piazzesi
Campiello della Feltrina
San Marco 2511.
Map 6 F3.
(041) 522 12 02.

Libreria Serenissima
Calle Casselleria,
Castello 5377.
Map 7 B1.
(041) 520 09 19.

Libreria della Toletta
Sacca della Toletta
Dorsoduro 1214.
Map 6 D3.
(041) 523 20 34.

Livio de Marchi
Salizzada San Samuele
San Marco 3157.
Map 6 E2.
(041) 528 56 94.

Paolo Olbi
Calle della Mandola, San
Marco 3653. **Map** 6 F2.
(041) 528 50 25.

Signor Blum
Campo San Barnaba
Dorsoduro 2840.
Map 6 D3.
(041) 522 63 67.

Teresa Porto
Rio Terrà dei Nomboli, San
Polo 2753. **Map** 6 E1.
(041) 523 13 68.

FOOD SHOPS

Aliani (Casa del Parmigiano)
Casaria, San Polo 240/A.
Map 3 A5.
(041) 522 08 25.

Drogheria Mascari
Ruga Rialto,
Calle dei Spezieri,
San Polo 381.
Map 3 A5.
(041) 522 97 62.

Pasticceria Marchini
Ponte San Maurizio
San Marco 2769.
Map 6 F3.
(041) 522 91 09.

What to Buy in the Veneto

Glass is the most popular Venetian souvenir, but there are many other possibilities, ranging from Carnival masks and ceramics to fabrics and lace. For food lovers there is a wide selection of local olive oils, honey, wines and preserves. In the Veneto many food producers sell direct to the public, while different craft and food specialities are found in individual towns and islands.

Modern vase of opaque glass

Traditional glass with gold overlay

Two-coloured goblet

Venetian Glass
In traditional rich colours of blue and claret, or in striking modern designs, you will find anything from scent bottles to chandeliers.

Gift box covered in marbled paper

Address book

Venetian Marbled Paper
Marbled paper is a Venetian speciality. The sheets of paper are dipped into liquid gum before adding the paint. You can buy a large range of stationery items covered in the paper, as well as paper by the individual sheet. Each sheet of marbled paper is unique.

Pretty trinket box

Sheets of marbled paper

Crafts from the Veneto
The ancient patterns of Burano lace are used to great advantage on table linen and to trim exquisite lingerie. Hand-painted vases, plates and bowls are produced in the picturesque old town of Bassano del Grappa.

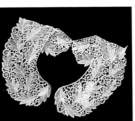

Delicate lace collar from Burano

Decorated ceramic vase from Bassano

Silver spoon with Venetian lion finial

Red and gold mask

Masks *(see pp30–31)*

Mask designs range from Commedia dell'Arte motifs to modern abstracts from young designers, and many are intricate and colourful. They are available all year, but at Carnival time you can buy them from street stalls.

Carnival mask

Colourful child's sweater

Clothing

As everywhere in Italy, stylish designer shops abound. Clothes for children are particularly bright and inventive. Velvet slippers, which are made in rich jewel-like colours, are worn at home as well as to dress up in at Carnival time.

Velvet slippers

Pasta

Attractively packaged dried pasta comes in many colours, shapes and flavours. Tomato, herb and spinach are the most popular varieties, but beetroot, garlic, artichoke, salmon, squid, and even chocolate can also be found in many shops.

Artichoke

Beetroot

Squid

Pasta shapes

Balsamic vinegar and extra virgin olive oil

Panettone

Amaretto biscuits

Delicacies from the Veneto

Panettone is the light yeast cake, flavoured with vanilla and studded with currants and candied peel, that is traditionally eaten at Christmas. Other local delicacies include olive oil from the shores of Lake Garda, vinegars, mountain honey from Belluno, fruit-flavoured liqueurs, grappa from Bassano (see p166), and after-dinner Amaretto biscuits.

Orange liqueur   **Lime liqueur**   **Pear liqueur**

ENTERTAINMENT IN THE VENETO

VENICE WAS ONCE one of Europe's liveliest night-time cities, and today it still has an impressive range of special events throughout the year. At every season there are some splendid festivals unique to Venice, and in late summer the normal city diet of opera, theatre and concerts is augmented by the International Film Festival and the Biennale, which rank among the best world-class cultural events. The day-to-day evening entertainment in Venice itself now tends to be far less frenetic than in the heyday of the Republic *(see pp46– 7)*, but there

Poster advertising the Film Festival

are a few clubs and discos, and many more across the causeway in Mestre. Or you could have a little flutter at the casino.

Whatever you choose, your enjoyment will be enhanced by the idyllic backdrop of Venice itself. The ultimate and quintessential Venetian romantic experience is, of course, a gondola ride by moonlight *(see p276)*. However, an evening's entertainment could more usually comprise the traditional stroll, or *passeggiata*, followed by a drink at a bar or café in one of the squares or amid the floodlit splendours of the Piazza San Marco.

PRACTICAL INFORMATION

INFORMATION ABOUT what's on in Venice can be found in *Un Ospite di Venezia*, a free Italian and English bilingual booklet which is published weekly during the summer and monthly in the winter. You should be able to get a copy at some hotels or from the main tourist offices, where there are also posters advertising forthcoming cultural events. The Tourist Board also publishes an annual month-by-month list of events called *Venezia Manifestazioni*. The Venetian local newspaper, *Il Gazzettino*, lists cinema performances, rock concerts and discos under *Spettacoli*.

For details of events and festivities in the other towns and cities in the Veneto, ask at the local tourist offices. Regional newspapers also often have listings of what's on in their area.

Music and coffee at Florian's café, Piazza San Marco *(see p246)*

BOOKING TICKETS

BOOKING IN advance is not part of the Italian lifestyle, where decisions are made on the spur of the moment. If you want to be certain of a seat you will have to visit the box office in person, as they usually do not take bookings over the telephone. You may

also have to pay an advance booking supplement, or *prevendita*, which is usually about 10 per cent of the price of the seat.

The price of a theatre ticket starts at about L15,000, though prices are likely to be five times as much for star-name performances. Tickets for popular music concerts are normally sold through record and music shops whose names are displayed on the publicity posters.

Whereas tickets for classical concerts are sold on the spot for that day's performance, opera tickets are booked weeks ahead. There are very few ticket touts, so it is almost impossible to obtain tickets when the box office has sold out. The **Goldoni** box office is open 9:30am–12:30pm and 4–6pm.

La Fenice opera house before the 1996 fire *(see p93)*

CINEMA AND THE FILM FESTIVAL

THERE ARE five cinemas in Venice, mainly showing dubbed versions of international films. These are known as *prima visione* (first run). The **Accademia** and the **Olimpia** occasionally show more interesting "art-house" films, and you will find these listed in *Un Ospite*.

The annual Film Festival, which takes place in August and September, is one of the major world cinema showcases and has been running since 1932. Screenings are held in two cinemas on the Lido, the **Palazzo del Cinema** and the **Astra**, and in several cinemas in Venice itself. Tickets are sold to the public direct from the cinema on the day of performance. The programme is can be obtained in advance from the tourist office, and you will see posters for the festival around the city.

Gondolier serenading on the Grand Canal

MUSIC AND THEATRE

LIKE MANY Italian cities, Venice makes good use of the most magnificent churches as concert halls. La Pietà *(see p112)* was Vivaldi's own church and is still used for concerts, as are the churches of the Frari *(see pp102–103)* and Santo Stefano *(see p93)*.

Other concerts are held from time to time in Scuola di San Giovanni Evangelista *(see p104)* and the Palazzo Prigioni Vecchie, the old prison attached to the Doge's Palace *(see pp84–9)*. During the summer, the garden of

Outdoor entertainment in the courtyard of the Doge's Palace

Ca' Rezzonico *(see p126)* and the courtyard of the Doge's Palace are also used as outdoor concert halls.

Unfortunately, La Fenice *(see p93)*, one of Italy's most charming opera houses, suffered a disastrous fire in early 1996. Formerly the venue for major operas, its future is now uncertain, although there are plans to rebuild the theatre as soon as money can be raised.

Venice's principal theatre is **Teatro Goldoni** where, not surprisingly, the repertoire is mainly drawn from the 250 or more comic works written by the eponymous dramatist, Carlo Goldoni (1707–93). The theatre also puts on a wide range of other productions, most of which are staged in

Italian. Performances run from November to June.

At Carnival time in February *(see pp30–31)*, the whole city takes on a party atmosphere as the streets are invaded by merry-makers in flamboyant fancy dress and outlandish masks. Numerous theatrical and musical events take place, both in theatres and in the streets and *campi*.

FACILITIES FOR THE DISABLED

ACCESS FOR disabled people is difficult everywhere in Venice, and theatres are no exception, although concerts are often held in easily accessible churches. For further advice, see page 261.

Masked reveller at Carnival time *(see pp30–31)*

THE BIENNALE AND OTHER EXHIBITIONS

V ENICE IS without doubt one of the leading art exhibition centres in Europe, offering shows on themes ranging from art history to photography, and frequently playing host to the world's major travelling exhibitions. There are excellent facilities for such exhibitions, and these include the Doge's Palace, the Museo Correr, the Palazzo Grassi, the Querini-Stampalia, the Peggy Guggenheim and the Fondazione Cini. *Un Ospite di Venezia* will give details, as will the tourist office and posters around the city.

One of the best and largest exhibitions is the Biennale, an international display of contemporary and avant-garde art, which is held from June to September in odd-number years (its centenary is 1995). The main site is the Giardini Pubblici *(see p121)*, where the specially built pavilions represent about 40 different countries. Another branch of the exhibition, known as the Aperto and showing the work of less established artists, takes place around the city in venues such as the old rope factory in the Arsenale *(see p119)* and the salt warehouse on the Zattere. The tourist office will have further details.

CASINOS, CLUBS AND DISCOS

I F YOU WANT to play roulette on your visit, there is a magnificent casino. In winter, from October to March, the casino is housed in the **Palazzo Vendramin-Calergi** on the Grand Canal *(see p61)* and you can sweep up to the stately entrance by gondola.

Exhibit by Larry Rivers at the 1992 Biennale exhibition

In summer the more prosaic *vaporetto* serves the casino's summer quarters on the Lido in the **Palazzo del Casino**.

The **Antico Martini** is the best-known late-night club. Open until 2am, it has live music in smart surroundings. A few other bars also feature live bands, including the **Paradiso Perduto** in Cannaregio. Discos are few and far between in Venice. You could try **El Souk**, near the Accademia, or go to the mainland, where Mestre has numerous discos. You will find these advertised in the *Spettacoli* listings in *Il Gazzettino*.

SPORT AND CHILDREN

V ENETIANS are very keen on rowing and sailing. There are several clubs in the city, and the tourist office will be able to give you information.

Most of the other sporting facilities are on the Lido, where you can ride, swim, cycle, and play golf or tennis.

In the city itself, there are few attractions for young children, but the mainland is more promising. Around Lake Garda there are plenty of watersports and a theme park, Gardaland *(see p205)*.

MUSIC AND THEATRE IN VERONA

V ERONA HAS two exceptional venues for theatre and music: the superb Arena *(see p95)*, and the 1st-century Teatro Romano *(see p198)* on the far side of the River Adige.

Both stage open-air performances during the summer months.

The Arena is a popular site for rock concerts, and is internationally renowned for its summer opera season. The Teatro Romano stages a succession of ballets and drama, including a Shakespeare Festival, in Italian translation. Tickets for the Teatro can be ordered by post; they are also sold at the box office at the Arena. Tickets to some events are free. Information about all the entertainment is given in the Verona newspaper, *L'Arena*.

Placido Domingo singing at the Verona Festival

OPERA AT THE ARENA

A LMOST EVERYONE will enjoy the experience of hearing opera in the magnificent open-air setting of the Arena. Real opera buffs should be aware, however, that Verona performances are very much "opera for all". You should be prepared for less-than-perfect acoustics, noisy audiences, and even small children running about. The opera season runs from the first week in July until the beginning of September, and every year features a lavish production of Verdi's *Aida*. Performances start at 9pm, as dusk is falling, and it is customary to buy one of the little candles that are on sale. Ten

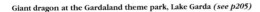

Giant dragon at the Gardaland theme park, Lake Garda *(see p205)*

Aida, **performed annually in Verona's Roman Arena**

minutes before the "curtain goes up", the whole Arena becomes a breathtaking sight, with a sea of flickering lights.

There are normally two intervals, when people eat the picnics they have brought with them, or buy *panini* and ice creams. Glass bottles are not allowed in the Arena, so if you are taking a drink make sure it is in a plastic bottle. Toilets are few and far between and have lengthy queues during the intervals.

Ticket prices are high: an unreserved, un-numbered, backless seat in the *gradinata*, or tiers, is L30,000, while the different types of *poltrone*, literally "armchairs", either on the steps or in the stalls, range from L120,000 to L200,000, with a first-night supplement of L50,000. If you opt for a cheap seat, arrive about two hours before the performance and sit about halfway down the tiers, where the acoustics are better. You can hire an air

cushion for about L2,000. Numbered seats are more comfortable, but seats lower in the Arena can be very hot and airless and the view of the stage is limited. You may prefer to sacrifice comfort for fresh air and a bird's-eye view. Unless you have a seat in the best stalls with the glitterati, there is no need to dress up.

Visitors flock to Verona to attend the opera season, so you need to book accommodation months ahead.

DIRECTORY

MUSIC AND THEATRE

La Fenice
Cassa di Risparmio,
Campo San Luca.
Map 7 A2.
((041) 521 01 61.

Teatro Goldoni
Calle Goldoni,
San Marco 4650.
Map 7 A2.
((041) 520 54 22.

CINEMAS

Accademia
Calle Corfù
Dorsoduro 1019.
Map 6 E3.
((041) 528 77 06.

Astra
Via Corfù, Lido.
((041) 526 02 89.

Olimpia
Campo San Gallo
San Marco 1094.
Map 7 B2.
((041) 520 54 39.

Palazzo del Cinema
Lungomare G Marconi
Lido. ((041) 272 65 00.

CASINOS, CLUBS AND DISCOS

Antico Martini
Campo San Fantin
San Marco 1980.
Map 7 A2.
((041) 522 41 21.

El Souk
Calle Corfù, Dorsoduro.
Map 6 E3.

Paradiso Perduto
Fondamenta della
Misericordia,
Cannaregio 2540.

Map 1 C4.
((041) 72 05 81.

Palazzo del Casino
Lungomare G. Marconi 4.
((041) 529 71 11.
○ May–Oct only.

**Palazzo
Vendramin-Calergi**
Strada Nuova,
Cannaregio 2040.
((041) 529 71 11.
○ Nov–Apr only.

SPORTS

Cycling
Giorgio Barbieri
Via Zara 5,
Lido.
((041) 526 14 90.

Golf
Alberoni
Lido.
((041) 73 10 15.

Rowing
Canottieri Bucintoro
Punta Dogana
Dorsoduro 15.
Map 7 B4.
((041) 522 20 55.

Tennis
Tennis Club Venezia
Lungomare G
Marconi 41/d.
((041) 526 03 35.

VERONA OPERA

Main box office
ENTE Arena
Piazza Brà 28
37121 Verona.
((045) 59 65 17.

Ticket agent
Cangrande
Via Giovanni della Casa 5
37122 Verona.
((045) 800 49 44.
FAX (045) 801 01 08.

SURVIVAL GUIDE

PRACTICAL INFORMATION 260-269
TRAVEL INFORMATION 270-279
VENICE STREET FINDER 280-293

PRACTICAL INFORMATION

THE ENORMOUS WEALTH of art and architecture found in Venice and the historic cities of Padua, Verona and Vicenza can dazzle and overwhelm. The best way to avoid cultural overload is to concentrate on sights in the morning, when they are most likely to be open, relax over your lunch as the Italians do, and leave any shopping or sightseeing of churches until the late afternoon or early evening. The inconsistency of museum opening hours and the fact

ENTE NAZIONALE ITALIANO PER IL TURISMO

Tourist Board logo

that some sights or large sections of them are closed for years for restoration can be frustrating. This is particularly true of Venice, where you may often see scaffolding and the signs *chiuso per restauro* (closed for restoration), so it is best to check opening hours with individual museums in advance. However, on the plus side, the principal sights are all within easy walking distance of one another, and exploring by boat and on foot is an exciting experience.

Tourists crossing the white stone Ponte della Paglia

TOURIST INFORMATION

MOST TOWNS in the Veneto have tourist offices, and in season Verona and Padua each have three. The offices in smaller towns may be of limited help. In contrast, the Verona offices publish a useful free booklet, *Passport Verona*, with information on what to see and do. Travel agents can supply information on city and other tours on offer. Tourist offices in Venice provide city maps, lists of accommodation, *vaporetto* maps and other printed material. Tourist offices and hotels also have leaflets on local entertainment and events *(see pp32–5)*. To obtain information prior to travel contact **ENIT** (Italian State Tourist Office) in your home country, or write to the **Azienda di Promozione Turistica di Venezia**. The

AZIENDA PROMOZIONE TURISTICA

A Tourist Information sign

Forum per la Laguna, a cultural association that promotes the lagoon area, also has an information service, the **Sportello della Laguna**, on Venice and the surrounding area.

GUIDED TOURS

CITY TOURS in Venice with English-speaking guides can be booked through many travel agencies, including **American Express** and **World Vision Travel**. The tours offered take from one to three hours, and are conducted either by foot, motorboat or gondola. In Verona and Padua half-day tours are organized in the tourist season by each town's tourist office. Boat trips along the Brenta Canal *(see pp182–3)* between Venice and Padua, in both directions, are available from April until the end of October.

MUSEUMS AND MONUMENTS

THE OPENING HOURS of museums, galleries and palaces change with alarming rapidity. To avoid disappointment ask at the local tourist office for a list of opening times or, if in Venice, consult the current edition of the free booklet *Un Ospite di Venezia*, available from most hotels. Civic museums are shut on Mondays, otherwise there is no real pattern to opening and closing times. Many places shut at 1pm or 2pm and do not re-open in the afternoon. The majority of museums charge an admission fee, but there are usually concessions for children, students and, in a few cases, senior citizens. Churches are normally open in the mornings from around 9am until noon, then again from mid-afternoon until 6 or 7pm.

A selection of local tourist information publications

A mechanically operated
wheelchair ramp across a bridge

VENICE FOR THE DISABLED

THE STEPPED BRIDGES of
Venice make it almost
impossible for the disabled to
get around the city – it is
difficult enough for a parent
with a pushchair. A further
problem are the *vaporetti* –
particularly the smaller,
sleeker *motoscafi* which are
especially hazardous for those
confined to wheelchairs.

One of the few aids for the
disabled is the *Veneziapertutti*
plan of the city, indicating
places of interest which can be
reached by *vaporetto*, or by
streets avoiding any bridges.
This is produced by the
University of Architecture in
Venice, Santa Croce 191. Few
of the sights have special
facilities for the disabled, but
one or two of the bridges in
the city have now been
adapted for wheelchairs by
the installation of a mechanically operated ramp.

The Venice tourist office
brochure that lists available
accommodation indicates
which hotels are suitable for
disabled guests.

ETIQUETTE

ANY ATTEMPT by visitors to
speak Italian is always
appreciated by local people.
Few people speak English in
the Veneto, but hotel recep-
tionists are usually helpful
and will readily offer to make
any enquiries and reservations on your behalf.

To avoid offence always
dress decently, particularly for
churches, and make sure you
are never drunk in a public
place. Smoking is common in
bars and restaurants but
banned on the *vaporetti*.

VISITING CHURCHES

BARE SHOULDERS and shorts
are frowned upon in
Italian churches and those
unsuitably dressed may well be
refused entry. Church interiors
tend to be very dark but there
are usually coin-operated light
meters to illuminate works of
art. Make sure you take plenty
of L200 and L500 coins.
Machines that provide recorded information on the church
and its artifacts are available
to hire, but the commentaries
are sometimes inaudible. The
majority of churches charge
an entrance fee or encourage
contributions. Photography is
forbidden in most churches.

Pedestrians shopping in Verona

TIPPING

ALWAYS KEEP L1,000 and
L2,000 notes handy for
porters, chambermaids, restaurant staff and custodians of
churches. Italian taxi drivers
do not expect a tip and there is
no need to tip a gondolier.

WCs

THERE IS A DEARTH of public
toilets in the Veneto. The
few in Venice are very incon-
spicuous. You will need L500
or L1,000 for those at the
station, or you can use toilets
in cafés and bars, or the
facilities in museums. Ask for
il bagno or *il gabinetto*. The
toilets are always short of
paper, so it is a good idea to
carry tissues with you.

Gondola with passengers

Students relaxing in the sun in Verona

IMMIGRATION AND CUSTOMS

EUROPEAN UNION (EU) residents and visitors from the US, Canada, Australia and New Zealand do not need visas for stays of up to three months. However, all non-EU visitors need to bring a full passport. British citizens may use a Visitor's Card. A visa is needed for stays longer than three months. Vaccination certificates are not necessary.

All visitors to Italy should, by law, register with the police within three days of arrival. Most hotels will register visitors when they check in. If in doubt, contact a local police department or phone the **Questura**.

Duty-free allowances are as follows: non-EU residents can bring in either 400 cigarettes, 100 cigars, 200 cigarillos or 500 grams of tobacco; 1 litre of spirits and 2 litres of wine; 50 grams of perfume. Goods such as watches and cameras may be imported as long as they are for personal or professional use. EU residents no longer have to declare goods, but random checks are often made to guard against drugs traffickers.

The refund system for Value Added Tax (IVA in Italy) for non-EU residents is complicated and is worth reclaiming only if you have spent at least L300,000 in a single establishment.

STUDENT INFORMATION

AN INTERNATIONAL Student Identity Card (ISIC) or a Youth International Educational Exchange Card (YIEE) will usually get reductions on museum admissions and other charges. Venice Municipality's Rolling Venice card for 14- to 30-year-olds offers, for a small fee, a package of useful books and information on the city; this includes alternative itineraries, haunts for the young, and hotels, theatres, shops and restaurants offering discounts to card holders.

Discount rail tickets for students are available from the Transalpino office at Venice railway station.

EDUCATIONAL COURSES

THE SOCIETA Dante Alighieri in Venice organizes monthly Italian courses for foreigners. The **European Centre for Training Craftsmen in the Conservation of the Architectural Heritage**, on the island of San Servolo, offers standard three-month or intensive two-week courses to Italian and foreign craftsmen.

The **Scuola Internazionale di Grafica** in Venice specializes in short summer courses in painting, printing and sketching, while **Zambler** offers Italian courses in Venice, with accommodation arranged if required. In Padua the **Istituto Linguistico Bertrand Russell** organizes courses in the Italian language, which run throughout the year.

NEWSPAPERS, RADIO AND TV

THE LOCAL NEWSPAPERS are the *Gazzettino* and the *Nuova Venezia*. European and American newspapers and magazines are available at the main news kiosks, normally a day or two after publication. The state TV channels are RAI Uno, RAI Due and RAI Tre. Satellite and cable TV transmit European channels in many languages, as well as CNN news in English. BBC World Service is broadcast on radio on 15.070 MHz (short wave) in the mornings and 648 KHz (medium wave) at night.

Newspaper stall selling national and international publications

Standard Italian plug

EMBASSIES AND CONSULATES

IF YOU LOSE your passport or need other help, contact your national embassy or consulate as listed in the directory below.

ELECTRICAL ADAPTORS

ELECTRICAL CURRENT in Italy is 220V AC, with two-pin, round-pronged plugs. It is probably better to purchase an adaptor before leaving for Italy. Most hotels that are graded above three star have electrical points for shavers and hairdryers in all bedrooms.

ITALIAN TIME

ITALY IS ONE HOUR ahead of Greenwich Mean Time (GMT). The time difference between Venice and other

The clock of San Giacomo di Rialto in San Polo, Venice

cities is: London: −1 hour; New York: −6 hours; Perth: +7 hours; Auckland: +11 hours; Tokyo: +8 hours. These figures may vary for brief periods in summer with local changes. For all official purposes the Italians use the 24-hour clock.

CONVERSION TABLE

Imperial to Metric
1 inch = 2.54 centimetres
1 foot = 30 centimetres
1 mile = 1.6 kilometres
1 ounce = 28 grams
1 pound = 454 grams
1 pint = 0.6 litres
1 gallon = 4.6 litres

Metric to Imperial
1 centimetre = 0.4 inches
1 metre = 3 feet, 3 inches
1 kilometre = 0.6 miles
1 gram = 0.04 ounces
1 kilogram = 2.2 pounds
1 litre = 1.8 pints

DIRECTORY

POLICE (QUESTURA)

Venice
Calle dei Fabbri, Campo San Marco 996. **Map** 7 B2.
((041) 522 54 34.

Vicenza
Viale Mazzini 213.
((0444) 33 75 11.

Padua
Via Riviera Ruzante 9/11.
((049) 66 16 00.

Verona
Lungadige Porta Vittoria.
((045) 809 06 11.

STUDENT INFORMATION

Comune di Venezia Assessorato alla Gioventù
San Marco 1529, Venice.
Map 7 A3.
((041) 274 76 37.

Transalpino
Ferrovia Santa Lucia Venice.
Map 1 B4.
((041) 524 13 34.

Ufficio Informativo Rolling Venice
Ferrovia Santa Lucia Venice. **Map** 1 B4.
((041) 524 28 52.
◯ Jul–Sep only

EDUCATIONAL COURSES

European Centre for Training Craftsmen in the Conservation of the Architectural Heritage
Isola di San Servolo Casella Postale 676 30100 Venice.
((041) 526 85 46.

Istituto Linguistico Bertrand Russell
Via Filiberto 6, 35122 Padua. ((049) 65 40 51.

Istituto Zambler
Campo Santa Margherita, Dorsoduro 3116/A, 30123 Venice.
((041) 522 43 31.

Società Dante Alighieri
Ponte del Purgatorio Arsenale, Castello, Venice. **Map** 8 F2.
((041) 528 91 27.

Scuola Internazionale di Gràfica
Calle della Regina Santa Croce 2213 30135 Venice.
Map 2 F5.
((041) 72 19 50.

EMBASSIES AND CONSULATES

Australia
Via Alessandria 215, Rome.
((06) 85 27 21.

Canada
Via Vittor Pisani 19 Milan.
((02) 675 81.

New Zealand
Via Zara 28, Rome.
((06) 441 71 71.

United Kingdom
Palazzo Querini Accademia Dorsoduro 1051 Venice. **Map** 6 E3.
((041) 522 72 07.

US
Via Principe Amedeo 2/10 Milan.
((02) 29 03 51.

RELIGIOUS SERVICES

Anglican
St George's Anglican Church, Campo San Vio Dorsoduro
Venice. **Map** 6 F4.
((041) 520 05 71.

Greek Orthodox
Greek Orthodox Church Ponte dei Greci Castello 3412 Venice. **Map** 8 D2.
((041) 523 95 69.

Jewish
Sinagoga, Ghetto Vecchio Cannaregio Venice. **Map** 2 D3.
((041) 71 50 12.

Lutheran
Chiesa Evangelica Luterana Campo Santi Apostoli Cannaregio 4443 Venice. **Map** 3 B5.
((041) 522 71 49.

Methodist
Chiesa Evangelica Valdese e Metodista, Campo S Maria Formosa, Castello 5170, Venice. **Map** 7 C1.
((041) 522 75 49.

Personal Security and Health

Venice is one of the safest cities in Europe. Violent crime is very rare and petty crime minimal in comparison with other main cities. Nevertheless, it is wise to take a few simple precautions, particularly against pickpockets, both in Venice and elsewhere in the Veneto. Leave valuables and any important documents in the hotel safe and carry only the minimum amount of money necessary for the day.

Make sure you take out adequate travel insurance before leaving for Italy, as it is very difficult to obtain once you are in the country.

Venice by night, not always well-lit but safe

Looking After Your Property

Traveller's cheques or Eurocheques are the safest way to carry large sums of money. Try to carry your cheque receipts and Eurocheque card separately to be on the safe side, and keep a photocopy of all vital documents such as your passport.

Safeguard against attracting the attention of pickpockets and bagsnatchers, particularly at railway stations, markets and on the buses. In Venice take extra care while waiting at the *vaporetto* landing stages; be especially vigilant when crowds are jostling to get on to the boats.

If you drive while in the Veneto, always remember to lock the car before you leave it and never leave valuables on display inside. Hired cars or those with foreign number plates are favourite targets of car thieves.

Personal Safety

Venice is uneventful by night and you can stroll through the streets without any threat. There is no red light quarter or any area that could be described as unsavoury. Women alone in Venice are unlikely to encounter anything more troublesome than the usual Latin roving eye. Elsewhere in the Veneto, in the less touristy towns particularly, unescorted females are likely to attract more attention.

Avoid unauthorized taxi drivers, who may not be insured and almost invariably overcharge. Airports are their favourite haunts. Make sure you take only official taxis which have the licence number clearly displayed *(see p278)*.

Police

The vigili urbani, or municipal police, are most often seen in the streets regulating traffic and enforcing local laws. They wear blue uniforms in winter and white during the summer. The *carabinieri*, with red striped trousers, are the armed military police, responsible for public law and order. *La polizia*, or state police, wear blue uniforms with white belts and berets. They specialize in serious crimes. Any of these should be able to help you.

In the event of theft go straight to the nearest police station *(polizia* or *carabinieri)* to make a statement. If there is a language problem, you should consult your nearest consulate *(see p263),* which you should also do in the case of a lost passport.

(see p278). *(see p263),*

EMERGENCY NUMBERS

Ambulance
Venice
(118.
Verona
(118.
Padua
(118.
Vicenza
(118.

Automobile Club d'Italia
(116.
Car accident and breakdown.

Fire
(115.

General SOS
(113.

Medical Emergencies
(118.

Police
(112.

Traffic Police
Venice
((041) 274 70 70.
Verona
((045) 50 03 33.
Padua
((049) 880 55 00.
Vicenza
((0444) 50 77 07.

MEDICAL PRECAUTIONS

Visitors from the European Union (EU) are entitled to reciprocal state medical care in Italy. Before you travel, pick up form E111 from the post

A group of Venetian policemen on the Riva degli Schiavoni

office, which covers you for emergency medical treatment. You may wish to take out additional medical insurance, as E111 does not cover repatriation costs or additional expenses such as accommodation, food and flights for anyone travelling with you. Visitors from outside the EU should take out a comprehensive insurance policy covering emergency medical treatment. If you are taking prescribed medication, take supplies or prescriptions with you.

Inoculations are not needed for the Veneto, but take sunscreen and mosquito repellent in the summer. Because of the canals, mosquitoes can be irksome in Venice. An electric gadget, from pharmacies or department stores, will repel insects in your room for up to 12 hours. Tap water is safe to drink, but locals often prefer mineral water, either fizzy *(con gas)* or still *(naturale)*.

Electric mosquito deterrent

MEDICAL TREATMENT

I F YOU ARE in need of urgent medical attention, go to the *Pronto Soccorso* (First Aid) department of the nearest main hospital. Standards of health care are generally better than those in the south of Italy, although not as high as in Britain or the US. There are usually queues at the emergency departments and many hospitals expect the patient's family or friends to help with his or her nursing.

Should you require a consultation with a doctor, ask the advice of your hotel or look in the yellow pages of the telephone directory, under *medici*. (A *dottore* is not necessarily a doctor of medicine.) If you have a serious medical complaint or allergy you should bring a letter, preferably translated, from your doctor at home.

Pharmacy sign

Many doctors in the region speak at least a little English. There are first aid facilities with the services of a doctor at airports and at most railway stations.

Dentists are expensive in Italy. You can find the nearest one in the yellow pages of the telephone directory, listed under *dentisti medici chirurghi*, or ask your hotel receptionist for his or her recommendation.

For insurance claims, make sure you keep all receipts for medical treatment and any medicines prescribed.

Pharmacies are open during the summer months from 8:30am to 12:30pm and 4pm to 8pm Monday to Friday, and from 9am to noon on Saturday. Winter hours are slightly shorter. All towns offer a 24-hour pharmacy service, with a night-time and Sunday rota. You will find the rota posted on the doors of pharmacies. Opening times can also be found in the local newspapers or, if you are in Venice, the booklet *Un Ospite di Venezia*.

Italian pharmacists are well-trained to deal with minor ailments and can prescribe many drugs without needing a doctor's prescription. The majority of pharmacies do not stock quantities of foreign medicines but can usually supply the local equivalent. Many of the words for minor complaints and remedies are similar in Italian, for example *lassativo* (laxative), *aspirina* (aspirin) and *tranquillante* (tranquillizer).

An ambulance boat on the Grand Canal

Banking and Local Currency

VISITORS TO THE VENETO have a number of options available to them for changing money. Banks tend to give more favourable rates than bureaux de change, hotels and travel agents, but the paperwork is usually more time consuming. Alternatively, credit cards or Eurocheques can be used for purchasing goods. When changing traveller's cheques you will need to show some form of identification.

Cash dispenser which also accepts VISA and MasterCard (Access)

CHANGING MONEY

BANKING HOURS can be erratic, especially the day before a public holiday, so it is safest to acquire some local currency before you arrive in Italy. Exchange rates will vary from place to place.

A more convenient way to change money is to use the electronic exchange machines. These are found at Marco Polo airport, Venice railway station and at several banks in the city. All major towns in the Veneto have foreign exchange machines. These machines have multilingual instructions and the exchange rate is displayed on the screen. You simply feed in up to ten notes of the same foreign currency, and you will get lire in return.

TRAVELLER'S CHEQUES

TRAVELLER'S CHEQUES are probably the safest way to carry large sums of money. Choose a name that is well known such as Thomas Cook, American Express or cheques

issued through a major bank. There is usually a minimum commission charge, which may make changing small sums of money uneconomical. Some establishments will charge you for each cheque.

Check the exchange rates before you travel and decide whether sterling, dollar or lire traveller's cheques are more appropriate for your trip. Bear in mind that it may be more difficult to cash lire traveller's cheques, especially in hotels, because they are not very profitable for the exchanger.

EUROCHEQUES

EUROCHEQUE CARDS can be used in any cashpoint machine displaying the Eurocheque logo. Eurocheques can also be used as direct payment for a wide variety of goods and services. Most up-market shops, hotels and restaurants in the popular tourist areas will accept Eurocheques, but it is worthwhile checking before you try. Alternatively, you can cash cheques at any bank displaying the Eurocheque logo. A Eurocheque card guarantees cheques up to a maximum amount of L300,000.

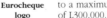

Eurocheque logo

CREDIT CARDS

CREDIT CARDS are not as widely used in Italy as they are in the rest of Europe. However, most establishments in the cities will accept them. VISA and Access (MasterCard) are the most popular, followed by American Express and Diners Club. Some banks and cash dispensers accept VISA or Access for cash advances, although interest is payable once the money is withdrawn. In Venice, cash dispensers

accepting credit cards can be found at the Banca d'America e d'Italia in the Calle Larga XXII Marzo (**map** 7 A3), and at the Cassa di Risparmio in Campo Manin (**map** 7 A2).

BANKING HOURS

BANKS ARE USUALLY open between 8:30am and 1:30pm, Monday to Friday. Most also open for an hour in the afternoon from about 2:35pm until 3:35pm. They close at weekends and for public holidays, and they also close early the day before a major holiday. Exchange offices stay open longer, but the rates are less favourable. The exchange offices at Venice airport and railway station stay open until the evening and at weekends.

Plaque of the Cassa di Risparmio in Campo Manin

USING BANKS

CHANGING MONEY at a bank can at times be a frustrating process, as it inevitably involves endless form-filling and queuing. You must apply first at the window displaying the *cambio* sign, then move to the *cassa* to obtain your Italian money.

For security, most branches have electronic double doors. Press the button to open the outer door, then wait for it to close behind you. The inner door then opens automatically.

CURRENCY

ITALY'S CURRENCY is the lira (plural lire) and is usually written as L or, confusingly, £. Lira means pound, so the English pound is referred to as the *lira sterlina*.

Initially, the thousands of units of currency may seem very confusing, but the distinctive colours of the notes make distinguishing between them easy. From time to time, however, familiar coins and notes are redesigned or even discontinued, although plans to alter the basic unit have not yet been implemented. You will find that the last three noughts are regularly ignored in spoken Italian: *cinquanta* will usually mean L50,000 and not, as you may think, L50.

Shop and bar owners are not keen to accept high-value notes for small purchases, so try to obtain some small denomination notes when changing money. Always keep a few coins in reserve for telephones, tips and coin-operated lights which illuminate works of art in churches *(see p261)*. If there is a dearth of small-denomination coins, you may occasionally be offered your change in sweets.

Bank Notes

All bank notes are issued by the Banca d'Italia. Each denomination is a different colour and carries a portrait of a historic person. As a further aid to identification, the notes also increase in size according to their value. The lira itself is never divided up into smaller units.

1,000 lire

2,000 lire

5,000 lire

10,000 lire

50,000 lire

100,000 lire

50 lire (old)   100 lire (old)   50 lire (new)   100 lire (new)   200 lire

Coins

Coins, shown here at actual size, are available in denominations of L1,000, L500, L200, L100 and L50. Three versions of the L100 and L50 coins are still in circulation, the two types shown here and an older design. All three are likely to remain legal tender until the introduction of the Euro as the single European currency.

500 lire

1,000 lire

Using the Telephone

YOU CAN FIND PUBLIC TELEPHONES on the streets of all the main towns in the Veneto, as well as at bars and post offices. In Venice there are public phones in most of the main squares and at virtually every *vaporetto* landing stage. Many of these now accept prepaid phonecards, so it is far easier and more convenient for visitors to make long-distance calls.

Telephone company logo

TELEPHONE OFFICES

TELEPHONE OFFICES *(Telefoni)* are run by the Italian telecom companies Telecom Italia (previously called SIP) and ASST. When making international or long-distance calls you may find it easier to get a connection using one of these offices. Each *Telefono* has several soundproof booths with a metered phone. You will be assigned a booth by an assistant and your call will be metered once you are connected to the number. No premium is charged, but you will find that the opening hours of *Telefoni* rarely coincide with Italy's cheap-rate

Telephone sign

calling hours. The calls are measured in *scatti* (units) costing L200 per unit. All major post offices and **Telecom Italia** offices have *Telefoni*. The *Telefono* at Venice's main post office *(see page 269)* is open every day until 6:45pm. If you need to send a telegram abroad or to anywhere in Italy, you can either go to any post office or call 186 for assistance.

CALL CHARGES

THE CHEAPEST TIMES to phone within Italy are between 6:30pm and 8am from Monday to Friday, after 1:30pm on Saturday and all day Sunday. International calls within

Europe are cheapest between 10pm and 8am on weekdays and Saturdays and all day Sunday. The cheapest rates for calls to Canada and the United States are from 11pm to 8am weekdays, and 11pm to 2pm at weekends. For the cheapest calls to Australia, phone between 11pm and 8am Monday to Saturday and all day Sunday. There are no cheap rates for Japan.

In general, it is far cheaper to dial direct for international calls, either from a payphone or from a *Telefoni*, rather than going through the operator or making collect or credit card calls. Telephoning from hotel rooms is usually expensive and is sometimes marked up by several hundred per cent. In general, it is more expensive to phone abroad from Italy than, for example, from the USA or the UK.

USING A TELECOM ITALIA COIN AND CARD TELEPHONE

1 Lift the receiver and wait for the dialling tone.

2 If you use coins insert them in the slot at the top. The slot for telephone cards is lower down.

3 The display shows how much credit is left.

4 Dial the number and wait to be connected.

5 If you still have credit and want to make a second call, press the "follow-on call" button.

6 If your telephone card is about to expire, place a new one in the telephone card slot. When the old card expires, it will feed through automatically.

7 After your call is finished, unused coins are returned from the left-hand slot. Cards are returned from the slot on the right.

Telephone cards have values of L5,000, L10,000 or L15,000.

To use a card, break off the marked corner and insert, arrow first.

L100

L200   L500

USING PUBLIC TELEPHONES

YOU CAN DIAL long-distance and international calls from public telephones. When making long-distance calls, always have at least L2,000 in change ready. If you don't put enough coins in to start with, the telephone disconnects you and retains your money. The most up-to-date payphones also take telephone cards (carta or scheda telefonica). You can buy these from post offices, newspaper kiosks and tobacconists (tabacchi) that display the black and white T sign.

Tabacchi sign

Recent changes in the Italian phone network mean that any Italian number you dial in Italy must now be prefixed by its area code, even if you are making a local call. When dialling Italian numbers from abroad, do not drop the zero from in front of the area code.

Using a public phone

MAIN TELEFONI

Venice
Ferrovia Santa Lucia. **Map** 1 B4.
Piazzale Roma. **Map** 5 B1.

Verona
Ferrovia Porta Nuova.

Padua
Piazzetta A Sartori 17a.

Vicenza
Via Napoli 11.

REACHING THE RIGHT NUMBER

To ring Italy from the UK, and Ireland dial 00 39 then the number, including the full area code. From the US and Canada, dial 0 11 39 and from Australia, dial 00 11 39.

- Dialling code for
  Venice   041
  Verona   045
  Vicenza   0444
  Padua   049
  Treviso   0422
- International directory enquiries   176
- International operator assistance   15
- Telegrams and cables in Italy and abroad 186

To reach the operator in your own country to place a reverse charge or credit card call dial 172 followed by: 0044 for UK; 1011 for AT&T, US; 1022 for MCI, US; 1877 for US Sprint; 1061 for Telstra, Australia; 1161 for Optus, Australia; and 1001 for Canada.

- *See also* Emergency Numbers, *p264.*

Sending Letters

THE ITALIAN POSTAL SERVICE is notoriously inefficient. Expect anything sent abroad to take some time, especially during the August holiday season. Postcards to the UK can take up to a month if sent during the summer, and letters sent within Italy can take up to a week to reach their destination. For urgent or important communications, it is better to use the more expensive express system.

You can buy stamps (francobolli) from any tobacconist which has the black and white T sign, as well as from post offices. Post office hours are

City letters   Other destinations

Italian post box

Post Office sign

usually 8:30am to 2pm, Monday to Friday and 8:30am to noon on Saturday and the last day of the month. Main offices stay open until early evening.

SENDING PARCELS

SENDING PARCELS from Italy can be extremely difficult. Unless certain rules are adhered to, it is unlikely that your package will be sent. The package must be placed in a rigid box, wrapped in brown paper and bound with string and a lead seal. You will also need to fill in a simple customs declaration form. Often a stationery or gift shop in the major towns will, for a fee, wrap your package. Very few post offices offer this service.

POSTE RESTANTE

LETTERS AND PARCELS should be sent care of (c/o) Fermo Posta, Ufficio Postale Principale, followed by the name of the town in which you wish to pick them up. Print the surname clearly in block capitals to make sure the letters are filed correctly. To collect your post, you need to show some form of identification and pay a small fee.

MAIN POST OFFICES

Fondaco dei Tedeschi 929, Venice.
Map 7 B1.
((041) 271 71 11.

Piazza Viviani, Verona.
((045) 59 09 55.

Piazza Garibaldi, Vicenza.
((0444) 32 24 88.

Corso Garibaldi, Padua.
((049) 820 85 11.

TRAVEL INFORMATION

THE EASIEST WAY to reach the Veneto is by air. Direct flights link Venice to major European cities, but there are no direct intercontinental flights. Visitors from outside Europe have to transfer at Milan or Rome. Venice's Marco Polo airport, 10 km (6.5 miles) north of the city, receives both domestic and European flights as well as some charter flights. The airport is small and not well equipped for the volume of traffic. Treviso and Verona have their own small airports, both of which receive flights from the

Alitalia aircraft

UK. Car drivers who plan to tour the Veneto must bear in mind that toll charges are expensive on European motorways. Visitors to Venice itself will have to leave their cars in one of the large car parks on the outskirts of the city because there are no streets for cars in the centre. Parking fees are heavy, and owners run the risk of leaving their cars unattended for the length of their stay. However, the region's rail network is good, and Venice railway station links the city to towns of the Veneto, and major European cities.

The quayside at Venice's Marco Polo airport

ARRIVING BY AIR

VENICE IS SERVED by two airports: Marco Polo for scheduled flights and Treviso for charter flights. The city is linked to London, Paris and all other major European cities by direct flights. Visitors from outside Europe must fly to Rome or Milan then take a connecting flight or a train to Venice. The alternative, which is usually cheaper, is to take a budget flight to London, Paris, Amsterdam or Frankfurt, and then a connecting flight to Venice from there.

Daily scheduled flights to Venice are operated by **British Airways** and **Alitalia** from London. PEX or SuperPEX generally offer the best deals in scheduled flights to Venice (Marco Polo), but these are subject to booking restrictions and need to be reserved in advance. They may also be subject to penalty clauses, so it is advisable to take out suitable insurance cover against unforeseen cancellation.

Many charter flights operate to Venice (Treviso). Specialists

such as **Sky Shuttle** in the UK offer charter flights and reduced prices on scheduled services flying into Venice (Treviso) and Verona.

If you wish to book flights during your stay, travel agents such as **American Express** or **World Vision** in Venice offer a good service.

PACKAGE HOLIDAYS

TAKING A PACKAGE holiday to the Veneto is more convenient but not always cheaper than going independently of a tour operator. It is always worth comparing the costs, particularly if you are intending to travel off-season when charter flights are at their cheapest. For visitors who prefer the convenience of a package holiday, Venice is offered as a single destination or as part of a two- or three-centre holiday with Florence and Rome. Transfer from the airport on arrival is usually included in the holiday price. Most tour operators tend to concentrate on Venice as a centre, though some offer

packages to Verona or touring trips of the Veneto taking in the popular villas, museums and art galleries.

USEFUL NUMBERS

Alitalia
Venice
[147 86 56 41 (domestic flights);
147 86 56 42 (international flights);
147 86 56 43 (information).

British Airways
Venice
[147 81 22 66.

Sky Shuttle
Air Travel Group (Holidays) Ltd
227 Shepherds Bush Road, London
W6 7AS. [0181-748 1333.

American Express
See p261.

World Vision Travel
See p273.

Airport Information
Venice
[(041) 260 92 60.
Verona
[(045) 809 56 66.
Treviso
[(0422) 23 03 93.

MARCO POLO AIRPORT (VENICE)

FACILITIES ARE LIMITED at the airport, but there is a hotel reservations office and a currency exchange office which is open all day. The only restaurant is 3 minutes' walk from the airport building.

Verona airport check-in desk

The most dramatic entry from the airport into Venice is by boat. The Cooperativa San Marco public water launch to San Marco and the Lido departs at hourly or two-hourly intervals depending on the time of day. Tickets are available from the office close to the exit of the arrivals hall. The journey to Venice takes about 50 minutes and costs around L15,000 per person one way. The boat stops only a short walk away from the San Marco *vaporetto* landing stage. Water taxis operating from the airport to San Marco take only about 20 minutes but a journey will cost around six times as much as the public launch. Beware of water taxi touts who will charge you a good deal more than the official fare.

The less spectacular but quicker and cheaper alternative to the lagoon crossing is the ATVO bus to Piazzale Roma. The service meets all scheduled flights and costs around L5,000. Cheaper still, but stopping along the way, is the public bus to Piazzale Roma, which departs every 30 minutes. There is also a land taxi rank at the front of the airport. The journey takes 15 minutes and the drop-off point is Piazzale Roma.

TREVISO AIRPORT

THIS IS A SMALL airport which receives charter flights from London (Gatwick) twice a week and from Amsterdam daily. An exchange office is open when flights are in operation, mainly in the afternoon. The coach service to Piazzale Roma in Venice,

which connects with flights, costs about L7,000 and takes approximately 45 minutes. Alternatively, you can take the public bus No. 6 which runs to Treviso station, where there is a regular rail service to Venice. For those on package tours the transport to Venice is pre-arranged and normally included in the overall price of the holiday.

VERONA AIRPORT

VERONA AIRPORT receives flights from London (Gatwick), Frankfurt and Paris. The currency exchange office opens on weekdays only. The bus service from the airport to Verona, which links up with scheduled flights, costs about L6,000.

PORTERS IN VENICE

UNLESS YOU ARE staying very close to your arrival point, you will have to take a *vaporetto* to the landing stage nearest to your hotel. Porters are very expensive; you will have to pay for the porter's boat fare, as well as for each piece of luggage – each piece costs the same as an adult.

The cost of a porter handling two suitcases, including your *vaporetto* fare, could amount to nearly L20,000. If there are no porters available, which is often the case, you can call your hotel and ask for a porter to meet you.

ARRIVING BY CAR

TO DRIVE your own car in Italy you will need an international Green Card (for insurance purposes) and your vehicle registration documentation. EU nationals who do not have the standard pink licence will need an Italian translation of their licence, available from most motoring organizations and Italian tourist offices. Requirements vary for visitors from non-EU countries, and drivers should check with their insurance companies before leaving for Italy. Insurance can always be bought at the border. This is also required to hire a car. *(See also p278.)*

CAR HIRE NUMBERS

IN ADDITION to those below, each major car hire company has an office at Venice, Treviso and Verona airports.

Piazzale Roma, Venice
Avis [C] *(041) 522 58 25.*
Hertz [C] *(041) 528 40 91.*
Thrifty [C] *(041) 522 30 00.*

Padua Railway Station
Maggiore [C] *(049) 875 28 52.*

Verona Railway Station
Avis [C] *(045) 800 66 36.*
Hertz [C] *(045) 800 08 32.*
Maggiore [C] *(045) 800 48 08.*

Vicenza Railway Station
Maggiore [C] *(0444) 54 59 62.*

Boat from Venice's Marco Polo airport into the city

Travelling by Train

ITALY'S STATE RAILWAY (Ferrovie dello Stato or FS) runs an extensive and efficient rail network throughout the Veneto. Services are regular, trains tend to be punctual and the cost of travel is very reasonable. The variety of trains ranges from the painstakingly slow *locale*, which stops at almost every station, through various levels of fast intercity services to the high-speed *pendolino*, which links Venice with Rome.

FS train in Verona station

A *pendolino* – Italy's fastest train

ARRIVING BY TRAIN

SANTA LUCIA railway station in Venice is the terminus for trains from Paris, Munich, Innsbruck, Vienna, Geneva, Zürich and other European cities. Passengers travelling from London have to change in Paris or Ostend. Fast intercity trains link Venice with Verona, Bologna, Milan, Rome and other major Italian cities.

Europe-wide train passes such as Eurail (US) or Inter-Rail for those under 26 (Europe) are accepted on the FS network. You may have to pay a supplement, however, to travel on fast trains.

SANTA LUCIA STATION, VENICE

STANDING AT the west end of the Grand Canal, Ferrovia Santa Lucia is a modern, well-equipped station. There are *vaporetti* landing stages below the steps of the station with boats going to San Marco and all stops en route. There is also a water taxi and

gondola service. Porters are not so easy to find, however. The bus and coach terminal and the only land taxi rank in Venice are in Piazzale Roma nearby (follow yellow signs).

Automatic ticket machines in the station are easy to use and display instructions in six languages. Notes in every denomination up to L50,000, coins and some credit cards are accepted. Tickets can be booked free of charge in advance through travel agents.

Multilingual display screens give information on arrivals, departures, costs of travel and details about city services and tours. A tourist office offers to make hotel reservations, but queues are long in summer. There is also a Rolling Venice office (*see p262*), a bank and bureau de change, an international telephone office, a left luggage facility, a cafeteria and bar, and a shop that sells international newspapers and magazines. Another useful facility is the *albergo diurno*. This is a daytime hotel where you can rest in a private room with an en-suite shower.

ORIENT EXPRESS

FROM MARCH to November the *Venice Simplon-Orient-Express* runs between London and Venice with stops at Paris, Düsseldorf, Cologne, Frankfurt,

Zürich, St Anton, Innsbruck and Verona. A one-way journey with cabin from London to Venice costs four to five times the price of a charter flight, but if you opt for the return trip, the outward flight to Venice is thrown in.

The Orient-Express logo

VERONA STATIONS

VERONA LIES at the intersection of the main railway lines from Venice to Milan and Bologna to Munich. The main station, Porta Nuova, lies south of the centre, connected to it by frequent bus services. Train information is available at the ticket office and automatic help points give information in English. Other facilities include a left luggage office, a bar, an automatic exchange machine and a newspaper shop which sells bus tickets.

The small Porta Vescova station, serving local stations to the east of Verona, is used mainly by locals.

PADUA STATION

PADUA IS ONLY 30 minutes by train from Venice. The station is in the north of the town, and local buses for the centre leave from outside the station. The main bus terminal, with services to Venice and other towns of the Veneto is at Piazzale Boschetti, 10 minutes' walk from the station. Padua's tourist office is within the station building. There is

Santa Lucia station in Venice – gateway to the Veneto

a left luggage office, restaurant, a tobacconist selling bus tickets and a currency exchange office open 9am to noon and 3pm to 5:30pm Monday to Saturday; 9am to noon Sunday.

VICENZA STATION

VICENZA, 55 minutes from Venice, is on the main railway line between Verona and Padua. The station is south of the city centre. Facilities include a bar and offices for left luggage, tickets, information and currency exchange open 8am to 12:30pm and 2pm to 6:30pm Monday to Saturday, 8:30am to noon and 2pm to 6pm Sunday.

TRAIN TRAVEL

IF YOU PLAN to travel around, there are passes allowing unlimited travel on the FS network. These include a ticket for unlimited travel (*biglietto turistico libera circolazione*) and the *biglietto chilometrico*, which allows 20 trips totalling no more than 3,000 km (1,865 miles) for up to four people. These are available from international and Italian **CIT** offices and from some travel agents. There are facilities for disabled travellers on some services.

Tickets for Local Journeys

Ask at newsstands on the station for a biglietto a fasce chilometriche *to the destination you require.*

Station of departure

Stamp ticket here

Machine for validating tickets

MACHINES FOR FS RAIL TICKETS

These machines are easy to use, and most have instructions in six languages on a printed panel.

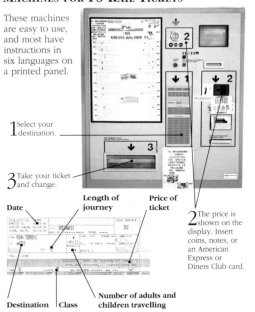

1 Select your destination.

2 The price is shown on the display. Insert coins, notes, or an American Express or Diners Club card.

3 Take your ticket and change.

Date

Length of journey

Price of ticket

Destination   **Class**

Number of adults and children travelling

TICKETS

ON ALL INTERCITY trains a supplement is charged, even if you have a rail card. Booking is obligatory on the *pendolino* and some other intercity services, and it is also advisable on other trains if you wish to travel at busy times. Buying your international city ticket at least five hours before travelling entitles you to a free seat reservation.

If you are travelling less than 200 km (125 miles), a short-range ticket (*biglietto a fasce chilometriche*) is available. The ticket is stamped with the destination you require and it must then be validated in one of the machines at the entrance to the platforms. Both outward and return portions of a ticket must be used within three days of purchase. Tickets can

be bought on the train but these are liable to a flat rate surcharge *and* a supplement based on the ticket price.

RAILWAY INFORMATION OFFICES

[147 88 80 88.
Use this national number for all rail enquiries in Italy.

BOOKING AGENTS

CIT
Via Giacomo Matteotti 12, Padua
[(049) 66 33 33.
London
[0171-258 8000.
Sydney
[(02) 299 4754.

World Vision Travel
Corso Porta Nuova 7, Verona.
[(045) 59 09 77.
See also p270.

Multilingual information board showing train departures

Getting Around Venice by Boat

F OR VISITORS TO VENICE, the *vaporetti* or waterbuses provide an entertaining form of public transport, although most journeys within the city can usually be covered more quickly on foot. The main route through the city for the *vaporetti* is the Grand Canal, and these waterbuses also supply a useful service connecting outlying points on the periphery of Venice and linking the city with the islands in the lagoon. The best value service from a visitor's point of view is the No. 1. This operates from one end of the Grand Canal to the other and travels sufficiently slowly for you to admire the parade of palaces at the waterside *(see pp56–71)*.

Vaporetto stop at the Giardini Pubblici *(see pp120–21)*

A *vaporetto* pulling into San Marco

The smaller, sleeker *motoscafo*

A two-tier *motonave* on its way to Torcello

If you are staying more than a few days, you can also save money by purchasing a weekly or monthly season ticket *(abbonamento)* which is available from ticket offices. Holders of Rolling Venice cards *(see p262)* can buy a *Tre Giorni Giovane*, or three-day youth pass, for L16,000.

The new "Isles Ticket" enables you to travel on No. 12 for a *one-way* run and stay for the day on the islands of Murano, Mazzorbo, Burano and Torcello. (You will, however, need to buy a ticket for the return trip.)

HOURS OF SERVICE

T HE MAIN ROUTES run every 10 to 20 minutes until the early evening. Services are reduced at night, particularly after 1am. From June to September the services are more frequent and certain routes are extended. Details of main lines are also given in the booklet *Un Ospite di Venezia* *(see p260)*. From May to September the main routes and island boats are very crowded.

Sightseeing from a *vaporetto* on the Grand Canal

THE BOATS

T HE ORIGINAL *vaporetti* were steam-powered (*vaporetto* means little steamer); today they are diesel-run motor boats. Although all the boats tend to be called *vaporetti*, strictly speaking the word applies only to the large wide boats used on the slow routes, such as No. 1. These boats provide the best views. The *motoscafi* are the slimmer, smaller and faster boats, such as No. 52. Some of them might look old and rusty, but they go at quite a pace. The two-tier *motonavi*, which look huge in comparison to the *vaporetti* or *motoscafi*, are used on routes to outlying islands and the Lido.

TYPES OF TICKET

T HE PRICE OF A TICKET depends not on the length of your journey but on the line you are taking. The faster *diretto* boats cost about half as much again as those which stop at every landing stage.

Tickets that are purchased on board, rather than at the kiosk found at each stop, are more expensive. If you buy a book of 10 or 20 tickets, the cost is no cheaper than single tickets, but does avoid the inconvenience of queuing at a ticket office for each journey.

You can save money, however, by buying a 24-hour or 72-hour ticket, which entitles the holder to unlimited travel on most lines.

THE MAIN ROUTES

① Confusingly called the *Accelerato*, this is the slow boat down the Grand Canal, stopping at every landing stage. The route starts at Piazzale Roma, travels the length of the Grand Canal, then from San Marco it heads east to the Lido.

⑧② A relative newcomer to the canals, the No. 82 is the faster route down the Grand Canal, making only six stops. It goes westwards as far as Tronchetto (the car park island), then eastwards along the Giudecca Canal to San Zaccaria. In season the line is extended to the Lido.

⑤② Taking the place of the old No. 5, the 52 skirts the periphery of Venice and takes in the island of Murano. It has also been extended to the Lido. The circular route provides a scenic tour of Venice, though to do the whole circuit you have to change boats at Fondamente Nuove.

③ A new seasonal line, this goes from Tronchetto, down the Grand Canal to San Zaccarie and returns via the Giudecca Canal.

④ Reverse route of No. 3, starting at San Zaccarie.

②③ Seasonal line to Murano from San Zaccarie.

①② Departing from the Fondamente Nuove, this line serves the main islands in the northern lagoon: Murano, Mazzorbo, Burano and Torcello. The service only runs about once an hour.

①④ A new line, this goes to Torcello and Burano from San Zaccaria (near San Marco). It is a much longer route than that from the Fondamente Nuove, going via the Lido, Punta Sabbioni and Treporti.

VAPORETTO INFORMATION

ACTV (Information Office)
Piazzale Roma, Venice.
Map 5 B1.
☎ *(041) 528 78 86.*

USING THE VAPORETTI

THE SERVICE is run by **ACTV** *(Azienda del Consorzio Trasporti Veneziano)*. In 1993 the waterbus system was given an overhaul; the map on the inside back cover of this guide reflects the changes made to the lines. Many maps on sale in Venice, therefore, will now be out of date. If you are not sure which boat to take to reach your destination, check with the boatman – the *vaporetti* crew tend to be very helpful.

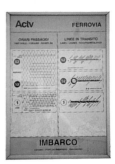

Timetable and routes at a *vaporetto* boarding point

1 Tickets are available at most landing stages, some bars, shops and tobacconists displaying the ACTV sign. The price of a ticket remains the same whether you are going one stop or doing the whole circuit, but some routes are more expensive than others and a variety of season tickets is available *(see* Types of Ticket*)*.

2 Signs on the landing stage tell you at which end you should board the boat.

3 Tickets should be punched at the automatic machines on the landing stages before each journey. Inspectors rarely board the boats and this makes it surprisingly easy for tourists (and Venetians) to hop on and off the boats without a validated ticket. However, there are steep fines for passengers without tickets, and there are notices in English to this effect in all the boats.

4 An indicator board at the front of each boat gives the line number and main stops. (Ignore the large black numbers on the side of the boat.)

5 Each landing stage has its name clearly marked on a yellow board. Most stops have two landing stages and it is quite easy, particularly if it is crowded and you can't see which way the boat is facing, to board a boat travelling in the wrong direction. It is helpful to watch which direction the boat is approaching from; if in doubt, check with the boatman on board.

Finding Your Way in Venice

VENICE IS SURPRISINGLY SMALL and most of the sights can be covered comfortably on foot. However, to avoid losing your way in the maze of little alleys, make sure you have the Street Finder *(see pp280–93)* handy. The gondola is the most romantic way to see the city, but prices are high, while the water taxi is the fastest means of travelling through the city and out to the islands.

GONDOLAS

GONDOLAS ARE a luxury form of transport used only by tourists (apart from Venetians on their wedding day). There are a number of gondola ranks throughout the city and plenty of gondoliers waiting for business.

Before boarding, check the official tariffs and agree a price with the gondolier. Prices are in the booklet *Un Ospite di Venezia (see p260)* and should also be available at gondola ranks. Official costs are around L70,000 for 50 minutes, rising to L90,000 after 8pm. However, gondoliers are notorious for overcharging, sometimes by double the official price: try bargaining, whatever the cost quoted. During the low season, or when business looks slack, you may be able to negotiate a fee below the official rate and a journey shorter than the minimum of 50 minutes. Another way of cutting costs is to share a gondola – five is the maximum number of passengers.

Gondoliers all speak a smattering of English and have taken basic exams in Venetian history and art. Do not expect your gondolier to burst into *O Sole Mio*, however; the most you are likely to hear are the low melodious cries of *Oe*,

The romance of an early evening gondola ride

Premi and *Stai* – the warning calls that have been echoing down the canals of Venice for centuries. If you want to go on a serenaded tour, join an evening flotilla with accompanying musicians, organized regularly from May to October. Hiring a gondola independently is more romantic, but will cost considerably more. Details are available from any local travel agent.

Sign for one of the *traghetti* across the Grand Canal

TRAGHETTI

TRAGHETTI are gondola ferries that cross the Grand Canal at seven different points, providing an invaluable service for pedestrians. Surprisingly, few tourists make use of this cheap, constant service. The points where the *traghetti* cross the Grand Canal are marked on the Street Finder maps *(see pp280–93)*. Yellow street signs show the way to the *traghetti*, illustrated with a little gondola symbol.

WATER TAXIS

FOR THOSE with little time and sufficient funds, the fastest and most practical means of getting from A to B is by water taxi. The craft are sleek, white or polished wood motorboats, all equipped with a cabin. They zip to and from the airport in only 20 minutes. There are 16 water taxi ranks, including one at the airport and at the Lido. Telephone numbers and official tariffs are listed in the booklet *Un Ospite di Venezia (see p260)*. Extra is charged for luggage, waiting, night service and for calling out a taxi. If the *vaporetti* are on strike, which is not uncommon, water taxis are like gold dust.

A water taxi

GONDOLA STANDS

San Marco (Molo)
[(041) 520 06 85.

Rialto (Riva Carbon)
[(041) 522 49 04.

Railway Station (San Simeone Piccolo)
[(041) 71 85 43.

WATER TAXI STANDS

Radio Taxi (all of Venice)
[(041) 522 23 03.

Ferrovia Santa Lucia
[(041) 71 62 86.

Piazzale Roma
[(041) 71 69 22.

San Marco
[(041) 522 97 50.

Crossing the Grand Canal by *traghetto*

WALKING IN VENICE

ONE OF THE GREAT pleasures of exploring Venice is walking. In the absence of traffic you soon get used to crossing streets and squares without so much as a glance to left or right. What you do have to contend with is the constant flow of tourists. The narrow alleys, particularly in the *sestiere* of San Marco, become extremely congested. However, the vast majority of tourists never venture beyond San Marco and it will be probably little more than a matter of minutes before you find yourself with only a few locals for company.

When sightseeing in Venice you will inevitably do a lot of walking, and a day taking in the sights can be extremely tiring. You need to allow only 35 minutes to cross the city from north to south on foot – provided you do not lose your way. Most visitors do, and this is, of course, part of the fun of exploring, but sensible shoes are a must, however short you think your journey may be.

Venice is so compact that you are never very far from the yellow signs that give directions to the key points of the city. Another useful landmark is the Grand Canal, which sweeps through the heart of the city in an inverted S-shape *(see p57)*.

The city has countless *campi*, or squares, which open out

Venice, city of bridges

An ornate Venetian door knocker

from the narrow alleys. Very few of these are equipped with public benches, but footsore tourists can sit at an open-air café. However, you will be expected to buy a drink, and drinks are expensive. Many of the main sights are concentrated in the *sestiere* of San Marco, either in Piazza San Marco *(see pp74–5)* or close by. Even the main sights in the *sestieri* beyond San Marco are, for most people, within comfortable walking distance of the main square. Apart from the Accademia and San Marco, the sign-posting is not very impressive, but the maps in this guide will help you find your way around.

In July and August, when temperatures are at their highest, it is wise to avoid walking around midday. You should also be prepared,

particularly at this time of year, for nasty smells which waft from some of the canals.

From October there is always the risk of high tides *(acqua alta)*, which cause flooding in the city. The first area to flood is Piazza San Marco. Duck-boards are laid out in the square, however, and along main thoroughfares. If you are not equipped with wellington boots you can always buy cheap knee-high plastic shoe covers from local shops.

ADDRESSES IN VENICE

FOR ANY NEWCOMER to the city of Venice, the system of addresses is initially very confusing. All buildings are numbered by the *sestiere* (administrative district) in which they fall rather than by the street. Hence a typical address would merely give the name of the *sestiere* followed by the number of the building, for example San Marco 2517 or Cannaregio 3499.

To locate an address it is, therefore, essential for you to establish the name of the street or square or, failing that, the nearest landmark. The Venetians resort to a book called *Indicatore Anagrafico*, which lists all the numbers in Venice and their corresponding streets. Better still is the more recent publication, *Calli, Campielli e Canali*, which also provides detailed maps of the city and islands.

You will find translations of Venetian words commonly used in place names in the Street Finder *(see p280)*.

A plethora of confusing signs in Cannaregio

Getting Around the Veneto

Taxi in Verona

DAY TRIPS CAN BE MADE from Venice by train or bus, and the city centres can be covered easily on foot or by local bus. Although the train and bus networks are excellent, the most practical and pleasant means of travel is by car, allowing total independence to explore the countryside. However, some of the roads between towns tend to be very congested in the summer, city centres are banned to tourist traffic, and the cost of petrol is high.

A city bus in central Verona

ON FOOT AND BY BUS

ALL THE CITIES of the Veneto are small enough to get around reasonably comfortably on foot. Limited traffic zones means that walking is pleasant and there are plenty of squares where you can sit and watch the world go by.

City buses are cheap and regular. Tickets, which must be bought prior to travel, are available from news-stands, bars, tobacconists and shops which display the bus company sign. There are also ticket vending machines in the streets, usually near stops, which take coins and L1,000 and L5,000 notes. A flat fee is charged for rides within the city and the suburbs. The ticket becomes valid only when you time-stamp it in the machine at the front or rear of the bus.

It is normally cheaper and quicker to travel between towns by train. In some cases the bus will take twice as long as the train, but there are a few towns such as Asolo where your only choice is a bus. In most cases the bus departure point is near the train station. You can usually buy a ticket valid for one, two or more hours of travel. Daily passes, or *tesserini*, are also available.

The city of Venice has excellent rail connections, but a limited bus service. The most popular routes connect nearby towns such as Mestre, Mira, Marghera and Stra.

TAXIS

TRAVELLING BY TAXI in the Veneto is not cheap. Meters show a fixed starting charge, then clock up every kilometre. There are extra charges for luggage, trips to the airports and journeys taken between 10pm and 7am, on Sundays and public holidays. Taxi drivers do not necessarily expect a tip – Italians give small tips or none at all.

Take taxis only from the official ranks, not from touts at railway stations and airports. In Venice the taxi rank is in

Rules of the Road
Drive on the right and, generally, give way to the right. Seat belts are compulsory in the front and back, and children should be properly restrained. You must also carry a warning triangle in case of breakdown. In town centres, the speed limit is 50 km/h (30 mph); on ordinary roads 90 km/h (55 mph); and on motorways 110 km/h (70 mph) for cars up to 1099cc, and 130 km/h (80 mph) for more powerful cars. Penalties for speeding include spot fines and licence points, and there are drink-driving laws as elsewhere in the EU.

One-way street

Piazzale Roma; in the Veneto towns of Verona, Vicenza and Padua, taxis can be found at the main piazzas.

CAR HIRE

IF YOU BOOK your car within the Veneto, local Italian firms such as Maggiore *(see p271)* tend to be cheaper than the international ones. Whichever company you choose, make sure that quoted prices include collision damage waiver, theft, breakdown service and IVA (Italian VAT, currently 19 per cent). Insurance against theft is usually an extra. To hire a car you must be over 21 and have held a licence for at least a year. Visitors from outside the EU need an international licence, though in practice hire firms may not insist on this.

DRIVING AND PARKING

CITIES in the Veneto have limited traffic zones and normally only residents and taxis can drive into the centre. Visitors can unload at their hotel, but must then park on the outside of town and come in by foot or bus. Some hotels have a limited number of parking permits, but this is no guarantee of a space. Your

Speed limit (on minor road)   **End of speed restriction**

Pedestrianized street – no traffic   **Give way to oncoming traffic**

Give way 320 m (350 yd) ahead   **Danger (often with description)**

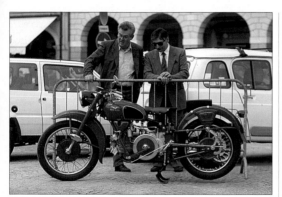

Moto Guzzi's classic Gambalunga in the market place at Montagnana

best bet is to telephone in advance and warn the hotel of your arrival.

Official parking areas are marked by blue lines, usually with meters or an attendant nearby. The *disco orario* system allows free parking for a limited period in certain areas. The cardboard discs, which you place on your windscreen, are provided by car hire companies, or can be purchased at petrol stations and also at supermarkets in the cities of the Veneto.

If your car is towed away, phone the **Polizia Municipale**, or Municipal Police.

In Venice parking is prohibitively expensive. The closest car parks to the centre are at Piazzale Roma, where space is at a premium. There is a huge car park on the Isola del Tronchetto, linked to Venice by *vaporetto*. The

Disco orario parking disc

cheaper parks at Fusina and San Giuliano in Mestre are open only in summer, for Carnival and Easter.

Many of the main roads are surprisingly old, with only a couple of lanes, and traffic is often very heavy. What looks like just a short trip on the map may take much longer than you would expect.

Autostrada tolls, which are levied on the motorways, are expensive. Payment can be made in cash or by pre-paid magnetic "swipe" cards called Viacards. These are available from tobacconists and all ACI offices.

PETROL

MOTORWAY SERVICE stations are open 24 hours a day. Petrol stations are scarce in the countryside and the majority do not accept credit cards. Many are closed all afternoon, all day Sunday and the whole of August. However, you will find that some of the self-service petrol stations have automatic machines which accept L10,000 notes.

BREAKDOWNS

THE ACI (**Automobile Club d'Italia**) provides an efficient 24-hour service which is also available to foreign visitors. The organization has basic reciprocal arrangements with affiliated associations in other countries such as the AA or RAC in Britain.

The picturesque but hair-raising Gardesana (see p204)

(see p204)

DIRECTORY

BUS INFORMATION

Belluno
Dolomiti Bus, Via Col da Ren
((0437) 94 11 67.

Padua
Autobus
ACAP Office
Ferrovia.
((049) 824 11 37.

Verona
Azienda Municipalizzata Trasporti
Via Torbido 1.
((045) 887 11 11.

Vicenza
Aziende Industriali
Municipalizzate
Via Fusineri 85
((0444) 39 49 09.

BREAKDOWN

Automobile Club d'Italia
Emergencies
(116.

Via Ca' Marcello 67
Mestre.
((041) 531 03 62.

Via della Valverde 34
Verona.
((045) 59 53 33.

Via degli Scrovegni 19
Padua.
((049) 65 49 35.

Viale della Pace 260
Vicenza.
((0444) 51 33 71.

TOWING AWAY

Polizia Municipale (Municipal Police)
Venice
((041) 274 92 98, or
(041) 522 45 76.

Padua
((049) 820 51 00.

Verona
((045) 807 84 11.

Vicenza
((0444) 54 53 11.

VENICE STREET FINDER

Aᴌᴌ ᴛʜᴇ sɪɢʜᴛs, hotels, restaurants, shops and entertainment venues in Venice have map references which refer you to this section of the book. The key map below indicates the areas of the city covered by the Street Finder, and includes the colour coding specific to each area. Following the map section is a complete index of street names *(see pp290– 93)*. The standard Italian spelling has been used on the maps throughout this book, but when exploring the city you will find that the street signs are often printed in Venetian dialect. Sometimes this means only a slight variation in the spelling (see the word Sotoportico/Sotoportego below), but some names look completely different. For example, Santi Giovanni e Paolo *(see Map 3)* is often signposted as "San Zanipolo". Major sights are labelled in Italian.

RECOGNIZING STREET NAMES

The signs for street *(calle)*, canal *(rio)* and square *(campo)* will soon become familiar, but the Venetians have a colourful vocabulary for the maze of alleys which makes up the city. When exploring, the following may help.

FONDAMENTA S.SEVERO

Fondamenta
A street that runs alongside a canal, often named after the canal it follows.

RIO TERRA GESUATI

Rio Terrà A filled-in canal. Similar to a *rio terrà* is a *piscina*, which often forms a square.

SOTOPORTEGO E PONTE SCRISTOFORO

Sotoportico or Sotoportego
A covered passageway.

SALIZADA PIO X

Salizzada A main street (formerly a paved street).

RIVA DEI PARTIGIANI

Riva A wide *fondamenta*, often facing the lagoon.

RUGAGIUFFA

Ruga A street lined with shops.

CORTE DEI DO POZZI

Corte
A courtyard.

RIO MENUO O DE LA VERONA

Many streets and canals in Venice often have more than one name: *o* means "or".

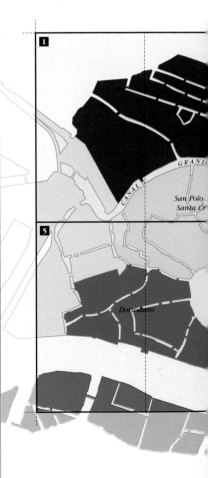

```
0 metres          500
0 yards           500
```

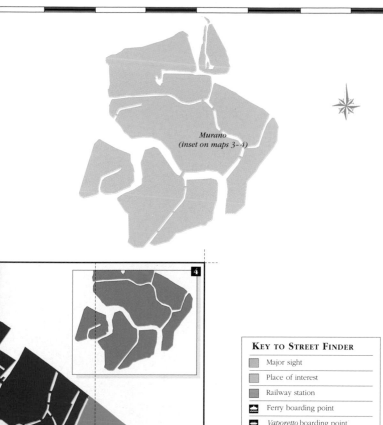

*Murano
(inset on maps 3-4)*

4

San Marco

Castello

8

KEY TO STREET FINDER

	Major sight
	Place of interest
	Railway station
⛴	Ferry boarding point
🚤	*Vaporetto* boarding point
	Traghetto crossing
	Gondola waiting point
	Coach station
i	Tourist information office
✚	Hospital with casualty unit
P	Parking
	Police station
✝	Church
✡	Synagogue
⊠	Post office
=	Railway line

SCALE OF MAP PAGES

0 metres	200
0 yards	200

SCALE OF MURANO INSET

0 metres	500
0 yards	500

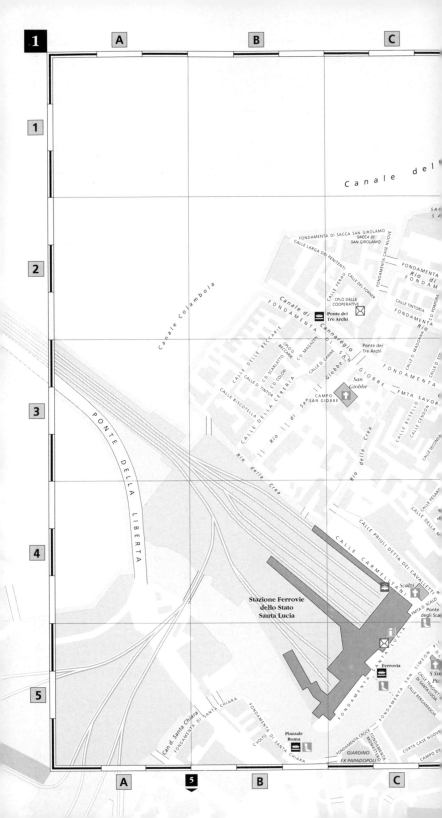

1

2

3

4

5

Canale del

FONDAMENTA DI SACCA SAN GIROLAMO
CALLE LARGA DEI PENITENTI

SACCA DI
SAN GIROLAMO

FONDAMENTA CASE NUOVE

FONDAMENTA
Rio di
FONDAM

CALLE FERAÙ
CALLE DEL FORNER

CALLE TINTORIA

Canale Colombola

FONDAMENTA

Canale di Cannaregio

CPLO DELLE
COOPERATIVE

Ponte dei
Tre Archi

FONDAMENTA
Rio

C D PORPORA

Ponte dei
Tre Archi

FONDAMENTA

CALLE DEL MADONNA

CALLE

CALLE DELLE BECCARIE

C D DO
BECCARIE

CALLE DELLO SCARLATTO

CALLE DEL TINTOR

C D COLORI

C D MAGAZEN

CALLE CANNE

San
GIOBBE

San
Giobbe

FMTA SAVOR

CALLE BUSELLO

CALLE CENDON

PONTE DELLA LIBERTA

CALLE BISCOTELLA

CALLE DELLA CERERIA

CAMPO
SAN GIOBBE

CALLE SECONDA

Rio di San Giobbe

Rio della Crea

CALLE PESARO

CALLE DELLA M

Rio della Crea

CALLE PRIULI DETTA DEI CAVALLETTI

CALLE CARMELITAN

Stazione Ferrovie
dello Stato
Santa Lucia

Scalzi

FMTA D SCALZI

Ponte
degli Scal

Ferrovia

FONDAMENTA SAN SIMEON PIC

S Sim
Pic

CALLE TRAGHETTO
DI SANTA LUCIA

FONDAMENTA SANTA LUCIA

CALLE BERGAMASCHI

Can d. Santa Chiara

FONDAMENTA DI SANTA CHIARA

C VOLTO DI SANTA CHIARA

Piazzale
Roma

FONDAMENTA CROCE
FONDAMENTA
MONASTERO

CORTE CASE NUOVE

GIARDINO
EX PAPADOPOLI

CAMPO DE

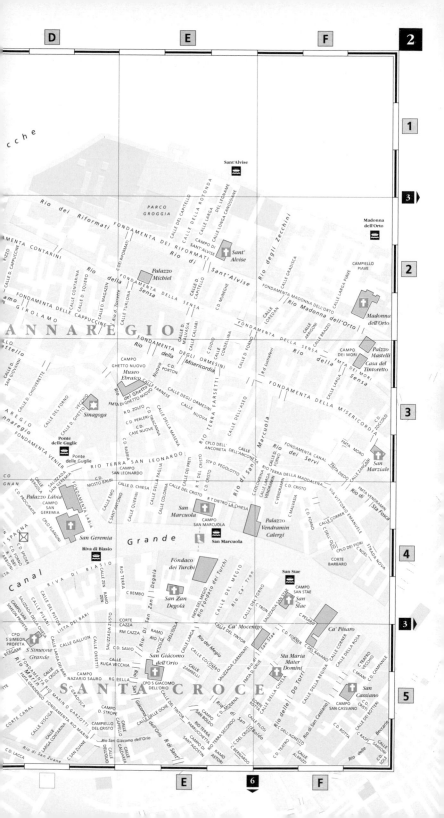

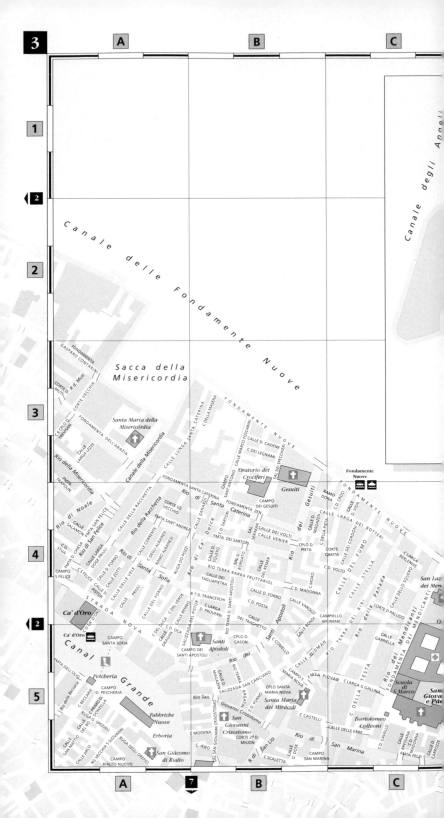

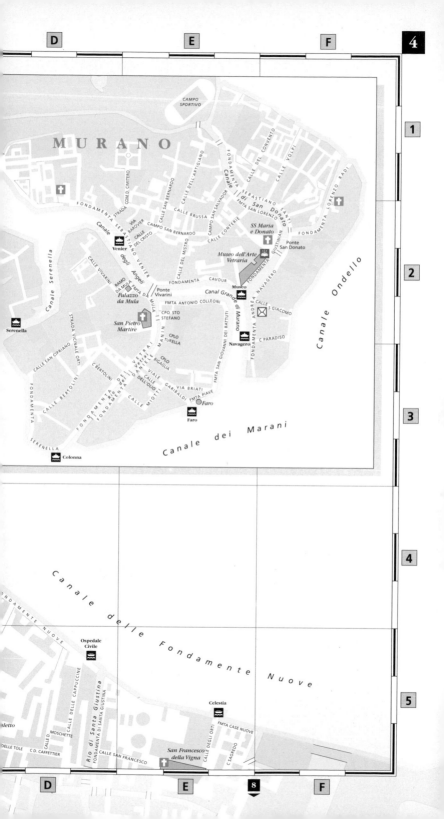

1

2

3

4

5

SANTA CROCE

GIARDINO
EX PAPADOPOLI

CAMPO SANT'ANDREA

CORTE DEGLI AM

CAMPO DEI
TOLENTINI

San Nicolò
da Tolentino

PIAZZALE
ROMA

Canale di Santa Chiara

Canale di Santa Maria Maggiore

Canale Scomenzera

FONDAMENTA PAPADOPOLI

FONDAMENTA
COSSETTI

FMTA CONDULMER

FONDAMENTA DEI TOLENTINI

FONDAMENTA SANT'ANDREA

C.RT SANT'ANDREA

C.NUOVA D.TABACCH

FONDAMENTA MINOTTO

CAMPAZZO
TRE PONTI

FMTA MAGAZEN

Rio del Malcanton

FMTA DEI GAFFARO

FONDAMENTA FABBRICA TABACCHI
Rio delle Burchielle
FONDAMENTA DELLE BURCHIELLE

CALLE BEI
PENSIERI

RIO NUOVO

C.D. MISERICORDIA

C.E BERNARDO
FMTA TRE PONTI
FMTA RIO NUOVO
FMTA PAZIEN

FONDAMENTA
DEL RIO NUOVO

CORTE E CORTE

RIO TERRA DEI PENSIERI

CORTE
CORRER

Rio della Cazziola

FMTA CAZZIOLA

CALLE LARGA RAGUSE

CALLE DELLA SACCA

Rio Nu

RIO DEL RIO NUOV

FONDAMENTA RIZZI

CORTE
CONTARINI

CALLE NUOVA

FONDAMENTA DELLE PROCURATIE

FMTA DI SANTA MARIA MAGGIORE

CALLE
PRIOL

C.VIOTTI
C.SPORCA

CALLE
CAPPELLO

CALLE RAGUSEO

CALLE NUOVA

FONDAMENTA DEI CERERI

FMTA DI S.

Rio del Tintor

FONDAMENTA ROSSA

FONDAMENTA FOSCARIN

Rio di S
Gri
d Ca

RIO
BIRRI

CALLE MADONNA

FMTA DJ S.M.MAGGIORE

C.CAMERINI

C.DELL'OLIO

CALLE DEI GUADIANI

RIO BIRRI

Rio dei Carmini

Santa Maria
dei Carmini

FONDAMENTA DELL'AZIERE

RIO TERRA DEI SECCHI

Rio delle Terese

CALLE DEL CRISTO

FMTA RUGHETTA

C.NUOVA

FONDAMENTA SANTA MARTA

C LARGA
S MARIA

FONDAMENTA DELLE TERESE

CALLE NUOVA TERESE

C.STRETTA

FONDAMENTA DEL SOCCORSO

Collegio
Armeno

CAMPO
DEI CARMINI

CO.

D O R S O

FONDAMENTA TRON

FONDAMENTA

Rio dell'Angelo Raffaele

CALLE SAN SEBASTIANO

RIO
dell'AVOGARIA

C.D. REMORCHIANTI

CPLO D.
STENDARDO

CAMPO
SAN
NICOLÒ

CPLO TRON
FMTA LIZZA
CALLE S.LORENZO
C.MAGGIORE

FONDAMENTA DI PESCHERIA

FONDAMENTA BARBARIGO

CALLE
MADDALENA

Angelo
Raffaele

CORTE
DEI VECCHI

CALLE
DEL DOLO

San
Sebastiano

CALLE DELL'AVOGARIA

CALLE BALASTRO

San Nicolò
dei Mendicoli

FMTA DEI BARI

Rio di San

CORTE
LARDONA

CPO ANGELO
RAFFAELE

CALLE
BEVILACQUA

CALLE NAVE
C.NUOVA
C.D. FRARI

CALLE CHIESA

FONDA

C DIETRO AI MEGAZZINI

SALIZZADA SAN BASEGIO

FONDAMENTA SAN BASEGIO

Stazione
Marittima

BANCHINA DEL PORTO COMMERCIALE

BANCHINA DI SAN BASEGIO

FMTA ZATTERE PONTE

CALLE
DEI MORTI

CALLE DELLA MASENA

CALLE DEI CARTI

San Basilio

Canale   di   Fusina

Sacca Fisola

FONDAMENTA   BEATA   GIULIANA

Mulino
Stucky

FONDAMENT

FONDAMENTA BEATA GIULIANA

CALLE DELLA SCUOLA

CALLE DEI FIGHERI

CALLE DEL VAPORETTO

CALLE DELLA SACCA

CALLE
FISOLA

CALLE
MONTALCONE

Canale   dei   Lavraneri

Rio di San Biagio

CALLE RIMINI

CALLE LARGA DEI LAVRANERI

CAMPO
DELLA
CHIESA

C.SERRAGLIA

GIUDECCA

FMTA SAN GERARDO SAGREDO

Can Sacca Fisola San

Biagio

CAMPIELLO
PRIULI

Rio delle Convertite

FMTA DELLE CONVERTITE

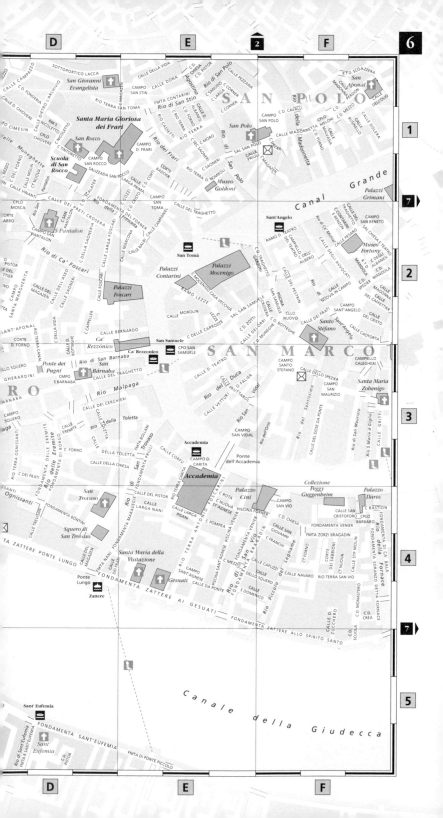

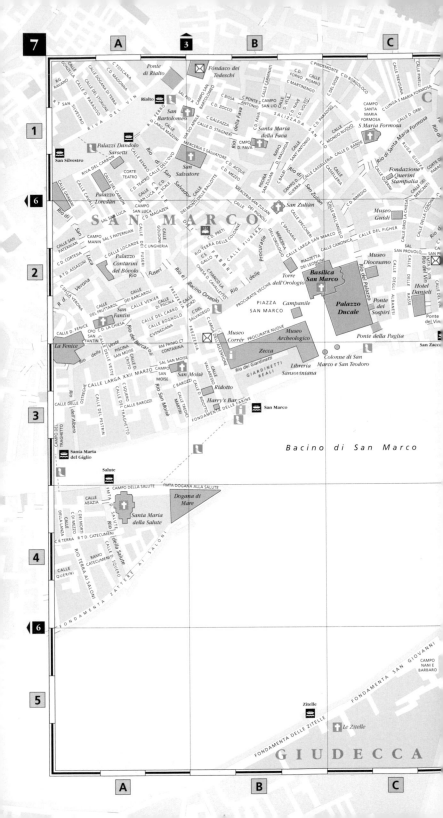

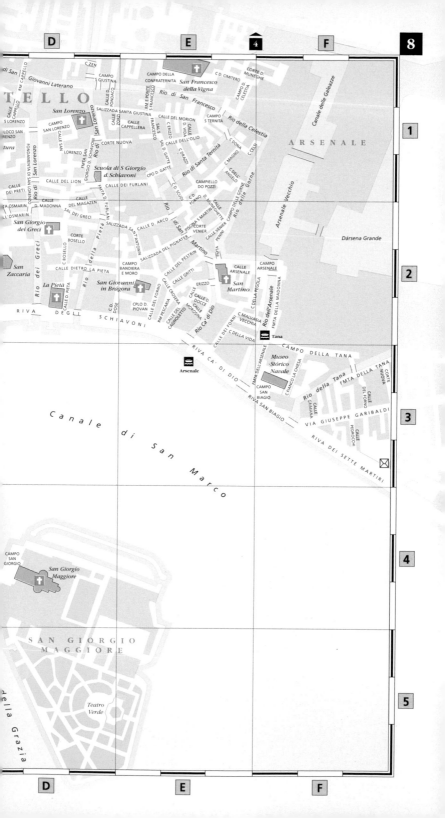

Street Finder Index

KEY TO ABBREVIATIONS USED IN THE STREET FINDER

C	Calle	**d.**	di, del, dell',	**R**	Rio	**Sta**	Santa
Can	Canale		dello, della,	**R T**	Rio Terrà	**Sto**	Santo'
Cpo	Campo		dei, delle, degli	**Rg**	Ruga/Rughetta	**SS**	Santi/Santissimo
Cplo	Campiello	**Fmta**	Fondamenta	**Sal**	Salizzada	**Stp**	Sottoportico
Ct	Corte	**Rm**	Ramo	**S**	San/Sant'		

XXII Marzo, Calle Larga 7 A3

A
Abazia, Calle 7 A4
Abazia,
  Fondamenta dell' 3 A3
Accademia Bridge 6 E3
Acque, Calle delle 7 B1
Agnello, Calle dell' 2 F5
Albanesi, Calle degli 3 A4
Albanesi, Calle degli 6 E1
Albanesi, Calle degli 6 F2
Albanesi, Calle degli 7 C2
Albanesi, Ramo 3 A4
Albero, Calle dell' 6 F2
Albero, Rio dell' 7 A3
Albrizzi, Calle 2 F5
Amai, Corte degli 5 C1
Anconeta, Calle dell' 2 E3
Anconeta,
  Campiello dell' 2 E3
Angeli, Canale degli 3 C2
Angeli, Canale degli 4 D2
Angelo, Calle dell' 7 C2
Angelo, Calle dell' 8 E1
Angelo Raffaele,
  Campo 5 B3
Angelo Raffaele,
  Rio dell' 5 B3
Archivio, Calle dietro l' 6 F2
Arco, Calle 3 A5
Arco, Calle dell' 8 E2
Arrigoni, Calle 2 F2
Arsenale, Calle 8 E2
Arsenale, Campo 8 F2
Arsenale,
  Fondamenta dell' 8 F3
Arsenale, Rio dell' 8 F2
Arsenale Vecchio 8 F1
Artigiano, Calle dell' 4 E1
Arziere,
  Fondamenta dell' 5 B2
Arziere, Rio dell' 5 B2
Ascensione,
  Calle Larga dell' 7 B3
Aseo, Calle 3 B5
Aseo, Calle dell' 2 E3
Aseo, Calle dell' 6 D2
Assassini,
  Rio Terrà degli 7 A2
Astori, Ramo 2 E5
Avogaria, Calle dell' 5 C3
Avogaria, Rio dell' 5 C3
Avvocati, Calle degli 6 F2

B
Badoer, Corte 6 E1
Bagatin, Rio Terrà 3 B5
Balastro, Calle 5 C3
Balbi, Calle 6 E2
Balbi, Calle 7 B1
Bande, Calle delle 7 C1
Bandiera e Moro,
  Campo 8 E2
Barba Fruttariol,
  Rio Terrà 3 B4
Barbarigo, Fondamenta 5 B3
Barbaro, Campiello 6 F4
Barbaro, Corte 2 F4
Barbo, Corte 6 D2
Barcaroli, Calle dei 7 A2
Barcaroli, Rio dei 7 A3
Bari, Calle Larga dei 2 D5
Bari, Fondamenta dei 5 A3
Bari, Lista dei 2 D4
Barovier, Via 4 E2
Barozzi, Calle 7 A3
Basego, Calle 5 C2

Basego, Corte 5 C2
Bastion, Calle 6 F4
Battello,
  Fondamenta del 1 C2
Battello, Rio del 1 C2
Beata Giuliana,
  Fondamenta 5 A5
Beccarie, Calle 3 A5
Beccarie, Calle delle 1 B3
Beccarie,
  Campiello delle 1 B3
Beccarie, Rio delle 2 F5
  continues 3 A5
Bella, Ruga 2 E5
Bembo, Calle 2 E4
Bembo, Calle 3 A4
Bembo, Calle 7 A1
Bergamaschi, Calle 1 C5
Bergami, Calle 2 D5
Berlendis, Calle Larga 3 C4
Bernardo, Calle 2 E5
Bernardo, Calle 5 B1
Bernardo, Calle 6 D2
Bertolini, Calle 4 D3
Bevilacqua, Calle 5 B3
Bezzo, Calle 6 D1
Biasio, Riva di 2 D4
Bigaglia, Campiello 4 E3
Biri, Rio Terrà dei 3 C4
Biscotella, Calle 3 B3
Bissa, Calle 7 B1
Bo, Calle del 3 A5
Bognolo, Calle 7 A2
Bollani, Fondamenta 6 E3
Bondi, Calle 3 B4
Bontini, Fondamenta 6 D4
Borgato,
  Salizzada Larga 3 B4
Borgo, Fondamenta di 6 D4
Borgoloco, Calle di 7 C1
Bosello, Calle 8 D2
Bosello, Corte 8 D2
Botta, Calle della 2 F5
Botteghe, Calle delle 6 D3
Botteghe, Calle delle 6 F2
Botteri, Calle dei 2 F5
Botteri,
  Calle Larga dei 3 C4
Bragadin, Fondamenta 6 E4
Brazzo, Calle 2 F2
Bressana, Calle 3 C5
Briati, Fondamenta 5 B3
Briati, Rio 5 C2
Briati, Via 4 E3
Brocchetta, Calle 6 D2
Brussa, Calle 4 E2
Burchielle,
  Fondamenta delle 5 B1
Burchielle, Rio delle 5 B1
Busello, Calle 3 C3
Businello, Calle 6 F1

C
Cadene, Calle delle 3 B3
Caffettier, Calle del 4 D5
Caffettier, Calle del 6 D2
Caffettier, Calle del 6 F2
Cagnoletto, Calle del 8 E2
Caldarer, Calle 2 E5
Calegheri, Campiello 6 F3
Caliari, Calle 2 E2
Camerini, Calle 5 B2
Campaniel, Calle 6 E2
Campanile, Calle del 2 F5
Campazzo, Calle 6 D1
Campo Sportivo 4 E1
Canal, Corte 2 D5
Canal, Fondamenta 2 F3
Canàl, Grande 2 D4

  continues 3 A5
  continues 6 F2
Canal, Rio Terra 6 D2
Cannaregio, Canale di 1 B2
Cannaregio,
  Fondamenta di 1 C3
Canne, Calle delle 1 B3
Canonica, Calle 7 C2
Canossiane,
  Calle Longa 2 E2
Caotorta, Calle 6 F2
Capitello, Calle del 2 E2
Capitello, Calle del 2 E2
Cappeller, Calle 6 D2
Cappellera, Calle 8 E1
Cappello, Calle 2 E5
Cappello, Calle 5 B2
Cappello, Calle 7 D1
Cappello, Ramo 7 D1
Cappuccine,
  Calle delle 2 D2
Cappuccine,
  Calle delle 4 D5
Cappuccine,
  Fondamenta delle 2 D2
Capuzzi, Calle 6 F4
Carbon, Calle del 7 A1
Carbon, Riva del 7 A1
Carità, Campo della 6 E3
Carità, Corte 3 C4
Carità, Rio Terrà 6 E4
Carmelitani, Calle 1 C4
Carminati, Calle 7 B1
Carminati, Salizzada 2 E5
Carmini, Campo dei 5 C2
Carmini, Rio dei 5 C3
Carro, Calle del 7 A2
Carrozze, Calle delle 3 C5
Carrozze, Calle delle 6 E2
Cartellotti, Calle del 5 C4
Casa del Tintoretto 2 F3
Case Nuove,
  Calle delle 2 E3
Case Nuove, Corte 1 C5
Case Nuove,
  Fondamenta 1 C2
Case Nuove,
  Fondamenta 4 E5
Cason, Campiello del 3 B5
Casselleria, Calle 7 C1
Cassetti, Rio 6 E1
Castelli, Calle 3 B5
Catecumeni, Ramo 7 A4
Catecumeni,
  Rio Terra de 7 A4
Cavalli, Calle 7 A1
Cavalli, Calle dei 6 F1
Cavallo, Calle del 3 C5
Cavour, Fondamenta 4 E2
Cazza, Corte 2 E4
Cazza, Ramo 2 E5
Cazziola, Fondamenta 5 C2
Cazziola, Rio della 5 B2
Ca' Bala,
  Fondamenta di 6 F4
Ca' di Dio, Rio 8 E2
Ca' di Dio, Riva 8 E3
Ca' Dolce, Rio di 3 B4
Ca' d'Oro, Calle di 3 A4
Ca' Foscari, Rio di 6 D2
Ca' Michiel, Rio di 6 F2
Ca' Tron, Rio 2 E4
Celestia, Campo della 8 E1
Celestia, Rio della 8 E1
Celsi, Calle 8 E1
Cendon, Calle 1 C3
Cerchieri, Calle del 6 D3
Cereri,
  Fondamenta dei 5 B2
Cereria, Calle della 1 B3

Chiesa, Calle 5 C3
Chiesa, Calle della 2 D4
Chiesa, Calle della 2 E4
Chiesa, Calle della 2 F5
Chiesa, Calle della 6 D3
Chiesa, Calle della 6 E1
Chiesa, Calle della 6 F4
Chiesa, Calle dietro la 7 A2
Chiesa, Calle drio la 7 C2
Chiesa, Calle fianco la 8 F3
Chiesa, Campo della 5 A5
Chiesa,
  Fondamenta della 3 A4
Chiesa,
  Rio Terrà dietro la 2 E4
Chiesa,
  Salizzada della 2 D3
Chiesa del Cavalletto,
  Calle fianco la 7 B2
Chiesa e Teatro,
  Salizzada 6 F2
Chiovere, Calle delle 6 D1
Chiovere, Campiello 6 D1
Chioverette, Calle delle 2 D3
Chioverette,
  Calle Lunga 2 D5
Chioverette, Ramo 2 D5
Cimesin, Ramo 6 D1
Cimitero, Calle del 8 E1
Cimitero, Strada
  Comunale del 4 D2
Colambola, Canale 1 B2
Coletti,
  Fondamenta Carlo 1 C1
Collegio Armeno 5 C3
Colleoni,
  Fondamenta Antonio 4 E2
Colombina, Calle 2 F3
Colombo, Calle 2 E5
Colonna, Calle 2 E4
Colonne,
  Rio Terrà delle 7 B2
Colori, Calle dei 1 B3
Comare,
  Campiello della 1 C5
Comello, Calle 3 B5
Condulmer,
  Fondamenta 5 C1
Confraternità,
  Campo della 8 E1
Contarina, Calle 2 D2
Contarina, Calle Larga 2 D5
Contarini, Corte 5 C2
Contarini, Fondamenta 2 D2
Contarini, Fondamenta 6 E1
Contarini,
  Fondamenta Gasparo 3 A3
Contarini e Benzon,
  Calle 6 F2
Conterie, Calle 4 E2
Convento, Calle dei 4 E1
Convertite,
  Fondamenta delle 5 C5
Convertite, Rio delle 5 C5
Cooperativa,
  Campiello delle 1 C2
Cordellina, Calle 2 E3
Cordoni, Calle dei 3 C4
Corfù, Calle 6 E3
Corner, Calle 2 F5
Corner, Calle 6 E1
Corona, Calle della 7 C2
Corrente, Calle 3 A4
Correr, Calle 5 B1
Correr, Corte 5 B1
Cortesia, Calle della 7 A2
Corti, Calle dei 6 E1
Cossetti, Fondamenta 5 B1
Crea, Calle della 6 F4
Crea, Rio della 1 B3

Crea, Rio Terrà della 1 C3
Cremonese, Calle 5 C1
Cristi, Calle dei 2 F5
Cristo, Calle de 2 E4
Cristo, Calle del 2 E3
Cristo, Calle del 2 E5
Cristo, Calle del 2 F4
Cristo, Calle del 4 E2
Cristo, Calle del 5 B3
Cristo, Calle del 6 E2
Cristo, Calle del 6 F2
Cristo, Calle del 7 A3
Cristo, Campiello del 2 D5
Cristo, Rio Terrà del 2 E3
Croce, Calle della 2 D5
Croce, Fondamenta 1 C5
Croci, Calle delle 3 C4
Crociferi, Oratorio dei 3 B4
Crosera, Calle 6 F2
Crosera, Calle 8 E2
Crotta, Fondamenta 2 D4

D

Dario, Sottoportico 2 D5
Diedo, Fondamenta 2 F3
Do Aprile, Via 7 A1
Do Pozzi, Campiello 8 E1
Do Pozzi, Ruga 3 A4
Do Torri, Rio delle 2 F5
Docce, Calle delle 8 E2
Dogana alla Salute,
  Fondamenta 7 A4
Doge Priuli,
  Calle Larga 3 A4
Dogolin, Calle 5 C3
Dolera, Calle 6 F1
Donà, Calle 6 E1
Donà, Calle 8 E1
Donà, Ramo 3 B4
Donzella, Calle 7 A1
Dose, Calle del 3 B5
Dose, Calle del 7 C1
Dose, Calle del 8 D2
Dose da Ponte,
  Calle del 6 F3
Dragan, Calle 3 A5
Drazzi, Calle 8 E1
Duca, Calle del 3 A4
Duca, Rio del 6 E3

E

Emo, Calle 2 D4
Erbe, Calle delle 3 C5
Eremite, Calle 6 D3
Eremite,
  Fondamenta delle 6 D3
Eremite, Rio delle 6 D3
Erizzo, Calle 8 E1
Erizzo, Calle 8 E2

F

Fabbri, Calle dei 7 B2
Fabbrica Tabacchi,
  Fondamenta 5 B1
Fabbriche Nuove 3 A5
Falier, Calle 6 D1
Farine,
  Fondamenta delle 7 B3
Farnese, Calle 2 E3
Farsetti, Rio Terrà 2 E3
Fava, Calle della 7 B1
Fava, Campo della 7 B1
Fava, Rio della 7 B1
Felzi, Fondamenta 3 C5
Fenice, Calle della 7 A2
Fenice, Fondamenta 7 A3
Ferau, Calle 1 C2
Ferro, Riva del 7 A1
Figher, Calle del 7 C2
Figheri, Calle del 5 A5
Filosi, Calle 2 F5
Fiori, Campiello dei 2 F4
Fisola, Calle 5 B5
Fiubera, Calle 7 B2
Flangini, Campiello 2 D4
Fóndaco, Calle del 8 D1
Fonderia, Calle della 6 D1
Fóndaco dei Turchi,
  Rio 2 E4
Fornace, Rio della 6 F4
Forner, Calle del 1 C2
Forner, Calle del 2 F5

Forner,
  Fondamenta del 6 D1
Forner, Piscina 6 E4
Forni, Calle dei 8 E2
Forno, Calle 6 D3
Forno, Calle del 2 D3
Forno, Calle del 2 D4
Forno, Calle del 2 E3
Forno, Calle del 2 E4
Forno, Calle del 2 F3
Forno, Calle del 2 F4
Forno, Calle del 3 A4
Forno, Calle del 3 A4
Forno, Calle del 3 B4
Forno, Calle del 3 B5
Forno, Calle del 6 D1
Forno, Calle del 6 D2
Forno, Calle del 6 E1
Forno, Calle del 6 F1
Forno, Calle del 7 B1
Forno, Calle del 8 E1
Forno, Calle del 8 E2
Forno, Calle del 8 F3
Forno, Corte 6 F4
Forno, Corte del 6 D2
Foscari, Calle 6 D2
Foscari, Calle Larga 6 D2
Foscarini, Calle Marco 3 B3
Foscarini, Fondamenta 5 C2
Foscarini,
  Rio Terrà Antonio 6 E4
Franceschi,
  Rio Terrà dei 3 B4
Franchi, Calle 6 F4
Frari, Campo dei 6 E1
Frari, Rio dei 6 E1
Frati, Calle dei 5 B3
Frati, Calle dei 6 D3
Frati, Calle dei 6 D4
Frati, Calle dei 6 F2
Frescada, Rio della 6 D2
Frezzeria 7 A2
Fruttarol, Calle 6 E3
Fruttarol, Calle del 7 A2
Fumo, Calle del 3 C4
Furlani, Calle dei 8 E1
Furlani,
  Fondamenta dei 8 D2
Fuseri, Calle dei 7 A2
Fuseri, Rio 7 A2
Fusina, Canale di 5 A4

G

Gabriella, Calle 3 C5
Gaffaro,
  Fondamenta del 5 C1
Galeazza, Calle 7 B1
Galeazze, Canale delle 8 F1
Gallina,
  Calle Larga Giacinto 3 C4
Gallion, Calle 2 D5
Gallo, Corte 5 C1
Garibaldi,
  Via Giuseppe 8 F3
Garibaldi, Viale 4 E3
Gatte, Campo delle 8 E1
Gatte, Salizzada delle 8 E1
Gesuiti, Campo dei 3 B4
Gesuiti, Rio dei 3 B4
Gherardini,
  Fondamenta 6 D3
Ghetto Nuovo, Campo 2 E3
Ghetto Nuovo,
  Fondamenta di 2 E3
Ghetto Nuovo, Rio del 2 E3
Ghetto Vecchio,
  Calle del 2 D2
Giardinetti Reali 7 B3
Giardinetti, Rio dei 7 B3
Giardino Ex
  Papadopoli 1 C5
  continues 5 C1
Giochin, Calle 2 D4
Giudecca, Canale della 6 E5
Giuffa, Ruga 7 C1
Giustinian, Fondamenta 4 E2
Goldoni, Calle 7 A2
Gorne, Campo delle 8 E1
Gorne, Rio delle 8 E1
Gozzi, Calle 6 E2
Gradenigo,
  Fondamenta 2 D5
Gradisca, Calle 2 D5
Gradisca, Calle 2 F2

Grazia, Canale della 8 D5
Greci, Rio dei 8 D2
Greci, Salizzada dei 8 D2
Grimana, Calle 8 F3
Grimani, Calle 7 A1
Gritti, Calle 6 F3
Gritti, Calle 8 E2
Groggia, Parco 2 E2
Grue,
  Fondamenta delle 2 E5
Guardiani, Calle dei 5 B2
Guerra, Campo della 7 B1

I

Isola, Ramo dell' 2 E5
Isola, Rio dell' 2 E5

L

Labia, Fondamenta 2 D4
Lacca, Calle della 2 D5
Lacca, Sottoportico 6 D1
Lana, Campo della 1 C5
Lanza, Calle della 7 A4
Lardona, Corte 5 B3
Larga, Calle 2 E5
Larga, Calle 2 F3
Larga, Calle 6 E1
Lavraneri,
  Calle Larga dei 5 A5
Lavraneri, Canale dei 5 B5
Le Zitelle 7 C5
Legname,
  Calle Larga del 2 E2
Legnami, Calle dei 3 A3
Leoncini, Piazzetta dei 7 B2
Lezze, Calle 6 E2
Lezze, Calle Larga 3 A3
Lezze, Ramo 6 E2
Lion, Calle del 8 D1
Lista di Spagna,
  Rio Terrà 2 D4
Lizza, Fondamenta 5 B3
Locande, Calle delle 7 A2
Loredan, Calle 2 F2
Lustraferri, Rio dei 2 F3

M

Maddalena, Calle 5 B3
Maddalena,
  Rio Terrà della 2 F3
Madonna, Calle 6 F1
Madonna, Calle 6 F2
Madonna, Calle della 1 C3
Madonna, Calle della 3 B4
Madonna, Calle della 3 C5
Madonna, Calle della 7 A1
Madonna, Calle della 8 D1
Madonna,
  Fondamenta della 5 B2
Madonna,
  Fondamenta della 8 F2
Madonna dell'Orto,
  Fondamenta 2 F2
Madonna dell'Orto, Rio 2 F2
Madonnetta, Calle 6 F1
Madonnetta, Rio della 6 F1
Magazen, Calle 6 D1
Magazen, Calle 6 F1
Magazen, Calle del 1 B3
Magazen, Calle del 2 D2
Magazen, Calle del 3 B4
Magazen, Calle del 3 B5
Magazen, Calle del 6 D2
Magazen, Calle del 6 D4
Magazen, Calle del 7 A2
Magazen, Calle del 8 D1
Magazen, Fondamenta 5 C1
Magazzini,
  Calle dietro ai 5 A3
Maggiore, Corte 5 B3
Magno, Calle 8 E1
Malcanton,
  Fondamenta 5 C1
  continues 5 C2
Malcanton, Rio del 5 C1
Malpaga, Rio 5 C3
Malvasia, Calle 2 F3
Malvasia, Calle 6 F1
Malvasia, Calle della 2 E2
Malvasia, Ramo della 7 B1
Malvasia Vecchia, Calle 8 E2
Mandola, Calle della 6 F2

Mandola,
  Rio Terrà della 6 F2
Manin, Campo 7 A2
Manin,
  Fondamenta Daniele 4 D3
Marani, Canale dei 4 E3
Maravegie,
  Fondamenta 6 D4
Marcona, Calle 6 E2
Marin, Rio 2 D5
Martinengo, Calle 7 B1
Masena, Calle della 2 E3
Masena, Calle della 3 B3
Masena, Calle della 5 C4
Mazzini, Calle Larga 7 A1
Megio, Calle del 2 E4
Megio, Fondamenta del 2 E4
Megio, Rio del 2 E5
Meloni, Campiello 6 F1
Mendicanti,
  Fondamenta dei 3 C5
Mendicanti, Rio dei 3 C5
Mercanti, Calle dei 7 C1
Mercerie 7 B2
Mezzo, Calle 6 E4
Mezzo, Calle di 6 D1
Mezzo, Calle di 6 F1
Mezzo, Calle di 7 A4
Mezzo, Calle di 7 B1
Miani, Calle 2 F5
Minotto, Fondamenta 5 C1
Miotti, Calle 4 D3
Misericordia,
  Calle della 1 C4
Misericordia,
  Calle della 5 C1
Misericordia,
  Canale della 3 A3
Misericordia,
  Fondamenta della 2 F3
Misericordia,
  Ramo della 1 C4
Misericordia, Rio della 2 E3
  continues 3 A3
Misericordia,
  Sacca della 3 A3
Mistro, Calle del 4 E2
Mocenigo Casa Vecchia,
  Calle 6 E2
Modena, Calle 3 B5
Modena, Calle della 2 E5
Molin, Calle 6 D1
Monastero, Calle del 6 F4
Monastero,
  Fondamenta 1 C5
Mondo Nuovo, Calle 7 C1
Monfalcone, Calle 5 B5
Monti delle Ballotte,
  Calle del 7 B1
Mori, Campo dei 2 F3
Mori, Fondamenta dei 2 F3
Morion, Calle del 8 E1
Moro, Calle 3 B4
Moro, Calle 6 E1
Moro, Fondamenta 2 F3
Morolin, Calle 6 E2
Morosina, Calle 8 E2
Morti, Calle del 5 C4
Morti, Calle dei 7 A4
Mosca, Campiello 6 D2
Moschette, Calle delle 4 D5
Mosto Balbi, Calle da 2 D4
Mula, Fondamenta da 4 E2
Mula, Ramo da 4 E2
Muneghe, Calle delle 2 E2
Muneghe, Calle delle 6 E3
Muneghe, Campiello 2 D5
Muneghe, Corte delle 8 E1
Muneghette, Calle delle 8 E2
Muneghette, Rio delle 6 D1
Murano,
  Canal Grande di 4 E2
Muti, Corte dei 3 A3
Muti, Rio dei 3 A3

N

Nani e Barbaro, Campo 7 C5
Nani, Calle Larga 6 E4
Nani, Fondamenta 6 D4
Navagero,
  Fondamenta Andrea 4 E3
Navaro, Calle 6 F4
Nave, Calle 5 B3
Nave, Calle della 7 B1

Nicoletto, Calle	6 D1	Pescheria,		Riello, Calle	2 D3	San Boldo, Rio di	2 E5
Noale, Rio di	3 A4	Fondamenta di	5 B3	Riello, Calle	5 B3	San Canciano,	
Noel, Calle	2 F4	Pestrin, Calle del	6 F2	Riformati, Calle dei	2 E2	Salizzada	3 B5
Nomboli, Rio Terrà dei	6 E1	Pestrin, Calle del	7 A3	Riformati,		San Cassiano, Campo	2 F5
Nova, Strada	2 F4	Pestrin, Calle del	8 E2	Fondamenta dei	2 E2	San Cassiano, Rio di	2 F5
Nova, Strada	3 A4	Pezzana, Calle	6 E1	Riformati, Rio dei	2 D2	Santa Caterina,	
Nuova, Calle	2 D2	Piave, Calle Larga	2 F2	Rimedio, Calle del	7 C1	Calle Lunga	3 A3
Nuova, Calle	2 E3	Piave, Campiello	2 F2	Rimini, Calle	5 A5	Santa Caterina,	
Nuova, Calle	5 B3	Piave, Fondamenta	4 E3	Rio Marin, Fondamenta	2 D5	Fondamenta	3 B3
Nuova, Calle	5 B3	Piccolo del Legname,		Rio Marin o Garzotti,		Santa Caterina, Rio di	3 B3
Nuova, Calle	5 C2	Rio	6 F4	Fondamenta	2 D5	Santa Chiara, Canale di	1 A5
Nuova, Corte	6 D1	Pietà, Calle della	3 B4	Rio Nuovo,		*continues*	5 A1
Nuova, Corte	6 F4	Pietà, Calle della	8 D2	Fondamenta	5 C1	Santa Chiara,	
Nuova, Corte	8 D1	Pietà, Calle dietro la	8 D2	Rio Nuovo,		Fondamenta di	1 B5
Nuova, Corte	8 F3	Pietà, Campiello della	3 B4	Fondamenta del	5 C2	San Cipriano, Calle	4 D3
Nuova dei Tabacchi,		Pietà, Rio della	8 D2	Rio Terrà, Calle	6 E1	San Cristoforo, Calle	6 F4
Calle	5 B1	Pignater, Salizzada del	8 E2	Rio Terrà, Calle	7 A4	San Domenico, Calle	6 E4
Nuova in Campo, Calle	6 F2	Pignoli, Calle dei	7 B2	Rizzi, Fondamenta	5 B2	San Donato, Canale di	4 E1
Nuova Sant'Agnese,		Pindemonte, Calle	7 B1	Rizzo, Calle	2 D2	San Fantin, Campo	7 A2
Calle	6 E4	Pinelli, Calle	7 C1	Roma, Piazzale	5 B1	San Felice, Calle	3 A4
Nuova Terese, Calle	5 A3	Pio X, Salizzada	7 A1	Rosa, Calle della	2 F5	San Felice, Campo	3 A4
Nuove, Canale delle		Piombo, Calle	7 B1	Rossa, Fondamenta	5 C2	San Felice,	
Fondamenta	3 A2	Piovan, Campiello del	8 E2	Rota, Calle	6 E4	Fondamenta	3 A4
Nuove, Fondamente	3 B3	Piovan, Fondamenta	3 B5	Rotonda, Calle della	2 E2	San Felice, Rio di	3 A4
Nuovo, Campiello	6 F2	Pisani, Calle	2 D4	Rotta, Calle	7 C1	Sant'Eufemia,	
Nuovo, Rio	5 C1	Pisani, Calle Larga	6 E4	Rotta, Corte	2 F5	Fondamenta	6 D5
		Piscina, Calle di	7 A2	Rotta, Corte	7 C1	Sant'Eufemia,	
		Pistor, Calle del	2 D4	Ruga Vecchia, Calle	2 D5	Fondamenta Rio	6 D5
O		Pistor, Calle del	3 A4	Rughetta, Fondamenta	5 B3	Sant'Eufemia, Rio di	6 D5
Oca, Calle dell'	3 A5	Pistor, Calle del	6 D5			Santa Fosca, Rio di	2 F4
Oche, Calle delle	2 E5	Pistor, Calle del	6 E1			San Francesco, Calle	4 E5
Ognissanti,		Pistor, Calle del	6 E4	**S**		San Francesco,	
Fondamenta	5 C3	Pistor, Salizzada del	3 B4	Sabbioni, Corte dei	6 F4	Ramo	8 E1
Ognissanti, Rio	6 D4	Pompea, Calle	6 E4	Sabbioni, Rio Terrà dei	2 D4	San Francesco, Rio di	8 E1
Ognissanti, Rio Terrà	6 D3	Ponte, Calle Da	6 E4	Sacca, Calle della	5 B5	San Francesco,	
Olio, Calle dell'	2 D5	Ponte Piccolo,		Sacca Fisola San Biagio,		Salizzada	6 E2
Olio, Calle dell'	2 F4	Fondamenta di	6 E5	Canale	6 E5	San Francesco,	
Olio, Calle dell'	4 E3	Ponte Sant'Antonio,		Sacche, Canale delle	1 C1	Salizzada	8 E1
Olio, Calle dell'	5 B2	Calle	7 B1	Sacchere, Calle	6 D1	San Gallo, Calle	7 B2
Olio, Calle dell'	6 F1	Porpora, Calle della	1 C2	Sacchere,		San Gerardo Sagredo,	
Olio, Calle dell'	8 E1	Porto Commerciale,		Fondamenta delle	6 D1	Fondamenta	5 A5
Olio, Fondamenta dell'	3 A5	Banchina del	5 A4	Sagredo, Calle	4 E5	San Geremia, Campo	2 D4
Ondello, Canale	4 F2	Porton, Calle del	2 E3	Salamon, Calle	3 A4	San Geremia,	
Orbi, Calle dei	6 E2	Posta, Calle della	3 B4	Saloni, Rio Terrà ai	7 A4	Salizzada	2 D4
Orbi, Calle dei	7 C1	Preti, Calle dei	2 E3	Salute, Campo della	7 A4	San Giacomo, Calle	4 F2
Orefici, Ruga degli	3 A5	Preti, Calle dei	7 B2	Salute,		San Giacomo dell'Orio,	
Ormesini, Calle degli	2 E3	Preti, Calle dei	8 D1	Fondamenta della	7 A4	Campo	2 E5
Ormesini,		Preti Crosera, Calle dei	6 D2	Salute, Rio della	7 A4	San Giácomo dell'Orio,	
Fondamenta degli	2 E3	Prima, Calle Larga	6 E1	Salvadego, Calle del	7 B2	Rio	2 E5
Orologio,		Primo Corte Contarina,		Sant'Agnese, Campo	6 E4	San Giobbe, Campo	1 B3
Merceria dell'	7 B2	Ramo	7 A3	Sant'Agnese, Piscina	6 E4	San Giobbe,	
Orseolo, Bacina	2 B2	Primo della Donzella,		Sant'Agostino, Campo di	2 E5	Fondamenta di	1 C3
Orseolo, Rio	2 B2	Calle	3 A5	Sant'Alvise, Campo di	2 E2	San Giobbe, Rio di	1 B3
Orsetti, Calle	2 D5	Priuli, Calle	3 A4	Sant'Alvise, Rio di	2 E2	San Giorgio, Campo	8 D4
Orso, Rio dell'	6 F3	Priuli, Calle	6 E1	Sant'Alvise, Sacca di	1 C2	San Giorgio	
Orti, Calle degli	4 E5	Priuli, Campiello	5 C5	Sant'Andrea, Campo	5 A1	degli Schiavoni,	
Orti, Strada Vicinale	4 D2	Priuli, Fondamenta	6 E3	Sant'Andrea,		Fondamenta	8 D1
Osmarin, Fondamenta	8 D2	Priuli detta dei		Fondamenta	3 B4	San Giovanni, Calle	6 F4
Osmarin,		Cavalletti, Calle	1 C4	Sant'Andrea,		San Giovanni, Calle di	2 D3
Fondamenta dell'	8 D2	Procuratie, Calle delle	2 D4	Fondamenta	3 B4	San Giovanni,	
Ospedale, Calle	3 C5	Procuratie, Calle delle	5 B2	Sant'Andrea, Rio Terrà	5 B1	Fondamenta	7 C5
Ostreghe, Calle delle	7 A3	Procuratie,		Sant'Angelo, Campo	6 F2	San Giovanni,	
Ovo, Calle dell'	7 A1	Fondamenta delle	5 B2	Sant'Angelo, Rio di	6 F2	Ruga Vecchio	3 A5
		Procuratie, Rio delle	7 B2	Sant'Antonin, Salizzada	8 E2	San Giovanni	
		Procuratie Nuove	7 B2	Sant'Antonio, Calle	2 D4	Crisostomo, Rio	3 B5
P		Procuratie Vecchie	7 B2	Sant'Antonio, Calle	7 B1	San Giovanni	
Pagan, Fondamenta	5 C1	Proverbi,		Sant'Antonio, Campo	3 B4	Crisostomo, Salizzada	3 B5
Paglia, Calle della	2 E3	Calle Larga dei	3 B4	Sant'Aponal, Rio Terrà	6 D2	San Giovanni dei Battuti,	
Palazzo, Rio del	7 C2			Santi Apostoli,		Fondamenta	4 E3
Paludo, Corte del	3 C4			Campo dei	3 B5	San Giovanni Laterano,	
Panada, Rio della	3 C4	**Q**		Santi Apostoli, Rio dei	3 B5	Rio di	8 D1
Papadopoli,		Querini, Calle	2 E4	Santi Apostoli,		San Girolamo,	
Fondamenta	5 C1	Querini, Calle	7 A4	Rio Terrà dei	3 B4	Fondamenta	2 D2
Paradiso, Calle	4 F2	Querini, Rio Terrà	7 C1	San Bárnaba, Rio	6 D3	San Girolamo,	
Paradiso, Calle del	7 A1			San Barnaba,		Fondamenta di Sacca	1 C2
Paradiso, Calle del	7 B1			Calle Lunga	5 C3	San Girolamo, Rio di	1 C2
Paradiso, Corte del	7 B2	**R**		San Barnaba, Campo	6 D3	San Girolamo, Sacca di	1 C2
Parrucchetta, Rio Terrà	2 E5	Rabbia, Calle della	2 E3	San Barnaba, Rio di	6 D3	Santa Giustina, Campo	8 D1
Pazienza, Calle della	5 C3	Racchetta, Calle della	3 A4	San Bartolomeo,		Santa Giustina,	
Pedrocchi, Calle	8 F3	Racchetta, Rio della	3 A4	Campo	7 B1	Fondamenta di	4 D5
Pegola, Calle della	8 F2	Radi,		San Basegio,		Santa Giustina, Rio di	4 D5
Pegolotto,		Fondamenta Lorenzo	4 F2	Banchina di	5 B4	Santa Giustina,	
Sottoportico del	2 E3	Ragusei, Calle	5 C2	San Basegio, Salizzada	5 B3	Salizzada	8 E1
Penini, Fondamenta	8 E2	Ragusei, Calle Larga	5 C2	San Basilio,		San Lazzaro dei	
Penitenti,		Raspi, Calle	2 F5	Fondamenta	5 B3	Mendicanti	3 C4
Calle Larga dei	1 B1	Rasse, Calle delle	7 C2	San Beneto, Campo	6 F2	San Leonardo, Campo	2 E3
Pensieri, Calle dei	5 B1	Ravano, Calle del	2 F5	San Bernardo, Calle	4 E2	San Leonardo,	
Pensieri, Rio Terrà dei	5 B1	Ravano, Ruga	7 A1	San Bernardo, Campo	4 E2	Rio Terrà	2 E3
Perdon, Calle del	6 F1	Regina, Calle della	2 F5	San Biagio, Campo	8 F3	San Lio, Campo	7 B1
Perleri, Calle dei	2 E3	Remer, Calle del	3 B4	San Biagio,		San Lio, Rio di	3 B5
Pesaro, Calle	1 C4	Remorchianti, Calle dei	5 A3	Fondamenta	5 C5	San Lio, Salizzada	7 B1
Pesaro, Calle	2 F4	Renier o Pistor, Calle	6 D2	San Biagio, Rio di	5 C5	San Lorenzo,	
Pesaro, Calle	6 F2	Rialto Bridge	7 A1	San Biagio, Riva	8 F3	Borgoloco	8 D1
Pescaria, Ramo	8 E2	Rialto Nuovo, Campo	3 A5	San Boldo, Campo	2 E5	San Lorenzo, Calle	5 B3
Pescheria, Campo della	3 A5	Ridotto, Calle del	7 B3			San Lorenzo, Calle	8 D1

San Lorenzo,
Calle Larga 8 D1
San Lorenzo, Campo 8 D1
San Lorenzo,
Fondamenta 4 E2
San Lorenzo,
Fondamenta di 8 D1
San Lorenzo, Rio di 8 D1
San Luca, Calle 7 A1
San Luca, Campo 7 A2
San Luca, Rio di 7 A2
San Luca, Salizzada 7 A2
Santa Lucia,
Fondamenta 1 C5
San Marco, Bacino di 7 B3
San Marco, Calle Larga 7 B2
San Marco, Canale di 8 E3
San Marco, Piazza 7 B2
San Marcuola, Campo 2 E4
San Marcuola, Rio di 2 F3
Santa Margherita,
Campo 6 D2
Santa Margherita, Corte 6 D2
Santa Margherita,
Rio di 5 C2
Santa Maria del Giglio,
Rio 6 F3
Santa Maria Formosa,
Calle Lunga 7 C1
Santa Maria Formosa,
Campo 7 C1
Santa Maria Formosa,
Rio di 7 C1
Santa Maria Maggiore,
Canale di 5 A1
Santa Maria Maggiore,
Fondamenta di 5 B2
Santa Maria Nova,
Campo 3 B5
Santa Maria Novo,
Campiello 3 B5
San Marina, Campo 3 B5
San Marina, Rio di 3 C5
Santa Marta, Calle Larga 5 A3
Santa Marta,
Fondamenta 5 A3
San Martin, Piscina 8 E2
San Martino, Rio di 8 E2
San Mattio, Calle 3 A5
San Maurizio, Campo 6 F3
San Maurizio, Rio di 6 F3
San Moisè, Campo 7 A3
San Moisè, Piscina 7 A3
San Moisè, Rio 7 A3
San Moisè, Salizzada 7 A3
San Nicoletto, Ramo 6 D1
San Nicolò, Campo 5 A3
San Nicolò, Rio di 5 A3
San Pantalon, Calle 6 D2
San Pantalon, Campo 6 D2
San Pantalon, Rio 6 D1
San Pantalon,
Salizzada 5 C1
San Paternian, Calle 7 A2
San Paternian,
Salizzada 7 A2
San Polo, Campo 6 F1
San Polo, Rio di 6 E1
San Polo, Salizzada 6 E1
San Provolo, Calle 7 C2
San Provolo, Campo 7 C2
San Provolo, Rio di 7 C2
San Provolo, Salizzada 7 C2
San Rocco, Campo 6 D1
San Rocco, Salizzada 6 D1
San Salvador, Campo 4 E2
San Salvador, Rio di 7 A1
San Salvatore, Merceria 7 B1
San Samuele, Campo 6 E3
San Samuele, Piscina 6 F2
San Samuele,
Salizzada 6 E2
San Sebastiano,
Fondamenta 5 C3
San Sebastiano, Rio di 5 C3
Santi Sebastiano,
Fondamenta 4 E1
San Severo,
Fondamenta di 7 C1
San Severo, Rio di 7 C1
San Silvestro, Rio Terrà 7 A1
San Simeon Piccolo,
Fondamenta 1 C5

San Simeon Profeta,
Campo 2 D4
San Simeon Profeta,
Campo 2 D5
Santa Sofia, Campo 3 A5
Santa Sofia, Rio di 3 A4
San Stae, Campo 2 F4
San Stae, Rio di 2 F5
San Stae, Salizzada 2 F4
Santo Stefano,
Campo 4 E2
Santo Stefano,
Campo 6 F3
San Stin, Campo 6 E1
San Stin, Rio di 6 E1
Santa Ternità, Campo 8 E1
Santa Ternità, Rio di 8 E1
San Tomà, Campo 6 E1
San Tomà, Rio Terrà 6 D1
San Trovaso, Rio di 6 E4
San Vidal, Campo 6 E3
San Vidal, Rio 6 E3
San Vio, Campo 6 F4
San Vio, Rio di 6 E4
San Vio, Rio Terrà 6 F4
San Zaccaria, Campo 7 C2
San Zan Degolà, Rio di 2 E4
San Zuane, Calle 2 D5
San Zuane, Rio di 2 D5
San Zulian, Merceria 7 B1
San Zulian, Piscina 7 B1
San Zulian, Rio di 7 B1
Sansoni, Calle 2 F5
Santissimo, Rio del 6 F3
Sanudo, Calle 6 E1
Saoneri, Calle 6 D2
Saoneri, Calle 6 E1
Saoneria, Calle della 6 D2
Sartori, Calle dei 3 B4
Sartori,
Fondamenta dei 3 B4
Sauro, Campo Nazario 2 D5
Savio, Calle del 2 E5
Savorgnan,
Fondamenta 1 C3
Savorgnan, Parco 2 D4
Sbiacca, Calle della 5 C2
Scalater, Calle della 6 D2
Scale, Calle delle 7 A1
Scaletta, Calle 3 B5
Scalzi Bridge 1 C4
Scalzi,
Fondamenta degli 1 C4
Scarlatto, Calle del 1 B3
Schiavoni, Riva degli 8 D2
Scoazzera, Rio Terrà 5 C3
Scoazzera,
Rio Terrà della 6 F1
Scomenzera, Canale 5 A1
Scudi, Calle degli 8 E1
Scuola, Calle della 5 A5
Scuola, Calle della 6 F5
Secchi, Rio Terrà dei 5A3
Seconda del Milion,
Corte 3 B5
Seconda delle Do Corti,
Calle 1 C3
Seconda Saoneri, Calle 6 E1
Secondo, Rio Terrà 2 E5
Senigallia, Calle 5 A5
Sensa,
Fondamenta della 2 E2
Sensa, Rio della 2 D2
Serenella, Canale 4 D2
Serenella,
Fondamenta 4 D3
Seriman, Salizzada 3 B4
Servi, Rio dei 2 F3
Sette Martiri, Riva dei 8 F3
Soccorso,
Fondamenta del 5 C3
Sole, Calle del 2 F5
Soranzo detta Fornace,
Fondamenta 6 F4
Soriana, Calle 5 C1
Sottoportico Molin,
Calle 6 F4
Sottoportico Scuro,
Calle del 1 C3
Spadaria, Calle 7 B2
Specchieri, Calle 7 B2
Specchieri,
Salizzada dei 3 B3

Speziali, Ruga degli 3 A5
Spezier, Calle 6 F1
Spezier, Calle dello 2 C4
Spezier, Calle dello 6 F2
Spezier, Calle dello 6 F3
Sporca, Calle 5 B2
Squero, Calle 7 A3
Squero, Calle dello 2 D2
Squero, Calle dello 3 B4
Squero, Calle dello 3 C4
Squero, Calle dello 6 E4
Squero, Calle dello 7 A4
Squero, Campo 6 D3
Squero,
Fondamenta dello 6 D3
Squero Vecchio,
Corte 3 A4
Stagneri, Calle degli 7 B1
Stella, Calle 3 C4
Stendardo,
Campiello dello 5 A3
Storione, Calle del 7 A1
Stretta, Calle 5 B3
Strope, Campo delle 2 D5
Stua, Calle della 3 A4

T
Tagliapietra, Calle dei 3 B4
Tana, Campo della 8 F3
Tana,
Fondamenta della 8 F3
Tana, Rio della 8 F3
Teatro, Calle del 2 F5
Teatro, Calle del 6 E3
Teatro, Calle del 7 A1
Teatro, Campiello del 6 F2
Teatro, Corte 7 A1
Teatro, Ramo del 6 F2
Teatro Vecchio, Calle 2 F5
Terese,
Fondamenta delle 5 A3
Terese, Rio delle 5 A3
Terrà, Calle Dogana di 7 A1
Terrà, Rio 2 E4
Terrà, Rio 6 E1
Testa, Calle della 3 C5
Tintor, Calle del 1 B3
Tintor, Calle del 2 E5
Tintor, Rio del 5 B2
Tintoretto, Calle 6 D1
Tintoria, Calle 1 C2
Tiracanna, Calle della 2 E3
Tole, Barbaria della 4 D5
Tolentini, Campo dei 5 C1
Tolentini,
Fondamenta dei 5 C1
Toletta, Calle 6 D3
Toletta, Calle della 6 D3
Toletta, Rio della 6 D3
Torelli, Calle 3 C5
Torrette, Rio delle 2 D2
Toscana, Calle 7 A1
Traghetto, Calle del 3 B4
Traghetto, Calle del 6 D3
Traghetto, Calle del 6 E2
Traghetto, Calle del 6 F2
Traghetto, Calle del 7 A3
Traghetto, Campo del 7 A3
Traghetto di Santa Lucia,
Calle 1 C5
Traghetto Garzoni,
Calle del 6 E2
Trapolin,
Fondamenta 3 A3
Tre Ponti, Campazzo 5 B1
Tre Ponti,
Fondamenta 5 C1
Tredici Martiri, Calle 7 A3
Trevisan, Calle 6 D4
Trevisan, Calle dei 3 A3
Trevisan,
Campiello dei 3 A3
Trevisana, Calle 7 C1
Tron, Calle 2 F4
Tron, Campiello 5 A3
Tron, Fondamenta 5 A3
Turella, Campiello 4 E3
Turlona, Calle 2 E2

U
Ungheria, Calle 7 A2

V
Vallaresso, Calle 7 B3
Vaporetto, Calle del 5 A5
Varisco, Calle 3 B4
Vecchi, Corte dei 5 C3
Vecchia, Corte 3 A3
Vele, Calle delle 3 A4
Vele, Calle delle 7 B1
Vendramin, Calle 2 F4
Vendramin, Calle Larga 2 F4
Vendramin,
Fondamenta 2 F4
Veneziana, Calle 7 A2
Venier, Calle 3 B4
Venier, Calle 7 A2
Venier, Calle 8 E2
Venier, Corte 8 E2
Venier, Fondamenta 2 D3
Venier, Fondamenta 6 E4
Venier, Fondamenta 6 F4
Venier,
Fondamenta Sebastiano
4 D2
Venier, Piscina 6 E4
Verde, Calle del 3 A4
Vergola, Calle 2 D4
Verona, Calle della 7 A2
Verona, Rio della 7 A2
Veste, Calle delle 7 A3
Veste, Rio delle 7 A3
Vetrai, Rio dei 4 D3
Vetrai,
Fondamenta dei 4 D3
Vetturi o Falier, Calle 6 E3
Vida, Calle della 3 C4
Vida, Calle della 6 D2
Vida, Calle della 6 E1
Vida, Calle della 8 E1
Vida, Calle della 8 E2
Vin, Calle del 7 C2
Vin, Fondamenta del 7 C2
Vin, Rio del 7 C2
Vin, Riva del 7 A1
Vinanti, Calle 6 D1
Viotti, Calle 5 B2
Visciga, Calle 2 D5
Vittorio Emanuele, Via 2 F4
Vivarini, Calle 4 D2
Volpi, Calle 4 F1
Volti, Calle del 3 B4
Volto, Calle 1 B5
Volto, Calle del 3 C4
Volto, Calle del 7 B1

W
Widman, Calle 3 B5
Widman, Campiello 3 C4

Z
Zambelli, Calle 2 E5
Zanardi, Calle 3 B4
Zancani, Calle 2 F3
Zattere ai Gesuati,
Fondamenta 6 D4
Zattere ai Saloni,
Fondamenta 7 A4
Zattere Allo Spirito
Santo, Fondamenta 6 E4
Zattere Ponte Lungo,
Fondamenta 5 C4
Zecca 7 B3
Zecchini, Rio degli 2 F2
Zen, Calle 2 D4
Zen, Calle 8 D1
Zen, Fondamenta 3 A4
Zen, Ramo 2 D4
Zitelle,
Fondamenta delle 7 B5
Zocco, Calle del 7 B1
Zoccolo, Calle dello 2 F3
Zolfo, Ramo dello 2 E3
Zorzi, Calle 7 B2
Zorzi, Calle 8 D1
Zorzi, Salizzada 7 C1
Zorzi Bragadin,
Fondamenta 6 F4
Zotti, Calle 3 A4
Zotti, Calle degli 6 E2
Zucchero, Calle dello 6 F4
Zudio, Calle 2 E3
Zusto, Salizzada 2 D5

General Index

A

A La Vecchia Cavana 241
Abano Terme 184
Abbazia Hotel 231
Abbazia di Praglia 184
Abbazia San Gregorio 70
Accademia Bridge 68
Accademia cinema 257
Accademia gallery 54, **130−33**
  Baroque, genre & landscapes 133
  Byzantine and international
    Gothic 132
  early Renaissance 132
  floorplan 130−31
  gallery guide 131
  Grand Canal 68
  high Renaissance 132−3
  Sala dell'Albergo 130, 133
  Visitors' Checklist 131
Acqua alta 51, 74
  See also Floods
Adam and Eve (Rizzo) 84, 89
Addresses, building numbers 277
Adoration of the Golden Calf
  (Tintoretto) 140
Adoration of the Magi (Il
  Pordenone) 174
Adoration of the Magi (Veronese)
  171
Adoration of the Shepherds
  (Bordone) 174
Adoration of the Shepherds
  (Conegliano) 127
Adoration of the Shepherds
  (Veronese) 116
Adria 185
Aeroclub G Ancillotto (Lido) 157
Age and Youth (Veronese) 89
Agli Alboretti Hotel 226, 230
  restaurant 241
Agnoletti (Treviso) 243
Agriturist Ufficio Regionale 224−5
Ai Do Draghi 247
Ai Do Mori Hotel 229
Ai Gondolieri 241
Ai Pescatori 241
Ai Pugni 247
Aida (Verdi), Arena (Verona) 195,
  256, 257
Air travel 270
Airports
  information 270
  Marco Polo (Venice) 270−71
  Treviso 271
  Verona 271
Al Bersagliere (Verona) 244
Al Capriolo (Vodo di Cadore) 245
Al Conte Pescaor 240
Al Gambero Hotel 229
Al Graspo de Ua 240
Al Salisa (Conegliano) 242
Al Sole Hotel 226, 229
Al Torresan (Vicenza) 244
Ala Napoleonica 74
d'Alemagna, Giovanni
  Accademia 133

d'Alemagna (cont.)
  San Zaccaria 112
Alessandro, Duke of Florence 101
Alex Hotel 229
Alexander III, Pope 82
Aliani, Casa del Parmigiano 251
Alighieri wine estate 208
Alitalia 270
Alla Bomba 247
Alla Botte (Portogruaro) 243
Alla Campagnola (Salò) 244
Alla Posta (Dolo) 242
Alpe del Nevegal 218
Altino, bishop of 40
Amarone 238
American Express 261
Ammannati, Bartolomeo, Benavides
  mausoleum 179
Andraz 215
Angelo della Città (Marini) 134
Angelo Raffaele 128
Angels in Armour (Guariento) 179
Annelie 251
Annigoni, Pietro, *La Strega* 166
Annunciation (Pisanello) 194
Annunciation (Titian) 174
d'Annunzio, Gabriele 69, 208
Antica Bessetta 240
Antica Locanda la Cappello
  (Belluno) 245
Antica Locanda Mincio (Valeggio
  sul Mincio) 244
Antica Trattoria alla Maddalena 241
Antica Trattoria Poste Vecie 240
Antica Trattoria Tre Visi (Vicenza)
  244
Antico Martini 240, 257
Aperitifs 239
The Apothecary's Shop (Longhi) 130
The Apotheosis of St Julian (Palma il
  Giovane) 95
Arche (Verona) 245
Arcimboldo (restaurant) 240
Arco dei Gavi (Verona) 194
Arena (Verona) 194−5
  opera 195, 256−7
Arquà Petrarca 184
Arrigoni, Abbot Onorio 141
Arsenale 45, 55, **119**
Art, Venetian 26−7
  See also Museums and galleries
Art exhibitions 256
Art galleries *see* Museums and
  galleries
Asolo 167
  map 164
Associazione Italiana Alberghi per
  la Gioventù (youth hostels)
  224−5
Assumption (Titian) 199
Assumption of the Virgin (Titian)
  102
Astor Hotel (Belluno) 233
Astra cinema 257
Augustus Terme Hotel (Padua)
  232

Austrian embassy 68
Austro-Hungarian Empire 216
Automobile Club d'Italia 279
Autumn, events 35
Avenzo, Jacopo, Oratorio di San
  Giorgio (Padua) 183
Azienda del Consorzio Trasporti
  Veneziano (ACTV) 275
Azienda di Promozione Turistica di
  Venezia 261

B

Baba-jaga (Verona) 245
Bacanal del Gnoco festival (Verona)
  32
*Bacchus and Ariadne Crowned by
  Venus* (Tintoretto) 87
Bacino Orseolo 74
Bacon, John H, *Romeo and Juliet*
  199
Balbi, Nicolò 66
Balo Coloc 251
Banks 266
Baptism of Christ (Conegliano) 118
Baptism of Christ (Giovanni Bellini)
  171
Bar Algiubagio 247
Bar Colleoni 247
Bar Cucciolo 247
Bar Dogale 247
Bar Gelateria Causin 247
Bar Gelateria Il Doge 247
Bar Gelateria Nico 247
Bar Gelateria Paolin 247
Bar Gelateria Riviera 247
Bar Gelateria Solda 247
Bar Ice 247
Bar La Palanca 247
Bar della Maddalena 247
Bar Mio 247
Bar Orologio 247
Bar Palmisano 247
Bar Pasticceria Vio 247
Bar Trono di Attila 247
Barattieri, Nicolò, San Marco and
  San Teodoro columns 77
Barbaro family 92
Barbarossa, Emperor Frederick 82
Barbesin (Castelfranco) 242
Bardolino 238
  grape festival 35
  maps 188, 204
  wine tour 208−9
Baroque architecture, *palazzi* 23
Barovier, Angelo, wedding cup 151
Barovier e Toso 251
Bars 246−7
Basilica di Monte Berico 171
Basilica di Sant'Antonio (Padua)
  161, **182**
Basilica San Marco 55, **78−83**
  Ascension and Pentecost Domes
    80−81
  atrium mosaics 80, **82**
  baptistry and chapels 83
  central doorway carvings 78

Basilica San Marco (cont.)
  façade mosaics 40–41, 78, **82**
  horses of St Mark 42, 78
  Mascoli Chapel 83
  Museo Marciano 82–3
  Pala d'Oro 41, 81, **83**
  Street-by-Street map 75
  Tetrarchs 79
  treasury 81, **83**
  Visitors' Checklist 79
Basilica dei Santi Maria e Donato
  (Murano) 151
Basilica (Vicenza)
  Street-by-Street map 168
Bassano del Grappa **166**, 239
  map 164
Bassano, Jacopo,
  Crucifixion 174
  Supper at Emmaus 167
Bathing, Lido 156
Beccerie Hotel (Treviso) 232
Befania 32
Belle Parti El Toulà (Padua) 243
Bellini cocktail 92, 239
Bellini family 27, 132
Bellini, Gentile, *The Procession in
  St Mark's Square* 133
Bellini, Giovanni 26
  Accademia 132
  Baptism of Christ 171
  Madonna with Child 140
  Madonna and Child with Saints
    27, 112, 115
  Pietà 74
  Portrait of a Young Senator 179
  San Giobbe 132
  St Jerome with Saints 143
Belloni family 61
Belluno 218
  map 212
Belvedere Hotel (Bassano) 231
Bembo, Cardinal Pietro 167
Benavides, Marco, mausoleum 179
Benetton 18, 51
Benvenuti, Augusto, Garibaldi
  monument 120
Berico, Monte 171
Bianco di Custoza 239
Bicycles, hiring (Lido) 156
Biennale International Exhibition of
  Modern Art 34, 49, **256**
  foundation 48
  International Film festival 157
  pavilions 49, 121
Bird in Space (Brancusi) 134
Birds, Po delta 185
Bisesti Hotel (Garda) 233
Boatyard, San Trovaso 28, 129
Bocca di leone ("lion's mouth"
  denunciation box) 42, 88, 129
Boccadoro (Padua) 243
Bolca 191
  map 188
Bon, Bartolomeo
  Campanile, Piazza San Marco 76
  Ca' d'Oro 144
  Santa Maria Gloriosa dei Frari
    102

Bon (cont.)
  Santi Giovanni e Paolo 116
  Santa Maria della Carità 130
  Santo Stefano 93
  Scuola Grande di San Rocco 106
Bonaparte, Napoleon *see* Napoleon
Bordone, Paris, *The Adoration of
  the Shepherds* 174
Bosco Chiesanuova 191
  map 188
Brancusi, Constantin, *Bird in Space*
  134
Brandy, Italian 239
Breakfast, hotels 223
Breganze 239
Brenta Canal, guided tour 182–3
Bridge of Sighs 89, 110, **113**
  Doge's Palace 85
British Airways 270
Browning, Pen 66, 126
Browning, Robert 66, 126
  Asolanda 167
Brustolon, Andrea
  Ca' Rezzonico 126
  carvings 218
Bucintoro 47
  plunder by Napoleon 119
  replica 118
Budget accommodation 224–5
Buildings, foundations 20–21
Buora, Giovanni, Ospedale Civile
  114
Burano 149, **150**
  shops 248
Buses, Veneto 278, 279
Byron, Lord 67
  Lido 156
  San Lazzaro degli Armeni 155
Byzantine architecture, *palazzi* 22
Byzantium
  conquest of 42
  trade links 40
  Venetian rule 37

C

Ca' 23 (*see also* Palazzi)
Ca' Corner della Regina 62
Ca' Corner-Martinengo-Ravà 64
Ca' (Palazzo) Dario 69, 135
Ca' (Palazzo) Foscari 22, 66
  Street-by-Street map 125
Ca' Foscarini 62
Ca' Genovese 70
Ca' Grande 69
Ca' Marcello 185
Ca' Mocenigo (San Stae) 105
Ca' da Mosto 63
Ca' d'Oro 55, **144**
  Grand Canal 63
Ca' Pesaro 62, **105**
  Baroque architecture 23
Ca' Rezzonico 54, **126**
  Browning home 66
  Museum of 18thC Venice 66, 126
  Street-by-Street map 125
Cable cars 209
Cabot, John 120

Cabot, Sebastian 120
Cafés 246–7
Caffè al Cavallo 247
Caffè Florian 247
  Street-by-Street map 74
Caffè Paradiso 121
Caffè Pasqualigo 247
Caffè Pedrocchi (Padua) 46, **178**,
  246
  Street-by-Street map 177
  tradition 19
Caffè Quadri 247
  Street-by-Street map 74
  Carnival fresco 30
Campanile (Piazza San Marco) 75,
  76
  rebuilding 21, 49
Campiello Barbaro 135
Campo d'Abbazia
  Street-by-Street map 139
Campo Francesco Morosini *see*
  Campo Santo Stefano
Campo Marzio Hotel (Vicenza)
  232
Campo dei Mori 138, **140**
Campo San Barnaba 126
Campo San Bartolomeo 94
Campo San Fantin 90
Campo Santa Margherita 127
  Street-by-Street map 125
Campo Santa Maria Formosa 114
Campo Santa Maria Mater Domini
  20–21
Campo San Polo 101
Campo San Simeone Grande 59
Campo Santo Stefano 93
Campsites and mountain refuges
  224–5
Canale di Cannaregio 137
Canaletto (Antonio Canale) 63
  Accademia 133
  drawings 113
  *St Mark's Basin on Ascension
    Day* 46
  *Upper Reaches of the Grand
    Canal* 29
  View of the Rio dei Mendicanti
    126
Canals
  Cannaregio 137
  dredging 21
  Grand Canal 57–71
  Rio San Barnaba 124
  Torcello 153
  See also Vaporetti
Cangrande I 42, 192
  monuments 193, 198, 207
Cangrande II 193, 194
Cannaregio area 136–45
  Street-by-Street map 138–9
Canon d'Oro Hotel (Conegliano)
  232
Canova, Antonio
  birthplace 167
  Museo Correr 77
  Palazzo Farsetti 64
  studio 69
  tomb 103

Cansignorio, tomb 198–9
Cantina del Vino già Schiavi 247
Canto della Stella festival
　(Desenzano) 32
Caorle 175
　map 164
　Regata di Santi Giovanni e Paolo
　34
Capella Scrovegni 180–81
Capo Reamol Hotel (Limone sul
　Garda) 232–3
Cappella del Rosario, Santi
　Giovanni e Paolo 116
Cappella di San Domenico, Santi
　Giovanni e Paolo 117
　Bianca Cappello 110
Capriccio (Lake Garda) 244
Caranto 20–21
Carnevale *see* Carnival
Carnival 32, 255
　costume 30
　masks 30–31, 253
　tradition 30
Carpaccio, Vittore
　Ca' d'Oro 144
　The Courtesans 77
　Cycle of St Ursula 54, 130, 133
　Healing of the Madman 100,
　133
　*Portrait of a Young Man in a Red
　Hat* 77
　St Paul 185
　Scuola di San Giorgio degli
　Schiavoni 118
Carpione, Giulio, Palazzo Chiericati
　(Vicenza) 170
Cars
　breakdowns 279
　documents required 271
　hiring 271, 278
　towing away 279
　see also Driving; Parking
Casa Adoldo 59
Casa Favretto 62
Casa di Giulietta (Verona) 199
　Street-by-Street map 197
Casanova 46, 87, 89
Casa Pigafetta (Vicenza) 170
　Street-by-Street map 168
Casa di Romeo (Verona) 199
Casa San Raffaele Hotel (Vicenza)
　232
Casetta Dandolo 65
Casetta delle Rose 69
Casinos 46, 256
　Lido 156
　Municipal 61
　see also Ridotto
Castagno, Andrea del, San Zaccaria
　112
Castelfranco 167
　map 164
Castello area 108–21
　Street-by-Street map 110–11
　walk 120–21
Castles
　Ca' Marcello 185
　Castel San Pietro (Verona) 202

Castles (cont.)
　Castello di Andraz 215
　Castello di Giulietta (Montecchio
　Maggiore) 190
　Castello Inferiore (Maròstica) 166
　Castello Porto-Colleoni (Thiene)
　166
　Castello di Romeo (Montecchio
　Maggiore) 190
　Castello Superiore (Maròstica) 166
　Castelvecchio (Conegliano) 175
　Castelvecchio (Verona) 193
　Fortezza del Quadrilatero 205
　Riva del Garda 205
　Rocca Scaligeri (Soave) 160, 190,
　206
Catullus 38, 206
Cavalletto e Doge Orseolo Hotel
　229
Cavallino, Festa della Sparesca 33
Cemetery, San Michele 151
Chess, *Partita a Scacchi* (Maròstica)
　35, 166
Children 256
　hotels 223
　restaurants 235
Chioggia 161, **185**
　map 164
Chioggia, Battle of 42, 43
Chioggia, San Domenico 185
Christ Bearing the Cross (A.
　Vivarini) 117
Churches in the Veneto
　Abbazia di Praglia 184
　Basilica di Monte Berico 171
　Basilica di Sant'Antonio (Padua)
　182
　Duomo (Belluno) 218
　Duomo (Caorle) 175
　Duomo (Castelfranco) 167
　Duomo (Citadella) 167
　Duomo (Conegliano) 175
　Duomo (Montagnana) 184
　Duomo (Padua) 176, **182**
　Duomo (Treviso) 174
　Duomo (Verona) 199
　Duomo (Vicenza)
　Street-by-Street map 168
　Eremitani (Padua) 179
　La Rotonda (Rovigo) 185
　Salò cathedral 208
　Sant'Anastasia (Verona) 197, **199**
　Santa Corona (Vicenza) 170–71
　San Domenico (Chioggia) 185
　San Fermo Maggiore (Verona) 194
　San Giorgio in Braida (Verona)
　203
　San Giovanni in Fonte (Verona)
　199
　San Lorenzo (Vicenza) 171
　Santa Maria (Grezzana) 190
　Santa Maria Antica (Verona) 198
　Street-by-Street map 197
　Santa Maria in Organo (Verona)
　203
　San Nicolò (Treviso) 174
　San Pietro (Belluno) 218
　San Pietro di Foletto (Follina) 167

Churches in the Veneto (cont.)
　San Pietro Martire (Sirmione) 207
　San Rocca (Feltre) 219
　Santo Stefano (Belluno) 218
　Santo Stefano (Verona) 202
　San Zeno Maggiore (Verona)
　200–1
　Scrovegni Chapel (Padua)
　180–81
Churches in Venice
　Basilica San Marco 78–83
　Basilica dei Santi Maria e Donato
　(Murano) 151
　cathedral (Torcello) 41, **152–3**
　Frari 102–3
　Gesuati 123, **129**
　Gesuiti (Santa Maria Assunta) 142
　Madonna dell'Orto 140
　opening hours 260
　La Pietà (Santa Maria della
　Visitazione) 111, **112**
　Il Redentore 129, **154**
　religious services 263
　La Salute 45, 71, **135**
　Sant'Anna 121
　Sant'Apollonia 113
　San Cassiano **101,** map 97
　San Fantin 90
　Santa Fosca (Torcello) 152–3
　San Francesco del Deserto 150
　San Francesco della Vigna 115
　St George's 123
　San Giacomo dell'Orio 104
　San Giacomo di Rialto 99, **100**
　San Giobbe 145
　San Giorgio dei Greci 111, **112**
　San Giorgio Maggiore 95
　San Giovanni in Bragora 118
　San Giovanni Crisostomo 143
　San Giovanni Evangelista 104
　Santi Giovanni e Paolo (San
　Zanipolo) 116–17
　San Giuseppe 121
　San Lazzaro degli Armeni 155
　San Lazzaro dei Mendicanti 114
　San Lorenzo 115
　San Marco 78–83
　Santa Maria Assunta 142
　Santa Maria dei Carmini
　(Carmelo) 124, 127
　Santa Maria dei Derelitti 115
　Santa Maria Formosa 114
　Santa Maria Gloriosa dei Frari
　102–3
　Santa Maria del Giglio 92
　Santa Maria della Grazia 155
　Santa Maria dei Miracoli 142
　Santa Maria di Nazareth 58, 130,
　145
　Santa Maria della Salute 45, 71,
　135
　Santa Maria della Visitazione 129
　See also La Pietà
　Santa Maria Zobenigo (del
　Giglio) 92
　San Marziale 141
　San Michele in Isola 151
　San Moisè 92

Churches in Venice (cont.)
San Nicolò (Lido) 157
San Nicolò dei Mendicoli 123, **128**
San Nicolò da Tolentino 104–1
San Pantalon 104
map 97
San Pietro di Castello 120
San Polo 101
San Rocco 104
San Salvatore 94
San Samuele 67
San Sebastiano 123, **128**
San Simeone Piccolo 59
San Simeone Profeta (Grande) 59
San Stae 105, map 97
Santo Stefano 93
San Trovaso 129
San Zaccaria 111, **112**
San Zanipolo 116–17
San Zulian 95
Scalzi (Santa Maria di Nazareth) 58, 130, **145**
visiting 261
Le Zitelle 154
Ciccarelli (Verona) 245
Cinemas 257
Lido 157
Cini Collection 134
Cini, Count Vittorio 95, 134
Cinzia e Valerio (Vicenza) 244
Cipriani, Giuseppe 92
Cipriani Hotel 154, **231**
restaurant 242
See also Locanda Cipriani, Villa Cipriani
CIT 273
Cittadella 167
map 164
Climbing and hiking, Dolomites 216
Club Alpino Italiano 214, 224–5
Coducci, Mauro
Palazzo Corner Spinelli 67
Palazzo Vendramin Calergi 61
Santa Maria Formosa 114
San Michele in Isola 151
San Pietro di Castello 120
San Zaccaria 111, 112
Scuola di San Giovanni Evangelista 104
Torre dell'Orologio 76
Coffee 239
Coins, Bottacin Museum (Padua) 179
Colleoni, Bartolomeo, statue 114
Colli Euganei *see* Euganean Hills
Colomba d'Oro (Verona) 233
Colonna di San Marco
Piazza San Marco 75, 77
Verona Street-by-Street map 196
Color Casa 251
Columbine 31
Columns of St Mark and St Theodore (Piazza San Marco) 46, 75, **77**
The Communion of St Lucy (Tiepolo) 143

Comune di Venezia Assessorato alla Gioventù 263
Conegliano 175
map 164
wine school 175, 239
Conegliano, Cima da
Adoration of the Shepherds 127
Baptism of Christ 118
St John the Baptist and Other Saints 140
Virgin and Child with Saints 175
Conservatory of Music 93
Constantinople, siege 42
See also Byzantium
Contarini family 68, 92
Contarini, Marino 144
Continental Hotel 231
Contino, Bernardino, Caterina Cornaro monument 94
Contrà Porti (Vicenza) 170
Street-by-Street map 168
Conversion table 263
Cooper, James Fenimore 64
Corderia (rope factory), Arsenale 119
Cornaro, Caterina, Queen of Cyprus 43, 143
Asolo 167
birthplace 62
monument 94
Cornaro (Corner) family 69
Corner, Marco, tomb 143
Corona Hotel (Cortina) 233
Coronation of the Virgin (Giambono) 132
Coronation of the Virgin (Guariento) 89
Coronation of the Virgin (Veneziano) 26, 131, 132
Correr, Abbot Teodoro 77
Correr Museum *see* Museo Correr
Corso Cavour (Verona) 194
Corte Capitaniato (Padua)
Street-by-Street map 176
Corte, Giusto Le, Santa Maria della Salute 135
Corte Sconta 241
Cortina d'Ampezzo 214
map 212
winter sports 211
Coryate, Thomas 203
Costanza, Tuzio 167
Council of Ten 129
Doge's Palace 88–9
ghetto decree 145
powers 42
San Servolo 154
The Courtesans (Carpaccio) 77
Credit cards 266
missing 265
Crodino 239
Crucifixion (Bassano) 174
Crucifixion (Memling) 170
Crucifixion (Tintoretto) 106
Crucifixion (Zevio) 183
Crusades 40, 42
Currency 266–7

Curtis family 69
Cycling 257

D

Da Arturo 240
Da Fiore 240
Da Romano 242
Da Silvio 240
Dal Cavalier (Auronzo di Cadore) 245
Dall'Amelia (Mestre) 242
Dalmatia, traders 113
Dandolo, Andrea (doge) 65, 83
Dandolo, Enrico (doge) 42, 65
Dandolo family 65
Danieli Hotel 110, **112–13**, 230
Terrace restaurant 241
Dante, *Paradiso* 192
Dante statue (Verona) 198
Street-by-Street map 196
Death in Venice 50, 156, 231
Deposito del Megio 60
Desenzano
Canto della Stella festival 32
maps 188–204
Diaghilev, Sergei 151
Dialectic (Veronese) 88
Diana Hotel (Valdobbiadene) 232
Direzione Compartimentale 58
Disabled travellers 261
hotels 224
restaurants 235
theatres 255
Do Forni 240
Do Mori 241, 247
Do Pozzi Hotel 229
Do Spade 247
Dogana di Mare 71, **135**
Doges
Dandolo, Andrea 65, 83
Dandolo, Enrico 42, 65
Donà, Leonardo 44, 76
election 43
Falier, Marin 43, 68, 89
Foscari, Francesco 59, 66, 102
Foscarini, Marco 63
Gritti, Andrea 59
Loredan, Francesco 68
Loredan, Leonardo 44
Manin, Ludovico 58, 65
Marcello, Nicolò, tomb 116
Mocenigo, Alvise 61
Mocenigo, Giovanni 37
Mocenigo, Pietro, tomb 116
Orseolo, Pietro 33, 74; relics 112
Tradonico, Pietro 113
Vendramin, Andrea, tomb 117
Venier, Sebastiano, statue 117
Vitale, Michiel II 113
Ziani, Sebastiano 41
Doge's Palace 55, 75, **84–9**
Bridge of Sighs 85
collegiate rooms 87, 88
Council chambers 87, 88
floorplan 86–7
Giants' Staircase 84
Gothic architecture 22
Porta della Carta 84

Doge's Palace (cont.)
 prisons 87, 89
 Sala del Consiglio dei Dieci 87, 88–9
 Sala del Maggior Consiglio 85, 87, **89**
 Scala d'Oro 86, **88**
 Sala dello Scudo 87, 88
 Secret Itinerary tour 87, 113
 Street-by-Street map 75
 Torture Chamber 85
 Visitors' Checklist 85
 wellheads 20, 86
Dolada (Belluno) 245
Dolomieu, Dr Deodat 46, 216
Dolomite Road (Strada delle Dolomiti) 214–15
Dolomites region 161, **211–19**
 fauna 217
 flora 217
 geology 216
 landscape 217
 map 212
 winter sports 32, 216
Donà, Leonardo (doge) 44, 76
Donatello
 Basilica di Sant'Antonio (Padua) 182
 Gattamelata statue 183
Donatello Hotel (Padua) 232
Don Giovanni (Losey) 171
La Donna Partigiana statue 120, 121
Dorsoduro area 122–35
 Street-by-Street map 124–5
Double Portrait (Tullio Lombardo) 144
Drinking Satyr (Il Riccio) 179
Driving
 Dolomites 214
 tips 214
 Veneto 278
 see also Cars; Parking
Drogheria Mascari 251
Due Torri Hotel Baglioni (Verona) 233
Duilio (Portogruaro) 243
Dunant, Henri 205
Duomo (Padua) 182
 Street-by-Street map 176
Duomo (Verona) 199
Duomo (Vicenza)
 Street-by-Street map 168
Duty-free allowances 262

E

Economy, Veneto 18
Educational courses 262
El Cantinon (Verona) 245
El Gato (Chioggia) 242
El Toulà (Cortina) 245
Electrical adaptors 263
Embassies and consulates 263
Emergencies, telephone numbers 264
Emile Massaro 251
Emilio Ceccato 251
Emo, Angelo 58
Emporio Armani 251

ENIT 225
ENIT UK 261
Enoteca Boldrin 247
Entertainment 254–7
 booking tickets 254
 ticket prices 257
Ernst, Max 134
Erberia (market) 99, 100
Esplanade (Lake Garda) 244
Este 184–5
 map 164
Etiquette 261
Euganean Hills 184
 map 164
Eurocheques 266
Europa e Regina Hotel 71, 229
European Centre for Training Craftsmen in the Conservation of the Architectural Heritage 154–5, 263
Evelyn, John 95, 203
Excelsior Palace Hotel 48, 157, **231**
Exhibitions, art 256

F

Falier, Marin (doge) 43, 68, 89
Falier Hotel 229
Fallopio, Gabriele 178
Falzarego 215
Favretto, Giacomo 62
Feast at the House of Simon (Strozzi) 133
Feast in the House of Levi (Veronese) 132–3
Feast of the Redeemer, Giudecca 34, 154
Feltre 219
 map 212
 Palio di Feltre 34
La Fenice 90, **93**, 257
Ferrari, Ettore, Vittorio Emanuele statue 111
Ferries, Lake Garda 205
Festa dell'Assunta (Treviso) 34
Festa Medioevale del Vino Soave Bianco Soave 33
Festa di Mosto (Sant'Erasmo) 35
Festa del Redentore 34, 154
Festa della Salute 35
Festa di San Marco 33
Festa di Santi Pietro e Paolo 34
Festa della Sparasea 33, 34
Fiaschetteria Toscana 241
Film festival 157, 255
Films, Venice setting 50
Fiorella 251
Flagellation (Signorelli) 144
Floods, Venice 50, 51, 74
 San Nicolò dei Mendicoli 128
Flora Hotel 227, 229
Fondaco dei Tedeschi 65
Fondaco dei Turchi (Natural History Museum) 60, **105**
 Byzantine architecture 22
Fondamenta Gasparo Contarini
 Street-by-Street map 139
Fondamenta Gherardini
 Street-by-Street map 124

Fondamenta della Misericordia
 Street-by-Street map 139
Fondamenta della Sensa 138, **141**
Fondamente Nuove 141
Fondazione Europea pro Venetia Viva 155
Fondazione Querini Stampalia 114
Food and drink
 amaretti 237
 anguille im umido 237
 antipasto di frutti di mare 236
 baccalà mantecata 236
 brodo di pesce 236
 carpaccio 236
 cheeses 237
 coffee 239
 faraona con la peverada 237
 fegato alla Veneziana 237
 fiori di zucchini 236
 gelati 237
 insalata mista 237
 polenta 237
 radicchio alla griglia 237
 risi e bisi 236, 240
 risotto alle seppie 236
 sardine in saor 237
 soft drinks 239
 spaghetti alle vongole 237
 tiramisù 237
 what to drink 238–9
 what to eat 236–7
 wine 238–9
 zuppa di cozze 236
 see also Restaurants
Foresteria Valdese 224
Forno di Zoldo 218
Fortuny y Madrazo, Mariano 94
Foscari family 62
Foscari, Francesco (doge) 59
 monument 102
Foscarini, Marco (doge) 63
Fossils, Museo Civico di Scienze Naturali (Verona) 203
The Four Seasons (Vivaldi) 47
Franchetti, Baron Giorgio 63, 144
Frari *see* Santa Maria Gloriosa dei Frari
Frederick, Archduke of Austria 69
Frederick I, Holy Roman Emperor 41
Frezzeria 91, 248
Friso, Alvise dal, San Nicolò dei Mendicoli 128
Fumiani, Gian Antonio, San Pantalon 104

G

Galileo 178
 telescope 44, 76
Gallerie dell'Accademia *see* Accademia gallery
Galleys, Venetian 44–5, 119
Gambello, Antonio
 Arsenale gateway 119
 San Zaccaria 112
Gambling at the Ridotto (Guardi) 30

Gambrinus Parco (Oderzo) 243
Garda 205
  map 188
Garda, Lake 187, **204–9**
  ferry trips 205
  maps 160, 188, 204
  Sardellata al Pal del Vo festival 34
  La Vecia festival 33
Gardaland theme park 205, 256
La Gardesana route 205
Gardini, Raul 135
Gardone Riviera 208
  map 188
Gattamelata statue (Padua) 183
Geneva Convention 205
German Institute 67
Germans, Veneto 19
Gesuati 129
Gesuiti (Santa Maria Assunta) 142
Ghetto 54, **145**
Giambono, Michele
  Coronation of the Virgin 132
  St Chrysogonus on Horseback 129
  St Michael 123
Giardinetti Reali
  Street-by-Street map 74
Giardini Pubblici 120–21
Giardino Giusti (Verona) 187, **203**
Giazza 160, **191**
  maps 188
Giordano, Luca 113
Giorgione
  birthplace 167
  *The Madonna and Child with
    Saints* 167
  The Tempest 131, 132, 167
Giorgione Hotel 227, 231
Giotto, Scrovegni Chapel 180–81
Giovanelli family 60
Giudecca 148, **154**
Giulietta e Romeo Hotel (Verona)
  233
*Giulietta e Romeo see Romeo and
  Juliet*
Glass blowing 51, 151
Glass 252
  factories (Murano) 150–51
Glory of St Dominic (Piazzetta) 117
The Glory of Saint Martial (Ricci)
  141
Gobbo of the Rialto, statue 99, 100
Golden Book 42, 150
Goldoni, Carlo 101
  statue 94
Golf 257
Gondolas
  crafting techniques 28–9
  decoration 28
  Grand Canal 58
  prices 276
  San Trovaso workshops 129
  shape 28
  sumptuary laws 47
Gondoliers
  attire 28
  Regata Storica 35, 50
Gothic architecture, *palazzi* 22
Gran Caffè Garibaldi (Vicenza) 170

Gran Viale Santa Maria Elisabetta
  (Lido) 156
Grand Canal 56–71
Grand Council 42, 43
  Doge's Palace 85–9
Grand Hotel (Gardone Riviera) 208
Grande Italia Hotel (Chioggia) 231
Grande Italia Hotel (Padua) 232
Grapes, wine-making 208–9, 238
Grezzana 190
  map 188
Grimani, Domenico 77
Grimani, Girolamo 64
Gritti, Andrea (doge) 59
Gritti Palace Hotel 70, 226, **229**
  restaurant 240
Grotte di Catullo (Sirmione) 207
Gruppo Italia 224–5
Guarana, Jacopo, Ospedaletto 115
Guardi, Antonio, Angelo Raffaele
  128
Guardi, Francesco
  Ca' d'Oro 144
  Gambling at the Ridotto 30, 126
  Nuns' Parlour 126
Guariento 26
  Angels in Armour 179
  The Coronation of the Virgin 89
Guggenheim, Peggy 48, 134
  Palazzo Venier dei Leoni 69
Guided tours 260

H

Harry's Bar **92**, 240, 247
  Grand Canal 71
Harry's Dolci 242, 247
Healing of the Madman
  (Carpaccio) 100, 133
Health 264
Henry III, King of France 89, 119,
  125
History 36–51
Holidays, public 35
The Holy Family with Saints
  (Veronese) 115
Holy Family (Veronese) 126
*The Holy House Transported from
  Nazareth to Loreto* (Tiepolo) 130,
  145
Honour, Hugh 142
Horse races, Palio dei Dieci
  Comuni 35
Horses of St Mark 46
  See also Basilica San Marco
Hospitals 265
Hostaria Da Franz 121, 241
Hostaria da Zorzi 247
Hôtel des Bains (Lido) 156, 231
Hotel du Lac (Gargnano) 232
Hotels
  Asolo 231
  Bassano del Grappa 231
  Belluno 233
  booking and paying 224
  budget accommodation 225
  Cannaregio 230–31
  Castello 230
  children 223

Hotels (cont)
  Chioggia 231
  chooser chart 228
  classification 223
  Conegliano 232
  Cortina 233
  disabled travellers 224
  Dorsoduro 230
  grades 223
  in historic buildings 224
  Lagoon Islands 231
  Lake Garda 232–3
  map, best hotels (Venice)
    226–7
  Padua 232
  parking 278–9
  prices 222–3, 225
  San Marco 229
  San Polo and Santa Croce
    229–30
  San Vito di Cadore 233
  Treviso 232
  Valdobbiadene 232
  Venice 222–31
  Verona 233
  Vicenza 232
  what to expect 223
  where to look 222
  words and phrases 312
  see also individual names

I

Ice cream parlours 246–7
Il Caffè 247
Il Desco (Verona) 245
Il Doge 247
Il Gelatone 247
Il Torcolo Hotel (Verona) 233
Immigration and customs 262
Industry, Veneto 18
International Chapters 224
International Exhibition of Modern
  Art *see* Biennale
International Film festival 51, **157**,
  255
International Red Cross,
  establishment 205
International University 154–5
Istituto Ciliota 224
Istituto Linguistico Bertrand Russell
  263
Istituto Zambler 263
Italian State Tourist Office 224

J

James, Henry 69
  Crucifixion (Tintoretto) 106
  Portrait of a Lady 111
  Riva degli Schiavoni 110
  Santa Maria della Salute 135
Jesurum 251
Jubanico family 92
Julius II, Pope 44

K

Kriss Internazionale Hotel
  (Bardolino) 233
Kublai Khan 42, 143

L

La Bottega dell'Arte 251
La Boutique del Gelato 247
La Braseria (Padua) 243
La Caravella 240
La Fenice et des Artistes Hotel 229
La Montanella (Arquà Petrarca) 242
La Pausa (Pieve di Cadore) 245
La Residenza Hotel 227, 230
La Tortuga (Lake Garda) 244
Labia family 143
Laboratorio Artigiano Maschere 251
Lace 150, 252
Ladinia Hotel (San Vito di Cadore) 233
Lagoon, Venetian
 early history 39
 hotels 228, 231
 islands 146–57
 maps 147, 148–9
 restaurants 241–2
Lake Garda see Garda, Lake
The Last Judgment (Tintoretto) 26, 140
Last Supper (Tintoretto) 101
Laura Biagiotti 251
Law, John 92
Layard, Sir Austen Henry 67
Lazise 208
Lazzaretto Vecchio 149, **157**
League of Cambrai 37, 44
 war with Venice 219
Le Bistrot de Venise 240
Legatoria Piazzesi 251
Leon Bianco Hotel 64
Leon Bianco Hotel (Padua) 232
Leoncino (Vicenza) 244
Leopardi, Alessandro, Colleoni statue 114
Lepanto, Battle of 44
Les Deux Lions del Hotel Londra Palace 241
Lessini, Monti 191; map 160
Liberi, Pietro 67
Libraries
 Biblioteca Marciana 77
 Fondazione Querini Stampalia 114
 Libreria Sansoviniana 75, 77
Libreria Serenissima 251
Libreria della Toletta 251
Libri, Girolamo dai, *Virgin Enthroned between St Zeno and St Lawrence* 203
Lido 148, **156–7**
 beaches 48
 Venice Film festival 35, 157
Lido Palace Hotel (Lake Garda) 233
Life of St Anthony (Titian) 183
Life of St Dominic (Tiepolo) 129
Linea d'Ombra 241
Lion of St Mark 17, 37, 74
 St Mark's column 77
 Torre dell'Orologio 76
Lippi, Filippo, *Madonna col Bambino* 134
Livio de Marchi 251
Lo Spuntino 247

Locanda Cipriani 242
Locanda Montin 241
Locanda San Lorenzo (Belluno) 245
Locanda San Vigilio (Lake Garda) 233
 Regina Restaurant 244
Locanda Sturion Hotel 229
Loggia del Capitaniato (Vicenza) 170
 Street-by-Street map 168
Loggia della Gran Guardia (Padua) 176
Lombardo, Pietro, Bishop Zanetti monument 174
Lombardo, Pietro
 Ospedale Civile 114
 San Giobbe 145
 San Giovanni Evangelista 104
 Santa Maria Gloriosa dei Frari 102
 Santa Maria dei Miracoli 142
Lombardo, Tullio
 Double Portrait 144
 Duomo (Belluno) 218
 fountain (Feltre) 219, 219
 Santa Maria dei Miracoli 142
 San Salvatore 94
Londra Palace Hotel 227, 230
 restaurant 241
Longhena, Baldassare
 Ca' Pesaro 62, 105
 Ca' Rezzonico 126
 Palazzo Belloni Battagia 61
 Santi Giovanni e Paolo 117
 Santa Maria dei Derelitti 115
 Santa Maria della Salute 71, 135
 Scalzi 145
 Scuola di San Nicolò dei Greci 112
 Tomb of Andrea Vendramin 117
Longhi, Pietro
 Accademia 133
 The Apothecary's Shop 130
 Ca' Rezzonico 126
Loredan, Francesco (doge) 68
Loredan, Leonardo (doge) 44
Losey, Joseph, *Don Giovanni* film 171
Lost Property offices 265
Lotto, Lorenzo
 page boys fresco 174
 Portrait of a Dominican 174
 Portrait of a Gentleman 132
 St Nicholas of Bari with saints 127
Luzzo, Lorenzo 219

M

Madonna di Ca' Pesaro (Titian) 27, 102
Madonna with Child (Giovanni Bellini) 140
Madonna and Child with Saints (B. Vivarini) 118
Madonna and Child with Saints (Giorgione) 167
Madonna and Child with Saints (Giovanni Bellini) 27, 112, 115
Madonna and Child (Sansovino) 144

Madonna of Nicopeia 83
Madonna dell'Orto 138, **140**
 restoration 51
Madonna with Saints (Montagna) 170
Majolica ware, Bassano del Grappa 166, 252
Malcésine 209
 maps 188, 204
Manin, Daniele 46, 47
 statue 91
Manin, Ludovico (doge) 58, 65
Mann, Thomas, *Death in Venice* 156, 231
Mantegna, Andrea
 Ovetari Chapel (Padua) 179
 Renaissance style 26
 St Sebastian 144
 St George 132
 Virgin and Child with saints 200
Mantua, Duke of 62
Maps
 Belluno 218
 best hotels (Venice) 226–7
 Brenta Canal 182–3
 Cannaregio 137
 Castello 109
 Dolomites 212–13
 Dolomite Road 214–15
 Dordosuro 123
 Eastern Castello (walk) 120–21
 Grand Canal 57
 Lagoon Islands 147, 148–9
 Lake Garda 204
 Medieval Venice 37
 Roads 12–13
 Roman Verona 38–9
 San Marco 73
 San Polo and Santa Croce 97
 Treviso 174
 Valpolicella wine tour 208–9
 Veneto 160–61; road map 12–13
 Veneto Plain 164–5
 Venice 14–15, 52–3, 54–5
 Venice Street Finder 282–9
 Verona 192–3
 Verona and Lake Garda 188–9
 Western Europe 10–11
 See also Street-by-Street maps
Marcello, Benedetto 61
Marcello, Nicolò (doge) 116
Marconi Hotel 230
Marina di Venezia agency 224
Marini, Marino, *Angelo della Città* 134
Markets 250
 cherry (Verona) 33
 Erberia 100; Street-by-Street map 99
 fish (Chioggia) 185
 Padua 176
 Pescheria 62, 100; Street-by-Street map 99
 Rialto, map 97
Marmolada, Mt 212
Maròstica 166
 map 164
 Partita a Scacchi 35, 166

Maròstica, Castello Inferiore 166
Marriage with the Sea festival 33
Martyrdom of St George (Veronese) 203
Martyrdom of St Lawrence (Titian) 142
Masks 30–1, 253
   Plague Doctor 30
Massari, Giorgio
   Ca' Rezzonico 126
   La Pietà 112
   San Marcuola 61
Mastelli brothers 140
Mastino II, tomb 198-9
Maximilian I, Holy Roman Emperor 44, 219
Mazzorbo 150
Medical insurance 264–5
Medical treatment 265
Medici, Cosimo de' 101
Medici, Lorenzo de' 101
Memling, Hans, *Crucifixion* 170
Menabuoi, Giusto de', Baptistry (Padua) 176, 182
Menardi Hotel (Cortina) 233
Mendigola island 123
Menus, fixed-price 234
Mercerie 95
   shops 248
Mestre 18, **175**
   map 164
The Miracle of the Slave (Tintoretto) 133
Miretto, Nicola, Palazzo della Ragione (Padua) 178
Missoni 251
Misurina 215
   map 212
Misurina, Lake 215, 216
Mocenigo, Giovanni (doge) 37
Mocenigo, Pietro (doge), tomb 116
Modena, Tomaso da, portraits of saints 174
Monaco and Grand Canal Hotel 229
Mondonovo 251
Money 266–7
Monsélice 185
   map 164
Montagna, Bartolomeo
   Madonna with Saints 170
   Pala di San Bartolo Madonna 170
   Pietà 171
Montagna, Bartolomeo, Museo Civico (Belluno) 218
Montagna Spaccata 190
Montagnana 184
   map 164
   Palio dei Dieci Comuni 35
   Villa Pisani 25
Monte, Monti *see under* individual names
Monte Berico, basilica (Vicenza) 171
Montecchio Maggiore 190
   Castello di Giulietta 190
   Castello di Romeo 190
   map 188
Montegrotto Terme 184

Monteverdi 45
   Proserpine Rapita 112–13
Montin Hotel 230
   restaurant 241
Mooring posts 29
Morosini, Admiral Francesco 104, 119
Morosini family 62, 63
Mosquitoes 265
Mosto, Alvise da 63
Mulino Stucky (Giudecca) 154
Murano 148, **150**
   shops 248
Museums and galleries in the Veneto
   Bottacin Museum (Padua) 179
   Casa di Canova (Asolo) 167
   Casa di Giorgione (Castelfranco) 167
   Casa di Petrarca (Arquà Petrarca) 184
   Casa di Tiziano (Pieve di Cadore) 215
   Castelvecchio (Verona) 193
   Eremitani (Padua) 179
   Garda museum 205
   Medieval and Modern Art Museum (Padua) 179
   Museo Archeologico (Adria) 185
   Museo Archeologico (Verona) 202
   Museo Archeologico Romano e Preromano (Pieve di Cadore) 215
   Museo Civico di Scienze Naturali (Verona) 203
   Museo Civico (Belluno) 218
   Museo Civico (Feltre) 219
   Museo Civico (Treviso) 174
   Museo Civico (Vicenza) 170
   Museo Concordiese (Portogruaro) 175
   Museo della Battaglia (Vittorio Veneto) 219
   Museo di Fossili (Bolca) 191
   Museo Etnografico (Giazza) 191
   Museo Lapidario Maffeiano (Verona) 194
   Museo Naturalistico-Archeologico (Vicenza) 171
   Museo Nazionale Atestino (Este) 184-5
   Natural History Museum (Verona) 203
   Natural History Museum (Vicenza) 171
   Rocca di Riva 209
   Scrovegni Chapel (Padua) 180–81
   Scuola del Santo (Padua) 183
   Solferino war museum 205
   Villa il Vittoriale (Gardone Riviera) 208
Museums and galleries in Venice
   Accademia gallery 123, **130–33**
   Ca' Mocenigo 105
   Ca' d'Oro 144
   Ca' Pesaro 105
   Ca' Rezzonico 126

Museums and galleries (cont.)
   Cini Collection 134
   Fondaco dei Turchi (Natural History Museum) 105
   Fondazione Querini Stampalia 114
   Galleria d'Arte Moderna 105
   Gallerie dell'Accademia123, **130–33**
   Giorgio Franchetti Collection 144
   Glass Museum 150–51
   Jewish Museum 145
   Lace Museum 150
   Libreria Sansoviniana 77
   maps 73, 75
   Museo Archeologico 75, 77
   Museo Correr 74, 77
   Museo Diocesano d'Arte Sacra 110, 113
   Museo Ebraico 145
   Museo dell'Estuario (Torcello) 153
   Museo Fortuny 94
   Museo Goldoni 101
   Museo dei Icone 112
   Museo Marciano (Basilica San Marco) 82–3
   Museo Orientale 105
   Museo del Risorgimento 77
   Mueso del Settecento 126
   Museo di Storia Naturale (Fondaco dei Turchi) 105
   Museo Storico Navale 118
   Museo del Tessuto e del Costume 105
   Museo Vetrario (glass) 150–51
   Museum of 18thC Venice 126
   Natural History Museum (Fondaco dei Turchi) 105
   opening hours 260
   Oriental Museum 105
   Peggy Guggenheim Collection 134
   San Lazzaro degli Armeni 155
   Scuola Grande dei Carmini 127
   Scuola Grande di San Marco 114
   Scuola Grande di San Rocco 106–7
   Scuola dei Merletti (lace) 150
   Scuola di San Giorgio degli Schiavoni 118
   Scuola di San Giovanni Evangelista 104
   Scuola di San Nicolò dei Greci 112
Mushrooms 35
Music and theatre 257
   Verona 256
Musset, Alfred de 113
Mussolini, Benito 208
Muttoni, Antonio, Villa Valmarana 171
Mystical Marriage of St Catherine (Veronese) 133

N
Napoleon 37
   Accademia 130
   Basilica San Marco 83

Napoleon (cont.)
  destruction of docks 119
  Doge's Palace 88
  Ghetto 145
  Giardinetti Reali 71
  Palazzo Balbi 66
  siege of Venice 46
Nature reserves
  Riserva Naturale Gardesana
    Orientale 209
  San Giorgio 185
  see also Parks and gardens
Negroponte, Antonio da, *Virgin
  and Child* 115
Nehmekhet, Prince, sarcophagus
  155
Newspapers 262
Nicolò, Duomo (Verona) 199
Niel, Joseph da 110
Nightclubs 257
Nuns' Parlour (Francesco Guardi)
  126
Nuptial Allegory (Giambattista
  Tiepolo) 126

O

Olimpia cinema 257
Opening hours
  churches 260
  museums and monuments 260
Opera (Verona) 34, **257**
Oratorio dei Crociferi 141
Oratorio di San Giorgio (Padua) 183
Orient Express 272
Orseolo, Pietro (doge) 33, 74
  relics 112
Ospedale Civile 114
Ospedaletto (Santa Maria dei
  Derelitti) 115
Un Ospite di Venezia 260
Ostaria al Bacco 241
Ostello Venezia 224
Osteria al Ponte del Diavolo 242
Osteria da Alberto 247
Osteria dalla Pasini (Treviso) 243
Osteria L'Anfora 243
Osteria Terrà Assassini 247
Ottoman Empire 44

P

Package holidays 270
Padova *see* Padua
Padua 19, 164, **176–83**
  Basilica di Sant'Antonio 161–2
  Caffè Pedrocchi 178
  Duomo and Baptistry 182
  Eremitani Museums 179
  Gattamelata statue 183
  maps 164
  Oratorio di San Giorgio 183
  Orto Botanico 183
  Palazzo del Bo 178
  Palazzo della Ragione 178
  Prato della Valle 183
  police (Questura) 263
  railway station 272–3
  Sagra di Sant'Antonio festival 34
  Scuola del Santo 183

Padua (cont.)
  Scrovegni Chapel 180–81
  Street-by-Street map 176–7
  tourist information 261
  University 177, 178
Paganelli Hotel 230
Pala di San Bartolo Madonna
  (Montagna) 170
Palaces *see Palazzi*
Palazzi 21, 22–3, 57
  Baroque 23
  Byzantine 22
  Gothic 22
  layout 23
  Renaissance 23
  see also Ca'
Palazzo Balbi 66
Palazzo Barbarigo 62, 67, 69
Palazzo Barbaro 69
Palazzo Belloni Battagia 61
Palazzo Bembo 65
Palazzo Bettoni, gardens 205
Palazzo del Bo (University, Padua)
  178
Palazzo Calbo Crotta 59
Palazzo Camerlenghi 65
Palazzo Capello Malipiero 67
Palazzo Capello-Layard 67
Palazzo dei Capitani (Garda) 205
Palazzo del Capitano (Padua)
  Street-by-Street map 176
Palazzo del Casino 257
Palazzo Centani (Zantani) 101
Palazzo Chiericati (Vicenza) 170
Palazzo del Cinema (Lido) 157, 257
Palazzi Communale (Padua) 177
Palazzo Contarini del Bovolo 91, **92**
Palazzo Contarini Fasan 70
Palazzo Contarini del Zaffo 68
Palazzo Corner-Contarini 60
Palazzo Corner Mocenigo 101
Palazzo Corner Spinelli 67
Palazzo (Ca') Dario 69
Palazzo Diedo 58
Palazzo Donà Balbi 60
Palazzo del Duca 68
Palazzo Ducale *see* Doge's Palace
Palazzo Emo 58, 61
Palazzo Erizzo 61
Palazzo Falier 68
Palazzo Farsetti 64
Palazzo Flangini 59
Palazzo Fontana Rezzonico 62
Palazzo (Ca') Foscari 66, 125
  Gothic architecture 22
Palazzo Foscari-Contarini 59
Palazzo Foscarini 63
Palazzo Franchetti Cavalli 69
Palazzo Garzoni 67
Palazzo Giovanelli 60
Palazzo Giustinian (Dorsoduro) 66,
  Street-by-Street map 125
Palazzo Giustinian (San Marco) 71
Palazzo Grassi 67
Palazzo Grimani 64
Palazzo Gritti 59
Palazzo Gritti-Pisani 70

Palazzo Gussoni-Grimani 62
Palazzo Labia 60, **143**
Palazzo Loredan (San Marco) 64
  Byzantine architecture 22
Palazzo Loredan (Dorsoduro) 68
Palazzo Maffei (Verona) 198
  Street-by-Street map 196
Palazzo Mangili Valmarana 63
Palazzo Manin-Dolfin 65
Palazzo Marcello 61, 66
Palazzo Michiel 141
Palazzo Michiel del Brusà 63
Palazzo Michiel dalle Colonne 63
Palazzo Mocenigo (Grand Canal) 67
  See also Ca' Mocenigo
Palazzo del Monte di Pietà (Padua)
  Street-by-Street map 176
Palazzo Moro Lin 67
Palazzo Morosini Brandolin 62
Palazzo Nani
  Street-by-Street map 125
Palazzo Papadopoli 64
Palazzo Patriarcale 120–21
Palazzo Persico 66
Palazzo Pesaro degli Orfei (Museo
  Fortuny) 94
Palazzo Pisani 93
Palazzo Porto-Colleoni (Vicenza)
  170
Palazzo Priuli
  Street-by-Street map 111
Palazzo Querini 60
Palazzo Querini Stampalia 114
Palazzo della Ragione (Padua)
  Street-by-Street map 177, 178
  wooden horse 178
Palazzo della Ragione (Verona) 198
  Street-by-Street map 196
Palazzo della Ragione (Vicenza) 170
Palazzo Sagredo 63
Palazzo Salviati 70
Palazzo degli Scrigni 68
Palazzo Soranzo 101
Palazzo Thiene (Vicenza) 170
Palazzo Tiepolo 71
Palazzo Treves Bonfili 71
Palazzo Trevisan-Cappello 110
Palazzo Tron 61
Palazzo Valmarana (Vicenza)
  Street-by-Street map 168
Palazzo Vendramin-Calergi 61, 257
Palazzo Venier dei Leoni 69, 134
Palazzo Zenobio
  Street-by-Street map 124
Palio dei Dieci Comuni
  (Montagnana) 35
Palio di Feltre 34
Palladian architecture 24–5
Palladio, Andrea 24
  Accademia courtyard 131
  Loggia del Capitaniato (Vicenza)
    170
  palazzi (Vicenza) 160, 170
  Palazzo Chiericati (Vicenza) 170
  Palazzo della Ragione (Vicenza)
    170
  Palazzo Thiene 170
  Ponte degli Alpini 166

Palladio (cont.)
  Quattro Libri (Four Books) 24
  Il Redentore 154
  San Francesco della Vigna 115
  San Giorgio Maggiore 95
  Teatro Olimpico (Vicenza) 172–3
  Veneto villas 163
  Vicenza 168–9
  Villa Barbaro 24–5, 161
  Villa Emo 167
  Villa Foscari (Malcontenta) 183
  Villa Godi Malinverni 166
  Villa Rotonda 165, **171**
  Le Zitelle 154
Palma il Giovane
  The Apotheosis of St Julian 95
  Oratorio dei Crociferi 141
Palma il Vecchio
  Sacra Conversazione 132
  St Barbara and Saints 114
La Pantofola 251
Paolo Olbi 251
Paolo Rossi 251
Paradise (D & J Tintoretto) 85
Paradiso Perduto 257
Parco Faunistico (Lake Garda) 205
Parking
  discs 279
  hotels 278–9
  prices 222
  see also Cars; Driving
Parks and gardens
  Giardinetti Reali 74
  Giardini Pubblici 120, **121**
  Giardino Giusti (Verona) 187,
    203
  Hruska botanical gardens
    (Gardone Riviera) 208
  Orto Botanico (Padua) 183
  Palazzo Bettoni 205
  Parco delle Rimembranze 121
  Rifugio Brigata Alpina Cadore
    botanical garden 218
  see also Nature reserves
Partita a Scacchi (Maròstica) 35, 166
Passeggiata 19
Passo del Pordoi 214
Pasticceria Dal Mas 247
Pasticceria Marchini 251
Pasticceria Vio 247
Pauly 251
Pedemonte 208
Pedrocchi café *see* Caffè Pedrocchi
Peggy Guggenheim Collection 134
Pensione Accademia Villa
  Maravegie 230
Pensione La Calcina 230
Pensione Seguso 230
Pensione Wildner 230
Pesaro, Leonardo 62
Pescheria (fish market) 62, 99, 100
Peschiera (town) 205
  maps 188, 204
Peschiera Hotel (Peschiera) 232
Petrarch (Francesca Petrarca) 110,
  163, **184**
  portrait 176
Petrol stations 279

Piana, Monte 216
Pianta, Francesco, Tintoretto
  caricature 107
Piazza delle Erbe (Padua)
  Street-by-Street map 177
Piazza Erbe (Verona) 192, **198**
  Street-by-Street map 196–7
Piazza delle Erbe (Vicenza) 169
Piazza San Marco 54, 74–5
  Campanile 21, 76
  Carnival 30
  street entertainers 31
  Street-by-Street map 74–5
Piazza dei Signori (Padua)
  Street-by-Street map 176
Piazza dei Signori (Verona)
  Street-by-Street map 196, 198
Piazza dei Signori (Vicenza)
  Street-by-Street map 168, 170
Piazzale Roma, car park 222
Piazzetta dei Leoncini 75
Piazzetta, Giambattista
  Gesuati 129
  Glory of St Dominic 117
Piazzetta, Giovanni, Accademia di
  Belle Arti 130
Picasso, Pablo, *The Poet* 134
La Pietà (Santa Maria della
  Visitazione) 111, **112**
  Vivaldi concerts 47
Pietà (Giovanni Bellini) 74
Pietro, Nicolò, *The Virgin and
  Child* 142
Pieve di Cadore 215
  map 212
Pieve di Livinallongo 215
Pigafetta, Antonio 170
Pink Floyd 50
Piombo, Sebastiano del, *St John
  Chrysostom and Six Saints* 143
Pisanello, Antonio
  Annunciation 194
  St George and the Princess 199
Piscopia, Elena 178
Plague 45
  deliverance from 35, 135
  Plague Doctor mask 30
Po delta 32, 185
Polésine 185
  map 164
Police, municipal 264, 279
Police (Questura) 263
Polignac family 68
Pollock, Jackson 134
Polo, Marco 42, 115, **143**
  Le Livre des merveilles 143
Ponte, Antonio da, Rialto Bridge 100
Ponte dell'Accademia *see*
  Accademia Bridge
Ponte Nuovo (Verona)
  Street-by-Street map 197
Ponte della Paglia 110, **113**
Ponte dei Pugni 126
  Street-by-Street map 125
Ponte di Rialto *see* Rialto Bridge
Ponte Romano, Verona 39, 202
Ponte San Michele (Vicenza)
  Street-by-Street map 168

Ponte dei Scalzi 59
Ponte Storto
  Street-by-Street map 98
Ponte di Veia 191
Il Pordenone, *Adoration of the
  Magi* 174
Porters, Venice 271
Porto di Lido 157
Porto, Luigi da, *Romeo and Juliet* 199
Portogruaro 161, **175**
  map 164
Portrait of a Dominican (Lotto) 174
Portrait of a Gentleman (Lotto) 132
Portrait of a Lady (Henry James)
  111
Portrait of Sperone Speroni (Titian)
  174
*Portrait of a Young Man in a Red
  Hat* (Carpaccio) 77
Portrait of a Young Senator
  (Giovanni Bellini) 179
Postal service 269
Poste Restante 269
Pound, Ezra 151
Poveglia 148, **157**
Il Prato 251
Prato della Valle (Padua) 183
Presentation of the Virgin (Titian)
  133
Principe Hotel 59
The Procession in St Mark's Square
  (Gentile Bellini) 133
Procuratie Nuove 74
Procuratie Vecchie 74
Prosecco 239
Proserpine Rapita (Monteverdi)
  112–13

Q

Quartiere delle Barche (Vicenza)
  Street-by-Street map 168
Quattro Fontane Hotel 231
Quattro Libri (Four Books)
  (Palladio) 24

R

Races
  Palio (horse races) 34, 35
  regattas 29, 34, 50
  su e zo per i ponti 33
  Vogalonga 33
Radio 262
Rail services
  Dolomites 213
  Verona 188
  see also Trains
Railway information offices 273
Railway stations 272–3
Rainfall chart 35
Rangone, Tommaso 95
Rape of Europa (Veronese) 88
Il Redentore 129, **154**
  Festa del Redentore 34
Regata di Santi Giovanni e Paolo,
  Caorle 34
Regata Storica 35, 50
  gondoliers 35
  Grand Canal 57

Regattas 29, 50
Relais & Châteaux 224
Renaissance architecture, *palazzi* 23
Restaurants
  Asiago 242
  Asolo 242
  Belluno 245
  Brenta Canal 242–3
  Cadore area 245
  Cannaregio 241
  Castelfranco 242
  Castello 240–41
  children 235
  Chioggia 242
  Conegliano 242
  Cortina 245
  Dorsoduro 241
  dress code 235
  Euganean Hills 242
  fixed-price menus 234
  Lagoon islands 241
  Lake Garda 244
  listings 235
  Oderzo 243
  opening times 234
  Padua 243
  Portogruaro 243
  prices 234–5
  reading the menu 235
  reservations 235
  Rovigo 243
  San Marco 240
  San Polo and Santa Croce 240
  smoking 235
  Treviso 243
  types 234
  vegetarian 234
  Venice 240–42
  Verona 244–5
  Vicenza 244
  wheelchair access 235
  wine 235
Restoration 51, 154–5
Rezzonico family 62, 126
Rialto Bridge 100
  early settlement 40, 55
  Grand Canal 65
  Street-by-Street map 99
Rialto markets 99, **100**
Ricci, Sebastiano
  Gesuati 129
  The Glory of Saint Martial 141
  San Marziale 138
Ricci, Sebastiano, Museo Civico
  (Belluno) 218
Il Riccio
  Ca' d'Oro 144
  Drinking Satyr 179
Ridotto **92**
  closure 46
Ridotto (Francesco Guardi) 126
Rio San Barnaba 126
Risorgimento movement 46
  Caffè Pedrocchi (Padua) 178
Ristorante alle Beccherie (Treviso)
  243
Ristorante Casa Rossa (Asiago) 242
Ristorante El Zoco (Belluno) 245

Ristorante Enoteca Marchi (Treviso)
  243
Ristorante Marco Polo (Padua)
  243
Ristorante Storione (Vicenza) 244
Riva del Ferro 65
Riva del Garda 205, **209**
  map 188
Riva degli Schiavoni 110, **113**
Riva del Vin 64
  Street-by-Street map 98
Riviera Bresciana 208
Rizzo, Antonio
  Adam and Eve 84, 89
  Giants' Staircase 84
  tomb 174
Roads
  Dolomites 213, 214
  Lake Garda 205
  Map 12–13
  Veneto Plain 165
  Verona 188
Rocca di Riva (Riva del Garda) 209
Rocca Scaligeri (Sirmione) 206
Rocca Scaligeri (Soave) 190
Rolfe, Frederick (Baron Corvo) 101
Rolling Venice 263
Roman Empire, history 38–9
Romeo and Juliet 199
Romeo and Juliet (Zeffirelli) 219
Rosa Salva 247
Rossi, Domenico
  Ca' Corner della Regina 62
  Gesuiti 142
  San Stae 105
La Rotonda (Rovigo) 185
La Rotonda, Villa (Vicenza) 171
Rovigo 185
  map 164
Rowing 257
Rubelli 251
Ruskin, John
  Hotel Daniele 110
  Ospedaletto 115
  Palazzo Gritti-Pisani 70
  San Moisè 92

S

Sacca della Misericordia
  Sacca Sessola 148
  Street-by-Street map 139
Sacra Conversazione (Palma il
  Vecchio) 132
The Sacrifice of Isaac (Giambattista
  Tiepolo) 115
Sagra di Sant'Antonio festival
  (Padua) 34
Sagredo family 63
Sailing Center Hotel (Malcésine)
  233
Salò, Gaspare da 208
Salute, La *see* Santa Maria della
  Salute
Salò 208
  map 188–9
Salone *see* Palazzo della Ragione
  (Padua)
Sant'Ambrogio di Valpolicella 209

Sant'Anastasia (Verona) 197, **199**
Sant'Angelo delle Polvere 148
Sant'Anna 121
Sant'Anna d'Alfaedo 191
  map 188
St Anthony of Padua 183
  relics 182
St Anthony's Basilica (Padua) 161,
  182
Sant'Apollonia, cloister 113
  Street-by-Street map 110
Sant'Aponal
  Street-by-Street map 98
Santi Apostoli 143
Sant'Ariano island 149
St Barbara and Saints (Palma il
  Vecchio) 114
San Barnaba
  Street-by-Street map 125
San Cassiano 98, **101**
San Cassiano Hotel 62
St Catherine of Siena, relics 117
St Christopher statue, Madonna
  dell'Orto 140
St Chrysogonus on Horseback
  (Giambono) 129
San Clemente island 148, **157**
San Clemente (Padua) 243
Santa Corona (Vicenza) 170–71
Santa Croce area *see* San Polo and
  Santa Croce
Sant'Elena island 120–21
Sant'Erasmo 149
  Festa di Mosto 35
Sant'Eustachio *see* San Stae
San Fantin 90
San Fermo Maggiore (Verona) 194
Santa Fosca (Torcello) 152–3
San Francesco della Vigna 115
San Francesco del Deserto island
  149, 150
St George and the Princess
  (Pisanello) 199
St George (Mantegna) 132
San Geremia 60
Santi Gervasio e Protasio *see* San
  Trovaso
San Giacomo dell'Orio 104
San Giacomo di Rialto 99, **100**
San Giobbe 145
San Giorgio in Alga island 148
San Giorgio in Braida (Verona) 203
San Giorgio dei Greci 111, **112**
San Giorgio Maggiore **95**, 134
San Giorgio sanctuary 118, 185
San Giovanni in Bragora 116
San Giovanni Crisostomo 143
San Giovanni Evangelista 23, **104**
Santi Giovanni e Paolo (San
  Zanipolo) 116–17
  monuments 42, 43
  Visitors' Checklist 117
St Jerome with Saints (Giovanni
  Bellini) 143
St John the Baptist and Other Saints
  (Conegliano) 140
St John Chrysostom and Six Saints
  (Piombo) 143

San Lazzaro degli Armeni island 149, **155**
San Lazzaro dei Mendicanti 114
San Lorenzo 115
San Lorenzo (Vicenza) 171
Santa Lucia railway station (Venice) 58, **272**
San Marco area 72–95
  Street-by-Street maps 74–5, 90–91
  see also Basilica San Marco, Column of St Mark, Festa di San Marco, Piazza San Marco, St Mark
San Marcuola 61
Santa Maria Antica (Verona) 197, **198**
Santa Maria Assunta see Gesuiti
Santa Maria della Carità 130
Santa Maria del Carmelo see Santa Maria dei Carmini
Santa Maria dei Carmini 124, **127**
Santa Maria dei Derelitti see Ospedaletto
Santa Maria Formosa 114
Santa Maria del Giglio see Santa Maria Zobenigo
Santa Maria Gloriosa dei Frari 54, **102–3**
  floorplan 103
  monks' choir 102
  monument to Titian 103
  Visitors' Checklist 103
Santa Maria della Grazia island 148, **155**
Santa Maria dei Miracoli 142
Santa Maria di Nazareth see Scalzi
Santa Maria in Organo (Verona) 203
Santa Maria della Salute 45, 55, **135**
  Grand Canal 71
  Titian 135
Santa Maria della Visitazione 129
Santa Maria Zobenigo (del Giglio) 90, **92**
St Mark
  feast of 33
  relics 40, 41
  winged lion 37
  see also San Marco
St Mark's Basilica see Basilica San Marco
St Mark's Basin on Ascension Day (Canaletto) 46
St Mark's Square see Piazza San Marco
San Marziale 138, **141**
Sanmicheli, Michele, San Giorgio in Braida (Verona) 203
St Michael (Giambono) 123
San Michele island 49, 148, **151**
San Michele in Isola 151
San Moisè 91, **92**
San Moisè Hotel 229
St Nicholas of Bari with saints (Lotto) 127
San Nicolò 224
  Lido 157
San Nicolò da Tolentino 104
San Nicolò dei Mendicoli 128
San Pantalon 104

St Pantalon Healing a Boy (Veronese) 104
St Paul (Carpaccio) 185
St Peter, statue (Verona) 202
San Pietro di Castello 120
  island 109, 120–21
San Pietro di Foletto (Follina) 167
San Polo 101
San Polo and Santa Croce area 96–105
  Street-by-Street map 98–9
San Rocco 104
St Roch 106
St Roch Curing the Plague Victims (Tintoretto) 104
San Salvatore 94
San Samuele 67
St Sebastian (Mantegna) 144
San Sebastiano 128
San Servolo island 149, **154–5**
  restoration 51
St Simeon Stock 127
St Simeon Stock Receiving the Scapular of the Carmelite Order from the Virgin (Giambattista Tiepolo) 127
San Simeone Piccolo 59
San Simeone Profeta 59
San Stae 61, **105**
Santo Stefano 93
Santo Stefano Hotel 229
Santo Stefano (Verona) 202
St Theodore, statue 41, 75, 88
San Trovaso 129
St Ursula Cycle (Carpaccio) 54, 130, 133
San Zaccaria 111, **112**
San Zanipolo see Santi Giovanni e Paolo
San Zeno Maggiore (Verona) 200–1
  cloister 200
  crypt 201
  Visitors' Checklist 201
  west doors 201
San Zulian 95
Sand, George 113
Sant'Angelo agency 224
Sanmicheli, Michele 64
Sant'Andrea 157
Sansovino, Jacopo
  burial place 83
  Ca' Grande 69
  Libreria Sansoviniana 76
  Logetta 76
  Madonna and Child 144
  Palazzo Manin-Dolfin 65
  San Francesco della Vigna 115
  San Salvatore 94
  Tribunale Fabriche Nove 63
Il Santo (Padua) see Basilica di Sant'Antonio
Sardellata al Pal del Vo, Lake Garda 34
Sardi, Giuseppe 59
Scaligeri dynasty 42, 166, 192, **207**
Scaligeri tombs (Verona) 198–9
  Street-by-Street map 197

Scalzi (Santa Maria di Narazeth) 58, 130, **145**
Scamozzi, Vincenzo
  Doge Marino Grimani monument 121
  Teatro Olimpico (Vicenza) 172–3
Scandinavia Hotel 230
Scarpagnino, Scuola Grande di San Rocco 106
Schiavonia, trade links 118
School of Craftsmanship (San Servolo) 51
Scrovegni Chapel (Padua) 180–81
  gallery guide 180
  Giotto frescoes 180–81
  Visitors' Checklist 181
Scuola della Carità 68
Scuola Grande dei Carmini 124, **127**
Scuola Grande di San Marco 114
Scuola Grande di San Rocco 106–7
  gallery guide 107
  Visitors' Checklist 107
Scuola Internazionale di Grafica 263
Scuola dei Merletti (Burano) 150
Scuola di San Giorgio degli Schiavoni 118
Scuola di San Giovanni Evangelista 104
  The Stories of the Cross 133
Scuola di San Nicolò dei Greci 112
Scuola del Santo (Padua) 183
Scuola dei Varotari 127
Scuola Vecchia della Misericordia
  Street-by-Street map 139
Scuole 127
Security 264
Self-catering 224–5
Selva di Cadore 219
La Sensa see Marriage with the Sea
Shakespeare festival (Verona) 34, 202
Shipyards, Arsenale 45, 119
Shops 248–53
  books and gifts 251
  department stores 251
  fabrics and interior design 251
  fashion and accessories 251
  food 251
  glass 251
  how to pay 248
  jewellery 251
  masks and costumes 251
  VAT exemption 248
  what to buy 252–3
  when to shop 248
  see also Markets
Signor Blum 251
Signorelli, Luca, *Flagellation* 144
Sirmione Peninsula 206–7
  castles 160
  Grotte di Catullo 206-7
  maps 188, 204
  Rocca Scaligeri 206-7
  San Pietro 207
  walk 207
Ski resorts
  Alpe del Nevegal 218

Ski resorts (cont.)
  Cortina d'Ampezzo 214
Skiing, Dolomites 32, 212
Sky Shuttle 270
Smith, Joseph 63
Snack & Sweet 247
Soave **190**, 239
  map 188
Società Dante Alighieri 263
Sofonisba (Trissino) 173
Solferino 205
  map 188
Soto Sopra 247
El Souk 257
Spas 184
Spavento, Giorgio, San Salvatore
  94
Spluga della Preta 191
Sportello della Laguna 261
Sports 256, **257**
Spring, events 33
Squero di San Trovaso 28, **129**
Stamps 269
Stazione Santa Lucia *see* Santa Lucia
  station
The Stealing of St Mark (Tintoretto)
  131
The Stories of the Cross (Scuola di
  San Giovanni Evangelista) 133
Strada delle Dolomiti 214–15
Strada del Vino Bianco 167
Stravinsky, Igor 48, 151
La Strega (Annigoni) 166
Street-by-Street maps
  Cannaregio 188–9
  Castello 110–11
  Dorsoduro 124–5
  Piazza San Marco 74–5
  San Marco 90–91
  San Polo and Santa Croce 98–9
  Padua 176–7
  Verona 196–7
  Vicenza 168–9
Strozzi, Bernardo, *Feast at the
  House of Simon* 133
Student information 262, 263
Summer, events 34
Sunshine, daily hours 33
Supper at Emmaus (Bassano) 167
Supper of St Gregory the Great
  (Veronese) 171

T

Taglioni, Maria 144
Tailor Made Tours 224
Taverna Aeolia (Vicenza) 244
Taverna San Trovaso 241
Taxis
  Veneto 278
  water 271, **276**
Tchaikovsky, Piotr Ilyitch 230
Teatro Goldoni 257
Teatro Olimpico (Vicenza) 172–3
  Anteodeon 172
  Odeon frescoes 172
  Scamozzi stage set 172
  Visitors' Checklist 173
Teatro Ridotto *see* Ridotto

Teatro Romano (Verona) 202
Telephones 268–9
  cards 268–9
  hotels 223
  tokens *(gettoni)* 268, 269
Telefoni 268, 269
Television 262
Temperature chart 34
The Tempest (Giorgione) 131, 132,
  167
Tennis 257
Teresa Porto 251
Thiene 166
  map 164
Tickets
  boat 274
  train 273
Tiepolo dell'Europa e Regina 240
Tiepolo family 71
Tiepolo, Giambattista
  Accademia 133
  The Communion of St Lucy 143
  Gesuati ceilings 123
  *The Holy House Transported from
    Nazareth to Loreto* 130, 145
  The Life of St Dominic 129
  Nuptial Allegory 126
  Palazzo Labia 143
  The Sacrifice of Isaac 115
  *St Simeon Stock Receiving the
    Scapular of the Carmelite Order
    from the Virgin* 127
  Scuola Grande dei Carmini 124
  Triumph of Faith 112
  Villa Valmarana 171
  Virgin with Saints 129
Tiepolo, Giandomenico
  Ca' Rezzonico 126
  Via Crucis 101
  Villa Valmarana 171
Time zones 263
Tintoretto, Domenico, *Paradise* 85,
  89
Tintoretto (Jacopo Robusti) 140
  The Adoration of the Golden Calf
    140
  *Bacchus and Ariadne Crowned
    by Venus* 87
  Crucifixion 106
  Doge's Palace 88
  Flight into Egypt 107
  house 136, 138
  The Last Judgment 140
  Last Supper 101
  The Miracle of the Slave 133
  Paradise 85, 89
  San Cassiano 98, 101
  San Giorgio Maggiore 95
  *St Roch Curing the Plague
    Victims* 104
  San Trovaso 129
  Scuola Grande di San Rocco
    106–7
  The Stealing of St Mark 131
  The Temptation of Christ 107
  tomb 140
  Triumph of Doge Nicolo da Ponte
    36

Tintoretto (cont.)
  Wedding at Cana 135
Tipping 261
Tirali, Andrea 58
Titian
  Annunciation 174
  Assumption 199
  Assumption of the Virgin 102
  Casa di Tiziano (Pieve di Cadore)
    215
  death 45
  house 141
  Life of St Anthony 183
  Madonna di Ca' Pesaro 27, 102
  Martyrdom of St Lawrence 142
  Portrait of Sperone Speroni 174
  Presentation of the Virgin 133
  Santa Maria della Salute 135
  statue 212
  Venus 144
Tito, Ettore, *The Council of Ephesus*
  145
Toilets 261
Tolls, motorway 279
Tombs
  Andrea Vendramin (Lombardo)
    117
  Nicolò Marcello (Lombardo) 116
  Pietro Mocenigo (Lombardo) 116
  Scaligeri 197–9
Tommaseo, Nicolò 93
Toni del Spin (Treviso) 243
Torcello 149, **152–3**
  cathedral 41, 152
  Museo dell'Estuario 153
  Santa Fosca 153
Toreuma, Claudia 179
Torre dei Lamberti (Verona) 106,
  198
Torre dell'Orologio 75, 76
Torre di Piazza (Vicenza) 170
  Street-by-Street map 168
Torre del Tormento (Vicenza)
  Street-by-Street map 168
Touring Club Italiano 224–5
Tourism, Venice 50
Tourist information 260–61
  entertainment 254
Tours
  Brenta Canal 182–3
  Secret Itinerary (Doge's Palace)
    87
  see also Guided tours
Tours by car
  around Verona 187–8
  Dolomite Road 214–15
  La Gardesana 205
  Valpolicella 208–9
  Valzoldana 218–19
Trade
  links with Schiavonia 118
  Mediterranean 44
Tradonico, Pietro (doge) 113
Traghetti 276
  Grand Canal 67, 100
Tragicomica 251
Trains 272–3
  see also Rail services

Transalpino 263
Transfiguration (Veronese) 184
Transport, public (Verona) 188
Trattoria alla Madonna 240
    Street-by-Street map 99
Trattoria da Piero Ceschi (Euganean
    Hills) 242
Trattoria Vecchia Lugana (Lake
    Garda) 244
Travel
    air 270
    boat 274–6
    car 271
    train 272–3
Traveller's cheques 266
    missing 265
Tre Pini (Rovigo) 243
Treviso 174
    airport 271
    Festa dell'Assunta 34
    maps 164, 174
Tribunale Fabricche Nuove 63
Trireme, Venetian 45
Trissino, G G, *Sofonisba* 173
Triumph of Doge Nicolo da Ponte
    (Tintoretto) 36
Triumph of Faith (Giambattista
    Tiepolo) 112
Trois 251

U

Upper Reaches of the Grand Canal
    (Canaletto) 29

V

Vacanze in Italia 224
Valdagno 190
    map 188–9
Valdobbiadene 167
    map 164
Valentino 251
Valle delle Sfingi 191
Valli 251
Valpolicella 238
    wine tour 208–9
Valpolicellore 33
Valzoldana 218–19
    map 212
Vaporetti 274–5
    Grand Canal 57–8
    information office 275
    main routes 275
La Vecia festival (Lake Garda) 33
Vendramin, Andrea (doge) 117
Venegazzù 239
Venetian Empire 37, 42–3
Venetian Gothic architecture 55
Venetian Institute of Sciences,
    Letters and Arts 93
Veneto
    buses 278
    car hire 278
    Dolomites 211–19
    driving 278
    economy 18
    entertainment 254–7
    exploring 160–61
    history 38–51

Veneto (cont.)
    industry 18
    Lake Garda 204–9
    maps 12–13, 160–61
    Padua 176–83
    portrait 17–19
    Roman 38–9
    taxis 278
    Verona 192–203
    Vicenza 168–73
    village festivals 34
    walking 278
Veneto Plain region 163–85
    map 164–5
Veneziano, Lorenzo 26
Veneziano, Paolo
    Byzantine Gothic art 26
    Coronation of the Virgin 26, 131,
    132
Veneziano, Paolo, Salò cathedral
    208
Venice
    Accademia gallery 130–33
    airport 270–71
    Arsenale 119
    Basilica San Marco 78–83
    Ca' d'Oro 144
    Doge's Palace 84–9
    entertainment 254–7
    foundation 40
    Frari 102–3
    getting around 274–7
    Ghetto 145
    Grand Canal 56–71
    history 36–51
    hotels 228–31
    Lagoon 146–57
    Palazzo Ducale 84–9
    Piazza San Marco 74–5
    police (Questura) 263
    population 18
    portrait 17–19
    railway station 272
    restaurants 240–42
    Rialto Bridge 100
    Santi Giovanni e Paolo 116–17
    Santa Maria Gloriosa dei Frari
    102–3
    St Mark's Basilica 78–93
    St Mark's Square 74–5
    San Zanipolo 116–17
    Scuola Grande di San Rocco
    106–7
    shops 248–51
    Torcello 152–3
    tourist office 261
    vaporetti 274–5
    walking 277
Venice Simplon-Orient-Express 272
Venier, Sebastiano (doge) 117
Venus (Titian) 144
Verona 160, **192–203**
    airport 271
    Amphitheatre 195
    Arco dei Gavi 194
    Arena 195
    Bacanal del Gnoco festival 32
    Casa di Giulietta 199

Verona (cont.)
    Casa di Romeo 199
    Castel San Pietro 202
    Castelvecchio 193
    cherry market 33
    Corso Cavour 194
    Dante statue 198
    Duomo 199
    fountain 198
    Giardino Giusti 187, 203
    history 38–9, 187
    Loggia del Consiglio 198
    maps 188 , 192–3
    Museo Lapidario Maffeiano 194
    music and theatre 256
    Museo Archeologico 202
    Museo Civico di Scienze Naturali
    203
    Opera festival 34, 256–7
    osterie 209
    Palazzo della Capitano 198
    Palazzo Maffei 198
    Palazzo della Ragione 198
    Piazza dei Signori 198
    Piazza Erbe 192, **198**
    police (Questura) 263
    Ponte Romano 202
    Ponte Scaligero 194
    railway station 272
    Roman 38–9
    Sant'Anastasia 199
    San Fermo Maggiore 194
    San Giorgio in Braida 203
    Santa Maria Antica 198
    Santa Maria in Organo 203
    Santo Stefano 202
    San Zeno Maggiore 200–1
    Street-by-Street map 196–7
    Teatro Romano 202
    Tomba di Giulietta 199
    Torre dei Lamberti 198
    tourist office 261
    Venetian lion 198
Verona, Fra Giovanni da, Santa
    Maria in Organo 203
Verona and Lake Garda region
    186–209
    map 188–9
Veronese, Paolo 123
    Adoration of the Magi 171
    The Adoration of the Shepherds
    116
    Age and Youth 89
    Dialectic 88
    Doge's Palace 88–9
    Feast in the House of Levi 132–3
    Holy Family 126
    The Holy Family with Saints 115
    Martyrdom of St George 203
    Mystical Marriage of St Catherine
    133
    Rape of Europa 88
    San Sebastiano 128
    St Pantalon Healing a Boy 104
    Supper of St Gregory the Great
    171
    Transfiguration 184

Veronese (cont.)
  Villa Barbaro 24–5, 161
Verrocchio, Andrea, Colleoni statue
  114
Via Crucis (Giandomenico Tiepolo)
  101
Via Garibaldi 120
Vicenza 160, **168–73**
  Basilica di Monte Berico 171
  Casa Pigafetta 170
  Contrà Porti 170
  map 164
  Museo Civico 170
  Piazza dei Signori 170
  police (Questura) 263
  railway station 273
  San Lorenzo 171
  Santa Corona 170-1
  Street-by-Street map 168–9
  Teatro Olimpico 172–3
  tourist office 261
  Villa Rotonda 171
  Villa Valmarana 171
Victoria Hotel (Bassano) 231
View of the Rio dei Mendicanti
  (Canaletto) 126
Villa Barbaro (Masèr) **24–5**, 161,
  167
  Bacchus Room 25
  Crociera 25
  Hall of Olympus 25
  Nymphaeum 24
  Room of the Little Dog 24
  Room of the Oil Lamp 25
Villa Cipriani Hotel (Asolo) 231
  restaurant 242
Villa Cortine Palace Hotel (Lake
  Garda) 232
Villa Fiordaliso (Lake Garda) 244
Villa Parco Hotel 231
Villa Santa Sofia wine estate 208
Villas
  Villa Alba 208
  Allegri-Arvedi (Cuzzano) 190
  Barbarigo 184
  Barbaro (Masèr) *See* Villa Barbaro
  Castello Porto-Colleoni (Thiene)
    166
  Emo (Castelfranco) 167
  Foscari (Malcontenta) 183
  Godi Malinverni (Thiene) 166
  Malcontenta *see* Foscari
  Palladian 24–5

Villas (cont.)
  Pisani (Montagnana) 25, 184
  Pisani (Stra) 182
  Rotonda (Vicenza) 25, 171
  map 165
  Thiene (Quinto Vicentino) 24
  Valmarana "ai Nani" (Vicenza) 171
  Il Vittoriale (Gardone Riviera) 208
  Widmann-Foscari (Mira) 183
Vini Da Gigio 241
Vino Vino 247
Virgin and Child with Saints
  (Conegliano) 175
Virgin and Child (Negroponte) 115
Virgin and Child (Nicolò) 142
Virgin and Child with saints
  (Mantegna) 200
Virgin with Saints (Tiepolo) 129
*Virgin Enthroned between St Zeno
  and St Lawrence* (Libri) 203
Visconti family, Milan 192, 202
Visconti, Luchino, *Death in Venice*
  48, 231
Visentini, Antonio 63
Visintini, Antonio 63
Vitale, Michiel II (doge) 113
Vittoria, Alessandro, sculpture 115
Vittorio Emanuele II 219
  statue 111
Vittorio Veneto 219
  map 212
Vivaldi, Antonio 47
  La Pietà 111, 112
Vivarini, Antonio
  Accademia 133
  Christ Bearing the Cross 117
  San Zaccaria polyptychs 112
Vivarini, Bartolomeo, *Madonna
  and Child with Saints* 118
Vogalonga 33
Vogliuder 63
Volta del Canal 66
Volumni tomb 179

W

Wagner, Richard 125
  Palazzo Giustinian 66
Walking
  Dolomites 214, 217
  eastern Castello 120–21
  Veneto 278
  Venice 277
Water
  drinking 265
  supplies 20

WCs 261
Wedding at Cana (Tintoretto)
  135
Wine
  Bardolino 208
  Conegliano wine school 175
  festivals 33
  labels 238
  recommended producers 238
  Soave 190
  types 238
  Valpolicella 208
  Valpolicella wine tour 208–9
  what to drink 238–9
Wine bars 247
Winter, events 32
Winter sports, Dolomites 32, 211
World Vision Travel 261, 273
World War I, battlefields 211, 216
World War II, Verona bridges 202

Y

Youth hostels, *see* Associazione
  Italiana Alberghi per la Gioventù

Z

Zandomeneghi, L and P, monument
  to Titian 103
Zanetti monument (Lombardo)
  174
Zattere 128–9
Zecca Street-by-Street map 74
Zecchini Hotel 226, 230–1
Zeffirelli, Franco, *Romeo and Juliet*
  219
Zelotti, Giambattista
  Castello Porto-Colleoni (Thiene)
    166
  Godi Malinverni (Thiene) 166
  Villa Emo (Fanzolo) 167
  Villa Foscari (Malcontenta) 183
Zen, Cardinal 83
Zevio, Altichiero da
  Crucifixion 183
  Oratorio di San Giorgio (Padua)
    183
Ziani, Sebastiano (doge) 41
Le Zitelle 154
Zoo, Parco Faunistico 205
Zoppe di Cadore, fresco 218
Zotto, Antonio del 94
Zuccarelli, Francesco, Accademia
  133

Acknowledgments

DORLING KINDERSLEY would like to thank the
many people whose help and assistance
contributed to the preparation of this book.

MAIN CONTRIBUTORS

Susie Boulton studied languages and history
of art at the University of Cambridge, where
she still has her home. She has been visiting
Venice for over 20 years and is the author of
several guide books on the city. Although a
specialist on Venice, she has also written
travel guides and articles on various other
cities and regions of Europe.

Christopher Catling has been visiting Italy for
over 22 years since his first archaeological dig
there while he was a student at Cambridge
University. He is the author of several guide
books on Italian cities and regions, including
*The Eyewitness Travel Guide to Florence and
Tuscany*.

ADDITIONAL CONTRIBUTOR

Sally Roy first got to know Venice while she
was at school in Rome and has been returning
to the country ever since. She read medieval
history at St Andrew's University, Edinburgh
and has contributed to several books on Italy
where she now spends six months of every
year.

ADDITIONAL ILLUSTRATIONS

Annabelle Brend, Dawn Brend, Neil Bulpitt,
Richard Draper, Nick Gibbard, Kevin Jones
Associates, John Lawrence, The Maltings
Partnership, Simon Roulstone, Sue Sharples,
Derrick Stone, Paul Weston, John Woodcock.

DESIGN AND EDITORIAL ASSISTANCE

Michael Blacker, Dawn Brend, Michael Ellis,
Irena Hoare, Annette Jacobs, Steve Knowlden,
Erika Lang, Gillian Price, Steve Rowling, Janis
Utton, Lynda Warrington, Fiona Wild.

RESEARCH ASSISTANCE

Hans Erlacher, Paolo Frullini, Oscar Gates,
Marinella Laini, Elizabetta Lovato, Fabiola
Perer, Sarah Sole.

INDEX

Indexing Specialists, 202 Church Road, Hove,
East Sussex, UK.

SPECIAL ASSISTANCE

Comune di Vicenza; Arch. Gianfranco Martinoni
at the Assessorato Beni Culturali Comune di
Padova; Ca' Macana; Cesare Battisti at the Media
Tourist Office, Venice; Curia Patriarcale Venezia;
D.ssa Foscarina Caletti at the Giunta Regionale
di Venezia; Jane Groom, Brian Jordan; Alexandra
Kennedy; Joy Parker; Frances Hawkins, Lady
Frances Clarke and John Millerchip of the Venice
in Peril Fund; the staff of the APT offices
throughout the Veneto, in particular Anna Rita
Bisaggio in Montegrotto Terme, Stephano
Marchioro in Padua; Anna Maria Carlotto, Virna

Scarduelli and Christina Erlacher in Verona,
Anselmo Centomo in Vicenza; Heidi Wenyon.

PHOTOGRAPHY PERMISSIONS

DORLING KINDERSLEY would like to thank the
following for their kind permission to
photograph at their establishments:
VENICE: Amministrazione Provinciale di
Venezia (Museo dell'Estuario, Torcello); Ca'
Mocenigo; Ca' Pesaro; Ca' Rezzonico; Caffè
Quadri; Collegio Armeni; Fondazione Europea
Pro Venetia Viva, San Servolo; Fondazione
Giorgio Cini (San Giorgio Maggiore); Peggy
Guggenheim Museum; Hôtel des Bains;
Libreria Sansoviniana; Museo Archeologico;
Museo Correr; Museo Diocesano d'Arte Sacra;
Museo Fortuny; Museo Storia Navale; Museo
Storico Naturale; Museo Vetrario, Murano;
Arch. Umberto Franzoi and staff at the Palazzo
Ducale; Procuratie di San Marco (Basilica San
Marco); Santi Giovanni e Paolo; San Lazzaro
degli Armeni; Santa Maria Gloriosa dei Frari;
Scuola Grande dei Carmini; Scuola Grande di
San Rocco.
VENETO: Arena Romano, Verona; Basilica,
Vicenza; Caffè Pedrocchi, Padua; Duomo,
Padua; Duomo, Vicenza; Giardini Giusti,
Verona; Museo Archeologico, Verona; Museo
di Castelvecchio, Verona; Museo Civico,
Malcésine; Museo Civico, Vicenza; Museo
Concordiese, Portogruaro; Museo dei
Eremitani, Padua; Museo Lapidario Maffeiano,
Verona; Museo dei Storia Naturale, Verona;
Ossuario di San Pietro, Solferino;
Sant'Anastasia, Verona; San Fermo Maggiore,
Verona; San Giorgio, Monsélice; San Giorgio
in Braida, Verona; San Lorenzo, Vicenza; Santa
Maria in Organo, Verona; San Pietro in
Malvino, Sirmione; San Severo, Bardolino; San
Stefano, Verona; San Zeno Maggiore, Verona;
Santuario di Monte Berico, Vicenza; Teatro
Olimpico, Vicenza; Università di Padova;
Contessa Diamante Luling-Buschette, Villa
Barbaro, Masèr; Conte Marco Emo, Villa Emo,
Fanzolo di Vedelago.

PICTURE CREDITS

t = top; tc = top centre; tr = top right;
cla = centre left above; ca = centre above;
cra = centre right above; cl = centre left;
c = centre; cr = centre right; clb = centre left
below; cb = centre below; crb = centre right
below; bl = bottom left; bc = bottom centre;
br = bottom right.

Every effort has been made to trace the
copyright holders, and we apologize in
advance for any unintentional omissions. We
would be pleased to insert the appropriate
acknowledgments in any subsequent edition
of this publication.

Works of art have been reproduced with the
permission of the following copyright holders::
© ADAGP, Paris and DACS, London 1995:
Intérieur Hollandais II (1928) by Joan Miró,

Maiastra by Constantin Brancusi, 134cr.

The publishers are grateful to the following museums, companies, and picture libraries for permission to reproduce their photgraphs: ACCADEMIA OLIMPICA, VICENZA: 172tr, 173crb; ACE PHOTO/AGENCY TORE GILL: 254b; ACE/ MAURITIUS: 257t; ANCIENT ART & ARCHITECTURE COLLECTION: 38c, 40 br, 40 tl; APT DEL BRESCIANO: 35b; ARCHIV FÜR KUNST UND GESCHICHTE: 26tl/c/cr, 30bl, 36, 43br, 44crb, 45bl, 45t, 46tl, 46tr, 48cla, 49clb, 50b, 54br, 130b, 131b, 131c, 132b, 133t, 30/31c; ARCHIVIO RAIMONDO ZAGO 49cl. ARCHIVIO VENEZIANO: Sarah Quill 29br, 51crb, 67cl, 106tr, 144t.

BENETTON: 51tl; BIBLIOTECA CIVICA DI TRIESTE (FOTO HALUPCA): 119b; BRIDGEMAN ART LIBRARY, LONDON: *Madonna and Child and Saints* (triptych altarpiece) by Giovanni Bellini (c.1431-1516), Santa Maria dei Frari, Venice 27tl/tr; *The Siege of Antioch* 1098 by William of Tyre. Bibliothèque Nationale, Paris 40cla; *Marco Polo with Elephants and Camels* from Livre des Merveilles, Bibliothèque Nationale, Paris, 42cb; *View of Venice* by Bernardo von Breitenbach, from Opusculum Sanctarum Peregrinationum in Terram Sanctam, Bibliothèque Nationale, PARIS, 8-9; *Family Tree of the Cornaro Family*, Italian School (18th century), Palazzo Corner Ca' Grande, Venice, 69tr; *Salome* by Gustav Klimt (1862-1918) Museo d'Arte Moderna, Venice, 105br; *The Nuns' Visiting Day* by Francesco Guardi (1712-93), Museo Ca' Rezzonico, Venice, 112bl; *St George Killing the Dragon* by Vittore Carpaccio (c.1460/5-1523/6), Scuola di San Giorgio degli Schiavoni, Venice, 118tl; *The Stealing of the Body of St Mark* by Tintoretto (1518-94), Accademia, Venice, 131t; *The Rape of Europa* by Francesco Zuccarelli, Accademia, Venice, 133c; *Marco Polo dressed in Tartar costume* (Italian, c.1700) Museo Correr, Venice/Giraudon, 4tr/115br; OSVALDO BÖHM: 20b, 20cl, 29bl, 41crb, 63tl, 79tl, 132c, 132t, 144c.

CEPHAS PICTURE LIBRARY: Mick Rock, 35cra, Mick Rock, 238tr; CIGA HOTELS: 70tl; CLAIRE CALMAN: 55cr; GIANCARLO COSTA: 47clb; JOE CORNISH: 15b, 209c, 216bl; STEPHANIE COLASANTI: 56, 195br.

CHRIS DONAGHUE THE OXFORD PHOTO LIBRARY: 3 (inset), 5tl, 76t, 156br, 280t; MICHAEL DENT: 82b, 252tl; DRAUGHTSMAN: 268tr.

E.T. ARCHIVE: Sala dei Prior Siena, 41tl; Baroque Hall of Mirrors, Palazzo Papadopoli, Venice, 64tl; *The Apothecary's Shop* by Pietro Longhi, Accademia, Venice, 130c; ELECTA, MILAN: 180cr, 181t/cl; ERIZZO EDITRICE SRL: 105clb; MARY EVANS PICTURE LIBRARY: 7 (inset), 9 (inset), 24tl, 39clb, 44bl, 47br, 47t, 53 (inset), 58cra, 58tr, 63c, 64c, 69ca, 143tr, 159 (inset), 221 (inset), 259 (inset), 32c.

GRAZIA NERI: 41b, 49tl, 50crb, 50tr, 65br, 92tl, 157b, 254t; Marco Bruzzo, 5tr, 32t, 35clb, 40tr, 166t; Cameraphoto 71tr, 115bl, 42/43c; PEGGY GUGGENHEIM MUSEUM, VENICE: 134b; THE RONALD GRANT ARCHIVE: 50cla.

HOTEL EXCELSIOR, VENICE LIDO: 48crb; ROBERT HARDING PICTURE LIBRARY: 216cl; THE HULTON DEUTSCH COLLECTION: 38br, 38tr, 39br, 43clb, 46br, 48bc, 49br, 61tr, 66b, 66cra, 69cl, 101c, 140bl, 181br, 199b

IMAGE BANK: Guido A. Rossi, 11 (inset); IMAGE SELECT: Ann Ronan, 44cl.

HUGH MCKNIGHT PHOTOGRAPHY: 71tl; MAGNUM PHOTOS/DAVID SEYMOUR: 48tr; MARKA: 37b; MORO ROMA: 30cl, 48/49c; MUSEO ARCHEOLOGICO, VERONA: 38bl; MUSEO CIVICO AGLI EREMITANI: 179t/c/b; MUSEO CIVICO DI ODERZO: 39t; THE MANSELL COLLECTION: 46crb, 47bl.

NHPA/GERARD LACZ: 217b; NHPA/LAURIE CAMPBELL: 217c; NHPA/SILVESTRIS FOTOSERVICE: 217crb; THE NATIONAL GALLERY, LONDON: 29t.

OLYMPIA/SELECT: 34b, 51br, 51clb, 157t, 255t; OLYMPIA/SELECT/LARRY RIVERS: 256t.

PERFORMING ARTS LIBRARY/GIANFRANCO FAINELLO: 256c.

THE ROYAL COLLECTION ©1994 HER MAJESTY QUEEN ELIZABETH 11: 46/47c.

JOHN FERRO SIMS: 167t; SCALA, FIRENZE: *Madonna di Ca' Pesaro* by Titian (1477/89-1576), S. Maria Gloriosa dei Frari, Venice 27, c/cr; *Ultimi Momenti del Doge Marin Faliero* by Francesco Hayez (1791-1881), Pinacoteca di Brera, Milan, 43t; *Banquet of Antony and Cleopatra* by Giambattista Tiepolo (1692-1770), Palazzo Labia, Venice, 60t; *Ultimi Momenti del Doge Marin Faliero* by Francesco Hayez (1791-1881), Pinacoteca di Brera, Milan, 68cra; *Crocifissione* by Tintoretto (1518-1594), Scuola Grande di S. Rocco, Venice,106c/cb; *S Michele* by Giambono (15th century), Accademia, Venice, 123b; *Il Trasporto della Santa Casa di Loreto* by Giambattista Tiepolo (1692-1770), Accademia, Venice, 130tr; *Presentazione al tempio* by Titian (1477/89-1576), Accademia, Venice,133b; *Intérieur Hollandais II* by Joan Miró (1928), Museo Guggenheim, Venice, 134c; *Madonna col Bambino* by Filippo Lippi (1406-69), Cini Collection, Venice 134t; *Annunciazione* by Vittore Carpaccio (1460 c.-1526), Ca' d'Oro, Venice,144b; Pala di San Zeno by Andrea Mantegna (1431-1506), San Zeno, Verona, 200cl; SCIENCE PHOTO LIBRARY: Earth Satellite Corporation,10 (inset); SETTORE BENI CULTURALI, PADUA: 180t/cla/clb; SPECTRUM COLOUR LIBRARY: 28b; STUDIO PIZZI: 45cla, 47crb; TONY STONE IMAGES: 214cla, 216t, 50/51c.

Phrase Book

IN EMERGENCY

Help!	Aiuto!	eye-**yoo**-toh
Stop!	Fermate!	fair-**mah**-teh
Call a doctor.	Chiama un medico	kee-**ah**-mah oon **meh**-dee-koh
Call an ambulance.	Chiama un' ambulanza	kee-**ah**-mah oon am-boo-**lan**-tsa
Call the police.	Chiama la polizia	kee-**ah**-mah lah pol-ee-**tsee**-ah
Call the fire brigade.	Chiama i pompieri	kee-**ah**-mah ee pom-pee-**air**-ee
Where is the telephone?	Dov'è il telefono?	dov-**eh** eel teh-**leh**-foh-noh?
The nearest hospital?	L'ospedale più vicino?	loss-peh-**dah**-leh pee-**oo**vee-**chee**-noh?

COMMUNICATION ESSENTIALS

Yes/No	Si/No	see/noh
Please	Per favore	pair fah-**vor**-eh
Thank you	Grazie	**grah**-tsee-eh
Excuse me	Mi scusi	mee **skoo**-zee
Hello	Buon giorno	bwon **jor**-noh
Goodbye	Arrivederci	ah-ree-veh-**dair**-chee
Good evening	Buona sera	**bwon**-ah **sair**-ah
morning	la mattina	lah mah-**tee**-nah
afternoon	il pomeriggio	eel poh-meh-**ree**-joh
evening	la sera	lah **sair**-ah
yesterday	ieri	ee-**air**-ee
today	oggi	**oh**-jee
tomorrow	domani	doh-**mah**-nee
here	qui	kwee
there	la	lah
What?	Quale?	**kwah**-leh?
When?	Quando?	**kwan**-doh?
Why?	Perchè?	pair-**keh**?
Where?	Dove?	**doh**-veh

USEFUL PHRASES

How are you?	Come sta?	**koh**-meh stah?
Very well, thank you.	Molto bene, grazie.	**moll**-toh **beh**-neh **grah**-tsee-eh
Pleased to meet you.	Piacere di conoscerla.	pee-ah-**chair**-eh dee coh-**noh**-shair-lah
See you soon.	A più tardi.	ah pee-**oo tar**-dee
That's fine.	Va bene.	va **beh**-neh
Where is/are ...?	Dov'è/Dove sono ...?	dov-**eh**/doveh **soh**-noh?
How long does it take to get to ...?	Quanto tempo ci vuole per andare a ...?	**kwan**-toh **tem**-poh chee voo-**oh**-leh pair an-**dar**-eh ah ...?
How do I get to ...?	Come faccio per arrivare a ...?	koh-meh **fah**-choh pair arri-**var**-eh ah..?
Do you speak English?	Parla inglese?	**par**-lah een-**gleh**-zeh?
I don't understand.	Non capisco.	non ka-**pee**-skoh
Could you speak more slowly, please?	Può parlare più lentamente, per favore?	pwoh par-**lah**-reh pee-**oo** len-ta-**men**-teh pair fah-**vor**-eh?
I'm sorry.	Mi dispiace.	mee dee-spee-**ah**-cheh

USEFUL WORDS

big	grande	**gran**-deh
small	piccolo	**pee**-koh-loh
hot	caldo	**kal**-doh
cold	freddo	**fred**-doh
good	buono	**bwoh**-noh
bad	cattivo	kat-**tee**-voh
enough	basta	**bas**-tah
well	bene	**beh**-neh
open	aperto	ah-**pair**-toh
closed	chiuso	kee-**oo**-zoh
left	a sinistra	ah see-**nee**-strah
right	a destra	ah **dess**-trah
straight on	sempre dritto	**sem**-preh **dree**-toh
near	vicino	vee-**chee**-noh
far	lontano	lon-**tah**-noh
up	su	soo
down	giù	joo
early	presto	**press**-toh
late	tardi	**tar**-dee
entrance	entrata	en-**trah**-tah
exit	uscita	oo-**shee**-ta
toilet	il gabinetto	eel gah-bee-**net**-toh
free, unoccupied	libero	**lee**-bair-oh
free, no charge	gratuito	grah-**too**-ee-toh

MAKING A TELEPHONE CALL

I'd like to place a long-distance call.	Vorrei fare una interurbana.	vor-**ray far**-eh oona in-tair-oor-**bah**-nah
I'd like to make a reverse-charge call.	Vorrei fare una telefonata a carico del destinatario.	vor-**ray far**-eh oona teh-leh-fon-**ah**-tah ah **kar**-ee-koh dell dess-tee-nah-**tar**-ree-oh
I'll try again later.	Ritelefono più tardi.	ree-teh-**leh**-foh-noh pee-oo **tar**-dee
Can I leave a message?	Posso lasciare un messaggio?	**poss**-oh lash-**ah**-reh oon mess-**sah**-joh?
Hold on.	Un attimo, per favore	oon **ah**-tee-moh, pair fah-**vor**-eh
Could you speak up a little please?	Può parlare più forte, per favore?	pwoh par-**lah**-reh pee-**oo for**-teh, pair fah-**vor**-eh?
local call	la telefonata locale	lah teh-leh-fon-**ah**-ta loh-**kah**-leh

SHOPPING

How much does this cost?	Quant'è, per favore?	kwan-**teh** pair fah-**vor**-eh?
I would like ...	Vorrei ...	vor-**ray**
Do you have ...?	Avete ...?	ah-**veh**-teh.. ?
I'm just looking.	Sto soltanto guardando.	stoh sol-**tan**-toh gwar-**dan**-doh
Do you take credit cards?	Accettate carte di credito?	ah-chet-**tah**-teh **kar**-teh dee **creh**-dee-toh?
What time do you open/close?	A che ora apre/ chiude?	ah keh **or**-ah **ah**-preh/kee-**oo**-deh?
this one	questo	**kweh**-stoh
that one	quello	**kwell**-oh
expensive	caro	**kar**-oh
cheap	a buon prezzo	ah bwon **pret**-soh
size, clothes	la taglia	lah **tah**-lee-ah
size, shoes	il numero	eel **noo**-mair-oh
white	bianco	bee-**ang**-koh
black	nero	**neh**-roh
red	rosso	**ross**-oh
yellow	giallo	**jal**-loh
green	verde	**vair**-deh
blue	blu	bloo
brown	marrone	mar-**roh**-neh

TYPES OF SHOP

antique dealer	l'antiquario	lan-tee-**kwah**-ree-oh
bakery	la panetteria	lah pah-net-tair-**ree**-ah
bank	la banca	lah **bang**-kah
bookshop	la libreria	lah lee-breh-**ree**-ah
butcher's	la macelleria	lah mah-chell-eh-**ree**-ah
cake shop	la pasticceria	lah pas-tee-chair-**ee**-ah
chemist's	la farmacia	lah far-mah-**chee**-ah
delicatessen	la salumeria	lah sah-loo-meh-**ree**-ah
department store	il grande magazzino	eel **gran**-deh mag-gad-**zee**-noh
fishmonger's	la pescheria	lah pess-keh-**ree**-ah
florist	il fioraio	eel fee-or-**eye**-oh
greengrocer	il fruttivendolo	eel froo-tee-**ven**-doh-loh
grocery	alimentari	ah-lee-men-**tah**-ree
hairdresser	il parrucchiere	eel par-oo-kee-**air**-eh
ice cream parlour	la gelateria	lah jel-lah-tair-**ree**-ah
market	il mercato	eel mair-**kah**-toh
news-stand	l'edicola	leh-**dee**-koh-lah
post office	l'ufficio postale	loo-**fee**-choh pos-**tah**-leh
shoe shop	il negozio di scarpe	eel neh-**goh**-tsioh dee **skar**-peh
supermarket	il supermercato	su-pair-mair-**kah**-toh
tobacconist	il tabaccaio	eel tah-bak-**eye**-oh
travel agency	l'agenzia di viaggi	lah-jen-**tsee**-ah dee vee-**ad**-jee

SIGHTSEEING

art gallery	la pinacoteca	lah peena-koh-**teh**-kah
bus stop	la fermata dell'autobus	lah fair-**mah**-tah dell **ow**-toh-booss
church	la chiesa	lah kee-**eh**-zah
	la basilica	lah bah-**seel**-i-kah
closed for the public holiday	chiuso per la festa	kee-**oo**-zoh pair lah **fess**-tah
garden	il giardino	eel jar-**dee**-no
library	la biblioteca	lah beeb-lee-oh-**teh**-kah
museum	il museo	eel moo-**zeh**-oh
railway station	la stazione	lah stah-tsee-**oh**-neh
tourist information	l'ufficio turistico	loo-**fee**-choh too-**ree**-stee-koh

STAYING IN A HOTEL

Do you have any vacant rooms?	**Avete camere libere?**	ah-**veh**-teh **kah**-mair-eh **lee**-bair-eh?
double room	**una camera doppia**	oona **kah**-mair-ah **doh**-pee-ah
with double bed	**con letto matrimoniale**	kon **let**-toh mah-tmee-moh-nee-**ah**-leh
twin room	**una camera con due letti**	oona **kah**-mair-ah kon **doo**-eh **let**-tee
single room	**una camera singola**	oona **kah**-mair-ah **sing**-goh-lah
room with a bath, shower	**una camera con bagno, con doccia**	oona **kah**-mair-ah kon **ban**-yoh, kon **dot**-chah
porter	**il facchino**	eel fah-**kee**-noh
key	**la chiave**	lah kee-**ah**-veh
I have a reservation.	**Ho fatto una prenotazione.**	oh **fat**-toh oona preh-noh-tah-tsee-**oh**-neh

EATING OUT

Have you got a table for ...?	**Avete una tavola per ... ?**	ah-**veh**-teh oona **tah**-voh-lah pair ...?
I'd like to reserve a table.	**Vorrei riservare una tavola.**	vor-**ray** ree-sair-**vah**-reh oona **tah**-voh-lah
breakfast	**colazione**	koh-lah-tsee-**oh**-neh
lunch	**pranzo**	**pran**-tsoh
dinner	**cena**	**cheh**-nah
The bill, please.	**Il conto, per favore.**	eel **kon**-toh pair fah-**vor**-eh
I am a vegetarian.	**Sono vegetariano/a.**	**soh**-noh **veh**-jeh-tar-ee-**ah**-noh/nah
waitress	**cameriera**	kah-mair-ee-**air**-ah
waiter	**cameriere**	kah-mair-ee-**air**-eh
fixed price menu	**il menù a prezzo fisso**	eel meh-**noo** a **pret**-soh **fee**-soh
dish of the day	**piatto del giorno**	pee-**ah**-toh dell **jor**-no
starter	**antipasto**	an-tee-**pass**-toh
first course	**il primo**	eel **pree**-moh
main course	**il secondo**	eel seh-**kon**-doh
vegetables	**il contorno**	eel kon-**tor**-noh
dessert	**il dolce**	eel **doll**-cheh
cover charge	**il coperto**	eel koh-**pair**-toh
wine list	**la lista dei vini**	lah **lee**-stah day **vee**-nee
rare	**al sangue**	al **sang**-gweh
medium	**al puntino**	al poon-**tee**-noh
well done	**ben cotto**	ben **kot**-toh
glass	**il bicchiere**	eel bee-kee-**air**-eh
bottle	**la bottiglia**	lah bot-**teel**-yah
knife	**il coltello**	eel kol-**tell**-oh
fork	**la forchetta**	lah for-**ket**-tah
spoon	**il cucchiaio**	eel koo-kee-**eye**-oh

MENU DECODER

l'acqua minerale gasata/naturale	**lah**-kwah mee-nair-**ah**-leh gah-**zah**-tah/ nah-too-rah-leh	mineral water fizzy/still
l'agnello	lahn-**yell**-oh	lamb
al forno	al **for**-noh	baked
alla griglia	ah-lah **greel**-yah	grilled
l'anguilla	lahng-**gwee**-lah	eel
l'aragosta	lah-rah-**goss**-tah	lobster
arrosto	ar-**ross**-toh	roast
il baccalà	eel bahk-kah-**lah**	dried salted cod
la birra	lah **beer**-rah	beer
la bistecca	lah bee-**stek**-kah	steak
il brodetto	eel-broh-**det**-toh	fish soup
il burro	eel **boor**-oh	butter
il caffè	eel kah-**feh**	coffee
i calamari	eel kah-lah-**mah**-ree	squid
il carciofo	eel kar-**choff**-oh	artichoke
la carne	la **kar**-neh	meat
carne di maiale	**kar**-neh dee mah-**yah**-leh	pork
i fagioli	ee fah-**joh**-lee	beans
il fegato	eel **fay**-gah-toh	liver
il formaggio	eel for-**mad**-joh	cheese
le fragole	leh **frah**-goh-leh	strawberries
il fritto misto	eel free-toh **mees**-toh	mixed fried fish
la frutta	la **froot**-tah	fruit
frutti di mare	**froo**-tee dee **mah**-reh	seafood
i funghi	ee **foon**-ghee	mushrooms
i gamberi	ee **gam**-bair-ee	prawns
il gelato	eel jel-**lah**-toh	ice cream
l'insalata mista	leen-sah-lah-tah **mees**-tah	mixed salad
l'insalata verde	leen-sah-lah-tah **vehr**-day	green salad

il latte	eel **laht**-teh	milk
i legumi OR **i contorni**	ee leh-**goo**-mee ee kon-**tor**-nee	vegetables
il manzo	eel **man**-tsoh	beef
la melanzana	lah meh-lan-**tsah**-nah	aubergine
la minestra	lah mee-**ness**-trah	soup
il pane	eel **pah**-neh	bread
il panino	eel pah-**nee**-noh	bread roll
le patate	leh pah-**tah**-teh	potatoes
le patatine fritte	leh pah-tah-**teen**-eh **free**-teh	chips
il pepe	eel **peh**-peh	pepper
la pesca	lah **pess**-kah	peach
il pesce	eel **pesh**-eh	fish
il pollo	eel **poll**-oh	chicken
il prosciutto cotto/crudo	eel pro-**shoo**-toh **kot**-toh/**kroo**-doh	ham cooked/cured
il riso	eel **ree**-zoh	rice
il sale	eel **sah**-leh	salt
la salsiccia	lah sal-**see**-chah	sausage
le seppie	leh **sep**-pee-eh	cuttlefish
secco	**sek**-koh	dry
la sogliola	lah **soll**-yoh-lah	sole
i spinaci	ee spee-**nah**-chee	spinach
succo d'arancia/ di limone	**soo**-koh dah-**ran**-chah/ dee lee-**moh**-neh	orange/lemon juice
il tè	eel **teh**	tea
la tisana	lah tee-**zah**-nah	herbal tea
il tonno	eel **ton**-noh	tuna
la torta	lah **tor**-tah	cake/tart
la trippa	lah **treep**-pah	tripe
vino bianco	**vee**-noh bee-**ang**-koh	white wine
vino rosso	**vee**-noh **ross**-oh	red wine
il vitello	eel vee-**tell**-oh	veal
le vongole	leh **von**-goh-leh	clams
lo zucchero	loh **zoo**-kair-oh	sugar
gli zucchini	lyee dzu-**kee**-nee	courgettes
la zuppa	lah **tsoo**-pah	soup

NUMBERS

1	**uno**	**oo**-noh
2	**due**	**doo**-eh
3	**tre**	treh
4	**quattro**	**kwat**-roh
5	**cinque**	**ching**-kweh
6	**sei**	**say**-ee
7	**sette**	**set**-teh
8	**otto**	**ot**-toh
9	**nove**	**noh**-veh
10	**dieci**	dee-**eh**-chee
11	**undici**	**oon**-dee-chee
12	**dodici**	**doh**-dee-chee
13	**tredici**	**tray**-dee-chee
14	**quattordici**	kwat-**tor**-dee-chee
15	**quindici**	**kwin**-dee-chee
16	**sedici**	**say**-dee-chee
17	**diciassette**	dee-chah-**set**-teh
18	**diciotto**	dee-**chot**-toh
19	**diciannove**	dee-chah-**noh**-veh
20	**venti**	**ven**-tee
30	**trenta**	**tren**-tah
40	**quaranta**	kwah-**ran**-tah
50	**cinquanta**	ching-**kwan**-tah
60	**sessanta**	sess-**an**-tah
70	**settanta**	set-**tan**-tah
80	**ottanta**	ot-**tan**-tah
90	**novanta**	noh-**van**-tah
100	**cento**	**chen**-toh
1,000	**mille**	**mee**-leh
2,000	**duemila**	**doo**-eh **mee**-lah
5,000	**cinquemila**	**ching**-kweh **mee**-lah
1,000,000	**un milione**	oon meel-**yoh**-neh

TIME

one minute	**un minuto**	oon mee-**noo**-toh
one hour	**un'ora**	oon **or**-ah
half an hour	**mezz'ora**	medz-**or**-ah
a day	**un giorno**	oon **jor**-noh
a week	**una settimana**	oona set-tee-**mah**-nah
Monday	**lunedì**	loo-neh-**dee**
Tuesday	**martedì**	mar-teh-**dee**
Wednesday	**mercoledì**	mair-koh-leh-**dee**
Thursday	**giovedì**	joh-veh-**dee**
Friday	**venerdì**	ven-air-**dee**
Saturday	**sabato**	**sah**-bah-toh
Sunday	**domenica**	doh-**meh**-nee-kah

DK EYEWITNESS ◉ TRAVEL GUIDES

TITLES PUBLISHED TO DATE

THE GUIDES THAT SHOW YOU WHAT OTHERS ONLY TELL YOU

COUNTRY GUIDES

AUSTRALIA • FRANCE • GREAT BRITAIN • GREECE:
ATHENS & THE MAINLAND • THE GREEK ISLANDS
IRELAND • ITALY • PORTUGAL
SPAIN • THAILAND

REGIONAL GUIDES

CALIFORNIA • FLORENCE & TUSCANY
FLORIDA • HAWAII • LOIRE VALLEY
NAPLES WITH POMPEII & THE AMALFI COAST
PROVENCE & THE COTE D'AZUR • SARDINIA
SEVILLE & ANDALUSIA • VENICE & THE VENETO

CITY GUIDES

AMSTERDAM • ISTANBUL • LISBON • LONDON
MOSCOW • NEW YORK • PARIS • PRAGUE
ROME • SAN FRANCISCO • ST PETERSBURG
SYDNEY • VIENNA • WARSAW

TO BE PUBLISHED IN SPRING 1999
MADRID • BUDAPEST • DUBLIN

CONTINUALLY UPDATED

Vaporetto Routes Around Venice

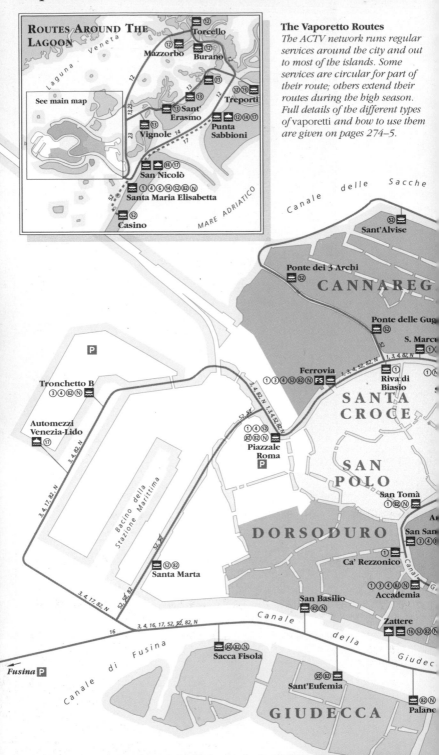

ROUTES AROUND THE LAGOON

The Vaporetto Routes

The ACTV network runs regular services around the city and out to most of the islands. Some services are circular for part of their route; others extend their routes during the high season. Full details of the different types of vaporetti *and how to use them are given on pages 274–5.*